Muslim Europe

Muslim Europe

*A Journey in Search of a
Fourteen Hundred Year History*

THARIK HUSSAIN

PENGUIN
VIKING

VIKING

UK | USA | Canada | Ireland | Australia
India | New Zealand | South Africa

Viking is part of the Penguin Random House group of companies
whose addresses can be found at global.penguinrandomhouse.com.

Penguin Random House UK,
One Embassy Gardens, 8 Viaduct Gardens, London SW11 7BW

penguin.co.uk

First published 2025
001

Copyright © Tharik Hussain, 2025

The moral right of the author has been asserted

Penguin Random House values and supports copyright.
Copyright fuels creativity, encourages diverse voices, promotes freedom
of expression and supports a vibrant culture. Thank you for purchasing
an authorized edition of this book and for respecting intellectual property
laws by not reproducing, scanning or distributing any part of it by any
means without permission. You are supporting authors and enabling
Penguin Random House to continue to publish books for everyone.
No part of this book may be used or reproduced in any manner for the
purpose of training artificial intelligence technologies or systems. In accordance
with Article 4(3) of the DSM Directive 2019/790, Penguin Random House
expressly reserves this work from the text and data mining exception

Set in 12.6/15pt Bembo Book MT Pro
Typeset by Six Red Marbles UK, Thetford, Norfolk
Printed and bound in Great Britain by Clays Ltd, Elcograf S.p.A.

The authorized representative in the EEA is Penguin Random House Ireland,
Morrison Chambers, 32 Nassau Street, Dublin D02 YH68

A CIP catalogue record for this book is available from the British Library

ISBN: 978–0–241–74282–2

Penguin Random House is committed to a sustainable future
for our business, our readers and our planet. This book is made from
Forest Stewardship Council® certified paper.

Contents

Picture Credits   vii
Maps   ix
Acknowledgements   xv

Introduction – *Larnaca, Republic of Cyprus*   1

PART 1
When Muslims Came to Europe

1   The Island of the Companions – *Girne and Kırklar, TRNC*   19
2   The *Wali's* Mosque – *Lefke, TRNC*   34
3   Among the Seekers – *Lefke, TRNC*   46
4   The Prophet Omer's Mosque – *Nicosia, Republic of Cyprus*   58
5   The 'Grandmother' of Muslim Europe – *Larnaca, Republic of Cyprus*   65

PART 2
The Children of al-Andalus

6   A Daughter of al-Andalus – *Palermo, Sicily*   87
7   The Corridors of Knowledge, Power and Pleasure – *Palermo, Sicily*   103
8   The Last Mosque Standing – *Hisn al-Hammah, Segesta and Mazara del Vallo, Sicily*   123
9   Ottoman Arab Malta – *Marsa, Malta*   137
10   Maimuna's Malta – *Rabat and Gozo, Malta*   156
11   Looking for the Moorish Maiden – *Sintra, Portugal*   173

CONTENTS

12	Rediscovering al-Gharb al-Andalus – *Mértola, Portugal*	185
13	The Christians Who Pray towards Makkah – *Mértola, Portugal*	198

PART 3
Europe's Caliphate Culture

14	The Caliphate Palace-City – *Córdoba, Spain*	215
15	The Caliphate's Jews – *Córdoba, Spain*	228
16	The Caliphate Mosque – *Córdoba, Spain*	248
17	The City of Poets – *Seville, Spain*	266
18	On the Nasrid Trail – *Granada, Spain*	285
19	The Muslim Alhambra – *Granada, Spain*	298

PART 4
Echoes of al-Andalus

20	The Village of Murids – *Órgiva, Spain*	313
21	The Blood Runs Deep – *Órgiva, Spain*	320
22	The Mosque-Churches of Toledo – *Toledo, Spain*	332
23	Madinat al-Yahud – *Toledo, Spain*	347
24	The Muslim Capital of Spain – *Madrid, Spain*	359
25	The Muslims in the Capital of Spain – *Madrid, Spain*	374

Glossary	381
Further Reading	387
Index	393

Picture Credits

Images 1, 4, 39, 42, 45 reproduced courtesy of Getty Images. Images 11 and 38 reproduced courtesy of Bridgeman Images. Images 3, 15, 19, 20, 24, 27, 30, 31, 33, 34, 40, 43, 46, 47, 50 reproduced courtesy of Alamy. Image 32 © 2015 Wilshire Boulevard Temple and Creative Ways.

The remaining photos, including those appearing on text pages, are in the public domain or are the author's own.

Maps

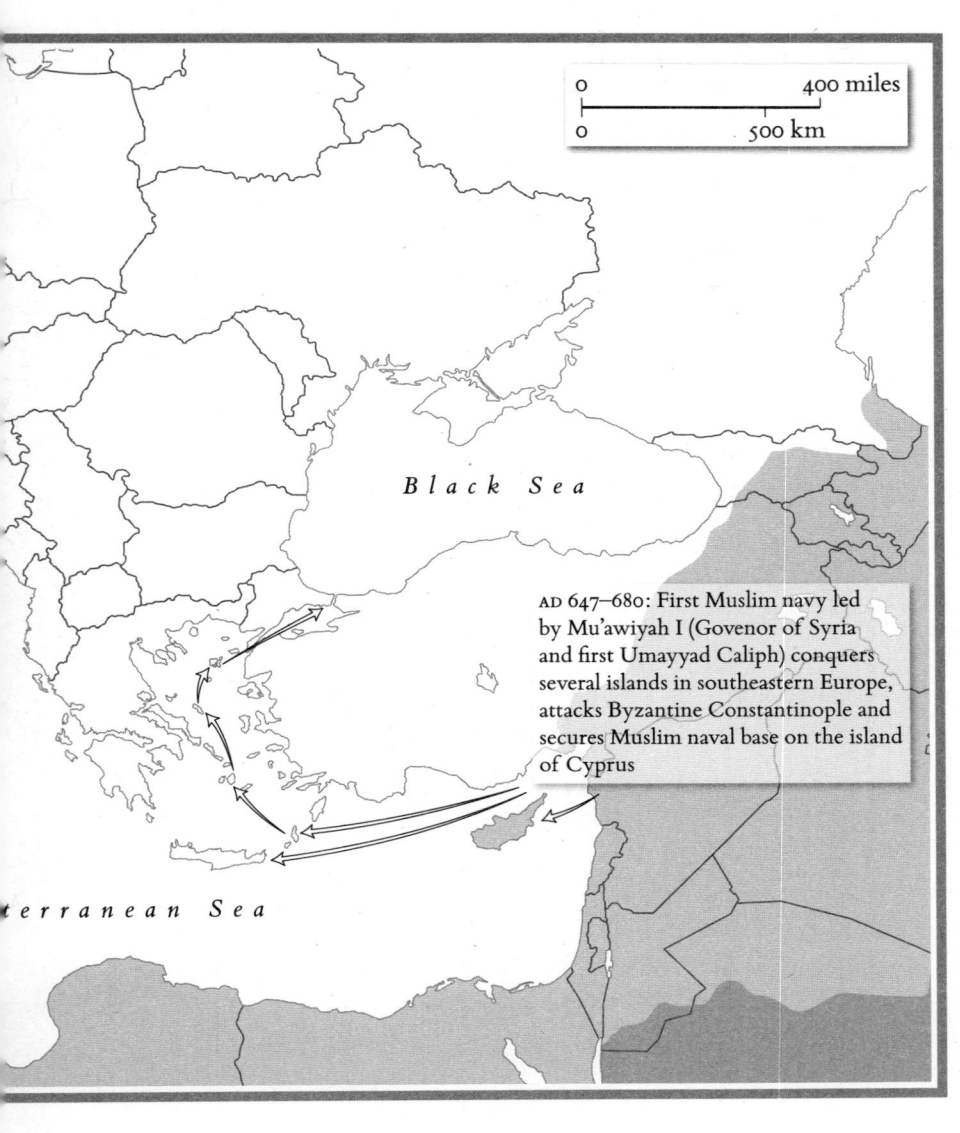

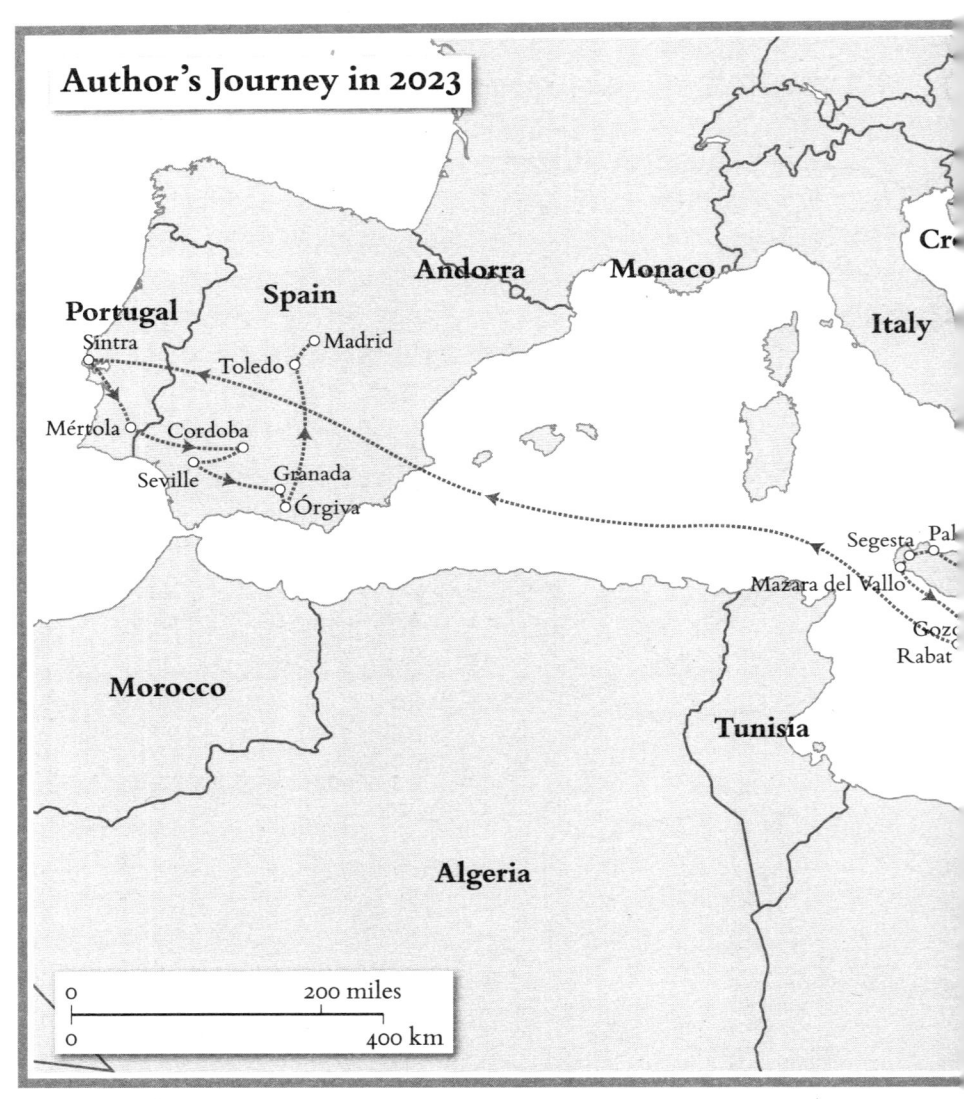

Acknowledgements

In writing this book, no one has been more important than my family, whose love, patience, and support have sustained me during the long years of research and writing. To my amazing wife, Tamara, who has endlessly humoured and encouraged me throughout this literary journey I feel so fortunate to be on – thank you for the love, patience, and strength you bring to our home and family, especially when I'm away doing this work. It means more than words can say. To my daughters Amani, Anaiya, Maya, and Nora, who bring so much joy, happiness, and fulfilment to our lives; raising them will always be my proudest and greatest achievement.

I also owe thanks to many others – too many to name individually – but some deserve special mention. My cousin, Nurul Uddin, has been a constant source of encouragement from the very beginning, and without his support this book would not have been possible. My dear friends Mevludin Sahinovic and Robert Scott, who always helped bring perspective when all I saw was darkness. My two baristas – Kheireddine Ammari at my local café and George Kerridge, formerly of the British Library – kept me fuelled with the perfect caffeine kicks and daily conversations during those long and often lonely days of research and writing. And all the kind and generous folk in the Muslim Historical Society of Britain network, especially my dear brother and mentor, Yahya Birt.

My heartfelt thanks also to my friend Professor Abigail Green at the University of Oxford for always being willing to open her contacts book for me. The same goes for my good friend Professor Todd Weir and all our colleagues at the Centre for Religion and

ACKNOWLEDGEMENTS

Heritage at the University of Groningen. I am also grateful to Sheikh Abdal Hakim Murad for his advice and guidance, and to my good friends Professor Ron Geaves and Dr Thorsten Kruse of the University of Münster, whose knowledge, expertise, and contacts in Cyprus were invaluable. Others who supported me during that leg include my friends Mehmet Ahmet, Syed Asam Abbas Hanif, Imam Şakir Alemdar, and Tania Peck of the Republic of Cyprus' Ministry of Tourism.

In Sicily, my thanks to Sheikh Dr Badri al-Madani, Paolo Valentino, and Marco Maria Giliberti. In Malta, to Ibtisam Sadegh, Professor David Zammit, and Jaafar Alloul, who were the most generous guides and travel companions. The same applies to Manuel Passinhas de Palma and Fabrizio Boscaglia in Portugal, whom I came to know through Abdoolkarim Vakil of King's College London, whose knowledge of Muslim Portugal was essential. In Spain, before I left, my friend Michael Mail from the Foundation for Jewish Heritage and Professor Brian Catlos both offered invaluable insight and connected me with many significant people on the ground. In Seville, Nabeel Abdalhaqq for his generosity with his time; in Córdoba, Youssef Fennouni and Sebastián de la Obra; in Granada, Ustadh Ali Keeler for his insight and wisdom; in Órgiva, Amadou Bamba Diawara and Muhammad Boulaich for sharing their stories with me. In Toledo and Madrid, my thanks to Jonathan Badichi and Dr Javier Castaño for their time and valuable perspectives.

I must also thank my two 'on-call' translators and hiking companions, Tawfiq Sleett and Mohamed Gaafar, for their patience and enthusiasm every time I sent them photos of random Arabic script to decipher. And my dear friend, brother, and mentor Sheikh Usama Hasan, for being so gentle with my ignorance and so generous with his support in the final stages of preparing this book.

A huge thank you, too, to my agent David Godwin, for taking me on, persisting with my ideas, believing I could actually write a history of an entire continent (ish), and then finding the perfect

ACKNOWLEDGEMENTS

commissioning editor at Penguin Viking in Connor Brown, whose belief, patience, and support were second to none. Thanks also to Greg Clowes, who stepped into that role towards the latter stages; to Laura Dermody for the incredible work that helped propel the book to whatever heights it has now hopefully reached; to the designers who created the most beautiful and powerful cover I could have asked for; and to the whole team at Penguin Viking for getting me over the line.

I am deeply grateful to the people of the countries I visited, and to the many unnamed individuals who helped me along the way — whether by giving directions to an obscure ruin or welcoming me into their homes and lives. I ask for their understanding, and, if necessary, forgiveness, for anything I have written that differs from how they remember things, including their histories.

Finally, as always, it is to my parents that I owe the most: to my mother, Rina Khanam, for giving me her spirit of adventure, and to my father, Mozir Uddin Ahmad, for his studious and bookish nature — qualities that shaped both this work and the person behind it.

Introduction

Larnaca, Republic of Cyprus

There are a series of framed photos above our dining table at home that span almost two decades of travel as a family. There is a picture of a white wooden *mashrabiya*-style bay window in Malta opposite the photo of an actual wooden mashrabiya window of ornate, delicate lattice, from one of the many crumbling Hijazi (of the Hijaz region of Saudi Arabia) merchants' homes in al-Balad, or Old Jeddah, Saudi Arabia. Another is of our two eldest daughters, aged three and five, high up on a hill in Sardinia's Parco Laconi, sitting on two stone ledges, staring out through the arabesque window frame of an ancient ruin known as Il Castello Medievale. Close by is another, from a time in Venice, when I didn't understand why such window frames sat alongside others shaped exactly like the arch in the picture below it. Taken at sunset, just before the *maghrib* call to prayer at the Great Mosque of Kairouan in Tunisia, the photo shows a seated figure in the cloak of a hermit, quietly reciting beneath one of the mosque's iconic horseshoe arches. Back then I also couldn't explain why that same horseshoe arch appeared on the dazzling churches all over the little island that separated Tunisia from mainland Italy; churches that had red, mosque-like domes and minaret-like bell towers. These aesthetic parallels in worlds I had been brought up to believe were completely different, even opposing — the Muslim East and the Judaeo-Christian West — seemed to me to make them perfect bedfellows, but I didn't know how.

The most significant picture on that wall, in the most decorative frame, is that of an Ottoman mosque, or *türbe*, with a thick, squat minaret and a large central dome. The sky behind is a cloudless palette of blues, pierced by the tall palms that rise up from the mosque's courtyard, where a small *wudu* fountain (for ritual ablutions) can be seen. Every time I stare at the poorly exposed photo of the Hala Sultan Mosque in Larnaca, southern Cyprus, I am transported back to that fateful day in September 2003, and, every time, the most vivid memory begins in the mosque's darkened prayer hall.

We were alone with the elderly guide; my wife Tamara, in her light-grey hijab, was holding our first daughter, a one-year-old, Amani, in her arms as we were not comfortable letting her crawl on the mishmash of dusty, eastern rugs covering the mosque floor. The imposing, Ottoman-style wooden *minbar* (pulpit) with its tall conical hood, topped by a crescent, felt unfamiliar to a Bangladeshi brought up in the South Asian mosques of 1980s and 1990s East London. It stood beside the mosque's sandstone *mihrab* – the niche where the imam stands – on top of which were some Arabic inscriptions. The guide, in a thick cloak, in spite of the heat, pointed to them with an extended finger but was unable to read anything. I was more concerned about the carvings beneath, and wondered why there were 'Jewish' Stars of David inside a mosque. The guide then shuffled slowly over to a neoclassical stone arch to the left of the mihrab and pointed to the large tablet above. It also had Arabic inscriptions on it, and again he was unable to tell us what they said. The old man then pulled back the curtains that covered the entrance to reveal a set of wooden doors behind an ornate green metal gate. Opening them with ancient-looking keys, he muttered something under his breath, as I held mine. Tamara had decided she wasn't coming in. The man stepped forward and then to one side to reveal a huge marble tomb, encircled by a green railing also draped with curtains. The sight caught me off guard and I took a step back. The old man had his hand out proudly pointing to what appeared to be large rocks at each end of the tomb, but I wasn't interested. Instead, I edged slowly back towards the entrance of the chamber. There I turned around and headed

INTRODUCTION

straight for Tamara and our baby. Tamara noticed the look of alarm on my face.

'What is it?' she asked.

'There's a tomb in there!' I said, barely able to suppress my fear. Tamara's eyes grew wide, and her face turned slightly pale.

'Come on, let's get out of here!' I said, leading our little family out of the dusty mosque and into the bright Cypriot sunshine, where we grabbed Amani's buggy and headed straight for our waiting taxi. It was only when we were sitting inside and heading back to Larnaca that I began to feel a sense of relief. I told our Greek driver, who had kindly waited for us, that the mosque was a strange place and not somewhere 'proper' Muslims would go. He nodded away in the rearview mirror. I continued by suggesting that was probably the reason why it was so empty. I then pulled out the booklet I had bought from the guide at the start of our visit and flicked to the back and the collection of old black-and-white and sepia-toned photos. Staring at the historical pictures of activities at the mosque, I noted the liberal attire of the community that once used the mosque and their observation of a festival called *Kurban Bayram* (Turkish for Eid al-Adha). This only reinforced my suspicions. I concluded – in my utter ignorance – that the mosque had probably been built by Shi'as. My rationale at that time was simple: only such deviants would put a tomb in a mosque.

The reason I had been so put out by the sight of a tomb 'inside' the Hala Sultan Mosque was because at that point in our lives, we had adopted a conservative approach to Sunni Islam popularly known as Salafism. This version of Islam claimed to offer a pure and cleansed *sunnah* – the example of how to live like the Prophet Muhammad – from which we get the term Sunni. The Salafi approach does this through a 'return' to the way Islam was practised by the most revered generations of Muslims, known as the *Salaf* or *as-Salaf as-Salih* – hence the name Salafism – which means the 'pious predecessors'. In Islamic tradition, these are the first three generations of Muslims and the belief is based on several highly revered *hadith* (traditions) that report the Prophet saying that the best of Muslims would be his own generation (*Sahabah*), then those that followed them (*Tabi'un*), and then the ones who followed them (*Tabi al-Tabi'in*). This meant, as far as any Sunni Muslim was concerned, to be a good Muslim we just needed to do what these three generations had done, and while many Sunnis often looked to other later Muslims for inspiration, Salafism's preoccupation with the first three generations meant it placed little or no value on those that came after, and therefore placed little or no value on much of later Muslim history. This simplicity is also what made the Salafi approach so appealing to many people.

Although various forms of Salafism have existed through the ages, the one that has become most popular today emerged from a movement that began in what is now Saudi Arabia, in the eighteenth century. It was founded by the reformer Muhammad ibn Abd al-Wahhab, who claimed to preach a pristine and pure Islam that rejected intermediaries between Muslims and God, and condemned the veneration of tombs, saints, holy sites, astrology and soothsayers, considering these practices as being among the biggest sins one could commit, *shirk* – equating others with God. *This* was the reason I had been so terrified of the tomb in the Hala Sultan Mosque that day. This particular brand of Salafism, also known as Wahhabism, became popular because of an alliance Abd al-Wahhab made in 1744 with a powerful local tribal leader called Muhammad ibn al-Saud, the founder of the first Saudi state.

Therefore, by the time the Kingdom of Saudi Arabia was formed in 1932 – a decade after the collapse of Islam's last Caliphate, the Ottoman Empire – Salafism had become the official creed of the Ibn Saud dynasty, the new rulers of Islam's holiest sites. Over the next century or so, as the Kingdom appointed itself leader of the Muslim world and its heads of state adopted titles historically reserved only for caliphs, like 'Custodians of the Two Holy Mosques' (in Makkah and Madinah), Saudi Arabia's global influence grew, and along with it the popularity of Salafism.

The idea of a purified, clear-cut and simple way to emulate the 'best Muslims' that ever lived was a highly appealing one. So, when Salafism came to the UK and began to embed itself as a popular alternative to the 'deviant' and 'corrupted' versions of Islam already being practised in 1990s and early 2000s East London, the choice was a simple one. Here was an approach that said I didn't need any of the baggage that had been picked up by 'Islam' after those three generations; I didn't need to worry about Muslim history to know how to practise Islam; I didn't need to concern myself with 'belonging' in this society, when all my role models lay elsewhere; I just needed to do what the Salaf did, and Salafism offered me a way to cut through all that nonsense and go straight to the sources to retrieve a pure, uncorrupted form of Islam. It made so much sense, and it was all I needed to be a happy Muslim. Having embraced Salafism, we decided to take it one step further and move to the country that 'birthed' both the creed and the religion, today's Saudi Arabia.

Our decision to move was not entirely about our relationship with Islam. It was one also born out of living in the midst of the vitriolic outpouring of Islamophobia and anti-Muslim hate in the wake of the 9/11 terror attacks in the USA in 2001. This had made it clear the extremists were right: Muslims didn't belong in the West and Islam was not compatible with Western society. With attacks on Muslims going up at an alarming rate in the wake of 9/11 and the community becoming the source of intense scrutiny by police, security forces and anti-terrorism authorities, we no longer felt safe in this society, so we did what the Salaf did in such circumstances: we began planning to make *hijrah*, to migrate for the 'sake of Allah', in other words to migrate for the betterment of our faith.

That is how we found ourselves in Cyprus in the late summer of 2003. The visit to the Hala Sultan Mosque was entirely unplanned, and only came about because the cheapest flight we could afford for a trip to explore the possibility of living in Saudi Arabia was with Cyprus Air, and it included a nine-hour layover in a place I had never heard of, Larnaca. In those days Saudi Arabia was completely closed to outsiders and so we were travelling there officially to just perform the smaller pilgrimage of *umrah*, but unofficially we were

INTRODUCTION

carrying out a recce ahead of a potential move to live there. The visit to the mosque came about because I was looking for something to fill the nine-hour layover that didn't involve sitting around in a tiny, ill-equipped airport with a one-year-old. I had found a reference to a 'mosque overlooking a salt lake' near the airport, and it was this picturesque description that appealed, nothing else. Our disappointment began on the way there, when from a distance we could see no lake, just a large, baked mud pit. We then arrived at the aesthetically underwhelming and dilapidated mosque and gardens to find it was not only surrounded by tombs, but for some bizarre reason had one 'inside' as well. The Salafi in me considered this a grave sin, and, given the creed's attitude to later Muslim histories, cared little for the heritage either, which is why we dismissed the brief Cypriot interlude as nothing more than a mistake. And as soon as we boarded the aeroplane for the second leg of our trip, we had all but forgotten about it.

Two years went by, during which the levels of Islamophobia and anti-Muslim hate across the West reached unprecedented levels, made all the worse in Britain by the 2005 7/7 London attacks. By the time we went out to live in Saudi Arabia in 2005, shortly after our second daughter, Anaiya, was born, the decision to leave Britain and Europe by making hijrah for a new life in the Promised Land made absolute sense.

During that year in Jeddah, I remember being surprised one afternoon to find the booklet I had been handed by the elderly guide in Hala Sultan, squeezed in among the small collection of books I had brought over from England: mostly, polemic ones telling me how to live my life as a true Salafi. Bored, I began browsing through the pages of *The Tekke of Hala Sultan*. At first nonchalantly, looking for pictures of what went on in that strange mosque at the very edge of Europe. Disappointed by the few, grainy, black-and-white images, I began reading some of the words and that's when I saw it, a sentence that made me sit up straight in my chair. At first, I assumed it was a typo, and then I tried to dismiss it as a deviant

INTRODUCTION

claim by the custodians of the mosque. But when I flicked back to the front cover, I saw the author's name, Ekaterini Chr. Aristidou, had 'Dr' in front. The book had not been written by one of the 'deviants' at the mosque. It had been written by an academic. I read it again. And then once more. There was no mistaking it, Dr Aristidou claimed the mosque I had visited and the tomb I had been so terrified of was the final resting place of the Prophet Muhammad's aunt. An actual Salaf. And not just any old Salaf, but a member of the most beloved group of Salaf, the Sahabah, and not just any old Sahabah, but one from the Prophet's actual family. Buried in Europe. Momentarily I was stumped. What did this mean? I flipped the booklet open again. Dr Aristidou now claimed the site I had visited had once been so significant that many Muslims considered it the third holiest site in Islam. Wow, I thought, leaning back on the chair. One of Islam's holiest sites was in Europe. As I tried to process this, a thousand questions began to run through my head. Who was this aunt? How did I not know about her? Why didn't I know about her? And were there others? There was just no way a woman from seventh-century Arabia would have travelled all that way by herself – the local laws in Saudi Arabia, which prided itself on re-creating those of Muhammad's seventh-century society, were a stark reminder of that. No woman here was allowed to travel alone without her *mahram* (male guardian). There had to be others, and if there were, and the very first generation of Muslims had indeed made it to Europe . . . I began to wonder what else lay out there.

The discovery of the story behind the Hala Sultan Mosque began a journey that saw me travel the length and breadth of the continent over the next two decades in search of its Muslim heritage. I met Europeans still speaking 'Arabic'; I came across palaces built by Italian emirs and Spanish caliphs; I visited towns where Muslim philosophers taught the world what Aristotle had really said; I stood in the ruins of Muslim cities that had street lighting and plumbing when London was a 'filthy, muddy squalor'; I learned that Europe's Muslim children in the ninth century were more literate than adults in Paris, Rome and Athens; I read that while Anglo-Saxons were using fried and crushed black snails to treat spider bites, Muslim physicians in Córdoba were being scientifically trained to perform caesareans. I came across the words of medieval Jewish poets pining for a Golden Age that came and went in Muslim Europe; I marvelled at the free Muslim hospitals in Spain and Portugal, a thousand years before the NHS; I even learned that an Anglo-Saxon king had once minted a coin with the *shahadah* (the Islamic declaration of faith) on it. What I didn't learn was why none of this was in my European history books.

Open any popular book on the history of Europe, and you will often find the continent's Muslim history – if included at all – relegated to a foreign invasion that gave us some nice things and left behind the odd cool monument, or depicted as a barbaric scourge. For example, Antony Alcock's *A Short History of Europe* (1998) confines Muslim history in Europe to just two pages about the Iberian Peninsula, mostly summarizing the birth of Islam and listing battle dates, without addressing the rich scientific, cultural and social contributions during the approximately 800 years of Muslim rule in that region. Similarly, John Hirst in *The Shortest History of Europe* (2009) offers a fleeting overview of Islam's arrival, echoing Alcock's limited perspective while acknowledging that Greek learning was preserved by Muslims. Yet he dedicates only one and a half pages to what he calls the 'most civilized part of Europe' in the Middle Ages, framing it as an 'invasion'. Jacob Field's *The History of Europe in Bite-Sized Chunks* (2019) compresses this entire epoch into just four paragraphs and also titles it 'The Arab Invasion of Europe'.

Sadly, this is not merely an issue with introductory texts; these books are part of a broader trend in popular histories that downplay or misrepresent the significance of Europe's Muslim culture. Even comprehensive works by established historians like Norman Davies and John M. Roberts are equally disappointing, if not more so given their status and repute. Roberts's *The Penguin History of Europe* is almost as brief in its coverage of Islam in Europe as the introductory texts: a miserly one page in a book of over

INTRODUCTION

750 pages. Meanwhile Davies's tome *Europe: A History* – nearly twice the length of Roberts's – has almost five pages dedicated to Muslims in Europe; however, a page and a half of this is a text box on the Mezquita in Córdoba (focused largely on its aesthetics), and several paragraphs are given over to discussing the *adhan* (the call to prayer), the legend of the Frankish knights Roland and Oliver, and the Muslim world's 'growing appetite for slaves', making it quickly apparent that there really isn't that much about medieval Muslim Europe after all. What makes this all the more frustrating is that both historians clearly appreciated the significance of Europe's Muslim presence. Roberts tells us that al-Andalus's golden age produced 'learned men and philosophers' that became 'Christendom's guides to the learning and science of the east'. Davies goes even further, telling us Muslims brought to Europe a 'civilization of the highest order', even acknowledging the role Toledo and Palermo played in the transmission of this civilization from Muslim to Christian European societies, and that European Islam – which he is the only one of these authors to acknowledge has been ever present – 'created the cultural bulwark against which European identity could be defined'.

This paucity of coverage combined with the consistent labelling of an 800-year presence as an 'invasion' – which, as Davies points out, is still here – perpetuates a post-Christian Eurocentric narrative that is anti-Muslim at its core and overlooks the complexities of intercultural relationships. These books neglect to address the rich tapestry of coexistence, the contributions of Muslim scholars, scientists and artists, and the historical context of anti-Semitism and anti-Islam that affected both Jews and Muslims in Europe. This misrepresentation and lack of visibility of Muslims in Europe's popular and, therefore, widely accepted histories allow other authors to feel justified in writing entire books about the apparent *Death of Europe* and lay the blame for this 'death' squarely at the feet of Muslims by declaring that 'Europe was never a continent of Islam'. Such authors – and their commissioning editors – appear oblivious to the fact that millions of

INTRODUCTION

Muslims are indigenous Europeans and that Europe still has its own Muslim countries: Bosnia and Herzegovina, Albania and Kosovo are all majority-Muslim nations, while other countries, like North Macedonia, Serbia, Romania, Bulgaria, Poland and Lithuania, as well as Cyprus, remain home to millions more, not to mention all those in Belarus, Ukraine and Russia. This hackneyed reductive narrative of medieval Muslim Europe has meant Muslims of Europe have not only been oblivious to their own rich history and heritage, but oblivious to its significance, be that to Europe, Islam or their own selves. When somebody like Hirst or Davies fails to mention Cyprus and the tomb of Hala Sultan, for example, they are not just neglecting to mention a historical mosque or grave – they are also failing to tell you that the very first generation of Muslims lived and died in Europe, i.e. they are failing to tell you that members of the first generation of Muslims were Europeans. The job of a historian is never just about relaying facts; it is as much about interpreting and contextualizing them; making clear their significance, symbolism and impact.

As my travels across the continent began to reveal the magnitude and scale of *my* European Muslim history, I also began to understand the scale and magnitude of the 1,400-year-old cover-up to deny it – a feat summed up best by the then Prince of Wales and now King of the United Kingdom, Charles III, during a lecture given at the University of Oxford in 1993. In the speech, the heir to the UK crown said this is because Europeans 'have tended to see Islam as the enemy of the West, as an alien culture, society and system of belief', and this is why 'we have tended to ignore or erase its great relevance to our own history'.

'The surprise, ladies and gentleman,' he explained, 'is the extent to which Islam has been a part of Europe for so long, first in Spain, then in the Balkans, and the extent to which it has contributed so much towards the civilization which we all too often think of, wrongly, as entirely Western. Islam is part of our past and our present, in all fields of human endeavour. It has helped to create modern Europe. It is part of our own inheritance, not a thing apart.'

INTRODUCTION

What the King did not discuss was the potentially dangerous effect of consistently denying this extensive and significant European heritage. Since that speech, Europe has witnessed a terrifying rise in violent extremism and terrorism committed in the name of Islam, with much of that violence taking place on European soil, perpetrated by European Muslims. This includes the 2004 Madrid train bombings, the 2005 7/7 London bombings, the 2015 Paris attacks and the 2016 Brussels bombings. Experts trying to understand the motivations of these Europe-based Muslims and the anger and resentment they harbour for these nations, all point to individuals feeling disconnected and detached from their European homes and cultures; what scholars of extremism call the 'alienation' the likes of ISIS and al-Qaeda seek to exploit. This stems from the way in which Muslims are consistently told they are not European and have no European history, heritage or anchorage to the continent; a perception reinforced by the aforementioned history books and theorists like Bernard Lewis, who claim Europe is 'Judaeo-Christian' (making a mockery of centuries of Christian-led anti-Semitism). Such assertions create what heritage theorists call a 'place identity' of Europe that excludes its Muslims and makes it impossible for them to develop a 'narrative of belonging' to their home nations or feel comfortable with the idea of 'Europeanness'. The popularization of that place identity also allows many politicians across Europe to brazenly dismiss Islam and Muslims as alien to the continent. This is why so many Muslims – including many of the overwhelming majority of Muslims who are not extreme – struggle to feel British, French, German, Spanish or simply European. If you keep telling an 'insider' they are an 'outsider', and you deny, delete or misrepresent that which makes them an insider, inevitably some will start to believe you. I did and that's why I was making my way to Saudi Arabia all those years ago.

There is no denying that other factors contribute to this alienation – socio-economic conditions, European foreign policy, and the involvement in or instigation of conflicts by European nations in Muslim-majority ones, to name a few – but I have often

INTRODUCTION

wondered just how different those European 'Muslims' responsible for the aforementioned atrocities and those non-Muslims adamant that Muslims are not Europeans might have felt had they gone to schools that taught them the history of Europe in its entirety, so that from an early age, as well as learning about Winston Churchill, Sigmund Freud, Alexander the Great and Aristotle, they were also taught about great Europeans like Ibn Rushd, al-Zahrawi and Abdu'r Rahman III. I wonder what their sense of belonging or, in the case of the non-Muslims, their sense of kinship towards the Muslims of Europe would have felt and looked like. I suspect it would have been radically different.

Europe's Muslim history began in Cyprus at places like the Hala Sultan Mosque in the seventh century, mere decades after the religion was established in Makkah, in what is now Saudi Arabia, and 1,400 years on it remains a European religion, a fact attested by its indigenous Muslim communities and their cultures. So, to employ the crude 'we-were-here-first' logic of many anti-immigrant movements, Muslims could be said to be more European than white people are 'American', yet because Europeans have been conditioned to see Islam as the enemy for millennia, very few are willing to accept there are indigenous European Muslims, and even fewer are willing to accept Islam as a European religion.

It was time to fix this, and to do that I needed to go back to the start, and revisit Europe's early Muslim history through European Muslim eyes, using a lens devoid of the anti-Muslim bias in popular European histories to try and undo some of that gross negligence – negligence I had fallen foul of during my past journeys in search of Muslim Europe. It was time to prove that Muslims actually came to Europe at a critical juncture in its cultural and intellectual development; one that had been on a downward trajectory called the Dark Ages since the end of the Graeco-Roman classical period, and it was in fact Muslim intervention that resuscitated Europe; had it not, it is almost certain, Europe would have lingered as a cultural and intellectual backwater long into the medieval and post-medieval era. Islam was no sideshow to Western European culture. It has been integral to its development for almost 1,400 years.

So, in 2023, two decades after first meeting Hala Sultan, I mapped a journey through five countries in the Mediterranean Basin where Europe's Muslim history had begun. I plotted a route through places of memory and history in Cyprus, Sicily (Italy), Malta, Portugal and Spain, to tell for the very first time a cohesive, connected and Muslim-Eurocentric version of the beginnings of Islam in Europe and what this *really* meant for the rest of the continent.

I would start in Cyprus, where the first period of Muslim presence lasted almost 300 years and the second period, which began in the sixteenth century, continues to this day. This makes it the only country on the route still home to indigenous European Muslims. In Cyprus I would go looking for the other Salaf reportedly buried there, as well as any other sites linked to that first generation of European Muslims and contextualize the significance of their arrival to the European narrative. I will also explore what that history means to the island's Muslims fourteen centuries on. After that, I will investigate four countries where the historical Muslim communities are no more but sizeable new ones have arrived in the last century or so. I will begin in the territories of the former Emirate of Siqilliya – Sicily, Malta and Gozo – where Muslims lived and ruled for over 400 years. Here the early Emirate gave way to what many believe was Europe's most enlightened medieval Christian kingdom, ruled by Norman kings who called themselves sultans and spoke Arabic. After this I will head to what was known as Gharb al-Andalus, now Portugal, where Muslims ruled for over 500 years, before ending my trip in Spain, known in the Muslim period as al-Andalus, which lasted eight centuries and was the very centre of that medieval Muslim culture which encompassed the Mediterranean Basin, a culture embodied by the 400-year rise of the Caliphate of Córdoba, one I refer to as the Córdoban 'Caliphate culture'. Like dominant modern cultures today where people in places as far apart as the USA, Germany and South Africa dress in similar clothes, listen to similar music, read similar books, live

INTRODUCTION

in similar houses and even eat similar foods, the Caliphate culture spread throughout the basin, affecting not just the European side but also the North African, which is why Muslims like the tenth-century traveller al-Maqdisi saw these countries as part of a 'province' with a distinct social, cultural, political and economic continuum, at the head of which sat 'al-Andalus, the excellent and marvelous'. It was this culture that resuscitated Europe by protecting its religious minorities and inspiring not just one but two Renaissances: a Jewish one in medieval Spain and a Christian one in late-medieval Italy and Spain.

My journeys through these five countries will mostly involve visiting spaces and monuments of memory, as I try to unearth each nation's long-forgotten Muslim history. Where possible I will stick to Muslim and Jewish sources, so glaringly absent in traditional popular histories of Europe, and speak to European Muslims and Jews on the ground in a bid to try and present for the first time a Muslim-Eurocentric perspective of the historical societies in each country. This will reveal the luminaries and traditions they gave birth to, and how that Córdoban Caliphate culture, which the German-Jewish historian Gustav Karpeles described as 'a very dreamland of culture', became manifest in each space. This perspective will also lay bare the roots of Europe's intrinsic Islamophobia, or what I call its anti-Muslim DNA (and anti-Semitism) that the future King Charles III alluded to and Muslims across the continent still experience so acutely. It will show how that 'DNA' emerged out of medieval anti-Muslim propaganda and myths and how it became solidified by a consistent denial of Europe's long and storied Muslim heritage. I will make my way to cities like Toledo and Palermo, to show how they became crucial corridors – after their Muslim periods – for the transference of Karpeles' 'dreamland of culture' into Christian Europe, which absorbed so much of medieval Muslim culture in spite of its Islamophobia that it inspired the much-lauded Christian Renaissance of the fifteenth and sixteenth centuries. This in turn inspired the later Enlightenment, in which the residue of its Muslim foundations remained strong, a fact the post-Enlightenment philosopher and thinker Friedrich Nietzsche was only too aware of when he described Europe's medieval Muslim culture as 'a civilization beside which even that of our nineteenth century seems very poor and very "senile"'.

What lay before me was a daunting task, but one I could see with each passing day was becoming more necessary and pressing. It was also one I had spent nearly two decades preparing for, which is why, when I left England for Cyprus in April 2023, exactly twenty years after my first trip, to revisit Europe's medieval Muslim history and Hala Sultan, I knew this time I wouldn't be scared of either.

PART I

When Muslims Came to Europe

I

The Island of the Companions

Girne and Kırklar, Turkish Republic of Northern Cyprus

'There are more than a thousand Companions buried here in Cyprus!'

'More than a thousand!?' I stared at Imam Sadruddin in disbelief.

The imam had deep bluish-grey eyes, short mousey-brown hair and a neatly combed pointy beard. Dressed in military-style khaki shirt, trousers, and matching desert boots, he looked nothing like an imam. When I walked into the tiny office attached to the Hazret Omer Türbe and mosque, I had assumed he was the security guard.

The *türbe* was my first stop in the Turkish Republic of Northern Cyprus (TRNC), a semi-autonomous state in the north-east of the island of Cyprus, recognized only by Turkey, and formed in the wake of the civil war between the island's Muslim Turks and Greek Orthodox Christians that devastated the island in the 1960s and 1970s.

Like most Cypriot Muslims, Imam Sadruddin was an ethnic Turk. I had come to the site in the company of a good friend and Professor of British Islam Ron Geaves, his son Dom and their friend Tony. The three of them were outside, leaning against a whitewashed wall, basking in the late-April sunshine. Ron, squinting through his fetching blue sunglasses, was pointing at the work up on the hill above us, where a new mosque was being built in the neo-Ottoman style, complete with a thick minaret. The current mosque structure didn't have one. In fact, it was not obvious at all that the tiny white and green building, precariously perched at the very edge of a rocky outcrop, was a mosque.

'Do people know where they are all buried?'

Imam Sadruddin shook his head and picked up his mug of coffee. His eyes began to soften. When I had first walked in, disturbing his mid-afternoon break with his friend, the *türbe*'s actual security guard, his demeanour had been stern, and I had felt like an intruder. Now as I sat on the well-worn leather sofa, close to the imam's imposing desk, I noticed the books on his shelves: there were ones on Islamic *fiqh* (jurisprudence) and hadiths – including the most famous hadith collection of all, *Sahih al-Bukhari*, which many Sunni Muslims consider second only to the Qur'an. I also noticed, much to my disappointment, there were no books about the *türbe*.

'Nobody really knows where these Sahabah are buried, because after the island was taken over by Christians again, everything was destroyed,' the security guard explained as the imam watched me carefully from behind his coffee.

The Prophet himself had made clear the Sahabah should be the most revered of the three generations of Pious Predecessors. For most Muslims, they were the best of the best. This is also why honouring them by performing *ziyara* (to visit – pilgrim-like – the sites linked to revered Muslim figures) to where they are reportedly buried is so desirable. Their burial on this island also proved that Islam arrived in Europe immediately.

Outside, a young couple had their arms around each other as they posed in front of the entrance to the mosque and *türbe* for a selfie. The sound of waves gently lapping against the craggy rocks could be heard beneath the hushed chatter of visitors coming in and out of the mosque. The traffic had gone from one or two people to a handful now as we approached the time for *asr*, the mid-afternoon prayer. I pointed to a framed black-and-white photograph resting on a large white air conditioning unit.

'Who is that?'

'That is old imam of *mescit* [mosque],' Imam Sadruddin said, 'very good man.'

'His grave is outside,' added the security guard, pointing in the direction of the two graves we had passed earlier. I noticed a tattoo on his hand that read 'Strength'.

'Oh, so that's whose grave it is! . . . My friends and I had wondered who was important enough to be buried here.'

I stared at the black-and-white picture of an old man, sitting on a reed mat, beneath the arches of the mosque's small courtyard, an unspoilt coastline curving away behind him. He wore a turban and was reading a large book. He looked every bit the sage he reputedly was. I noticed several other pictures of him placed around the room. They had all been taken from different angles, during the same sitting. My favourite had the imam in profile, with the sun behind him, creating a nice silhouette where only his face and beard were illuminated. This hung opposite a busy noticeboard with a leftover Ramadan calendar pinned on it.

The historical imam was Şeyh Hacı Osman Yeşilbaş, who is revered because of the many mystical experiences he had during his residency at the *türbe* in the 1940s. The *hoca* – as imams are known locally – was a dervish who had previously been based at a *madrasa* – Islamic school – in Paphos. During his time at the Hazret Omer Türbe, it was believed he often summoned the *jinn* – supernatural beings, popularized in the West through the caricature of the 'genie' – as well as the inhabitants of the tomb, who would then gallop past the *türbe* on horseback during the night, occasionally stopping to 'throw' the *hoca* around in some kind of mystical game of catch, with the *hoca* as the ball. Another miracle attributed to the powerful *hoca* was that he knew the exact time of his death, and reportedly dug his own grave just before he passed away. The grave, now a smart, square-shaped tomb with a marble headstone, was one of two surrounded by a circular stone wall a hundred metres or so from the mosque on the grassy slopes of the pleasure gardens being constructed outside, complete with colourful blooming flowers and carefully laid-out pathways.

PART I: WHEN MUSLIMS CAME TO EUROPE

Hazret Omer, according to the information tablet at the mosque's entrance, had been an actual Companion of the Prophet Muhammad. He would have sat and spoken to Muhammad the way I was now speaking to the imam and his friend. This was no ordinary tomb, and like the one I had stumbled upon twenty years ago, across the border in the island's south, is believed to be among three such places where members of that first revered generation are buried. Omer and the six other unnamed Companions were buried here between AD 647 and 649 said the sign (which overlap with the years 26 through to 29 in the Islamic calendar), a mere fifteen years or so after the Prophet Muhammad's death in 632. In other words, the first generation of Muslims made it to Europe, and by Islamic calculations there were over 1,400 years of European Islamic history.

According to the marble inscriptions, Omer was the commander of a fleet that 'entered Cyprus from where the Mausoleum is now present and here, he and his six soldiers were killed in a battle with Byzantines' before being buried in a cave and forgotten. Then after the Ottoman conquest of the island – known as Qubrus by the Sahabah – in 1571, the Turks, read the inscription, 'found the cave with the help of the rumours and built a mausoleum'. The complex built by the Ottomans had also included a mosque and caretaker's chambers. It is on those foundations that the current building now stands.

I had never heard of this Omer before my visit to Cyprus and asked the imam what else was known about him. Why was he afforded the honorific *hazret*? The imam shrugged his shoulders.

'We don't know anything about him, only that he was Sahabah.'

'What about his name?'

Again, the imam shrugged his shoulders.

'Where are you from?' he asked, diverting the conversation.

'London, England.'

'Londre?' The imam smiled. 'My brother is in Londre!'

'My brother is also in London,' said the security guard less enthusiastically.

'How is life in Britain?' he asked.

I told them things were difficult in the wake of Brexit, before

THE ISLAND OF THE COMPANIONS

trying to bring the conversation back to the Companions buried in the *türbe*, but they were now more interested in talking about Britain.

There is no historical evidence of an Omer leading any Muslim fleet to Qubrus. The only Omer 'involved' in the Muslim conquest of the island was Umar ibn al-Khattab, the second Caliph of Islam, who actually stopped the conquest happening sooner. According to tradition, Umar, who led the early Muslim community for a decade between 634 and 644, was the first ruler approached by the then governor of Syria, Mu'awiyah ibn Abi Sufyan, about developing a navy. Mu'awiyah had explained his concern about the frequent Byzantine attacks along the Syrian coast, launched by the eastern Christian empire from their naval base of Qubrus. He claimed the barking of their dogs and the crowing of their cocks could be heard in the villages of Homs. Mu'awiyah, who would later found Islam's first ruling dynasty, the Umayyads, was ambitious and intelligent, and having led armies to help conquer lands from Palestine right through the Levant, the man reportedly dubbed the 'Caesar of Arabia' by Muhammad smelt blood. He knew the Byzantines were in retreat and wanted to capitalize, but to do so meant the fledgling Caliphate, born in the desert, far from coastal waters, would have to take to water for the first time. The Muslims had sprinted out of the Hijaz region of Arabia at a phenomenal pace, bringing vast areas formerly ruled by the Persian Sassanid dynasty and the Byzantines quickly under their sway, so that within two decades of the Prophet Muhammad's death, their empire or Caliphate stretched from India in the east right to the very edge of Europe in the west. No other movement or empire in history had witnessed expansion on such a scale in such a short period of time, but until now it had all been done on terra firma.

Umar, being a desert-dweller, was suspicious of the sea and sought the advice of his governor in Egypt, Amr ibn al-As, who wrote back with a terrifying description of the sea as an unpredictable, violent and volatile 'creature' which tossed sailors around like 'insects clinging to a twig'. The response scared the Caliph so much he forbade Mu'awiyah from putting any Muslims to sea. Had the report from Ibn al-As been favourable, there is every chance Muslims would have been in Europe even earlier. It was only when Mu'awiyah's cousin Uthman became Caliph in 644 that permission was finally granted, and Mu'awiyah was able to build the world's first Muslim navy and land in Qubrus around 647, though no records show that any of his commanders were called Omer.

With the time for the mid-afternoon asr prayer upon us, I asked the imam where the wudu facilities were. The security guard leant out of the doorway and pointed to a small outdoor ablution area, beneath a white arch. I wandered over, placed my sandals on the brown wooden shoe rack and sat down on one of the low marble-tiled seats. Behind me the traffic of people began to grow. A middle-aged man in a red T-shirt leant against the railing looking out to sea, two South Asian women wearing coloured headscarves walked towards the mosque, and beneath its portico a young dad in sunglasses, his arm around a cute little toddler, was chatting with his friend as they both removed their shoes to enter the mosque. I twisted the silver head of the cheap taps and after a short, sharp gurgle, as if clearing its throat, it spat out a gush of water followed by a steady stream. I left the cool water running for a few seconds and closed my eyes. The murmur of the visitors began to fade as I slowly centred myself and made the *niyyah* (intention) to perform wudu ahead of the *salah* (formal prayer). The water felt wonderfully refreshing in the Cypriot heat as I washed my right hand three times, before doing the same with my left. A cool breeze came in off the sea, caressing my wet skin, as it began to dawn on me that this would actually be the first time I would be praying in one of the island's mosques. Such was the unease we had felt on that brief visit to Larnaca two decades ago that we didn't even pray inside the Hala Sultan Mosque.

I didn't recognize the imam when I entered the mosque. As he knelt in front of the ancient, plain, sandstone mihrab, gone was the military attire, replaced by a long, white, robe-like jacket and the green and white pointed turban of the *murid* (student mystic).

Behind him, in the corner, were a set of marble steps to a small green gate that led to the tombs. This was covered by a miniature *sitara* (curtain), the highly decorated section of the *kiswa* that hangs over the doors of the Ka'aba in Makkah, Saudi Arabia. A book called *Hakkani Kulliyati* on the mosque's small brown cupboard made clear which *tariqa* (Sufi order) the imam belonged to. It had been authored by Seyh Muhammed Nazim Adil El-Kibrusi, better known as Sheikh Nazim, the late and former Grand Sheikh of the Naqshbandi Haqqani Sufi order. A native of Larnaca in the south of the island, Sheikh Nazim was one of Europe's indigenous Sufi *awliyah* – literally, 'friends of God', a term reserved for individuals who have reached such a high station in their religious and spiritual journey they are said to be closer to God than normal human beings, and as a result have privileged insights into things. The term is also reserved for great teachers, sheikhs or mystics. This is particularly common within more spiritually inclined Sufi traditions of Islam. In the English language – though not entirely accurately – the term *wali* (singular of awliyah) is often equated with the idea of a saint.

There were about five of us in total who lined up to pray, including the young bearded dad who had now removed his sunglasses. Behind us in a small curtained area, I could hear the women who would also be taking part. After a little while, the imam recited Surah (chapter) *al-Ikhlas* three times, followed by Surah *al-Fatihah,* and soon the *muezzin* made the *iqama*, signalling the start of the congregational prayer. The afternoon prayer like the one in the middle of the day is not read out loud, so as soon as the imam said the *takbir* – the phrase *allahu akbar*, or 'God is the greatest' – a wonderful calm descended on the congregation and we slowly went through the graceful stages of the salah to the sound of gently lapping waves outside. After the prayer was finished, the imam led us in a round of *salawat* (praise and blessings) for the Prophet, before handing out *tasbih*, the Islamic aide-memoire that resembles Christian rosary beads. There were not enough to go around, so I used my fingers, and upon completion got up and shook hands with all those in the congregation, before stopping to admire the tombs of the Companions one last time. All seven sat on a raised platform inside one of the mosque's arches, almost directly behind its mihrab. Each sarcophagus was dressed in fine green silks and shaped like a bar of Toblerone, long and triangular. They were all topped with green silk turbans that featured the *bismillah* ('In the name of God') embroidered in the style of an Ottoman *tughra,* and had small red pin-badges in the shape of the Prophet's sandal attached to them: the universal Sufi symbol as it signifies the following in his footsteps.

Tombs of Hazret Omer and his six comrades, believed to have been buried on the island between AD 647 and 649

'Shall we go see the cave?' asked Ron, who had come into the mosque to get me.

'Can we still access it?' I asked.

'Yes, it's just around the corner.'

Ron had recently bought a holiday home close to the Hazret Omer Türbe, in the hills overlooking the town of Kyrenia (known as Girne in the TRNC). Resembling a cross between Raymond Briggs's Father Christmas and Bill Bryson, Ron was an Islamophile who had been 'flirting' with the religion since the seventies. This is why the TRNC suited him so well: being notoriously liberal in its practice of Islam meant that Ron could live in a Muslim 'country', safe in the knowledge that no one would bat an eyelid should he wish to enjoy a glass of wine. In fact, most would probably join him.

We left the mosque to find the other two, who had also respectfully stayed outside while the prayer was going on. Heading down to the water's edge, we passed a small boy in a camouflage top and a black baseball hat. He was bent over a red bucket, his green fishing rod lying beside him.

'No fish, no fish!' he shouted as we passed him, making us laugh.

The ledge that ran beneath the mosque's western wall was made of concrete and stone slabs battered by the elements, some beginning to break away into the wash. At the end was a sign made from thick plastic acetate. The text repeated what the earlier sign had said, before explaining that part of the cave where the bodies had been buried was now underwater. It also claimed the bodies had been found without any 'tiny deformation' after 925 years: a common claim for the remains of holy people in almost every religion.

I looked down at the craggy, coral-like rocks near the cave's narrow entrance covered by trails of melted wax from candle offerings.

'Have you been all the way inside?' I asked Ron, looking nervously at the claustrophobia-inducing narrow shaft beyond the small entrance gate.

'I did try but a very irate wife told me to get back down. You can stick your head up to see the original space the bodies were apparently kept in . . . it is quite feasible that they were holed up in there,' Ron explained.

'Alrighty then, off we go,' I said, lunging into the cave and noticing a mezzanine-like ledge. This was where the original, undecayed bodies had reputedly been found. I could see the ceiling had been concreted over, making the space even smaller, and found it difficult to imagine seven adult bodies lying there.

PART I: WHEN MUSLIMS CAME TO EUROPE

There are no surviving records of when the bodies were discovered, if at all, with some versions of the story claiming the tomb was a *makam türbe* – an empty mausoleum built to create a place of pilgrimage and help spread Islam in the locality. What *is* certain is that the caves were revered by the local Greeks and Turks long before the legend of Hazret Omer, with the latter travelling to the site to perform ziyara just as I had, but the reason for this is no longer known. Meanwhile, the Christian Greeks believed it was a shrine dedicated to a saint called Aghia Phanontes. Both communities would light candles and oil lamps when they came and some left money and attached coloured cloth to the railings.

I emerged from the gloom of the cave into the blinding sunshine to find the imam in his third outfit of the day: full motorcycle gear. He was done for the afternoon and would return for the sunset prayer. I went over to say goodbye.

'When they are finished,' he said, pointing to the workmen constructing the new mosque, 'this will be museum. All *namaz* [daily prayers] will be in there.'

The imam unclasped the strap of his helmet and put on his gloves.

'There are three sites,' he said, 'but Hala Sultan is the most important.'

I smiled as he fastened the leather chin strap of his helmet and thanked him. I knew he wanted to get away so I didn't ask him why. Instead, we embraced, before he sped off through the newly built promenade, past the grave of his illustrious predecessor, his moped briefly drowning out the noise of the builders working on his new mosque.

I left my hotel at the northern edge of Lefkoşa (Nicosia) and turned onto the Famagusta (known as Gazimağusa in the TRNC) highway, passing the recently built Hala Sultan Camii, a huge neo-Ottoman mosque opened by the Turkish president, Recep Tayyip Erdoğan, in 2018 and named after the revered historical *türbe* in the island's south. I was headed in the direction of the TRNC's only airport, the Yeni Ercan Havalimanı, in search of the Kırklar Türbesi or 'Forty Tombs', which lay five kilometres further south, near the United Nations Buffer Zone. Also known as the Green Line, this is the 180-kilometre demilitarized strip established in 1964 to act as a border between the two warring factions in the north and the south of the country. I stepped out of the car to be hit by a huge gust of wind – the Cypriot sun was nowhere to be seen today, and the sky above was pregnant with grey clouds. The *türbe* sat in a barren, windswept spot surrounded by fields with nothing to block the wind as it came rushing across the open scrubland. I looked around, but couldn't see a soul. As I wandered towards the *türbe*'s entrance I noticed an old man kneeling beside a low outer wall, building a tiny structure using loose roof tiles.

'Salaams, are you the *türbe*'s *hoca*?' I asked.

'Yes,' said the *hoca* looking up.

After a brief introduction, Hoca Omer explained that he was building a house for the mosque cat, which had recently given birth to several kittens and, with the storm coming, needed a shelter. I asked him about the tomb, which had again been found by the Ottomans in the sixteenth century. The forty inhabitants – hence the name – like Hazret Omer in Kyrenia were martyred Companions of the Prophet.

'How did the Ottomans know they were Sahabah?' I asked.

A loud thunderclap in the distance announced the imminent downpour.

'They guessed,' said the *hoca*, without a hint of sarcasm or irony.

Hoca Omer looked as if he was in his fifties, and had a wavy, bushy beard. Like Imam Sadruddin, he wore camouflage attire, and admitted very little was also known about the origins of these tombs.

'They guessed?' I asked, cupping my ears to hear his response as the wind began to pick up.

'When you go down, you will see . . . the Ottomans, they don't do such a structure . . .'

PART I: WHEN MUSLIMS CAME TO EUROPE

The imminent storm was sending the birds in the garden's trees into a frenzy, their screeching becoming louder, almost desperate, as if they knew what was coming. This made it even more difficult to hear what the *hoca* was saying.

'The arches, and the number of arches, like eight camels, like eight gates.' Hoca Omer was alluding to the popular belief among Muslims that there are eight gates to heaven, named after the virtues that allow believers to enter. These are the gates of prayer, struggle (in God's way), charity, fasting, repentance, self-control, submission and remembrance.

'We've never seen such a thing, so we guess this is unordinary, not ordinary but unordinary, and the people generally they say . . . plus Mawlana Sheikh Nazim, he said most of the Sahabah they came with Hala Sultan . . . so we believe, we believe so.'

'Sheikh Nazim came here?'

'Many times!'

The *hoca* explained that Sheikh Nazim, whose teachings Imam Sadruddin also followed, had spent years campaigning to get the *türbe* opened and accessible for ziyara, but it was difficult during the Kemalist period of the country when practising religion was deeply frowned upon. He explained that none of the names of the forty Companions were known and admitted that Omer was also made up. The only Companion's name known with certainty is Umm Harâm's in the south. Hoca Omer had been coming to the complex every day from his home in Famagusta for ten years, though he didn't always stay for all the daily prayers. The war and the introduction of the Green Line had killed off the local villages, where empty mosques stood alongside empty houses, so there was no one to come and pray here.

This was a far cry from the *türbe*'s heyday when Muslims and Christians revered the site. On holy days, like the first Friday of *Rajab* (the seventh month in the Islamic calendar), huge festivals took place around the *türbe,* with vendors selling fruit, *lokma*, nuts, *şamişi, bulgur köftesi* and fruit juices. People came from far and wide on foot, donkey or cart. The Muslim men prayed in the mescit and made vows. Candles were bought at the entrance of the *türbe* and then, in small groups, worshippers wandered through it chanting '*Allahumme salli ala*'. When they approached an iron spear set into the vault by the south-west wall, they would grab it and make a request, before leaving the *türbe* walking out backwards as a sign of respect for the *shuhada* (martyrs) who died for Islam. The *türbe* was also where local villagers came to pray for rain during periods of drought. An animal was brought along for sacrifice and the villagers would start the march towards the *türbe*, praying and singing hymns the whole way. The sacrificed animal was used by the women to cook a *herse* (a kind of bulgur biryani), as the men and children prayed for rain in the mescit. After the prayer, they would visit the *türbe* before eating the food and returning to their homes.

I felt the first drops of the oncoming storm – it seemed as though all those ancient rain prayers were about to be answered, so I quickly ran past the small garden of fig, olive, mulberry and citrus trees, where the screeching of birds was now deafening, and walked up to the main door of the *türbe* to enter its small mosque.

Kırk means forty in Turkish, a number that is very significant in many religious traditions, but especially Islam. It was at the age of precisely forty that Muhammad first began to receive divine revelations from Allah and became the Prophet. In the Qur'an, the prophet Musa (Moses) spent forty days on Mount Sinai, where he received the famous ten commandments, and according to the Qur'an it was for forty years that Musa and his people were lost in the desert. The age of forty is deemed the point at which a human being becomes spiritually and intellectually mature according to the Qur'an, and a Muslim who prays consistently in congregation for forty days virtually guarantees avoiding punishment. Most Muslims mourn the dead for forty days, which is why on the fortieth day after the murder of Hussein, the Prophet's grandson, Shi'a Muslims set off on a pilgrimage to Karbala, in Iraq, the site of his martyrdom. The name of the pilgrimage is *Arbaeen*, which means forty in Arabic.

As I approached the *türbe*'s entrance to the right of the mosque's tall wooden minbar, I passed framed verses of the Qur'an, including Surah *al-Fatihah*, commonly read at gravesides by the locals. In between the rumbles of thunder, I could hear Qur'anic recitation playing on a loop inside the *türbe*, where a small set of stairs descended beneath a snow-white arch. The *türbe* had a wide corridor with a raised rectangular tomb immediately on the right. Like those at the Hazret Omer Türbe, it had velvety green covers, with embroidered Arabic calligraphy, and green and white turbans topping the tombstone. The floor had a thick blue carpet and bright uplights to illuminate the space. To the left, on a cheap bookshelf, were a prayer rug, some prayer books, a set of brown tasbih beads and a small Roadstar speaker playing the recitation. I counted eight gates – in the shape of four small arches – leading off on each side, just as Hoca Omer had described it. I had to crawl through them to enter the attached chambers, where a long and continuous raised 'tomb' ran the entire length of the wall, also covered in green and embroidered with Arabic verse. I couldn't see the iron spear that locals once held during their wishing ceremony. Everywhere I wandered, the Qur'an could be heard, giving the space a reverential feel, but as Hoca Omer had said, this felt like no other Muslim space I had ever been in. The structure, carved mostly out of the rock, felt pre-Islamic, like an ancient temple or burial chamber.

The Kırklar Türbesi site had been revered by the island's Christians who knew it as Aghioi Saranda – the Forty Saints – and sits in a cemetery dating from the island's classical period, where later a church was built. The mosque and additional buildings were added after the Ottoman arrival in the sixteenth century to create a *türbe*, with the earliest records showing this was probably done by an Es-Şeyh el-Hac Abdülgafur Efendi in 1742 for followers of the Mevlevi order of Sufis – the order based on the teachings of the great Persian poet, scholar and sage Jalal al-Din Muhammad Rumi. Abdülgafur Efendi's original brick and wood complex was vast and included several guest rooms, a kitchen, stable and barn, toilets, a coffee house and residential cells for the dervishes – in other words, a Sufi lodge. The dervishes at the lodge would leave out a jar of water every night in the belief that the martyrs rose up from their graves to pray in the mosque. However, just like the Hazret Omer Türbe, there is no concrete or tangible evidence linking the site to the island's first Muslim period. All the connections emerged in later, local traditions, the most popular of which offers a narrative incorporating all three sites claiming to be graves of Sahabah. It says that Muslims first set foot on Qubrus near the Hazret Omer Türbe in Kyrenia, then, as they advanced inland, a great battle took place close to where the Forty Sahabah Türbe is, and this is when the forty martyrs were killed and buried there. The tradition claims that the Muslim army then marched south to Larnaca, where Umm Harâm fell from her horse and died.

I sat on a small stool in the middle of the main room, and considered the possibility that actual Sahabah were buried here. I tried to imagine their lives: their immense faith and the challenges they faced. A howling in the chimney-style vent reminded me the storm was now here and brought my ziyara to an end. On my way out I prayed two *rakat* (segments of a prayer) in the *türbe*'s small mosque, before continuing to the front door, where I was greeted by the sight of violently swaying trees and the sound of creaking wooden doors struggling to stay shut. Giving one last salaam to the Forty Sahabah who may or may not be buried here, I sprinted to my car.

2

The Wali's Mosque

Lefke, Turkish Republic of Northern Cyprus

So far on this journey, I had seen the imprint of a wali on both the major sites reportedly linked to the very first group of awliyah in Islam, the Companions. Both Imam Sadruddin and Hoca Omer were clearly followers of Sheikh Nazim al-Haqqani, and it was apparent from my conversation with Hoca Omer that the sheikh had revered these sites. Then there was the fact that even where the sheikh had been born, in Larnaca in 1922, also claimed to be the final resting place of a Sahaba. A truly European wali and mystic, during his lifetime Sheikh Nazim is credited with reviving the ancient Naqshbandi Haqqani Sufi order as its Grand Sheikh. He did this by focusing his teachings and guidance towards the people of Europe and the West, which is why every centre or *dargah* (lodge) he established is found in the western hemisphere. In that respect, the sheikh, who passed away in 2014, had been living proof that such Muslim mystics and the Islamic traditions they represent remain indigenous to Europe. It therefore came as no surprise to learn that the sheikh's final resting place in a small town called Lefke (Lefka), in the north-west of the TRNC, also claims to have a direct link back to as-Salaf as-Salih.

The drive to Lefke was less than an hour from Lefkoşa (Nicosia) and took me along the roof of the island, through a rural landscape dotted with fruit and honey farms, past a number of seemingly sleepy villages like Yılmazköy (Skylloura), Yeşilyurt (Pentageia) and Güzelyurt, where I was able to stop and admire forgotten church-mosques, with gothic features and Christian iconography that had been chipped away when places like St George's Church (Agios Georgios) became the Ramazan Camii, and St Nicholas's Church (Agios Nikolaus) became the Fatih Camii. These churches had been converted to mosques during the civil war of the 1960s and 1970s that split the country in two: the Muslim north and the Orthodox Christian south. This was why almost every village harboured a harrowing tale of displacement and forced migration, like Skylloura, which until the 1960s was a mixed village with a Christian Greek majority. However, following the outbreak of intercommunal violence in 1963, several Muslim villagers were abducted and murdered by the Christian Greek militia. This scared the village's remaining 300 or so Muslims, who fled to the capital and other Muslim villages. Then, in 1974, during the advance of the Turkish army, which came to the aid of the Cypriot Turks, it was the turn of the Christian Greeks to flee. Today, the entire village is Muslim and has been renamed Yılmazköy, meaning 'indomitable' or 'undaunted'.

The finest leg of the drive to Lefke came towards the end, just as the north-western mountain range began to appear over the horizon between Yeşilyurt and Denizli, when the road gives way to spectacular views across the blue waters of Güzelyurt Körfezi.

Born Mehmet Nazim Adil, on 21 April 1922, just under seven months before Islam and the world's longest familial dynasty was dissolved, bringing to an end the 623-year-old Ottoman Empire, Sheikh Nazim came from mystical royalty. On his father's side he is said to be descended from Sheikh Abdul Qadir Gilani, founder of one of the oldest Sufi orders in the world, the Qadiriyyah (or Qadiris); and on his mother's side the sheikh's bloodline goes back to Rumi. With such powerful ancestry, the sheikh was always destined for greatness, it seemed, which is why today he is remembered as one of the most influential modern Sufi sheikhs.

The murids I spoke to all seemed to think Sheikh Nazim chose to situate his dargah in Lefke because his teacher, Sheikh Abdullah al-Faiz ad-Daghestani, had ordered him to build it there. I arrived in Lefke, convinced the sheikh and his teacher did not choose the site by accident — that's just not how awliyah work. You see, the sheikh had chosen a site right next to the town's oldest mosque, called the Piri Mehmet Pasha Mosque or Pir Paşa Camii, and when I looked up its history, I was left in no doubt.

The Pir Paşa Camii is named after the twenty-seventh Grand Vizier of the Ottoman Empire, a deeply spiritual statesman who, like Sheikh Nazim, came from strong Sufi lineage. His father, Chelebi Khalifa, was a famous sheikh in the Halveti order, as well as a poet and scholar who served under two of the greatest Ottoman sultans: Selim I and his son, Sultan Suleiman the Magnificent, during whose rule the Muslim empire is said to have reached its cultural and intellectual zenith. But Piri Mehmet Pasha died in 1532, long before Qubrus was taken by the Ottomans. It was his grandson, Mehmet Bey Ebubekir, the Sanjak Bey of the Ottoman administrative region of Paphos, who gave the mosque its current name to honour his illustrious grandfather. The story goes that while visiting Lefke in 1571, Ebubekir came upon what was then a dilapidated mosque, dating back to the seventh century and the island's period of the Companions. Local lore says the reason the mosque survived for almost 700 years after the Muslims had left is because a treaty between the Muslims and Christians stated that the mosque — which sat on the site of the Agios Georgios church — was to be left alone. Ebubekir then had it repaired or replaced with the current building. If the legend is true, the mosque would have been built by members of the as-Salaf as-Salih, maybe even Sahabah. This would make it the only such mosque in Cyprus and Europe. I was certain *this* was the reason why Sheikh Nazim chose his site: to reconnect the Muslims of Europe to their fourteen-centuries-old heritage.

The modern mosque has a thick, sand-coloured brick minaret, built in the early Ottoman style. This sits on a large base detached from the main mosque, as if they don't belong together. The mosque is painted snow white and has a gently sloping, tiled apex roof and several arches at the entrance holding up a small porch. The interior is unusual in that it has a series of stone arches supporting a wooden roof, and ironically – given the history – resembles that of a church. The plain white mihrab stands out against the green minbar, a colour used throughout for its associations with the Muslim concept of paradise and with the Prophet Muhammad. This is why, among other things, the flags of Saudi Arabia and Pakistan are green and the dome beneath which the Prophet Muhammad is buried, in the city of Madinah in Saudi Arabia, is also green. In spite of the Piri Mehmet Pasha Mosque's potential significance, there were no signs up about its history. To most that pass by, it is just another Ottoman-era mosque.

The Naqshbandi Haqqani Sufi order is a branch of the larger Naqshbandi Sufi order, which emerged around the twelfth century in Central Asia but traces its lineage back to the first and fourth caliphs of Islam, the Prophet Muhammad's close friend Abu Bakr, and his cousin and son-in-law, Ali. Followers of the Naqshbandi order can be found across Asia and the Levant, and as far east as China, though Sheikh Nazim's branch is distinctly European and American.

The narrow road leading up to the dargah wound its way behind the mosque, where an elderly murid sat selling baggy patterned tops and colourful prayer hats, before passing beneath a large corrugated tin roof that spanned the width of the road. Hanging from it, close to a small grocer's, was a banner with the words 'One Love' and 'One Soul', flanked by a picture of the great sheikh himself. A boy in an orange top came through kicking a football, and a furry white cat yawned on top of a wall. I entered the men's side of the dargah, which was an extension of the main building – a two-storey whitewashed traditional Cypriot house – closely followed by a swallow nesting in the rose of the light fitting in the porchway. I noticed a glass lean-to, where two figures were fast asleep, no doubt exhausted from all the late-night prayers. One was entirely cocooned in a black sleeping bag, and the other curled up, foetus-like. I stood in the corridor, which had whitewashed walls covered in Arabic, English and Turkish incantations. To my left was the dargah's mosque, and directly in front a doorway that led out to the garden; above this was another, large picture of Sheikh Nazim. In the garden it was a hive of activity: people of all creeds and colours, many in bright, patterned waistcoats and green hats, wandered around as two young men prepared fresh bread in the communal kitchen, where a large clay oven had 'Bismillah' inscribed across the top.

The men's section of the dargah of the Naqshbandi Haqqani Sufi order in Lefke, Turkish Republic of Northern Cyprus

I sat on a bench next to an elderly murid in a green hat faded with age. He wore a number of large rings on his hand and had a thick beard and moustache. I gave him my salaams; he smiled and nodded before noticing my backpack, and, using the shiny wooden walking stick he was leaning on, pointed to the back of the mosque and the lean-to. I was to leave my bag there. Thanking him, I walked into the elaborately decorated mosque with its

Ottoman-style wood minbar and mihrab, surrounded by an explosion of decoration and Arabic inscription. I gently pushed open the doors to the lean-to, and was met by a musty smell and the sound of low snoring. The room was filled with the belongings of other murids, and so, after carefully placing my rucksack in a corner, I left, quietly closing the doors, leaving my belongings and the smell in the room.

I returned to the bench to find the old murid now dozing. The garden had citrus trees, flowers and a number of large palms; one of these had no head, but a winding stairway had been installed beside it. In the far corner was the *musafirhane* (lodgings for travellers) with bathrooms on the ground floor. I went over and peered into a large room where murids had set up camp with a mattress and their belongings. It looked full and smelt worse than the lean-to. On my return, I noticed the *türbe* of Sheikh Nazim for the very first time. The tomb was covered with a thick patterned green-velvet throw and a richly decorated red and gold covering of calligraphy. A string of lights hung down from the ceiling, behind which I could see the green universal symbol of the Sufi: the outline of the 'shoe' of the Prophet Muhammad. Only half of the huge tomb was visible; the other half was in the women's side of the dargah.

I stared at the tomb for a while, trying to read some of the inscriptions, until I was interrupted by the call to prayer, a gentle, melodious adhan, emanating from the Piri Mehmet Pasha Mosque. This prompted a tall white man in his twenties to climb the winding stairway leading up to the decapitated palm. Dressed all in black, except for a bright-orange and maroon hat, when he reached the top the fading sunlight made his beard and moustache appear reddish, and at first I wasn't sure what he was doing. It was only when he lifted his arms to either side of his head that I realized he was the dargah's muezzin. What came next, as he excitedly shouted the adhan, might only be described as the exclamations of an enthusiastic novice: loud, proud and very passionate. I listened with interest, before concluding the eloquent muezzin at the Piri Mehmet Pasha was in no danger of losing his job anytime soon!

PART I: WHEN MUSLIMS CAME TO EUROPE

The congregation for the maghrib sunset prayer was much larger than I expected and one of the most colourful. There were murids in bright-red, muted-yellow and vibrant-purple waistcoats, each matched with equally loud, patterned hats. As I sat observing, a sudden hush descended, and after a slight commotion, the dargah's current sheikh and the Haqqani order's new Grand Sheikh, Mehmet 'Adil ar-Rabbani, entered in full imam regalia. Also believed by his followers to be a wali, Sheikh Mehmet was the son of Sheikh Nazim, and was chosen by his father to take over his role after his death. I tried to catch a glimpse of the sheikh, but he quickly assumed his position in front of the mihrab. The iqama was given and soon we prayed the three rakat of maghrib, followed immediately by the sing-songy *dhikr* praising the Prophet and God using various incantations. As we did this, I realized why the mosque was so full. It was a Thursday night, but as it was now after sunset, according to Islamic tradition it was *actually* Friday, the holiest and most blessed day of the week for Muslims. This was why the congregation had swelled so much. Many people had travelled from far and wide to be here tonight, because it was also the night a weekly dhikr took place.

Sheikh Mehmet is of Tatar descent on his mother's side, and was born in the former Umayyad capital of Damascus, Syria, where he spent much of his youth with his father, receiving teaching from his father's mentor, Sheikh ad-Daghestani.

After the salah, I got my first glimpse of Sheikh Mehmet as he wandered into the courtyard. Surrounded by murids and no longer in his imam attire, he was wearing a long, green waistcoat over a loose-fitting blue shirt and a pair of beige-coloured chinos. The sheikh was not particularly tall and had an entirely white beard that complemented his neatly trimmed moustache. On his head he wore a simple green-velvet hat. In truth, there was nothing very 'sheikh-like' about him, and had it not been for the reverential behaviour of his followers, I might've mistaken him for just another devotee at the dargah, albeit one who wore a tired expression. I watched as he passed the murids lining his route back to his quarters. Every so often one or two boldly stepped forward, bowed and took the sheikh's hand in an attempt to kiss it and touch it to their foreheads. But each time, the sheikh quickly retracted his hand. This happened again and again until he reached the porch leading to his private quarters, where he stopped. Everyone now shuffled forward to get a better look. I peered over the tops of several heads. The sheikh was conversing quietly with a rotund older murid in a green pointed hat, wrapped in a white turban. He clearly had an elevated status for he was addressing the sheikh directly. The murid pointed to a young man beside him in black jeans and asked the sheikh to bless him. The sheikh closed his eyes, placed a hand on the man's small white hat, and began slowly reciting under his breath. Once he had finished, he removed the

The Grand Sheikh of the Naqshbandi Haqqani Sufi order, Mehmet 'Adil ar-Rabbani, prays for a murid, as others watch on

hand and the young man bowed profusely, as the sheikh moved on to do the same to another man.

'This is a special place,' Arif said, shovelling pieces of chicken, potato and bulgur wheat into his mouth with a spoon, tonight's dinner at the dargah.

Arif was the first person I had spoken to since arriving. We were sitting on wooden benches at tables inside the small communal dining area, next to the kitchen. Above us were images of the Ka'aba, in Makkah, and the Prophet Muhammad's grave and mosque in Madinah. A bright solitary bulb hung in the middle of the room, from a long, dust-covered wire, and all around us was the low hum of chatter in Spanish, English, Turkish, Arabic, Malay, German and French. The murids came from all over the world, but mostly the West, like Arif, who was born Caeser and was from England.

'I embraced Islam back in 1992, through a childhood friend called Brian . . . It all began, as many good stories do . . .' Arif smiled before delivering his punchline: 'late at night in a kebab shop.'

We both laughed at this.

'Where?' I asked.

'In Rotterdam,' Arif said, before explaining that Brian had found Wahhabi Islam and although that piqued Arif's interest in the religion, he found it too harsh, and then one day he met an Indonesian who was talking about mystical Islam and someone called al-Khidr.

'I'm like, who is this, and what is this?' Arif said.

Al-Khidr, also known as 'the Green One', is a mystical figure most commonly associated with the mysterious individual sent to teach Moses in Surah *al-Kahf* in the Qur'an. In Sufism, al-Khidr is very much alive, and numerous prominent Sufis through the ages have claimed to have had a personal encounter with him, including Sheikh Nazim's great ancestor Abdul Qadir al-Gilani, and the Andalusian mystic and Sufi master Muhyi ud-Din Ibn Arabi. Furthermore, many Sufi orders, including the Naqshbandi Haqqani, claim that al-Khidr is part of the order's spiritual chain.

I took a large spoon of delicious potato and bulgur and put it in my mouth. Arif was dressed in loose, striped clothing. On his head was a heavily embroidered hat. He looked every bit the seeker and wayfarer. The small dining area was even busier now as a group of South Americans arrived and tried to find seats. They greeted and embraced other murids warmly, before placing bowls of grapes, strawberries and sliced oranges on all the tables, including ours. We both thanked them.

'So, it was the Green One that brought you to Sufism, huh?' I asked.

Arif responded with a simple 'Bismillah' as he placed a juicy black grape in his mouth.

Learning about Sufism made it clear to Arif that Wahhabism wasn't for him, and in time a friend called Ifti suggested he come out to Lefke in northern Cyprus. The pair arrived at the dargah and immediately made themselves busy in order to gain *barakah* (blessings) as most murids do. That's when disaster struck.

'We were cleaning, when I accidentally caught Ifti's eye, quite badly. He needed two stitches in his cornea!'

I winced, as somebody offered me a cup of red Turkish tea. I mouthed a 'thank you'. The tea was steaming hot and already had sugar in it. Arif was smiling at me. I was about to hear the first of many miracles performed by the great wali Sheikh Nazim.

'The doctors said Ifti wasn't to travel for a month. He had come to only visit for a few days.' Arif explained how awful he felt. So he went to the sheikh for help and advice.

'You should have seen the sheikh's face when he saw Ifti's eye. He lost the plot!'

Arif grinned at the memory. When Sheikh Nazim had calmed down, he removed the bandage over Ifti's eye, whispered a prayer, and spat directly into it. I looked up from my tea.

'Ifti goes back to the doctor, and the doctor is astonished: "This will heal in a week!" he said to Ifti.'

Others were also now listening to the story; one or two nodded sagely. Sheikh Nazim kept repeating this for a week, and the eye healed in record time, explained Arif – something that left the doctors amazed. But that wasn't the end. When Arif met up with Ifti a year later and tried to apologize for what he had done, his friend told him not to bother.

'He said his sight is better now than before the accident! I was astonished . . . That's the miracle of Sheikh Nazim!'

A murid in a green body-warmer and a wine-red hat was smiling and nodding as he finished off the last of his bulgur wheat. Another said, '*Subhanallah*' (glory be to God) upon hearing the end of the story. I looked at Arif with his neatly trimmed box-beard and nodded. Arif got up and patted me on the back.

'Miracle of Sheikh Nazim, my brother,' he repeated, before leaving.

I sat for a while thinking about the story Arif had just told me. I came from a South Asian culture steeped in the cults of local awliyah, the most famous being the man credited with bringing Islam to Bengal, the thirteenth-century Turkic warrior saint Hazrat Shah Jalal, whose tomb and dargah sat in the centre of the main town near my place of birth, Sylhet. Stories about awliyah performing miracles were nothing new to me, but I had always assumed they were things that had happened in the past or to Muslims of a particular persuasion, not those educated in the rational, critically inclined West like myself, and yet here was Arif, exactly like myself, convinced his wali had been a miracle performer.

I got up and made my way to Sheikh Nazim's tomb again. This time there were two murids seated beside it. One had a small cup of tea resting next to him. The string of lights had been turned on, and as they flashed on and off, I was reminded of the lights that draped the front of South Asian houses when someone is about to get married. This was deliberate; many of the most famous mystics throughout history considered death like a 'marriage', including the sheikh's great ancestor Rumi, as it symbolized a return to their Beloved and the final union with The One. I sat on the bench opposite, next to a young man holding an empty food bowl.

'Didn't fancy eating with the rest?' I asked, after giving him my salaams.

'No, no, it's not that,' he replied in perfect English, 'I've been doing this since Ramadan.'

'Doing what?'

'Eating my dinner while staring at the shrine.'

'Why?'

'I don't know, I just feel a calmness in my soul.'

I smiled. The tomb watcher was originally from Afghanistan, though I suspected he now lived in England, judging by his accent. He had actually married a local Greek-Cypriot girl, who had converted to Islam and whose family were originally from the south. He explained that being at the dargah felt right and he now wanted to move to Lefke with his family, something many murids had done over the years, though the numbers had grown smaller since the passing of Sheikh Nazim in 2014, whose death anniversary, or *urs* – which has the literal meaning of 'wedding' – was around the corner on 7 May, one of the most important nights in the calendar of the Naqshbandis. It explained why the dargah was getting busy.

'More and more people will be arriving in the coming days.'

'So is the dargah not normally very busy?'

'Not like it used to be. Since the death of Sheikh Nazim, the numbers have definitely dropped,' he explained with sadness, 'Sheikh Mehmet is a different sheikh, you see . . .' His voice trailed off, as he continued to stare at the tomb with its dancing lights. I didn't press him on the matter so I also watched the lights dance for a while.

3

Among the Seekers

Lefke, Turkish Republic of Northern Cyprus

The dhikr began slowly, building up to a gentle rhythm. The sheikh led, loudly telling us the specific incantation or Qur'anic surah to repeat at each interval. The lights of the mosque had been turned off. The main prayer hall was so packed I found myself pushed into the small room adjacent. There were about twenty of us in this room, all crammed together; many of them I had not seen at the dargah earlier.

I closed my eyes and tried to find the rhythm. The phrase was *'la ilaha illallah'* – 'there is no god but God' – the most important phrase in Islamic belief, as it testifies absolute monotheism and the Oneness of God, what Muslims call *tawheed*. The more experienced murids in the main hall began the chorus, instantly finding a collective rhythm and giving the chant a weighty feel as it drifted around the room. Each repetition had a rhythm that I listened for carefully, before jumping in myself.

Eyes closed, I repeated over and over again:

'*La ilaha illallah, la ilaha illallah, la ilaha illallah, la ilaha illallah.*'

Closing my eyes narrowed my focus. I could no longer see the glare from the phone of the man to my right, nor hear the noise of the children in the courtyard outside. The more I repeated those mystical words, the more I was caught up in the communal rhythm of the congregation. This went on for several minutes: each of us, heading deeper into the rhythm, delving further and further until we no longer had to think about the words we were saying; we no longer had to think about the rhythm – we were the rhythm.

And then, a solitary voice came from the other room. It was the sheikh; he was now repeating the phrase slower, bringing us back, like a conductor with his orchestra. We all made the transition, slowly latching on to the new emphasis in the phrase; novices like me took a little longer. The sheikh added a new phrase after every third repetition of the tawheed declaration. This one offered salutation to the Prophet Muhammad. I listened the first time, and tried to jump on the rhythm the second time, but found myself stumbling a little, so I listened again. Just as I prepared to join in, the sheikh ended the round, and could be heard telling the murids which surahs to now recite in silence. Always ending with *al-Fatihah*, the first chapter of the Qur'an, and the one most often repeated by Muslims. I read it silently, everybody did. The only noise now was the gentle snoring of the large man to my left, the rhythm of the dhikr having lulled him to sleep.

Now the chant was much easier.

'*Allah! Allah! Allah!*'

Over and over again. The key this time was not the rhythm, but where we the collective took the chant; how that ebbed and flowed. We began slowly, as if waiting for everyone to jump on board, then after a minute the driver switched gears and the rhythm was heavier; the repetition of God's most important name much quicker. With only one familiar word to repeat, everyone in the room – except the snoring man – joined in. The energy for this round was noticeably electric. Another few minutes and there was another switch in gear, a much slower one that led straight into the repetition of the word '*Hu!*'

'*Hu! Hu! Hu!*'

This comes at the end of God's name, '*Allahu*', which when shortened to '*hu!*', meaning 'he', felt and sounded the same as exhaling. This dhikr was meant to feel as natural as breathing so that, with every breath, the body was naturally calling God. The man beside me was now whistling through his nose. I tried shuffling away from him, but felt the elbow of another person. I couldn't see in the dark, and with nowhere to physically go I went further into the rhythm. The short, sharp '*hu!*' mimicked how it felt when your pulse races while running. The orchestrators began to speed things up, before switching to '*Haq*' – 'Truth' – one of God's ninety-nine names in the Qur'an.

'*Haq! Haq! Haq!*'

The snoring of the man beside me grew quieter – his nose no longer whistling. Now we repeated '*Hay-yu!*', though I thought I heard some saying '*Qayyum*'. Both were among the ninety-nine names of Allah and meant the everlasting and the self-sustaining – two of God's greatest names. Soon there was a second pause, and more surahs were recited silently.

When the audible dhikr recommenced, it was with the phrase '*Allahu, Allah Haq*', in a slow, low rhythm; after a minute, we switched to '*Allahu, Allah Hayy*', though the rhythm stayed the same. This then seamlessly transitioned into '*Allah Hayy, ya Qayyum*', so that it was not clear what went first, '*Allah Hayy*' or '*ya Qayyum*', not that it mattered – when these names were used to call upon God, it virtually guaranteed a response, according to tradition.

There was a further pause, but this time there was nothing read in silence as we were led into a lengthy pattern of repetition, where we called upon God using one of his ninety-nine names three times before calling upon Him as Allah. We did this twice with each name: *Hafeez* (Protector), *Rahman* (Compassionate), *Lateef* (Gentle) and *Ghaffar* (Oft-Forgiving).

We did this using twenty names in a pattern that went:

'*Ya Rahman, ya Rahman, ya Rahman, ya Allah;*

'*Ya Rahman, ya Rahman, ya Rahman, ya Allah.*'

We would then switch to the next name. The consistency and gentle rhythm made it easy to follow, and soon I could no longer hear the snoring of the man beside me as I called upon the Granter of Security (*Mu'min*); I no longer felt the urge to shake him awake, as I called upon the All-Knowing (*Alim*), and by the time I repeated the last round by calling upon the Peaceful One (*Salaam*), I no longer felt the frustration I had earlier towards him.

There was another pause; something was said in the main prayer hall that I couldn't make out as we switched our focus from God to the Prophet and his family. Reciting a *dua* (a prayer of supplication or request), we asked Allah to bestow his grace, honour and mercy on Muhammad and his family over and over again. This type of dhikr mirrored the dua Muslims make during salah in the seated position known as *tashashud* (testimony of faith) and is inspired by verses in the Qur'an where Muslims are encouraged to ask Allah to confer blessings upon the Prophet.

After several minutes of doing this, the murids fell silent and a lengthy dua could be heard being made by the sheikh. The call to recite al-Fatihah was followed by the salawat for the Prophet again, but this time it was louder and noisier, and I could hear movement. I opened my eyes and was momentarily blinded by the lights, which had been turned back on. When my vision returned, I saw everyone moving towards the main prayer hall, where the chanting was loudest. All of us from the smaller room chanted and followed them, to find several human chains had been created by murids placing their right hand on the right shoulder of the murid in front. Each chain led towards the mihrab, where the most senior murid at the head of the chain placed his hand on the sheikh. I couldn't see if the sheikh was facing us or towards Makkah, as there were just too many chains and too many people. I joined a chain and continued praising the Prophet and his family. I looked around and realized the chains all emanating from the sheikh, fan-like, resembled the rays of the sun, at the centre of which was Sheikh Mehmet. The chains had physically and spiritually connected each and every one of us in the room through the sheikh and the dhikr. It was a powerful way to end the thirty-minute session.

When everyone began to disperse, several of the murids went straight to the mosque window that looked onto Sheikh Nazim's tomb. Some had their hands out in front, as if making dua or offering a prayer in its direction, while others simply stood and reflected. The noise of the dargah was back to its pre-dhikr levels: kids could be heard chasing each other in the street outside, women called for their husbands near the doorway, murids who had not seen each other for quite some time hugged and greeted, and I could hear the snoring again.

I went and sat near the back of the mosque, leaning against the wooden wall. I could see Arif speaking with someone; he had changed his clothes and was now wearing a long Moroccan-style *djellaba*. I lifted my hand in greeting when he saw me. He did the same and smiled. As the mosque began to empty with some murids going home and others walking towards the musafirhane or the tomb, those sleeping in the mosque started preparing their beds for the night. One by one, they headed to the back of the mosque and returned carrying a sleeping bag, a blanket and a pillow. I followed and made my bed where I had been sitting. I placed my bag at the head and, having secured my sleeping spot for the night, went out to the nearby shops to see if I could grab something to snack on before bedtime.

I unwrapped the pack of large hazelnut wafer and offered it around to all the murids at the table. Although some had left for an early night after the dhikr, many lingered with tea and coffee, including Shamsuddin, a young convert from Finland, who had arrived at the dargah four months ago and intended to stay for a year. We were sitting with a broad-shouldered murid of African descent, now living in Germany, who asked me why I was in Cyprus. I told him.

'Don't you think it's crazy we have Sahabah in Europe?' I asked.

'Yeah, yeah, bro, there are a lot of places that we don't know about, *alhamdulillah* [praise be to God] . . .' said the German-African.

'No, but I mean, especially when you think of this idea that Islam is something new . . . but actually, we have Sahabah buried right here.'

I broke off another piece of the wafer and offered it around. I was keen to understand what that heritage meant to these murids who came to Lefke in search of guidance and blessings. What did they think about this history? I mentioned the mosque too, and how it might just be the oldest in Europe if the story of its pre-Ottoman origins could be proved. They both nodded wisely, but said nothing. All around us spoons clinked against the delicate rims of little Turkish tea glasses; hundreds of them lined a shelf near a large, battered kettle, which seemed to always be filled with red tea.

The burials of Sahabah on the island proved Islam arrived in Europe straight away. In fact, of all the three Abrahamic faiths, only Islam and Christianity could claim that their first generation – the pioneers of their respective faiths – were European. Islam then, was as European a religion as Christianity.

'You have Barnabas also,' said the German-African, reinforcing this point.

'The Sahabah of Isa,' Shamsuddin said, sipping some nettle tea and using the Islamic name for Jesus.

Shamsuddin used to be called Pekka – the Finnish equivalent of Peter – and was from Helsinki. He was given his 'Muslim' name by Sheikh Nazim's former student Sheikh Hassan Dyck, the founder of the German branch of the order based in Berlin at the Ottoman Hostel. Shamsuddin and Arif were typical of the kind of Muslims I had come upon during my stay at the dargah: young, educated Westerners who had embraced Islam and the Haqqani order after much careful and critical consideration.

'Oh yes, Saint Barnabas, of course. He's buried in erm . . .' I tried to remember.

'Above Famagusta,' Shamsuddin said, covering his mouth to stop the wafer crumbs spilling out.

The island was proof that Islam and Christianity were truly European religions. Barnabas had been a Cypriot Jew who reportedly sold all his land and gave the money to the Apostles in Jerusalem, to be used in the cause of spreading Isa's message. According to Christian tradition he was martyred in Salamis, the town Mu'awiyah's men sacked, six kilometres north of Famagusta. Barnabas is considered the founder of the Cypriot Orthodox Church. It was my Naqshbandi friend Abbas in London who had first told me about Barnabas's tomb and that his grave was also a place the Sufis of the Naqshbandi Haqqani tarikah liked to go and perform ziyara at. It was not a huge surprise to find Muslims of a Sufi persuasion making ziyara at the tomb of a disciple of Isa. For Muslims, Isa is considered second only to Muhammad in importance, but as a prophet. He is mentioned twenty-five times in the Qur'an and is so significant in Islam that it is Isa who Muslims believe will return at the end of time, which is why it is said a vacant grave remains next to Muhammad, Abu Bakr and Umar under the Green Dome at the Prophet's Mosque in Madinah, awaiting his natural death and burial. For many Muslims, Isa represents the true spirit of God and this is why he lived his life the way he did: an immaculate conception who barely ate, barely slept, did not marry or raise a family. In that respect he was the ultimate ascetic, proving how little we really need the material. This is why for many Muslim ascetics Isa (the Qur'anic version) was a Sufi master, and why the great mystics like Attar, Rumi, Hafez and Ibn Arabi all spoke about him in glowing and reverential terms.

At around mid-morning the next day, I found myself caught off-guard by an unexpected gathering for prayer in the mosque. I checked the time; it was 9.40 a.m., between the sunrise *fajr* prayer and the midday *dhuhr* prayer. I asked one of the murids what was going on and he explained that it was the supererogatory *salat ad-duha*. This was an optional prayer reportedly performed by the Prophet between sunrise and noon, most famously upon his re-entry to Makkah as its conqueror in 630, having been forced to flee his place of birth with his small band of followers eight years earlier after his enemies began plotting to kill him. The Prophet and his community moved to a small oasis town called Yathrib that lay 340 kilometres to the north of Makkah. This migration, or hijrah, marks the start of the Islamic calendar, as it was in Yathrib that the persecuted Muslims and their Prophet were able to establish the first Islamic state, which is why Yathrib was later renamed

Madinat-an-Nabi, or the City of the Prophet (then shortened to just Madinah). Over the next eight years the Muslim community engaged in several battles against their enemies in Makkah, slowly growing in size and confidence as more and more local tribes embraced Islam. Thus, when the Prophet returned to Makkah in 630, it was at the head of an army numbering 10,000, and after a minor skirmish he entered his hometown for the first time since his exile, virtually unopposed, before he reportedly performed salat ad-duha. This is why it is also known as the Victory Prayer and was something later Muslim commanders would do upon entering a newly conquered city. The prayer is not considered one of the five daily obligatory prayers but it was a popular practice of Sheikh Nazim, which explained why so many of the murids were keen to observe it. Especially on a Friday.

After the duha prayer, I watched as the dargah's head chef, a short, stocky murid in frayed green top and baggy trousers, wandered over with a fold-up table and placed it on the bench nearest to the mosque's garden entrance. When the murids filed out of the mosque, many positioned themselves close to the table, but none sat on the actual bench. The chef wandered over again, this time carrying a huge round tray above his head. When he lowered it on the table, it was filled with piles of sweet biscuits and sugary treats: there were chocolate-covered biscuits, wafers, shortbread and Danish biscuits. A cup of black tea arrived in a large glass mug and soon Sheikh Mehmet emerged from the mosque. He was dressed exactly the same as yesterday, only the colours had changed: today it was a dark-green waistcoat and a black hat, married with a navy shirt. The sheikh sat down and began sipping his tea, as those standing around watched his every move carefully. More murids emerged from their mid-morning prayer through the mosque exit, each being careful not to turn his back on the sheikh as they positioned themselves around the small courtyard. What followed next was an extremely awkward period of silence as all those around the edge, hands reverentially clasped in front or behind, watched the elderly sheikh eat his elevenses. The only noise was the sound of the birds in the palm trees and the swallow returning with food to feed its chicks. This was punctuated by the odd bark of a neighbourhood dog. I was mesmerized. I had never seen anything like it. Had it not been for the sheikh's relaxed demeanour, I would have felt sympathy for him, having to sip tea and try and enjoy a biscuit or two, in front of such an intimate and intimidating audience. Eventually, and mercifully, a large German murid emerged from the mosque and sat next to the sheikh, his head slightly bowed as he did this. He began speaking to the sheikh with the authority of someone of high rank at the dargah, maybe one of the voices I had heard leading the dhikr last night. After discussing the situation in Germany he spoke about the Prophet's tomb in Madinah, expressing his anger at the 'humiliation' of the pilgrims who wanted to properly honour the beloved Prophet, but couldn't because of the Saudis and their 'abhorrent policies'. The elderly dervish was referring to the ultra-conservatism of the Saudi government, which saw dedicated guards patrol the area around the most important tomb in Islam, on the lookout for any attempts by pilgrims to 'pray towards' the grave itself. In the past, I had seen pilgrims being physically manhandled and halted in such attempts by the guards, usually an angry, rotund, late-middle-aged man with a thick scraggy beard.

After about twenty minutes, the sheikh got up and headed towards his private quarters. No sooner had he left the courtyard, pulling his hand sharply away from those in the line grabbing it, than the waiting murids pounced on the tray of biscuits in a bid to try and nab a half-eaten one or one touched by the lips of their beloved sheikh.

'Look!' said a murid in a brown hat, barely able to contain his excitement, as he held up a half-eaten chocolate biscuit for his friend to see. I kept hearing the word *barakah* repeated by the murids as, one by one, they gleefully grabbed something they had seen the sheikh touch. It was quite a scene.

I knew the mosque would be full to bursting for the *jumu'ah* prayer, the Friday prayer performed in congregation, so I got in early and managed to find myself a spot close to the minbar. Sheikh Mehmet arrived wearing his 'Friday best', a long, pristine navy robe and a large white turban wrapped around a green pointed hat, on the right side of which, tucked neatly into the lily-white fabric, were three freshly picked roses: a red, a pink and a yellow one. The sheikh stood right in front of the steps of the minbar and began leading us in a loud salawat. As he neared the end, one of his dervishes handed him the microphone, which he used to announce that we should all perform the sunnah optional prayers. After this, the adhan for jumu'ah was given and the red and green embroidered curtain covering the entrance to the minbar was pushed to one side. The sheikh ascended halfway up the stairs and began delivering his Friday sermon, which he did in Arabic in two parts, as is the convention. The sheikh then came down and led us in the two rakat for jumu'ah, which was followed by more standing salawat, a dua, further salawat and finally a laboured sermon in English, after which he was mobbed by murids. I was due to leave after the jumu'ah and started to feel that I would not have a chance to greet or speak with the sheikh, and so, after waiting for a while, I went out to load up my car.

When I returned to say goodbye to my new murid friends, I noticed the sheikh was holding court in one of the rooms near the dargah's entrance. Iskendar, a convert murid originally from Glastonbury, urged me to use the opportunity to see the sheikh before I left. I pointed to the long queue of families and young men, which included a woman with an unwell child. Iskendar told me to sit down and approached the doorman – the chef from earlier. He explained to him that I would like to see the sheikh as I was leaving today. The chef turned to me.

'Leaving today?' he asked.

I nodded.

'Okay!' he said.

I was not sure where this placed me in the queue but could see it made Iskendar very pleased that I would get to meet the sheikh before I left. I was glad too. I watched as a large South Asian family emerged from the room, and the chef turned to the young Brits; one of them was on the phone and his friend reprimanded him as they walked into the sheikh's room. The woman with the sick child was next. When they emerged, after fifteen minutes or so, the chef turned to me.

I stepped into the small room to find Sheikh Mehmet sitting on a chair having his right shoulder massaged by a large dervish. It was not the scene I was expecting and I was momentarily flummoxed and unable to say anything, but mercifully remembered to salaam them all. Behind the sheikh were a series of CCTV screens, and another dervish, who appeared to be taking notes. I was not sure of the protocol and, not seeing a chair, seated myself on the floor in front of the sheikh. I explained to him who I was, why I came to the dargah and what kind of places I was keen to visit. The sheikh told me in slow, deliberate English about the places where Sahabah are reputedly buried. I thanked him and explained that I had visited the *türbe* of Hazret Omer and the tombs of the Forty Sahabah and that my next stop would be the Hala Sultan Mosque in Larnaca. The sheikh appeared pleased with this.

'The most important is Hala Sultan!' he exclaimed, repeating what all the other *hoca* had said.

I nodded.

Like others at the dargah, the sheikh also mentioned visiting St Barnabas's tomb before pointing me to St Andrew's Church, named after another Apostle of Jesus, who reportedly came ashore there after going off course en route to the Holy Land. There was no tomb to visit, so I wondered what the sheikh meant. His English – probably his fourth language – was not easy for me to understand. I got the impression he was suggesting there were Sahabah buried there in unmarked graves and wanted to ask for clarity, but I could see this was a very quick turnaround situation, especially as I had not been on the original list to see him today. So, instead, I explained why I was writing my book and what purpose I hoped it would serve. The sheikh smiled, looked me in the eye and told me he was pleased to hear what I was doing, and that it was a good thing. I then revealed my anxiety and fears about the task and responsibility I felt. The sheikh listened patiently, all the time smiling at me. He then reached out his hand and touched my bowed head and made a dua for Allah to give me success and comfort before smiling at me again. My time was up. I smiled back and gave the sheikh my salaams, being careful not to turn my back on him as I walked out of the room.

Outside, Iskendar had now been joined by Shamsuddin and the Afghani murid. When I emerged, they were excited to know what had happened. I described the exchange, which was overheard by the German murid who had been by the sheikh's side earlier.

'Sheikh [Nazim] used to say that if she [Umm Harâm] had not come to Cyprus, then Islam would not have come here. There is much barakah at Hala Sultan,' he said, looking straight at me.

I thanked him for his wisdom, before again thanking all the murids for their hospitality and kindness.

'They say those that leave the dargah are like boomerangs – they always come back! See you soon, brother Tharik!' the Afghani guy said waving at me.

I smiled and waved back as they all watched me leave. I wasn't so sure I would come back. But I also wasn't so sure I wouldn't.

4
The Prophet Omer's Mosque
Nicosia, Republic of Cyprus

I had to read it twice to make sure. I even considered looking it up on my phone. The see-through sign, featuring the logos of the City of Nicosia, the European Union, the University of Nicosia and the Research Innovation Foundation, insisted the mosque in front of me 'was named Ömeriye Mosque in honour of the prophet Omar who, according to tradition, passed by Cyprus and stayed overnight in a church'. I searched my brain, firstly for a prophet of Islam called Omar, and secondly for one that had come to Cyprus. I came up with nothing. I stared at the sign again. Yes, there was no mistaking it, the sign was convinced Muslims believed in a prophet called Omar who had visited Cyprus.

I was in the southern half of the world's last divided capital city, Nicosia, the capital of both the TRNC and the Republic of Cyprus. To get here I had crossed the 'border', or Green Line, the UN-patrolled buffer zone. Ironically, in a city brimming with Islamic sites of heritage, mostly in the northern half of the city, the only one claiming to have a connection with the very first generation of Muslims that came to ancient Qubrus sits in the south.

I looked out across the vast car park of the Ömeriye Mosque, towards its thick, tall minaret, which, unlike conventional Ottoman minarets, had two balconies. The minaret stood against the northern wall of what had once been St Mary's Church, where according to

THE PROPHET OMER'S MOSQUE

the sign the 'prophet' Omar spent the night in the seventh century. I felt immense disappointment that such a monumental error had not only been made, but put out on public display and undersigned by some of the biggest authorities in local heritage. The mosque had not been named after a prophet at all. It had been named after a caliph, the second Caliph Umar Ibn al-Khattab. Prophets and caliphs were two entirely different categories of human being, and in Islamic theology to mix up the two was a cardinal sin. Any mortal human being could become a caliph, and through the ages there have been admirable and honourable ones, as well as awful and despotic ones. But prophets spoke directly (via angels) with God. No caliph would ever claim, or has ever claimed, to have that kind of divine access, not even the most mystical of Muslim rulers. Prophets were in an entirely different stratosphere of humanity and mixing the two up so casually was just negligent. What made the mistake even worse of course was that Caliph Umar was the caliph who famously shut down Mu'awiyah's naval exploits because of his fear of the sea, so even he could not have possibly come to Nicosia. Somebody needed to be fired.

It wasn't clear at first if the mosque building was open – the door was slightly ajar, but nobody appeared to be going in or out. I had arrived an hour or so before the asr prayer and could see several people floating around outside. The mosque had a large courtyard, with a covered area, beneath which were several rolled-up plastic mats; a skinny African, wearing a black tracksuit and speaking on his phone, was using one of these as a pillow. The mosque's gate had the most delightful and welcoming message. It made clear that the mosque toilets were open to all and the mosque would also provide free cold and hot drinking water, as well as free books. I wasn't sure if anyone had ever enquired about the free 'hot' drinking water, but I loved the sentiment. The message of openness also made me wonder why the authors of the tourist sign hadn't bothered to consult anyone at the Ömeriye Mosque before writing about the mosque. According to locals, the reason it was called the Ömeriye was because that was the name the Ottomans found it being referred to when they arrived in 1570; it was reportedly also where they first prayed in the city. The fact that it was being referred to as Ömeriye convinced the Ottomans that there was once a mosque on the site, possibly named in honour of the caliph – before that it had most likely been a monastery. Thus, like the Piri Pasha in Lefke, this was a mosque potentially first built by Sahabah.

I made my way towards the mosque's outdoor wudu facilities, a series of cheaply plumbed indoor kitchen taps over a grubby basin. I had been walking in the early afternoon heat for quite some time so the cool of the water felt wonderfully refreshing. I then went over to the entrance, beneath two large gothic arches and a shaky-looking lean-to, added to extend the *musafir* (travellers') prayer area. I took my sandals off and placed them on the shelf. A South Asian man with a sweaty face was asleep on the opposite side of the porch. I gave the heavy dark-wood doors a gentle nudge and much to my delight they opened. I stepped into the vast hall with its tall apex ceiling held up by a series of beautiful gothic arches that disappeared into the distance, creating a rainbow-like effect. The mosque's minbar was positioned on my right in the centre and I could see just beyond it, peering over its stairs: angled to face south-east, and completely out of sync with the building, the simple mihrab, cut from MDF wood and painted a mellow yellow. This alluded to the fact that before the Ottomans converted it into a mosque, it had been the Church of Saint Mary of the Monastery of the Augustinians, which reportedly dates back to at least the fourteenth century.

A man stood in the middle of the vast hall phoning while vacuuming the brand-new green carpet with lines that ran parallel to the mihrab in a way that jarred with the church's physical architecture, leaving no doubt in anyone's mind that this was not a purpose-built mosque. The noise of the vacuum cleaner meant he didn't hear me coming in, so I quietly went about taking a few pictures before standing to pray my two rakat in a discreet spot. As I raised my hands for the takbir, I realized the bookshelf in front of me was exclusively filled with Bengali Islamic literature.

'*Walaikum as salaam*, are you Bengali?' he asked in a dialect from the south of the country. He was responding to my salaams after I had finished praying.

'Yes, I'm from Sylhet,' I said, continuing in Sylheti-Bangla.

'*Subhanallah*, I thought you were Syrian,' he said, now grinning from ear to ear and revealing a set of slightly reddened, *paan*-stained teeth. He then turned off the vacuum, so we could hear each other.

Shiraz was from Lokkhipur in the south, which explained why I found myself having to really pay attention to what he said to understand his Bengali. A broad, stocky man, he explained that it was a tight-knit community here with most of the Bangladeshis familiar with each other. After carefully placing the vacuum's hose down on the floor, Shiraz sat down beside me and took off his prayer hat, revealing a smooth shiny head. He had a thick beard and gentle eyes, and wore a red top and jeans. I could see he was exhausted, but not physically.

'Who were you speaking to?' I asked.

'My wife,' began Shiraz, wiping the sweat from his brow and settling down beside me, 'I told her I'm coming home. That I've had enough, I just can't do this any more, *bhai* [brother], not at my age.'

I said nothing. I could tell he needed to just talk.

'I'm stuck, bhai, I paid eight *lakh* [800,000 Bangladeshi taka] to come to Europe, and now I'm sleeping in a mosque waiting for a hearing. I just want to go home.'

Shiraz looked thoroughly defeated as he held his *thokhi* – prayer cap – in one hand, slowly wiping his face with the other.

He wasn't employed by the mosque; they had let him stay there because of his situation. In return, he was helping out by hoovering the brand-new carpet that had taken three days to lay, such was the vastness of the mosque's interior. Shiraz had paid the equivalent of £7,000 to be smuggled into the north of the island – a small fortune for someone in his circumstances. He had been promised he would be brought to the European side and left in a position to apply for legal status, but instead he was abandoned in a refugee camp.

'I couldn't take it, so I escaped and made my way to the island of Aya Napa, but with no papers and no status I was working like a dog for almost no money . . . what kind of life is that, bhai?' Shiraz asked.

We both knew his was a familiar tale. Even when he remortgaged his whole life to pay the £7,000 in Bangladesh, he had known there was a chance this could happen.

'After two months, I ran away from there and came to Nicosia, where I gave myself up to the authorities . . . I had had enough, I didn't care if they sent me back, I just want to go home now.'

Shiraz looked at the clock and slowly picked up the vacuum cleaner again, just as another Bangladeshi man walked past. Shiraz told me the other guy had been here sixteen years. He had arrived through similar circumstances. The man was also helping out at the mosque, but was here through choice, as a volunteer. Many Bangladeshis had firmly established themselves in Nicosia, that much had been apparent to me from seeing the various Bangladeshi grocery stores while wandering the streets of both halves of the city. The stores were exactly like the small Bangladeshi grocers' shops I had grown up with in the East End of London, each with a small meat counter for fresh halal meat and chicken, large white, deep freezers containing cuts of frozen Bangladeshi fish, and all the spices and fresh fruit and veg needed to cook our curries. These were places where the single men came and chatted on their lunch breaks or in between jobs. The small community of Cypriot-Bangladeshis were definitely finding their feet; the only difference between them and the early British-Bangladeshis was how they all got here. While my father's generation of men had been actively invited to come to Britain by their former imperial master to help address the post-war and post-colonial labour shortages in a country also reeling from two devastating world wars, men like Shiraz had not been invited. They came because they were desperate and they came through avenues fraught with danger.

'He has his papers and legal status; he runs his own *hijama* [cupping] business,' Shiraz said, raising his hand to acknowledge the man who glanced over at us as he fiddled with electric cables near the mosque's minbar.

'What about your debt?' I asked, feeling uncomfortable for pointing out the painfully obvious.

'What can I do, *bhai*? . . . It is in Allah's hands now,' he said, before switching on the vacuum cleaner and continuing his gradual and slow attempt to clean up the excess fluff that covered much of the newly laid hall.

Both Shiraz and the other man had gambled when they paid the fixers promising to bring them to Europe. For the other man it had worked out; for Shiraz it had not.

Shiraz stops to take a call while hoovering the new carpet inside the Ömeriye Mosque in Nicosia, Republic of Cyprus

The adhan was called while I was still inside the mosque, and so I stood to perform the sunnah four rakat before the compulsory four done in congregation. I was expecting to hear the sound of worshippers entering the mosque as my forehead hit the new carpet, the fluff from which stuck to it. But no one entered the mosque. The only noise was that of Shiraz vacuuming. By the third raka I knew something wasn't right, and could hear the Bangladeshi man who had been working on the electrics asking Shiraz who I was. As I did my salaams to end the prayer, turning my head first towards the right and then my left, I realized I had been sitting all this time in a closed mosque. I could now hear the muffled noise of the congregation gathering under the porch outside, and when I stepped through the slightly ajar front door – much to the surprise of several worshippers – I was greeted by a large congregation, numbering around a hundred and filling every row beneath the porch. The *jama'at* (congregation) was almost exclusively made up of non-European immigrants from Arab, African and South Asian countries, with the two latter comprising the majority. Each person in the congregation looked like an honest, hardworking labourer in scruffy clothes, their faces deeply tanned by the Cypriot sun under which they spent long hours every day; and all of them were young men. There was just a handful of older men with their young sons in the congregation. This was in complete contrast to my experiences on the other side of the border, where the congregations for the daily prayers were tiny and almost entirely made up of local elderly men preparing to meet their maker and therefore eager to start the conversation early. Here, the older men were locally established Arabs, who had moved to the country long ago, and now had wives and children. The most observant Muslims in this land divided along religious lines were the ones living on the non-Muslim side; the irony was not lost on me as I performed the first congregational *sajdah* (prostration) and my forehead slowly edged towards the floor. I stopped it inches from the tired, reddish carpet and held my breath. It was now obvious why the mosque had spent so much money and effort replacing the carpet; like the busy roads of Nicosia and Lefkoşa, the Ömeriye Mosque's carpet received a lot of traffic, and it smelt horrendous.

5

The 'Grandmother' of Muslim Europe

Larnaca, Republic of Cyprus

When (Sheikh) Mehmet Nazim was a child, he would sometimes go missing from his home near the Djami Kebir Mosque in Larnaca. His parents, both descended from great mystics themselves, knew exactly where he had gone, so after confirming he was definitely not in any of the town's ancient Ottoman mosques, *hans* (caravanserai) or bazaars, they would send someone to walk the hour and a half along the coastal road, towards the famous salt lakes to the south of Larnaca, created according to legend by a scorned Lazarus. The errand boy would make his way to the lakes' southernmost banks and the site of the most revered Islamic sanctuary on the island, the Hala Sultan Mosque. Mehmet's mother and father knew that was where he would be, at the back of the revered ancient mosque, where his grandfather was *hoca* for many years, and where the young Mehmet spent so much of his youth. But it wasn't his grandfather the youthful Mehmet would go to see. It was another 'grandparent'. Mehmet would come to the Hala Sultan to 'talk' to his 'grandmother', Umm Harâm, the seventh-century maternal aunt of the Prophet Muhammad.

'There it is, Thorsten!'

I was barely able to contain my excitement as the iconic Hala Sultan Mosque's thick minaret and dome slowly came into view, peering out from an oasis-like huddle of palms on the other side of the grey waters of Larnaca's huge salt lake.

'According to some, the third holiest site of Islam!' I continued.

'Yaaah . . .' Thorsten said.

Since 2015, Dr Thorsten Kruse had been heading up a number of religious heritage projects across the divided island, focusing on the most vulnerable sites in the south and the north. I met the academic at the German University of Münster's Institute for Interdisciplinary Cyprus Studies after I gave a keynote address on Europe's Muslim Heritage at a conference in Lund, Sweden. Following the talk, Thorsten explained his desire to make the Islamic heritage of Cyprus more visible, and I knew immediately that in the tall, broad German I had found a kindred spirit.

'Gosh . . .' I said slowly, 'twenty years, Thorsten.'

Thorsten smiled but said nothing.

'Depending on who you ask, it is either the third *or* fourth holiest site in Islam!'

I laughed.

'If someone asks, I always say it's in the top five!' Thorsten said.

I had wanted to spend time in Cyprus with Thorsten because his work had made me realize that not only was Cyprus home to more Muslim heritage than even I had imagined, but much of it was disappearing.

Up ahead a man in hiking gear, sunglasses and a baseball hat slowly made his way along the footpath that followed the edge of the lake.

'I remember when I first read that, I nearly fell off my chair: Makkah, Madinah and . . . the Hala Sultan in Larnaca, Cyprus!'

We both roared with laughter as Thorsten indicated right, turning onto Türbe Road. Every Muslim knew the three holiest sites in Islam. The Prophet had made that clear in a hadith when he said that anyone who prays in the Ka'aba's mosque has their salah multiplied 100,000 times; for the Prophet's Mosque in Madinah it is 1,000; and for salah performed in al-Aqsa in Jerusalem the reward was multiplied 500 times. He didn't mention the Hala Sultan, as it didn't exist during his time. That is not to say the sanctuary has no links to the Prophet.

The word *hala* comes from the Arabic *khala* – maternal aunt – because the Hala Sultan Mosque is believed to be the final resting place of Umm Harâm bint Milhân (Malik) ibn Khâlid al-Ansariyya al-Khazrajiyya, an aunt of the Prophet Muhammad. This is because his mother, Amina, and Umm Harâm were 'milk siblings', i.e. they were breastfed by the same person, which in Islamic tradition makes you siblings. The tomb was therefore not just the tomb of any old Sahabah or wali: it was a tomb of a member of the family of Muhammad, whose journey and death in Qubrus he prophesied – a prophecy repeated in no fewer than six hadiths, all of which relate the same narrative with slight variations: Muhammad visits Umm Harâm one day, and falls asleep in her lap. When he wakes, he smiles and tells his aunt, much to her delight, that he has had a dream in which she would be among the first Muslims to cross the seas and become martyred in the new lands.

When Uthman granted Mu'awiyah permission to build a navy and set sail to invade the Byzantine island of Qubrus in 647, he did so on one condition: Mu'awiyah had to take 'his wife with him'. The wise old caliph knew that way the ambitious and headstrong Mu'awiyah would not take any unnecessary risks. As a result, others on the campaign did the same. Mu'awiyah's fleet left from Akka (Acre in Syria) in the spring of 647, with his wife Fakhita on board his flagship just as the caliph had requested. Also on board was the wife of Ubada ibn as-Samit, an elderly woman whose *kunya* (teknonym) was Umm Harâm (mother of Harâm), and whose actual name was either Rumaysa or Ramla. Upon landing in Qubrus, a 'beast' was brought for Umm Harâm to ride, which threw her off, breaking her neck and killing her instantaneously – thus fulfilling the prophecy of Muhammad.

This was the reason why the Hala Sultan Mosque was so deeply revered by Sheikh Nazim and all the *hoca* and dervishes I had met on this journey. It was also the reason why the Ottomans revered the site – in fact, historically, every time an Ottoman ship passed the *türbe*, it would lower its flag and salute her with a gun salvo. Umm Harâm's story, verified by the second-holiest scripture in Islam, was incontestable evidence that the first generation of Muslims – nay, members of the Prophet Muhammad's family – had made it to Europe. Islam was in Europe a mere sixteen years after the death of its founder. Even Christianity took longer to get here, arriving in Europe – at the earliest – within forty years of the death of Jesus, while modern Judaism was first recorded in Europe around 300 BC. Muslims were therefore European quicker than Christians or Jews. As far as I was concerned, Islam *was* a European religion.

The Hala Sultan Mosque viewed from across the salt lakes of Larnaca, Republic of Cyprus

'This is the real *maq'am* [shrine] where she's buried, where she fell off horse and died . . . *shahid*!' Imam Şakir Alemdar said, using the Arabic word for martyr.

'One thousand four hundred years ago, Muslims came with

over three hundred ships, very big armada, and it's Roman Byzantine time, they came . . . and took everything.'

The imam made a sweeping gesture, suggesting the conquest was an easy one.

'Like superpower!'

Imam Şakir wore a long white turban wrapped around a green pointed hat, which flowed down the back of his clerical robes. He had a gentle yet strong voice and his surname meant 'flagbearer', because four generations back one of his grandfathers had been the local carrier of the Ottoman standard.

'So we believe a lot Sahabah and Tabi'un are buried in Cyprus because they ruled Cyprus for three hundred years, from seventh century until tenth century . . . Even in tenth century they didn't leave, they lost power, but they stayed!'

'So they built communities here?' I asked.

'They had cities, villages everywhere! . . . When they came, they ruled for three hundred years. They were dominant. They had everything! *Ya'ni* [literally, 'mean', but used like 'erm' in conversations], this part of the history is not well documented,' explained the *hoca*, who had been the Hala Sultan Mosque's guardian for fifteen years.

As Thorsten and I followed him across the mosque's main prayer hall, I noticed again the two large Stars of David on the mihrab with roses in their centre, from all those years ago. The mihrab looked exactly as it did in 2003. The square, white prayer hall and sandstone pillars were also the same. The only visible change was the green paint on the women's wooden *mahvil* (balcony), the minbar and the windows, which all used to be a bland beige. They were now the favoured colour of the Prophet. The mosque also felt lighter and airier with all its windows and doors flung wide open, a far cry from how I remembered it. Imam Şakir stood where the guide had been that day, in front of the gothic arch and the green iron gates. After pointing up to the inscription and telling us it dated the current building to 1813 and featured the *tughra* of the then reigning Ottoman sultan, Mahmut II, he opened the gate. The fear I had once felt was now replaced with excitement. My story was about to come full circle.

'I have to close the gate, otherwise it becomes a funfair inside!' said Imam Şakir, as he led us into the chamber, shutting the gate behind us.

'So these are the actual stones?' I asked, pointing at the huge square piece of rock 'suspended' above the apexed stone sarcophagus I had struggled to even look at in 2003.

Imam Şakir nodded.

I now knew the story well. The tomb was covered in richly embroidered and colourful Islamic rugs, beneath thick green curtains that had been tied back in a style that resembled a four-poster bed.

'On the night she was buried,' began the imam, 'it is believed this stone came to cover her.'

Imam Şakir described the story of how Umm Harâm's gravestones came to Cyprus, one of her many reported miracles. In his version – there are many – Umm Harâm buys three large stones from some nuns in a monastery while on a journey through Palestine. The nuns, wondering how she will carry them home, offer the stones to Umm Harâm for free. She accepts and tells them, 'They will be taken from here in due time.' Then, on the night she dies, the three stones miraculously cross the sea to come and cover her grave. One by her head, the second at her feet, and the third across the top.

'It is believed that it is protecting her tomb,' continued Imam Şakir, 'you won't find it anywhere. It is part of her miracle.'

I wasn't entirely convinced. As a Brit, I thought the way the stones were positioned resembled a late-Neolithic dolmen, but I didn't say anything. The room where Sheikh Nazim would come and sit as a child to speak with Umm Harâm was covered with the same wine-red patterned carpet as the mosque's main hall. The walls were exposed sandstone with windows on one side, looking out to several graves beneath a porch, which blocked much of the sunlight, making the room dark, just as I remembered it.

The first recorded mention of Umm Harâm's tomb is made by

the twelfth-century Persian traveller Ali ibn Abu Bakr al-Harawi in his *Kitab al-ishara ila ma 'rifat al-ziyara*, a kind of medieval guide for Muslim pilgrims, hence the word *ziyara* in the title. He tells us that Cyprus 'contains the tomb of Umm Harâm, daughter of Milhan, sister of Umm Sulaym', but al-Harawi does not mention actually visiting it or where it might be. He also mentions none of the other burial sites revered today as being the tombs of Companions. However, he does report seeing 'written on a rock . . . embedded in the eastern wall' of a church, the bismillah followed by Surah *al-Ikhlas* and the words 'This is the tomb of Urwa ibn Thabit, who died in the month of Ramadan in the year 29 AH', the Islamic year in which Umm Harâm died. This suggests that while the exact locations of the graves of those first European Muslim martyrs are now lost to us, their graves *were* marked, and in the case of Urwa some even had elaborate tombstones.

'We have *masjid* [here] before, the last structure is around three hundred years ago . . . but for one thousand four hundred years her place is visited, and I believe there must be a masjid here before!'

Imam Şakir explained that although no concrete records survive proving this is the location of Umm Harâm's actual grave or that there was a mosque here before the Ottoman conquest in 1570, he was convinced there was a mosque here from the seventh century, which meant, like the Piri Pasha and the Ömeriye, this too was a mosque potentially first built by Sahabah. There was certainly a mosque built on Qubrus by Mu'awiyah and, according to the records, a *medina* too (an urban centre or town), where he stationed a garrison. However, no further details are provided as to the size or location of either of these, and it is believed his son and successor, Caliph Yazid I, had both destroyed.

The earliest mention of a tomb and mosque on the current site is in a seventeenth-century Ottoman document that tells us from '1658 to 1661 a Şeyh Abdurrahim Efendi carried out the duties of *türbedar* [keeper of the *türbe*] of Ümmül Harâm, foster-aunt of the Prophet, a *türbe* which stood near the salt lake in the *kaza* [district of authority of a judge] of the Tuzla [a neighbourhood of Larnaca]'. The earliest person to describe the tomb and mention its miraculous stones is the Dutch traveller and artist Cornelis de Bruijn, who visited the tomb in 1683 but mistakenly claimed it housed 'the grave of Mina, mother of their prophet Mahomet'. De Bruijn does, however, note that the site is revered by Muslims and local Christians.

I asked if local Christians still revered the tomb.

'They come here and they leave children's clothes – small shoes or something – even today I find here and there baby clothes in bags!'

The *hoca* laughed.

'I have been asked many times to pray for Greek-Cypriot Christians who say that only Hala Sultan can help us . . . Greek-Cypriots, they really love this place too!'

The reputed tomb of Umm Harâm bint Milhân (Malik) ibn Khâlid al-Ansariyya al-Khazrajiyya, an aunt of the Prophet Muhammad who is believed to have died on the island around AD 647

I was not surprised to hear this as I came across similar practices at both Christian and Muslim shrines across the world in places as different as the Balkans and Thailand, where human beings, regardless of their actual faith, arrive hoping some of the holiness of the site rubs off on them.

After visiting the tomb, the *hoca* invited us to his office and we left the mosque, stepping onto the neatly paved pathways, past young rose bushes, mulberry and pomegranate trees. I noticed two families in the garden; one appeared to be Jewish.

'Cyprus is very popular with Israelis,' Thorsten said, when I pointed this out. 'The country is close and safe for them, with lots of beaches.'

'Really?' I asked, genuinely oblivious to this.

The family wandered around the mosque, making no attempt to enter it as the children ran off chasing each other towards the short palm trees.

A black and gold tapestry of the ninety-nine names of Allah hung in a gold frame above Imam Şakir's large desk, which was piled high with books in English, Turkish and Arabic: several on Islamic theology, but the vast majority on the Muslim heritage of Cyprus. The desk had a glass top, underneath which was a historical map of Cyprus. Like the imam, it was busy. On the far wall was a black-and-white picture of his teacher, Sheikh Nazim. The *hoca* took a seat on his small leather armchair, and with the door now closed appeared visibly relaxed. I wanted to know more about his teacher, the man I kept coming across on this trip in search of the island's earliest Muslim presence. Imam Şakir began by telling me he saw the sheikh in a dream and this prompted a journey to Lefke, where the sheikh immediately stupefied him.

'He looks at me and says: "Hmm, you are reading Qur'an?" Nobody knew except Allah that I'm reading Qur'an!' said Imam Şakir, chuckling to himself at the memory.

The *hoca* was eighteen at the time, and having grown up in a typical post-Kemalist family had barely started to explore Islam, yet the sheikh's insight told him this was the teacher he was looking for. He remained by the sheikh's side for the rest of his teacher's life. The sheikh was a funny, warm and humane person who hated waste, explained Imam Şakir, especially in people. He wanted to help everyone, and that was what made him a master. I asked what made him a mystic.

'You could feel his spirituality . . . you could see many different things in his dhikr, around him happening and . . . you can call it extra-terrestrial . . . but these are real!'

'So, when he is doing dhikr you can see things around him?'

'Yes, for inexperienced people this sounds off, but it was normal, I saw it many times when I was with him, not just in dhikr but other times when I am with him too.'

I asked the imam to elaborate. He thought for a while, then told me about a 4×4 the sheikh had brought over from the UK, because he knew it could take him anywhere. The imam and the sheikh would often load up the car and head into the mountains, off road, with the sheikh dictating where to go.

'In some places the grass is higher than the car! And he tells me: "I pass from here yesterday."'

Thorsten and I laughed out loud.

'Pass from where? We cannot understand what he is talking about.'

Thorsten and I looked at the *hoca* confused. He explained that sheikhs don't act rationally. He *was* there the day before, because he travels through the world and universe in ways we do not understand.

'What he means, ya'ni, might not be in your dimension.'

The *hoca* then used the story of Musa and al-Khidr to make his point. He believed we all had this capacity: to better our insight. It was just about unlocking it. He then picked up his phone.

'Like this phone, it has many functions, taking photos, recording, making calls, internet . . . now this is perfectly normal! But for somebody fifty years ago, forget about one thousand, he will go crazy and say, "What is this?" They will call you a magician!'

Like a smartphone, the *hoca* believed human beings had mental and spiritual potential they could unlock with the help of a master like Sheikh Nazim.

'This is what the real awliyah, the real sheikhs or saints, teach us, and Sheikh Nazim was, *mashallah* [as God has willed it] . . . Erm, an extremely powerful one, mashallah.'

There was a pause, and I decided to ask the *hoca* about something I had been waiting to ask him since we met. What did he know about the reported relationship between Sheikh Nazim and the current king of the United Kingdom?

The *hoca* thought for a while.

'I heard, I didn't see myself.' The imam was choosing his words very carefully. 'Sheikh Nazim saying that Charles has accepted Islam, I hear him say his name is "Hussain" and he is going to be king, and King Hussain will meet with the *Mehdi* [descendant of the Prophet who will come at the end of time].'

'And you personally heard Sheikh Nazim say this?'

'I heard him say he's [Charles] a Muslim and his name is Hussain.'

Thorsten and I exchanged glances. I had mentioned the rumour, instigated by a Turkish TV interview Sheikh Nazim did in January 1994, to Thorsten on the way over, and we both expected the *hoca* either to dismiss it out of hand or to have no plausible knowledge about the alleged conversion of the then Prince of Wales. Neither of us expected this. The *hoca* explained this was during one of Sheikh Nazim's many visits to London, when he heard that they met discreetly around the time of Princess Diana's death, but he didn't know the exact details of the meeting. I asked if it was true that the king of the UK was now observing *taqiyya*.

'Definitely! He has to!'

Thorsten had a confused expression on his face. We explained that the practice of taqiyya is when one's Muslim faith can be kept hidden because it is too dangerous to reveal it.

'The tabloids were saying he had lost his mind, he was not fit to be a king, etc. They knew. They knew,' continued the *hoca*.

Princess Diana died in 1997, but King Charles's fascination with Islam began much earlier. In the summer of 1971, the young prince sat for the artist Derek Hill, who introduced him to the majesty and beauty of Islamic art and architecture. In the mid-1980s, he met Professor Keith Critchlow, an expert in the field and a 'sacred geometer' – someone who believed in the sacredness of geometric shapes and proportions. Author of the seminal book *Islamic Patterns*, Critchlow taught the young prince the spiritual dimension of Islamic art and architecture, and it was under Critchlow's tuition that Charles first began to study Sufism. The two of them went on to found The Prince's Foundation School of Traditional Arts, one of the most significant institutes nurturing classical Islamic art and architectural traditions anywhere in the West today. Charles also became a huge admirer of at least two prominent European converts to Islam: the French philosopher and intellectual René Jean-Marie-Joseph Guénon (Abdalwahid Yahia), who was inducted into the Shadili Sufi order, and the famous English convert and scholar Martin Lings (Abu Bakr Siraj al-Din), who joined the Alawiyya Sufi order and whose highly-acclaimed biography of the Prophet, *Muhammad: His Life Based on the Earliest Sources*, Charles read cover to cover. In 1993, he became a patron of the then fledgling Centre for Islamic Studies at the University of Oxford, where he would give his fascinating lecture, 'Islam and the West', describing 'a powerful feeling of disenchantment, of the realization that Western technology and material things are insufficient, and that a deeper meaning to life lies elsewhere in the essence of Islamic belief'. I read the speech many years later and was left gobsmacked. The prince was the first major Western leader to publicly call out the collective amnesia the 'West' had suffered since the medieval period about its own intellectual and cultural history; he was the first to concede that there was a huge 'debt' Western Europe owed to Islamic culture, stating that the failure to admit this stemmed 'from the straitjacket of history which we have inherited'. The prince then went on to describe how Western Europe has repeatedly denied that 'not only did Muslim Spain gather and preserve the intellectual content of ancient Greek and Roman civilization, it also interpreted and expanded upon that civilization, and made a vital contribution of its own in so many fields of human endeavour – in science, astronomy, mathematics,

THE 'GRANDMOTHER' OF MUSLIM EUROPE

algebra (itself an Arabic word), law, history, medicine, pharmacology, optics, agriculture, architecture, theology, music . . .' before adding, 'the surprise, ladies and gentlemen, is the extent to which Islam has been a part of Europe for so long . . . and the extent to which it has contributed so much towards the civilization which we all too often think of, wrongly, as entirely Western'. He did this, according to Imam Şakir, just four years before embracing Islam and giving his allegiance to Sheikh Nazim.

King Charles is not the first English monarch to have flirted with Islam. In 774, the Anglo-Saxon King Offa of Mercia minted a gold coin that featured the Islamic declaration of faith in Arabic around the edges and the king's title, 'Offa Rex', in Latin in the middle. During the medieval period, no fewer than two kings of England threatened conversion to Islam. First Henry II told Pope Alexander III he would 'become an infidel' if the pope did not rein in his nemesis Thomas Becket, the Archbishop of Canterbury, and then, in 1215, his son King John I, also annoyed with a pope, this time Innocent III, for placing England under an interdict and excommunicating him, tried to create an alliance with the Muslim Almohad caliph Muhammad an-Nasir, the most powerful Muslim ruler of Europe, by offering to place England at the caliph's disposal and 'adhere faithfully to the law of Muhammad'. In Tudor England, Queen Elizabeth I had such amicable relations with North Africa that an ambassador of the Saadi sultan Abu al-Abbas Ahmad al-Mansur arrived in London in 1600 to conclude an alliance that would have seen England help the Muslims retake Spain from the Catholics. A painting of the ambassador still hangs in the Shakespeare Institute as a reminder of the astonishing moment. Elizabeth also tried to create an alliance with the Shi'a ruler of Persia, Shah Tahmasp, and had commercial treaties and very warm relations with the Ottoman sultan Murad III. Then there was the infamous relationship between Queen Victoria and her *munshi* (secretary) and teacher, Abdul Karim, who taught her Urdu and Arabic, and exposed her to Islam, leading to the Empress of India developing sympathies for the religion. More recently, an actual member of the royal, albeit extended, family, Sir Archibald Hamilton, 5th Baronet of Trebishun and 3rd Baronet of Marlborough House, converted to Islam in 1924, changing his name to Abdullah.

The *hoca* explained that Sheikh Nazim had many aristocratic followers across Europe, and they would all come to his headquarters in London. Aristocratic converts, like Sir Abdullah Hamilton, were nothing new to Islam in the West. Along with other influential aristocrats such as Lord Headley and Lady Evelyn Cobbold, they were part of, arguably, Britain's first *real* indigenously Muslim community, formed around the end of the Victorian era from about 1887, firstly in Liverpool and continued at the country's first purpose-built mosque, the Shah Jahan Mosque in Woking, Surrey. Sheikh Nazim would have known about this community and in all likelihood made ziyara to the graves of Sir Archibald and Lord Headley, as he was a frequent visitor to the Brookwood Cemetery, where they are buried, in what is considered the country's oldest recognized Muslim cemetery, founded in 1884 as the Muhammadan Cemetery. The Brookwood Cemetery is also home to a huge Turkish-Cypriot burial ground, which is connected to the Ramadan Mosque in Shacklewell Lane, East London, a mosque Sheikh Nazim helped to establish in 1977 and where the funeral of one of the last Ottoman princesses and wife of the last Nizam of Hyderabad, HIH Hayriya Aisha Durr-i-Shahvar, was held in 2006. The daughter of Abdulmejid II, the last Ottoman caliph, HIH Durr-i-Shahvar, is also buried in Brookwood, beside her mother Mehisti Hanim, the caliph's fourth wife.

We returned to the story of the *hoca*'s teacher's frequent visits to see his grandmother.

'When they find him, he is in the tomb! If people asked him why he went there all the time, he would tell them it was to speak with his grandmother,' explained the *hoca*.

I asked what he meant by 'speaking' with his grandmother.

'When he was coming here as a child, ya'ni, he is *seeing* her.'

Thorsten and I exchanged glances.

'You mean, not metaphorically but literally?'

The imam nodded away. What about him, I asked, had he ever seen her? The imam smiled, and began with the story of how he became the *hoca* at the *türbe*. It started with a call from Sheikh Nazim in 2006 when the *hoca* was living in England doing his sheikh's work. After saying hello, Sheikh Nazim wanted to know if he was coming. It was another of those strange mystical episodes when the sheikh appeared to have already experienced the moment but the *hoca* had not. When the sheikh then demanded he return to Cyprus because Hala Sultan had 'ordered' him to come, and was 'waiting' for him to become imam of the *türbe*'s mosque, the imam said he nearly crashed his car, which he was driving whilst on the call. He knew the sheikh was not talking in metaphors: she had *actually* asked. The appointment was not random. It was ordained. So, after settling his affairs in England and uprooting his family, Imam Şakir arrived back in Cyprus in late August 2008. At first, though, he had no access to the site, so he led prayers outside the complex. Then in the month of Ramadan, the holiest month of the year for Muslims, the *hoca* finally entered the *türbe*.

'I entered the tomb saying the bismillah with my two friends, and right there in front of the tomb's door is Hala Sultan!'

'*Subhanallah*,' I said, a shiver running down my spine.

The *hoca* was quiet, as if reliving the moment.

'How did you know it was her?'

The *hoca* smiled.

'As soon as I saw her again, I knew I had seen her before, but I forgot it.'

The *hoca* first met Hala Sultan in 1974, aged six, when he visited the *türbe* with his family.

'I was walking between the legs of the elders. I remember I saw a lady, grandmother, very big lady, with dark skin. I remember her face, so clear! I see now: she's wearing a grey outfit with cover and her face is like moon and when I turned inside the tomb, in the left-hand corner of the tomb, she is looking at me like this.'

The *hoca* made a warm facial expression.

'I'm trying to understand who she is . . . I wasn't scared, I didn't feel scared.'

The *hoca* explained that this memory only came back to him when he stepped into the mosque in Ramadan 2006.

'I saw it [the memory] again like a video! . . . It was a very beautiful surprise for me.'

'Did your friends see anything?'

The *hoca* shook his head.

'So, you have the *noor* [light]?'

The *hoca* didn't see it as a gift or a special insight. For him it was just confirmation of his calling.

'So, he was right, she *was* waiting for you!' I exclaimed.

'Exactly,' said the *hoca*, clapping his hands together.

I asked if that was the only time he had seen her. The *hoca* smiled again, as if each nugget he was sharing was a little secret he was telling only us. He had actually seen her many times since and when I asked if he speaks with her, he told me he does, but not through words.

'I have asked her on a couple of occasions about some issues I had and she responded, "*Alhamdulillah*".' He smiled, making his eyes narrow.

I believe him. I am not entirely sure why, but I do.

'This was the centre of Turkish-Cypriot life until recently,' the *hoca* said, an air of slight resignation in his voice.

Although Kemalist attitudes eradicated many of the practices, especially widespread pilgrimage to Hala Sultan – with some locals equating it with performing the *Hajj*, a pilgrimage to the Ka'aba, the house of Allah, in Makkah – many people still came here on the biggest festival days right up until the split in 1974, which in essence was the final nail in the coffin. After the war it became too dangerous for Muslims to even venture south, let alone set off on a pilgrimage, and for decades the Hala Sultan, though still somewhat revered by locals, lay neglected and overlooked. Forgotten even. This is why for the first two or three years of his tenure at the *türbe*, the *hoca*'s congregation was tiny.

'Now every Friday the mosque is full!' exclaimed the *hoca* proudly, his voice much more upbeat.

'Now Hala Sultan's importance is coming out again, soon she will be very important for spreading mercy and love to the West, because there is a misconception of Islam in the West, she is God's mercy! She is sleeping at the gates of Europe, this is something designed by Allah fifteen centuries ago,' the *hoca* said, 'it is not random!'

He then explained why he believed *she* was specifically chosen and not someone else, not a male Companion but a woman.

'If it had been a main male Companion, it would not have been as effective. He would have been viewed as a warrior, but she is a "mother" character,' said the *hoca*.

Cyprus had a long history of female cults, the most famous being the cult of the Greek goddess Aphrodite, which emerged on the island during the early Bronze Age, with the Temple of Aphrodite in Paphos the centre of the cult. The cult of Aphrodite is said to have emerged from that of the Cypriot fertility goddess Astarte, a deity also of sexuality and war. Other female cults on the island included those of Ariadne and of the Greek goddesses Demeter, Kore, Hera and Athena. With the advent of Christianity in the fourth century, these were replaced in Cyprus by the likes of the Virgins St Paraskevi, St Catherine, St Helena and St Marina – with one theory claiming the site of the Hala Sultan was once dedicated to St Marina, before Umm Harâm's *türbe* was built.

For the *hoca* the fact that Hala Sultan was a woman, an aunt of the Prophet and a 'grandmother' of his great teacher – a maternal, loving, nurturing personality – made her much more appealing and accessible not just to the female-cult-loving Cypriots, but to all of Europe.

'If you want to give the "mercy" message of Islam, she is the best person. She is not seen as a conqueror; she is seen as a source of love.'

PART I: WHEN MUSLIMS CAME TO EUROPE

Imam Şakir Alemdar, whose ancestor had been an Ottoman flagbearer, is the current imam of the Hala Sultan Mosque

I realized it didn't actually matter that Cyprus was historically a haven for female cults, and that some commentators viewed Umm Harâm as just a Muslim version of that. It didn't even matter that she might not be buried at this very spot. None of it mattered, because, as the *hoca* said, there was a reason why it is only her story and her name that have survived from that epoch. There was a reason why her narrative had been passed down and no other, and maybe some of us were just not qualified enough to understand why.

As I got up from the leather armchair, my legs unsticking themselves, I showed the *hoca* my copy of Aristidou's *The Tekke of Hala Sultan*, urging him to look inside, where I had written the date of my visit.

'September 2003?' he asked, raising his eyebrows.

'My whole journey . . .' I said slowly, 'through Islam in Europe was started by Hala Sultan!'

The *hoca* looked up at me from behind his narrow spectacles, his eyebrows still raised in genuine surprise.

'Mashallah!' he finally said.

★

THE 'GRANDMOTHER' OF MUSLIM EUROPE

After securing Cyprus, Mu'awiyah followed this up by taking Crete, Rhodes, Kos and the Dodecanese islands. This set alarm bells ringing in Byzantium and Emperor Constans II took it upon himself to crush the upstart maritime power, sailing out in 655 to confront the Muslims at the famous Battle of the Masts (or Phoenix), only to narrowly escape with his life, when Mu'awiyah's fleet annihilated the Byzantines. Had it not been for the outbreak of civil war in the heart of the Caliphate with the murder of Mu'awiyah's cousin, Caliph Uthman in 656, the Muslim navy would have been sailing for Constantinople. The respite for the Byzantines would only be temporary though. Mu'awiyah returned to the Levant in 661, this time as caliph, setting up his capital in Damascus, which would become the seat for the dynasty he established upon his ascension to the Caliphate, the Umayyads. Two more caliphs had come and gone in that time: Ali, who was also murdered, and his son Hasan, who abdicated. The man who some believed the Prophet prayed would one day lead the *ummah* (Muslim community) was now in charge. Mu'awiyah might well have seen this as divinely ordained and, after consolidating his power, restarted his campaign against the Byzantines, picking off more islands in the Mediterranean before sending a fleet to blockade Constantinople in 674. Mu'awiyah laid siege to the walled city for four years, and was only repelled by the unstoppable and mysterious Byzantine weapon known as Greek fire – a kind of ancient napalm that would continue to burn in water, making it deadly during naval warfare. The message, though, had been delivered: a new superpower now reigned supreme in the waters the Muslims still called Bahr ar-Rum – the 'Sea of the Romans' – and the Byzantines would do well to steer clear of it. When the Caesar of Arabia died in 680, buried in the Prophet's shirt, his phenomenal leadership and political genius had stabilized an empire on the verge of collapse; Mu'awiyah had expanded the Muslim empire to become one of the largest in the world, and in taking the island of Qubrus secured a strategic base that would ensure his descendants made the most of their foothold on the continent. Mu'awiyah had made Islam European faster than any of the other Abrahamic faiths: he had brought Islam to Europe a mere sixteen years after the death of its founder, more than twice as fast as Christianity and several centuries quicker than Judaism.

PART 2

The Children of al-Andalus

6

A Daughter of al-Andalus

Palermo, Sicily

It was a brilliantly sunny day as I made my way along the narrow Via Maqueda on my first day in Palermo. Tall neoclassical apartment blocks with wrought-iron balconies and Graeco-Roman features loomed overhead, providing slivers of welcome shade; beneath them were rows of clothes and shoe shops, many selling the kind of light, flowing dresses ideal for a Sicilian summer. A Bangladeshi woman, her hair covered by a light scarf, used a long wooden pole to bring down a green and blue dress for a female tourist in a pair of tortoise-shell sunglasses. As I passed the shop entrance, I peered in to see her young children sitting inside, playing on electronic devices. Squeezed in between the apartment blocks were huge churches, mostly dating from the fifteenth and sixteenth centuries, also in the neoclassical style infused with later baroque-rococo. Some of the shops had their shutters down; these were heavily graffitied, as were the walls leading down narrow alleys. Bored-looking men sat on stone benches, flanked by small myrtle bushes in grey metal planters, and cafés spilled out onto the pavement. One of these, on the corner of Via dei Candelai, was the Bar del Centro, where Sheikh Dr Badri al-Madani, the imam of Moschea di Tunisia, sat drinking an espresso.

'The mosque was opened in 1990,' said the imam from behind a pair of large sunglasses after we had embraced and salaamed one another.

He spoke English slowly and deliberately; one of four languages he had mastered.

PART 2: THE CHILDREN OF AL-ANDALUS

The imam explained he worked for the Tunisian government, and it was their mosque. I was surprised by this. I had expected to hear the typical migrant-community-owned story. Tunisians were among the first immigrants to Italy in the modern era. From around the 1960s, small groups began arriving in the west of Sicily at towns like Mazara del Vallo, the part of the island closest to Tunisia. I had imagined Moschea di Tunisia had been founded by one of these waves. I asked the imam to elaborate. He leaned in.

'To try and control the Muslims here,' he said in a conspiratorial tone.

The imam then glanced either side of us. A man was cycling slowly up and down playing loud dance music from a speaker on his bike.

'Really?' I asked, a little shocked.

The imam leaned in again and explained that the former president of Tunisia, Zine El Abidine Ben Ali, was worried about Islamic fundamentalism. The mosque was his attempt to monitor Tunisian extremists that had escaped to Palermo.

'At the time there are only Tunisians that come here for commerce and those that "escaped" . . . Ben Ali makes the mosque to see who comes to the mosque.'

'Wow!' I said, genuinely astonished that the first mosque opened on the island since its ancient Islamic period was intended to spy on Muslims.

The imam explained that between 1990 and 2011 the mosque served its purpose, but after the Arab Spring toppled Ben Ali, it was abandoned by the Tunisian authorities and the local Maghrebi community took over the building — a deconsecrated church — until he arrived.

'I had never been to Balermo, so in 2021 one of my friends [at the Ministry] said to me we need an imam in Balermo; you should go. I think "why not?"' the imam said, unable to pronounce the P in Palermo, just like his North African ancestors who had conquered the town and called it Bal'harm.

The imam had only been in Palermo for a year and a half and explained that he had to be sensitive and tactful in replacing the old custodians, who had no legal right over the property.

'After I got rid of the Maghrebi man, I formed a new team: young men, students to who I say, "you are the future" ... There is now a small madrasa and we also teach Arabic, fiqh and Qur'an to adults every Friday before *khutbah* [sermon] and Saturday evening.'

The imam showed me his phone. On it was a Facebook page he had made for the mosque. He scrolled through, revealing videos and photos of him giving khutbahs; attending interfaith events; the mosque's muezzin giving the adhan; and of an 'open' *iftar* (meal to break the daily fast in Ramadan) event with non-Muslims. I was impressed.

I asked Dr Badri, who was born in Ksibet El-Mediouni, a coastal village close to Sousse, where the Muslim conquest of Siqilliya (as Sicily was known to the Muslims) was launched almost 1,200 years ago, what he knew about the island's Muslim history.

'Ibn al-Furat was a *Maliki* and *Hanafi* scholar with an open mind,' began the imam, naming the two Islamic theological schools al-Furat was versed in. 'They came with an army of Berbers, men from al-Andalus, Arab Tunisians and different Africans, and they brought to Sicily many good things: culture, science, engineering, medicine.'

I nodded away as Dr Badri reeled off what Muslims brought to Sicily.

The Muslim presence in Sicily actually began earlier, again with that brilliant Umayyad and Caesar of Arabia, Mu'awiyah, whose general occupied the island in 667. By then, Mu'awiyah was the undisputed Caliph of Islam and trying to keep the Byzantines on their toes. But expanding so much so quickly had its pitfalls, and the occupation of Siqilliya was short lived – just a month – with Mu'awiyah having to call back his troops to help secure his other newly conquered territories along the North African coast in what was known as Ifriqiya. Yet, even this brief occupation had a lasting impact on the hearts and minds of the Muslims. Mu'awiyah's

PART 2: THE CHILDREN OF AL-ANDALUS

continued pursuit of the Byzantines had exposed the weakness of the hitherto formidable Christian empire. The victory at the Battle of the Masts, followed by the attempt on the capital of 'Rum' – as it was known to the Muslims – and Mu'awiyah's securing of Cyprus as a garrison, along with other smaller islands in the Bahr ar-Rum, had signalled the end of Byzantine naval supremacy in those waters, giving later Muslim rulers the confidence to penetrate further into Europe.

Mu'awiyah's brief occupation of Sicily created another significant legacy for medieval Muslims. Just like his first campaign in Cyprus, several members of the Salaf were martyred in Siqilliya, including, once again, a female relative of the Prophet Muhammad. This immediately elevated the island to a place of ziyara, and it was also featured in al-Harawi's great book of medieval Muslim pilgrimage sites. Al-Harawi identifies four major sites of ziyara in Siqilliya. In Marsa Ali (Marsala) he writes that there are 'seven of the Companions, may God be pleased with them, in a single tomb'. In the mountainous town of Prizzi is buried one of Mu'awiyah's most celebrated generals, Hassan ibn Mu'awiya ibn Hudayj al-Sakuni. In the island's eastern city of Catania, there is a cemetery where 'thirty men from the Successors' are buried, but the most interesting tomb, says al-Harawi, is the one in the western half of the city of Trapani. This is the tomb of 'A'isha, daughter of Junada ibn Uways ibn Junada, the brother of Abu Dharr', one of Muhammad's nieces, and just like Umm Haram's, A'isha's tomb had been attached to a mosque and the most revered on the island. These tombs and the brief foray also presented later Muslim would-be conquerors with their very own Reconquest narrative.

I asked the imam if he knew anything about the whereabouts of such tombs, but he shook his head slowly. The locations of the tombs are long forgotten.

According to the founding legend of the Emirate of Siqilliya, the opportunity to take the island in 827 was presented by a double-crossing Byzantine naval commander called Euphemius, who had fallen foul of the emperor and developed ambitions of ruling the island himself. Euphemius turned up in Kairouan to present the Aghlabid Emir Ziyadatallah with an offer to pay a handsome yearly tribute, if he helped Euphemius conquer Siqilliya. At first, Ziyadatallah was hesitant. He had just spent three years quashing an internal military revolt, and there was the small matter of a peace agreement between his Emirate and the Byzantines. His council, though, in particular Kairouan's respected *qadi* (legal judge), Asad ibn al-Furat, saw in Euphemius's proposal an opportunity to advance Aghlabid domains and further spread the word of Islam. Ibn al-Furat, an intelligent and astute adviser, also pointed out that this new and noble cause would give Ziyadatallah's fractured fighting force a common purpose to unite under.

Though acknowledging the Abbasid Caliphate in Baghdad, the Aghlabids, like all the rulers in the Mediterranean, also paid homage to the Umayyad Emir of Córdoba, Abdu'r Rahman II. The Iberian Umayyad dynasty's meteoric rise, following the murder of almost their entire tribe, made it clear the 'sons of caliphs' — as they liked to refer to themselves — were caliphs-in-waiting. This is why the Aghlabid fleet of 200 ships that set sail from the Bay of Sousse for Mazara del Vallo, at the western edge of Sicily, were later joined by a hundred Umayyad ships sent by Abdu'r Rahman II from Córdoba.

'They called Balermo, Bal'harm, and there were three hundred mosques. The big cathedral was the Masjid al-Kabir.'

Imam Badri was quoting the famous words of the tenth-century Muslim geographer, and Fatimid spy, Ibn Hawqal, who claimed Bal'harm was home to 301 mosques. His contemporary, the great tenth-century Palestinian geographer al-Maqdisi, claimed 'the Muslims have no island more splendid, more prosperous, or with more cities'.

Sicily's Muslim period lasted just over two centuries: a brief and brilliant time that would completely alter the island and lay the foundations for one of Europe's most fascinating Christian kingdoms, the Arab-Normans of Sicily, who took over from the Muslims and went completely native.

PART 2: THE CHILDREN OF AL-ANDALUS

'They also spoke Arabic and dressed like Arabs . . .' began the imam, before pausing. 'They used the Muslims, because they saw the Muslims had intelligence so they used them to learn all of this through people like al-Idrisi, Ibn Hamdis and Muhammad Siqilli.'

As the imam spoke his hands spoke too, making the gold watch on his wrist wink in the Sicilian sunshine.

The Normans first arrived on the shores of the Emirate of Siqilliya in Messina, in 1038, initially alongside the Byzantines, but soon they broke away and conquered the island for themselves over a period of about fifty years, so that by 1091 Sicily was again Christian, but, as the imam pointed out, with a distinctly 'Muslim' air. The reason for this was very simple. During the 200 years or so of Muslim rule, first under the Aghlabids, then the Shi'a Fatimids and their viceroys, the Kalbids, Sicily flourished like never before. New agricultural techniques included systems of hydraulic irrigation which took water from streams, rivers, springs and wells and directed it through ditches and channels that criss-crossed the country to bring water to fields, mills, gardens and settlements all over Sicily. Meanwhile in urban areas like Palermo underground channels called *qanat* served its people, ensuring water reached every corner of the city. This is the reason why many historical local Sicilian terms linked to hydro-technology originated from Arabic, like *gebbia* to mean reservoir (from *jabiya*) and *saia* (from *saqiya*) to mean a water channel. Combined with the abundance of new crops, these techniques introduced by the Muslims meant, during the Emirate period, Sicily underwent what historians have called a green revolution, making it both self-sufficient and a bustling hub of international trade. Citrus fruits such as the famous Sicilian lemon appear for the first time, along with dates and sugar cane, henna for dyeing and ceremonial use, mulberry trees to breed silkworms for silk, sumac seeds for tanning, and papyrus plants for creating rope and, of course, high-quality paper. All of it enters medieval Europe for the first time. The Muslims also improved fishing techniques, in particular tuna fishing, which would become so important for Sicily; they developed the mining industry and laid the foundation for Italian silk production, which would later flourish. During this time Sicily's living standards were among the highest in the world.

The Muslims also built sophisticated cities where communities of highly literate Jews, Christians and Muslims lived side by side, and where poets, mystics, scholars and artists gathered. Muslim pilgrims came from far and wide to visit and learn from the mystics and perform ziyara at the tombs of Companions, Successors and saints. So luminous was the Emirate's capital of Bal'harm during its most stable period, under the rule of the Kalbids between the tenth and eleventh centuries, that for some visitors it was comparable with Constantinople and the Umayyad capital of Córdoba in Spain. When the Normans conquered the Emirate of Siqilliya, they knew they had inherited a culture far superior to their own, and to start with changed almost nothing. Thus Sicily transitioned so seamlessly from an enlightened Muslim rule to enlightened Arab-Norman Christian rule that when the Spanish Muslim traveller Abu'l-Husayn Muhammad ibn Ahmad ibn Jubayr wandered through the island in 1184, more than a century after Norman rule had started, the culture and aesthetics of Siqilliya felt so familiar to the Andalusian that he described it as a 'Daughter of al-Andalus', and compared Palermo to the great city of Córdoba.

Imam Badri had an impressive CV; I knew this because he sent it to me before we met. It revealed he had studied literature as an undergrad and had a Master's in Islamic science from the prestigious al-Zaytouna University in Tunisia, as well as a doctorate. He was attached to the Tunisian Ministry of Religious Affairs, had a wealth of endorsements and certifications in traditional Islamic jurisprudence, and was the grandson of the founder of the Tunisian Sufi order Tarikat al-Madaniyya, to which Dr Badri remained attached. This was no ordinary imam; what then, I wondered, was he doing here in Palermo?

'Everybody in Tunisia knows me, they ask me to become minister, but I don't want to . . . I want to stay free to do work in *dawah* [literally, 'to invite' to the faith] and be active in society.'

This was one of the key principles of the Madaniyya order, an offshoot of the larger Shadiliyya order, whose founder, Sheikh Muhammad ibn Khalifa al-Madani, believed Sufism shouldn't be something that stays hidden and private but a part of everyday life.

'I am a Sufi, but I believe Sufism and Islam is not for the *zawiya* but for the outside.'

A zawiya was another term for a lodge, of which there were many in North Africa, a region historically popular with Sufis, just as Siqilliya had been, even under the Normans. In one of the most fascinating accounts from his time in Siqilliya, Ibn Jubayr describes spending the night in a stunning zawiya called Qasr Sa'd, east of the capital, Bal'harm. The Andalusian arrives at the zawiya – 'known for its grace and blessedness being visited by men from all countries' because it was surrounded by the tombs of 'ascetics and pious' people – on a Friday evening, in the holy month of Ramadan. Qasr Sa'd was a fortified zawiya, a common sight, says Ibn Hawqal, when he visited the island in 973. These fortified lodges began life as lookout posts to watch for Byzantine naval attacks, but over time started housing communities of Islamic mystics, or Sufis, known as *murabitun*, who lived there observing an austere lifestyle. Ibn Hawqal called such a fortification a *ribat*, and they were mostly concentrated along the coast near Bal'harm as well as at Sciacca and Agrigento, with some evidence ribats were also built in the interior. The name *murabitun* is where the modern Sicilian word *murabbitu*, to describe a hermit or a teetotaller, and the Sicilian family name Morabito are said to come from.

Had the Sufi tradition been revived in modern Sicily, I asked the imam, were there any active tariqas here?

'No,' said the imam, before adding with a smile, 'but I hope there will be some in the future!'

As in historical al-Andalus, Sufism became so widespread and established in the Emirate of Siqilliya that, by the start of the tenth century, would-be mystics came from all over the world – just as they still do today in northern Cyprus – to study and learn from the great Siqilliyan Sufi masters, spending time in zawiyas like Qasr Sa'd. Among the most famous Sufi masters of the tenth century was Abu Uthman Sa'id ibn Sallam al-Kirkinti, from Agrigento (as the last name suggests), who was also a respected legal scholar. He spent time studying with mystics in Nishapur in Iran, and also led prayers at the Ka'aba in Makkah as the official sheikh of the mosque there. His contemporary Abd al-Rahman ibn Muhammad ibn Abd Allah al-Bakri al-Siqilli was educated at the holiest city in Imam Badr's native Tunisia, Kairouan. Al-Siqilli also authored several treatises on Sufism, as did the mystic Atiq ibn al-Samantari, who lived in Siqilliya a century or so after both Ibn Sallam and Abd al-Rahman.

A woman begging in a combination of Italian and French stopped beside us and held out her hand. The imam reached into his pocket and pulled out some change. The woman took it and moved on swiftly, without thanking him. It was almost time to visit his mosque and so I asked Imam Badri about a rumour I had heard that a historical 'mosque' can be found inside one of the stunning Arab-Norman churches of Palermo, the Chiesa di San Giovanni degli Eremiti – Church of St John of the Hermits. The imam wasn't sure.

'But this is possible,' he said, before nonchalantly adding, 'the same thing is in my mosque here – underground there is a mosque.'

'Really? . . . In your mosque?' I asked. 'And how old is the church?'

'More than one thousand years . . . But this, it's like a secret place. And the Christians tried to cover this . . .'

'How do you know it's a mosque?'

'There is mihrab and there is *qibla* . . . It's a little bit obscure, I go there secretly because for me I think that Allah has sent me to Palermo, *alhamdulillah*, to renovate Islam in Sicily . . . I am a Sufi and I want us to live in peace,' he smiled, revealing a set of clean white teeth.

The route to the imam's mosque took us along Via del Celso, which had a small Bangladeshi grocery store, called Sonar Bangla – 'Golden Bengal' – on the corner. The narrow alley was grubby and the walls heavily graffitied; the only redeeming feature was an ornate black iron street lamp overhead. As we walked, the imam told me his plans to create a centre for training other imams at the mosque.

'This is the best way to avoid ignorance and extremist factions creeping in.'

He also wanted to make it a site of heritage for people to visit. As the alley narrowed, I noticed that all the windows at ground level had thick metal security bars.

Interior of Moschea di Tunisia, the first mosque established in Sicily (1990) since the expulsion of Muslims in the thirteenth century

One of the most interesting things about Ibn Jubayr's visit to the zawiya of Qasr Sa'd is his assertion that the mosque at the very top of the fort is 'one of the finest mosques in the world'. Noting its oblong shape, with long arcades, Ibn Jubayr counted forty beautiful lamps made from brass and crystal inside the mosque, which was furnished with mats so beautiful that even he – a globetrotting traveller – had never seen anything like them. It was Ramadan and so Ibn Jubayr would have taken part in the supererogatory late-night *tarawih* prayers after arriving at Qasr Sa'd and breaking his fast. He then spent 'the most pleasing and agreeable night in that mosque'. It is quite an accolade, given the great mosques Ibn

Jubayr would have no doubt prayed in during his journey to and from Makkah and Madinah.

I told the imam how astonished I was to learn Ibn Jubayr claimed that Siqilliya was once home to one of the finest mosques in the world, and that this wasn't even the main mosque of Palermo. The imam nodded but didn't say anything. There was nothing to say; none of the ancient mosques of Siqilliya have survived. Like the imam's secret 'mosque', only scant remains are found scattered across modern Sicily. For example, in the Church of St Mary of the Admiral, in the heart of Palermo's old town, which like the smaller San Cataldo church beside it has windows covered in Islamic-inspired geometric patterns, and bright-red domes – distinctive traits of Sicily's Arab-Norman churches – are two beautifully carved calligraphic 'well-wishing' Qur'anic verses. These are found on a tall, slender, reddish-brown and grey Corinthian marble pillar, near the back of the church. Ibn Jubayr actually visited the church, built between 1146 and 1151 by one of the great *Amir al-Umara* – admirals – George of Antioch, and described it as 'beyond dispute the most wonderful edifice in the world'. The Andalusian was there on Christmas Day and noted the beautiful local Christian women in all their finery and wearing henna, but didn't mention the inscriptions, as the pillar was added four centuries later, during its baroque expansion. A similar example can be seen in another place the Andalusian visited, the then Great 'cathedral mosque' of Bal'harm – now Palermo Cathedral. Ibn Jubayr prayed tarawih there, not knowing it would be one of the last times the Ramadan night prayers would be held at the mosque, which was torn down the following year. The only echo of it being a mosque can be seen on a pillar beneath the cathedral's famous fifteenth-century portico – yet again, a later addition – where verses from the Qur'an's Surah *al-A'raf* ('The Heights') are beautifully inscribed inside a raised, ornate arabesque frame. In all likelihood, both pillars – added long after the initial churches were constructed – came from mosques that had stood elsewhere in the city, and were torn down later.

Verses from the Qur'an's Surah *al-A'raf* ('The Heights') on a pillar at the entrance of the Cathedral of Palermo and (*right*) Qur'anic verses on a pillar inside the Church of St Mary of the Admiral

At the top of the road, the peach-coloured facade of Imam Badri's mosque came into view: a rectangular two-storey building in the neoclassical style, complete with decorative plaster wreaths like those on a Wedgwood vase, giving the main entrance, held up by two Corinthian pillars, the feel and look of a Graeco-Roman temple, except for a white plastic sign that read in Arabic: 'Masjid Balermo'.

'Look, I added the *hilal* like the original mosque,' Imam Badri said, pointing to the small green fence surrounding the front, where thick bars were topped with small crescents. Before I could ask, he showed me a diagram of the building on his phone. It featured a tall white minaret, where now there are a series of derelict buildings, and fencing similar to what was in front of me. I didn't know if this was a picture of what he believed the original mosque looked like or if this was a proposal for what he hoped the mosque *would* look like.

The imam and I entered through a side door, leading into his office, where a decorator in stained white overalls was sitting on the floor scrolling his phone. The main prayer hall, like the exterior, had a neoclassical style with moulded pillars and wreaths on all four walls, as well as a beautiful arch and trim along the top. It resembled the walls of a library in a stately home, except here the niches didn't contain leatherbound copies of Tolstoy, Cervantes or Shakespeare, but copies of the Qur'an and small collections of *tafsir* (commentaries on the Qur'an) and hadiths, in the Arabic language. The mosque building underwent major renovation work in the late 1980s after it was given to Ben Ali. Old pictures reveal a decaying shell with no roof. A large green and white wooden archway had been installed at an angle near the old altar; the mosque's mihrab had a chandelier of faux-crystal teardrops hanging from the centre, and a small wooden pulpit, where Imam Badri stood to deliver his Friday sermons. Narrow and compact, Sicily's first post-Muslim-expulsion mosque was smaller than I expected. I asked how many people could pray there.

'Maybe one hundred,' he replied.

'And on jumu'ah?'

'On Fridays we also put some mats outside.'

The imam then showed me some of his renovation plans – where the new wudu area and entrance for women would go; at present, women prayed behind a screen at the back of the mosque. We then walked outside and the imam pointed to the five derelict properties attached to the mosque. He hoped to purchase them and turn them into his heritage and training centre.

'I want to keep building bridges, that's why at events, I always speak about Siqilliya's Islamic history and how we lived together and that we can do so again. I want to show that we are not here to fight, but to live together,' explained the imam as we started to head back in.

I asked about the 'secret' mosque.

'Can I see it?'

'No, there is too much work now,' Imam Badri said.

Noticing my disappointment, he led me to the front again, where he pointed to a small archway at the foot of the building, beneath an air conditioning unit.

'Look, it is down there.'

PART 2: THE CHILDREN OF AL-ANDALUS

I peered in, but all I could see in the darkness were some large rocks.

'There is a lot of work to do.'

'You have been down there?'

The imam nodded, but seemed reluctant to say much more; I didn't push him. This was his thing and I didn't want him to think I was going to take it away from him. I had no doubts he had big plans to reveal it one day; maybe invite the island's press, his friend the Archbishop and other dignitaries. Imam Badri knew the impact heritage like this could have in validating his mosque's presence and that of the new Sicilian Muslim community. Born along the coast to which many expelled Sicilian Muslims fled in the twelfth and thirteenth centuries, Imam Badri, I suspected, felt his 'calling' to Sicily was some kind of return.

'I want to put this mosque on the tourist map, to make it a place to visit.'

'That would be amazing,' I said, genuinely hoping he pulled it off, 'what a great story that would be: Palermo's first mosque since the Muslim period sits on the site of an actual mosque from that period!'

The imam smiled; he had seen the headline in his mind's eye many times already.

Located at the south-western edge of the historical Albergheria district, the Church of Saint John of the Hermits was on one of my favourite little streets in Palermo, a quiet little road of picturesque two-storey terraced buildings with wrought-iron balconies and painted shutters. The view south down Via dei Benedettini resembled a postcard. Sun-bleached banana leaves leaned over the bougainvillea clambering up the black iron fence of the church garden. Towering above this, like the mirage of a minaret, was the church's iconic red-domed bell tower, flanked by two giant palms.

Built around 1132 by the Arab-Norman King Roger II, as part of the monastery he dedicated to San Giovanni before it was donated to the Benedictine monks, from around the fourteenth century the monastery and church experienced a gradual decline and eventually fell into disrepair. By the sixteenth century a decision was made to secularize the church, with the former chapter house being turned into a hall.

I walked through the green garden of the church, past a large stone trough, where goldfish swam. Young banana trees offered shade to small pomegranate bushes, as myrtle and palms lined the stone footpaths leading up to the church. I had grown up in northern Europe, where entering the grounds of a church had filled me with dread as a child: dark, dingy and overgrown with weeds, where the only ornamental features were neglected gravestones. Not here: the hermitage churchyard felt different; the carefully landscaped garden, blending water features with strategically planted blooming flowers and fragrant, fruit-bearing trees, felt familiar. I stepped into the church building, which was barren inside with exposed bricks and mortar. It was built in a classic Latin cross plan with a single nave, above which were the church's two largest red domes; the other three were on top of the bell tower and the former sanctuary and diaconicon. The flooring was unfinished and much of it ran along raised metal walkways. With little to see in the main church building, I made straight for the annex. The hermitage church was my favourite of all the Arab-Norman churches in Palermo, for many reasons; the location – away from the main tourist traffic – meant every time I visited, I felt like I had the entire place to myself, which was just as well, as the complex was modest in size, diminutive even, adding to its charm. Soon enough, I was again all by myself in the 'Arab Room'.

It was when he measured the decaying church for the first time, in 1877, that the suspicions of Giuseppe Patricolo, Professor of Design and Architecture at the University of Palermo, were first aroused. Noticing irregularities along the southern wall, he felt something didn't quite add up. Later, when he came back as Director of the Royal Office for the Conservation of Monuments of Sicily and began excavating in preparation for restoration works, he noticed unusual details behind the existing architecture and structure. These included ancient traceries that resembled those he had seen in Islamic architecture in Cairo, where his son, Achille, worked as the curator of the Islamic Museum. Soon a 'motif' he was convinced was a faithful reproduction of one he had seen in the Ibn Tulun Mosque in Cairo turned up. By 1882, Patricolo was ready to publish his document on the discovery of *The Arab Monument*. In it he claimed that the rectangular hall-like building I now stood in had begun life as one of the 300 or so mosques Ibn Hawqal had seen in Bal'harm. To support the claim, as well as citing various architectural discoveries Patricolo pointed to the Arab Room's south-east orientation, towards the Ka'aba in Makkah. In 2019, further excavations revealed that the current church structure was built over the site of an ancient Muslim cemetery.

I placed my phone flat on the floor. The white line on the black compass app settled slightly more south than east, but it was definitely pointing south-east. The back wall, the one Patricolo claimed would have featured the mosque's mihrab, was indeed pointing towards Makkah. I felt a tingle up my spine. I was standing where Siqilliyan Muslims had once prayed. A woman in denim shorts and green sensible shoes nervously peered into the hall before stepping in with her husband. They stood for about thirty seconds on the terracotta floor tiles, admiring the faint remnants of a fresco on the eastern wall that showed a (headless) Madonna on a throne flanked by two saints, before disappearing. I stared at what might have once been the mihrab wall, now featuring two slit windows either side of two half-visible arches and a rectangular window above. I wondered when the last Muslim prayer had taken place here. Tempted, I sat down on the bench to assess the flow of traffic, but nobody came for a whole five minutes. I placed the compass on the floor one more time; the phone screen again confirmed the hall's south-east orientation. I stood up and listened for any footsteps. Nothing. Then, looking straight ahead, I closed my eyes and raised my hands either side of my head, before quietly saying the takbir. A tingle ran up my spine again.

7

The Corridors of Knowledge, Power and Pleasure

Palermo, Sicily

Among the places that dazzled the Muslim traveller Ibn Jubayr the most in Bal'harm were the Arab-Norman kings' palaces. These were in the 'higher parts' of Bal'harm, dotted around its very outer edges 'like pearls encircling a woman's full throat'. The reason why the Iberian was so utterly in awe of these pleasure palaces was because of how familiar they looked and felt to a man used to courtly life in al-Andalus. Ibn Jubayr had recently been appointed secretary to the Almohad ruler of Granada, Abu Sa'id Uthman ibn 'Abd al-Mu'min, and, according to legend, it was a meeting with al-Mu'min that led to the travels that would eventually bring him to Sicily in 1184. The story goes that when al-Mu'min met Ibn Jubayr for the first time, he offered the pious Muslim a cup of wine, which the Valencian politely refused. Outraged, al-Mu'min forced Ibn Jubayr to drink seven cups of wine in front of him. But by the time his new secretary had finished, the sultan was so overcome with guilt, he filled the seven cups with gold dinars and told Ibn Jubayr he could spend the money as he saw fit. Also filled with guilt for drinking the wine, Ibn Jubayr asked to be allowed to perform the Hajj as a form of penance. It was on the return leg of his pilgrimage that Ibn Jubayr was shipwrecked off the coast of Sicily and forced to spend time on the former Muslim-ruled island.

PART 2: THE CHILDREN OF AL-ANDALUS

The Arab-Normans modelled their pleasure palaces on those built by Muslim rulers in cities like Fustat (now in Cairo), Baghdad, Damascus and Córdoba, and one of the finest sits in Palermo's Zisa district, an area named after the Zisa palace, a stunning marriage of Norman and Islamic art, architecture and engineering. Zisa is actually a corruption of al-Aziz, the name it was given by King William I, who began its construction in 1165 but died before it was completed by his son, William II, the following year. Still visible in Arabic on the building, the name al-Aziz is one of the most revered in Islam. It means 'noble, mighty, splendid and glorious' and is one of the ninety-nine names of Allah in the Qur'an. Al-Aziz is just one of the palace's many allusions to Islamic divinity.

Once outside the ancient medieval walls of Bal'harm, al-Aziz used to sit surrounded by sweeping green hunting grounds and hidden gardens, with mini-pavilions and kiosks in what the Arab-Norman sultans called *Jannat al-ard*, or 'paradise on earth'. Now the palace sits within the sprawling modern city limits, overlooking what might only be described as a disappointing homage to that 'paradise', the Giardino della Zisa. Next to the palace is the pretty twelfth-century Chapel of the Holy Trinity, also built by King William I on the site of a mosque. As with many of the Arab-Norman churches, it features an iconic red dome, resting on a *tambour* of small windows above two large *muqarnas* reliefs – both inspired by mosque architecture. The church used to have a covered passage that linked it directly to the king's pleasure palace.

I stood in the Zisa's dusty courtyard and looked up to the very top, where once upon a time a series of Arabic inscriptions ran all the way along the edge, but all I could now see were the battlements added much later. I stared at the majestic, rectangular monument with its two turrets integrated at each end; its gothic arches and austere architecture were unmistakably Norman from the outside, and I realized that's why it felt so familiar. I had grown up in London's East End borough of Tower Hamlets – so named because the neighbourhoods of my youth, like Stepney Green, Bow and Bethnal Green, had once been little hamlets in the vicinity of the White Tower built by another Norman, William, the Duke of Normandy, a distant cousin of the Sicilian Williams, who is remembered as 'William the Conqueror'. He built his tower the year he ruthlessly took England in 1066, just as his distant cousins were slowly taking the Emirate of Siqilliya. While the Arab-Normans assimilated into the existing Muslim culture, adopting much of its enlightened, progressive and tolerant traits, the first Norman King of England took a very different approach. The Conqueror replaced all of the traditional Anglo-Saxon aristocracy and religious clerics with his own Norman people, by either imprisoning or killing them. He took away their land, imposed heavy taxes on locals and introduced laws that discriminated against the natives. The taxes were used to build more Norman towers across the country as French replaced English in the court, and within twenty years nearly a fifth of the native Anglo-Saxon population were starved or killed. Unsurprisingly, William was viewed by locals as little more than a cruel, foreign tyrant.

The ties between the two Norman kingdoms at each end of the continent were strong. William II was married to Joan 'of England', a daughter of the Norman King Henry II of England. After William's death, the Zisa was where his bastard cousin Tancred imprisoned Joan as he seized the island's throne. This enraged Joan's brother Richard (of Lionheart fame), who had just been crowned King of England, and he arrived in Italy in 1190 on his way to the Third Crusade, demanding his sister be freed and her dowry be returned. When Tancred refused, Richard took the city of Messina. The warning was heeded, and Tancred promptly freed Joan along with her dowry. Richard would later offer her in marriage to Saladin's brother, al-Malik al-Adil Sayf ad-Din or 'Saphadin'.

I opened a picture of London's White Tower on my phone and held it up to the Zisa. It was uncanny. The exterior was exactly like a Norman keep. The Tower of London was an iconic ever-present feature of my life; I have visited it numerous times with family and friends, and even written about it for travel guides, but I never expected to encounter its twin on the other side of

PART 2: THE CHILDREN OF AL-ANDALUS

The front of the Arab-Norman pleasure palace, al-Aziz, known today as the Zisa, which was built in 1165 blending Norman and Islamic artistic and architectural styles

the continent, and I certainly didn't expect the twin to have a Muslim soul.

Begun at great expense and speed by William I, the Zisa's outer facade is decorated on all four sides by three tiers of cusped arches framed in rectangles, except at the front, where three large gothic arches, one nearly two storeys high, announce the once magnificent main entrance in front of which today there is an empty rectangular space with a protruding oblong island of concrete in the middle. This was once a picturesque water feature filled with stunning tropical fish, where in the middle, as if afloat, there was a small rectangular pleasure *chiosco* (kiosk) – from the Arabic *kushak* – that resembled a miniature al-Aziz, connected to the grounds by a dainty little bridge. Visitors arrived to the sound of calming, gentle water as it flowed through a long, thin channel from the palace into the fish pool, before entering beneath the magnificent arch that announced in *naskh* Arabic script – still visible today – that the palace is called 'al-Aziz' and was completed by Sultan '*Musta'izz*', or 'glorious by the grace of God' – William II's Arabic dynastic name. The Zisa's most enduring Islamic feature is known as the Sala della Fontana, or Fountain Room, a sumptuous quadrangle space with marble-covered walls and muqarnas niches on three sides. In the middle, opposite the grand arches of the entrance, positioned so it is the first thing that greets the visitor, is a beautiful marble fountain beneath a large cone-shaped muqarnas hood. Water cascades over a series of marble chevrons, before entering the channels that lead all the way out to the pool. Beneath the muqarnas is a dazzling gold mosaic framed in geometric Islamic shapes featuring three interlaced circular friezes: one in the middle with two archers, their bowstrings pulled back ready to fire – hinting at the monarch's favourite pastime – while the two on either side feature beautiful peacocks, their feathers on display, beneath a palm tree.

I became fascinated by the Sala della Fontana after learning it had been the inspiration for the stunning Arab Hall built by the British Victorian artist and orientalist Fredric Leighton – who reputedly visited the Zisa during his many trips to Italy – at his home in London's fashionable Holland Park in 1877. The Arab Hall was famous for its stunning tiles and glazed Arabic inscriptions, which the artist, like many Victorian orientalists, 'acquired' through questionable channels from across the Muslim world, including his fellow orientalist and friend Sir Richard Burton. The controversial explorer, who famously performed the Hajj masquerading as a Muslim, was prepared to 'have a house pulled down' if necessary, and wrote, quite nonchalantly to Leighton, about one batch he had sent to the artist containing tiles he had 'taken from the tomb (Moslem) of Sakhar, on the Indus'. Like most members of the European colonial classes, the looting and defacing of a holy tomb, sacred to a subject (and therefore inferior) race, was not an ethical dilemma for Burton or Leighton. Like the Zisa, there is a fountain in Leighton's Arab Hall, only his is contained within the building and no channels lead out. The niches are also different: plainer and lacking the beautiful muqarnas of William's al-Aziz, which was constructed by Muslim artisans.

The Fountain Room was one of the many regal spaces where

Sultan Musta'izz would hold court, in a hall inspired by the Islamic concept of heaven, surrounded by Arabic inscriptions. One of his guests was the twelfth-century Archbishop of Salerno Romuald Guarna, who had crowned William II in the Cathedral of Palermo and was a student of medicine, history, law and theology at the Schola Medica Salernitana, Christian Europe's most important medieval medical school, and an important corridor for the translation and transfer of cutting-edge Islamic medical knowledge from books like those the archbishop would have seen on the shelves of the libraries the Arab-Norman kings had inherited from their Muslim predecessors and continued to build. Efforts to translate this knowledge had been going on for almost a century in Italy by the time the archbishop visited the Zisa. This was largely led by the brilliance of Tunisian-born Constantine the African, who studied medicine in Egypt and oversaw the translation from Arabic into Latin of numerous groundbreaking medical treatises, including those by the great Persian physicians and polymaths Ibn Sina (Avicenna) and al-Razi (Rhazes), and the Iberian physician and philosopher Ibn Rushd (Averroes) – books that would revolutionize Western medicine. One of the founding texts of the archbishop's medical school in Salerno, the *Liber Pantegni*, was basically a translation of *Kitab al-Maliki* by the tenth-century Persian physicist and psychologist Ali ibn al-Abbas al-Majusi. The book is later mentioned by Chaucer, which points to its wider dissemination. One of the first translators of the book was Stefano of Pisa, who tells us that the best and brightest scholars of medicine were in Sicily and Salerno, and were either Greeks or Arab-speakers, like the Arab-, Greek- and Latin-speaking Admiral Eugenius of Palermo, who was carrying out translations of Arabic into Latin for William I (ruled 1154–66). Many of these translators, such as Plato of Tivoli, often worked in Spain too.

This attitude towards the Muslim intellectual tradition was embraced by all the Arab-Norman monarchs, reaching unprecedented heights during the lengthy reign of the last of the Norman kings of Sicily, Frederick II – the 'Renaissance man'. Ruler of Sicily from 1198 until his death in 1250, Frederick institutionalized the medical school in Salerno and founded the university at Naples, where the medieval Christian philosopher Thomas Aquinas, who would revolutionize Christian thinking, was taught logic and natural philosophy by a Peter of Ireland – most likely an Anglo-Norman – and first accessed the works of the Córdobans Maimonides and Ibn Rushd, via whom he came to understand Aristotle. Frederick is also known to have sent works on logic and physics translated from Arabic to the University of Bologna, which later became a major centre for education and intellectual exchange during the region's Christian Renaissance between the fourteenth and seventeenth centuries when the likes of the fifteenth-century Polish Renaissance astronomer Nicolaus Copernicus studied there. Copernicus, who was credited for centuries with changing our understanding of the cosmos, by placing the sun at the centre of the universe as opposed to the earth (the ancient Greek Ptolemaic model), also studied at the universities of Padua and Ferrara. In his book *De Revolutionibus Orbium Coelestium* or *On the Revolutions of the Heavenly Spheres*, published just before his death in 1543, Copernicus cites five Muslims, including Ibn Rushd, whose works he would have first encountered in Latin translation at these universities, along with key medieval Muslim mathematical tools developed for astronomical calculations, like spherical trigonometry. Without the latter, Copernicus could not have developed his ideas, the most revolutionary of which was the heliocentric model of the cosmos, which up until 1957 was believed to have been his own original idea. That was the year an Austro-American scholar, Otto Neugebauer, came across the works of the late fourteenth-century Syrian astronomer and timekeeper at the Umayyad Mosque in Damascus, Ibn al-Shatir, whose lunar model Neugebauer realized was identical to that of Copernicus, only the Syrian had lived a century before the Pole. Neugebauer and his colleagues went on to also discover near-identical parallels with Copernicus's work on planetary movement and that of the thirteenth-century Persian polymath Nasir al-Din al-Tusi. Neither Ibn al-Shatir nor al-Tusi was mentioned by Copernicus. Neugebauer and his colleagues concluded that the likelihood of

Copernicus independently coming up with these same ideas was 'all but impossible'; instead they believed the much-celebrated Pole must have come across the works of the Syrian and Persian in translated or unattributed form in Italy. Copernicus's example is typical of how many Christian Renaissance men credited as innovators, pioneers and trailblazers were in truth (knowingly or unknowingly) simply plagiarists who had failed to credit their Muslim predecessors. If we consider that the Christian Renaissance happened during the height of the Crusades and the Inquisition, when anti-Muslim sentiments were rife across Christian Europe, and the days of Spanish and Italian *convivencia* – coexistence – a distant memory, it is easy to see how and why that rupture in the intellectual continuum between medieval Muslim Europe and the Christian Renaissance could have happened. Nobody wants to give credit to the enemy, which might also explain why, even after Neugebauer's discovery, almost every major popular astronomical text continues to credit Copernicus with placing the sun in the centre of our universe, and nobody remembers the fourteenth-century Syrian astronomer who kept the time at the Umayyad Mosque in Damascus.

The half-Norman, half-German monarch Frederick, though talented, was reportedly not the most attractive of men; according to the Syrian writer and historian Sibt ibn al-Jawzi, he was bald, his body was covered in red hair, and he had green eyes like a snake, but couldn't see very well. Most cuttingly, al-Jawzi says had Frederick been a slave, he would not have fetched even 200 dirhams. What the Renaissance man lacked in physical attributes, Frederick, who was also the Holy Roman Emperor and the King of Germany, made up for in charisma and intelligence (he could speak six languages, including Arabic), which is why he was known to his contemporaries as *stupor mundi*, or the 'wonder of the world', and it was under the patronage of this curious, cultured and worldly Christian monarch that the convergence of al-Andalusian and Sicilian translation channels was accelerated.

Frederick's most prolific translator was a man called Michael Scot, who as the name suggests was born in Scotland, around

1175. Scot studied in Durham, Oxford and Paris, before making his way to Iberia to work as a translator. His first stint in Italy was in Bologna before he headed south to join Frederick's court. He translated from Arabic into Latin, among others, the works of Aristotle and his Arab commentators Ibn Sina and Ibn Rushd. Scot also translated vast Arabic works on astrology, astronomy, mathematics, alchemy and other sciences, for which he was rewarded with a place in Dante's *Inferno* for knowledge of alchemy and the magic of the Arabs. Other translators at Frederick's court included Theodore of Antioch, who had studied in the great Muslim intellectual capital, Baghdad, and was a gift sent to him by al-Kamil, the Ayyubid sultan and nephew of Saladin. Then there was John of Palermo, who mainly translated Arabic books on mathematics by the likes of the tenth-century Iraqi polymath Hasan Ibn al-Haytham. Many of these translators had ties to the efforts that had begun in earnest in neighbouring Christian Iberia through institutes such as the Toledo School of Translators. Collectively, they would become the primary channels through which Europe's Islamic knowledge was transferred to the continent's Christian North. The Norman connection meant Sicily also became the primary channel for England to access this rich Muslim intellectual tradition. When Roger II's Chancellor of the Exchequer, Thomas Brown, arrived to serve Henry II in England, he proposed the adoption of the revolutionary and much simpler Indo-Arab numerical system he had been using in Sicily. Henry though wasn't interested, yet the eventual popularizing in England and Christian Europe of what is today the most widely used 'language' in the world almost certainly came about because of Sicily and the Muslim Mediterranean. It is believed that the modern number system was introduced to England by the twelfth century, by Adelard of Bath, dubbed 'the first English Scientist', who also translated from Arabic extensive works on astrology, astronomy, philosophy, mathematics and alchemy. Adelard is said to have learned Arabic while travelling in Sicily and Spain, where the Indo-Arab numbers had replaced the classical Roman ones.

PART 2: THE CHILDREN OF AL-ANDALUS

Another person credited with popularizing the numbers across the continent is the thirteenth-century Pisan Leonardo Bonacci – 'Fibonacci' – who learned Arabic during his formative years in Algeria, but almost certainly picked up the number system in Sicily as a guest of Frederick II, to whom he dedicated at least one of his books, also dedicating another to Michael Scot.

Adelard, who travelled so extensively to seek out the 'studies of the Arabs', was actually one of Henry's tutors, dedicating his *De Opere Astrolapsus* to the monarch and expressing his admiration for Henry's desire to appreciate 'the writings of the Latins' and 'the opinions of the Arabs'. Muslim culture would have been familiar to Henry from an early age. His grandfather had a physician called Petrus Alphonsi, who had been born a Sephardic Jew in Muslim Spain, spoke Latin, Hebrew and Arabic, and even wrote the first credible account of the Prophet Muhammad's life in Latin. Henry was also tutored by William of Conches, another medieval scholar who studied Islamic philosophy and science. The king's appreciation for Islamic knowledge saw him encourage travelling Arab scholars to frequent his court, and he would often ask diplomats heading to Sicily and the Middle East to bring back specific manuscripts for his library. These channels – strengthened by Henry marrying his daughters to Christian rulers in Spain and Sicily – also led to some of England's most famous buildings being influenced by the architecture of Muslim Europe, including Durham Cathedral, where the nave and Galilee chapel share features with the Great Mosque of Córdoba and the Aljafería Palace in Zaragoza, Spain. Likewise the rebuilt east end of Canterbury Cathedral – popularly described as 'early English' – with its striped columns and stone vaulting, is a clear fusion of local styles and those found in Muslim Europe. Most fascinatingly, Henry may well have built England's very first 'Muslim-style' pleasure palace and garden for his mistress, Rosamund Clifford. Said to have been inspired by buildings such as the Zisa in Sicily, the palace called Everswell had Islamic-style fountains and courtyards and featured three interconnected pools; it resembled nothing ever seen before in Northern

Europe. Sadly, the palace is no more, having been destroyed in the early eighteenth century to make way for Blenheim Palace; the only remnant is a rectangular pool known as Fair Rosamund's Well.

What has remained, though, is quite possibly Henry's most enduring legacy: English Common Law, the framework of which he established towards the end of his life. This framework has so many parallels with classical Islamic law, especially that observed in Muslim Sicily, that legal historians believe Henry may well have borrowed elements from it to create English Common Law. Henry would have been familiar with the Sicilian legal system from people like Brown, who lived through the period in which Roger II formalized the Arab-Norman legal framework by adopting elements of the existing Islamic law of the island. Historians point to features including judicial impartiality, trust (*waqf*), the primacy of law over state, contractual freedom, individual rights and, most notably, trial by jury. Henry's institutionalizing of a twelve-man jury system to uncover the truth bears more than a striking resemblance to the *lafif* in Islamic Maliki jurisprudence. The *lafif*, which was developed between the eighth and eleventh centuries within the Maliki legal system – one of the four main Islamic Sunni schools and the one that was popular in Sicily and Iberia – requires twelve members of the community to swear by God to tell the truth as they analyse the facts of a case before arriving at a unanimous verdict. All of which makes his threat to the pope of conversion to Islam in 1168 seem all the more curious.

I stepped out of the blistering mid-afternoon sun into the dark coolness of the Zisa's north wing. The grand main entrance and the Fountain Room were not accessible as they were being renovated, so I went upstairs to its Islamic museum. Inspired by, among others, the palaces of North Africa's Hammadid Islamic dynasty, and built with engineering from ninth-century Fustat, the original Muslim capital of Egypt, the techniques and aesthetics of the Zisa are now seen all over the Mediterranean. As I wandered up, I noticed the building was full of niches with muqarnas hoods that

PART 2: THE CHILDREN OF AL-ANDALUS

resembled the mihrabs I had seen in the Ottoman mosques of northern Cyprus. I was hoping the museum would contain interesting items from Sicily's Emirate period, but unfortunately these were little more than a collection of cheap domestic artefacts, like amphoras and bowls. The most fascinating object was from the later period: the white marble tombstone of a Christian woman called Anna, the mother of a priest, Grisanto, who had died in 1148. Discovered in Palermo's Church of the Archangel Michael, and decorated with mosaic patterns in red, green and gold, the tombstone had been inscribed in no fewer than four languages: Hebrew, Latin, Greek and Arabic – reflecting the multilingual and multiconfessional society the Arab-Normans inherited and nurtured.

The marble tombstone of Anna, a Sicilian Christian woman who died in 1148, featuring the four languages of the Muslim Emirate and later Arab-Norman kingdom

The top floor was the coolest part of the Zisa and is a testimony to the intelligent airflow system still working, nine centuries on. It was built facing north-east to allow the cooling sea breeze to enter via its upper windows and the three large arches along the ground floor, where the rectangular pool of water – key to its natural, medieval 'air conditioning' system – and canals helped cool the air as it entered the palace. Then clever wind tunnels, ventilation ducts and carefully positioned windows distributed the air throughout the different rooms. Meanwhile, a large wooden mashrabiya kept the Sicilian sun's hot rays out. The top floor offered spectacular views over the new public Zisa Gardens, opened in 2005 on land that was once part of the *Jannat al-ard*, complete with a 130-foot canal running through the middle. Dating from the 1950s, and lying beyond a Renaissance arch with baroque features and a row of *dammusi* – small stone dwellings said to have Arab origins – less than two decades on the 'garden' appeared dusty and neglected. I noticed a jogger slowly moving along mostly dirt and sand tracks; nobody else was inside the modern interpretation of 'paradise on earth'. Once upon a time, visitors like Ibn Jubayr and the archbishop would have come up here to be treated to the spectacular views over the vast heavenly gardens, stretching for miles around al-Aziz; they would've heard the jubilant cries of the king's hunters with each successful kill far down below, and looked out towards the silhouette of bell towers and minarets of Bal'harm in the distance, a place of 'wealth and splendour' and an 'elegant city, magnificent and gracious, and seductive to look upon', according to Ibn Jubayr: a view now obscured by ugly post-war high rises. They might have also looked to the right, past the forest of fruit trees, landscaped pathways and pleasure gardens, and noticed, deliberately tucked away, William II's personal addition to that necklace of 'pearls encircling' the 'throat' of the city: the Palazzo della Cuba, or the Cube Palace, the Arabic name of which we no longer have. My next stop.

The Cuba, on the busy Corso Calatafimi, once the most famous ancient road out of Palermo, sat hidden behind a decrepit wall, with a faded baroque entrance. Unlike the Zisa, it was not visible from the street, and when I arrived at its tiny office to explain I was a journalist seeking information on the Cuba in English, it caused a major panic. None of the elderly attendants spoke English, and as one old man kept loudly repeating 'Journalist!', a woman in a floral blouse scampered off only to reappear with two ancient guidebooks to Sicily, each complete with its own film of dust. I smiled and took them from her, flicking through to find there was nothing about the Arab-Norman pleasure palaces in either one. Politely handing them back, I mouthed a 'thank you' and headed into the complex.

In many ways, William II's pleasure palace was a miniature of the Zisa: tall, monolithic, with two square turrets integrated into the outer wall, and the iconic arched Norman windows, only much smaller and oriented differently. I was again reminded of the White Tower on the banks of the River Thames. Walking up the metal stairwell that led into the Cuba, I noted the dark waterline all the way around the outer wall; where the Cuba's decorative features abruptly ended. Unlike the Zisa, the Cuba used to sit in a lake, like an island, with water lapping at its walls, so that the only way to get to it was by boat.

When Ibn Jubayr visited William II's court, he noted that similar to many Muslim rulers, the Arab-Norman king had a number of concubines, like a harem. The Muslim traveller even claims that many of them had been persuaded to embrace Islam by the king's Muslim handmaidens. I looked around the smaller, more intimate, fort-like Cuba with its protective moat; it seemed the perfect place to keep just such a harem. While William held court at the Zisa, welcoming travellers there from far and wide, maybe the Cuba tucked away in this corner of *Jannat a l-ard* was where William had kept all his beautiful *houris*, locked up and far from prying eyes.

'I wonder if this was where William kept his women?'

The question stopped Svitlana, a PR manager from Ukraine, dead in her tracks.

'Really?'

Svitlana's eyebrows rose above the rim of her sunglasses.

'You imagine this?' she asked.

'Maybe? . . . after all it was very private, around here was water.'

I pointed out of the windows to the ground below and the space around the Cuba. Svitlana looked out.

'You have to admit it would be a great location for it,' I added.

Svitlana and I got talking when she asked if I could take a

picture of her beneath the only surviving architectural feature of note inside the roofless Cuba: the remnants of a dazzling muqarnas above a niche of two windows that is yet another testimony to the artistic and architectural exchange across the region between Christians and Muslims. The exquisitely carved feature includes a series of details found in Almohad and Almoravid architecture across the Maghreb and in parts of Iberia, such as the highly ornate interlocking T-cells decorated with vegetal patterns, including the acanthus, a hallmark of Almoravid decoration.

Dressed in a loose white shirt, a black skirt and gold strapped sandals, Svitlana wore bright-red lipstick and a floppy sun hat with designer sunglasses. She looked every bit the European tourist, only she was not where the hordes were.

'That's interesting, so he lived in the palace and you think this could've been where he kept his women?'

I laughed and shrugged my shoulders. William's main palace in medieval Palermo, the Palazzo dei Normanni, was at the other end of the Corso Calatafimi, a fifteen-minute walk from where we stood. Almost nothing is known about the Cuba's actual use by William II but if this had been his harem, it would have taken no time at all for the Arab-Norman king to gallop here on horseback whenever he felt the need to come and lie with one of his favourite concubines.

'In that respect, he was also like the Arab and Muslim kings, with his harem – you know what a harem is?'

Svitlana nodded, excitedly.

'I know harem. Are you talking about, like, Norman kings?'

It dawned on me that Svitlana had assumed I was theorizing about some pre-Norman Muslim history of the palace.

'Yes, yes, William II,' I explained, adding that it was William who built the palace, so it wasn't here during the Emirate of Siqilliya.

'Amazing!'

Svitlana clapped her hands in delight and smiled from ear to ear as we stared at to two chamber-like spaces near the back of the building.

PART 2: THE CHILDREN OF AL-ANDALUS

'Maybe that's where he would sleep with them, in those two rooms.'

The lack of renovation at the Cuba made it difficult to imagine anything, so we walked over to the small rectangular ruins of two chambers either side of the entrance at the back. We then turned to look at where the *diwan* (reception hall) would have been, and the internal fountain – like any good Arab palatial court. It was almost certainly Muslim architects William commissioned to build the palace.

'Oh, I love history,' she said, when I asked Svitlana what had brought her to the hidden, and frankly dilapidated, monument, far from the beaten track.

'Not everybody understands,' she added.

Svitlana was like me. Obsessive about history and heritage. Both of us could see it would take the uninformed visitor no more than five minutes to wander along the walkways above the ruined foundations of the Cuba's interior. There were no explanatory signs and no old photos. This was why Svitlana had stopped underneath the muqarnas – there was nothing else for a visitor to be drawn to.

'You need time to imagine in historical places,' Svitlana said to me, as we both meandered along the cheap, scaffolded walkway.

I nodded in agreement.

We walked out of the Cuba's shell through the back exit, and as we stepped on to the dusty floor of what would have been the bed of the pleasure lake that once surrounded the Cuba, I pointed out the dark watermarks again. I then walked several feet away from the Cuba, asking Svitlana to do the same.

'Look up there, can you see it?'

Svitlana raised her right hand above her glasses against the bright sunlight and stared intently along the upper rim of the Cuba, where intermittently, just as it had once been along the top of the Zisa, there were strips of surprisingly legible Kufic Arabic, yet another clue that the builders had been Muslim.

'The words tell us William, who was fluent in Arabic, built this in 1180; on the Zisa, he is called *Musta'izz*.'

Svitlana nodded silently. She was concentrating.

'Wow,' she said eventually. 'There is no way I would have known that was there.'

Svitlana was right. With no signs and no pointers, most visitors would easily miss the Cuba's most intriguing and most complete feature of all.

As we both now headed towards the exit, Svitlana wanted to know what other 'hidden' Islamic heritage there was in Palermo. I jokingly asked her how long she had, which obviously doesn't translate well into Ukrainian, as she gave me a literal response of having set aside five whole days to explore the city. I laughed, before telling her about the pillars inscribed with verses from the Qur'an, as well as the 'ghost' mosque in the Hermitage church, before asking if she had seen the muqarnas roof in the main Norman palace. When she nodded, I told her that she absolutely could not miss the Zisa – the older sibling of the Cuba.

It was quite a sight. All thirty of us, craning our necks to stare up at the dazzling honeycombed ceiling of the Cappella Palatina – the Palace Chapel – inside the Palazzo dei Normanni, the greatest Arab-Norman muqarnas ever constructed. The honeycombed masterpiece, commissioned by Roger II, sits in the middle nave of the Cappella Palatina and is believed to have been made by Fatimid artisans. If ever there was an Arab-Norman ode to Islamic culture, this was it. I had come to the palace *only* to see this and had expected something special, but nothing quite on this scale. Begun in 1132 and taking almost a decade to carve, the entire rectangular piece, measuring 43.8 by 22 feet is carved from dense wood with a series of recessed panels running through the centre, where delicate, lobed cupolas inside eight-pointed stars are inscribed with white Kufic script. This vast central feature is framed by a cascading series of muqarnas. The entire piece is then covered in a thin layer of plaster where Muslim artisans painted scenes from Islamic and Christian cultures. The result is a kaleidoscope of animal and human figures playing chess, juggling, wrestling and hunting; there are scenes from Eastern fables like the fateful lovers Layla and

Majnun, dancers, lute players, camels, falconers, warriors, even mermaids and knights slaying dragons. At the centre of it all sits a prince on his throne, surrounded by a court of people drinking, listening to music and watching dancers wearing veils. The entire thing resembled the ceiling of a Muslim palace.

I rubbed my neck as I took a break from trying to zoom into the niches using my phone; the ceiling was very high and every time I did this, the lens would shake, making my head hurt. A guide with a small group walked past.

'This is the best-preserved medieval monument in the world . . . and it shows the cohabitation between people who were always at war,' he said.

I resisted the urge to correct him. This popular tendency to polarize Muslims and Christians (and to a lesser extent Jews as well) in European history is yet another way in which the continent's Muslim heritage has been grossly othered. The establishment of a historical narrative where Muslims and Christians are eternal enemies ultimately means – in a post-Christian Europe – Islam and Muslims remain the continent's eternal enemy. Yet time and again in European history we see this is simply not the case, be that in the alliances and intermarriages of Muslim and Christian rulers in Iberia and the dukes and khans of the Baltic and the Crimea, or in the relationship of the Venetians with the Ottomans. Throughout European history Muslims and Christians have loved as much, if not more, than they have warred.

Roger II's ceiling was the ultimate testimony to this, proving that the Arab-Normans of Sicily didn't passively absorb the Islamic culture they inherited and lived in the midst of; they actively sought it out across the wider Muslim world to which they were connected geographically, culturally, politically and commercially. Of course they warred with some, but it was certainly not *just* about war. By the early thirteenth century, in the court of Frederick II, Arab influence surpassed that of the Greeks, a dominance that intensified following his visit to the East and the cultivation of political and intellectual ties with North African and Near Eastern rulers. For example, in 1232, the Sultan of Damascus sent an embassy to Frederick with a tent planetarium full of mechanical astral bodies made from gold and shimmering jewels, and during the Crusade he eventually led in 1227, Frederick came to an agreement to share control of the Holy Land with the Ayyubid sultan al-Kamil. This saw Jerusalem, Nazareth and the corridor leading to the Sea of Jaffa given to Frederick as King of Jerusalem, while the Ayyubids retained control of the Aqsa Mosque and the Dome of the Rock. Frederick also maintained personal contact and correspondence with eminent Muslim scholars, seeking their expertise on various problems in mathematics, physics and philosophy. Among these were Alam al-Din al-Hanafi, a distinguished mathematician sent to his court by al-Kamil, and the Sufi philosopher of al-Andalus, Abd al-Haqq Ibn Sab'in, to whom Frederick addresses his *al-Masai'l al-Siqilliya*, or *Sicilian Questions*. These are a series of philosophical questions about such topics as the eternity of the world, divine knowledge and the art of logic. The response from Ibn Sab'in makes clear just how brilliantly educated and well read he was, and how broad his knowledge base. Citing thinkers as diverse as the Muslims al-Ghazali and al-Farabi, the Greeks Aristotle, Plato, Zeno of Elea and Anaxagoras, and even the Babylonian Berossus, the dialogue is a real glimpse of the intellectual heavyweights both men were and the extent of their learning. Under the Holy Roman Emperor, this rich cultural exchange radiated from Sicily, spreading its influence to northern Italy, Germany and Provence.

Built between the eleventh and twelfth centuries, the Royal Palace of Palermo was constructed on the foundations of the Emirate rulers' palace. The Palatine Chapel was added in 1130 by Roger II and is a heady mix of Byzantine and Islamic-inspired mosaics and architecture. The sanctuary resembles a domed basilica, and boasts three apses and six pointed arches with the apex of the dome above the altar featuring a mosaic of Christ Pantocrator. Almost every inch of the upper regions, barring the muqarnas ceiling, is covered in a series of shimmering mosaics, including illustrated scenes of St John in the desert wilderness and moments in Christ's life, as well as images of the five Greek saint fathers of the Church, intertwined with Greek, Latin and Arabic inscriptions.

After Ibn Jubayr visited the Royal Palace in 1184, he recalled walking 'across royal courts' past 'towering palaces and well-set piazzas and gardens'. He remembers seeing a 'hall set in a large court enclosed by a garden and flanked by colonnades'; he found himself marvelling at its length and at the 'height of its belvederes'. All of it left the highly travelled Muslim quite amazed. He also met the king's commissioner, who arrived 'walking majestically between servants' carrying the 'train of his robes'. The 'stately old man with a long white moustache' spoke 'supple Arabic' and typified the Muslims employed by the Arab-Norman kings. Ibn Jubayr's reception offers a glimpse of how the myriads of scholars, poets, philosophers, musicians and artists that patronized the Arab-Norman courts might have been received. Of all these, probably none are as famous as Muhammad al-Idrisi, a Muslim geographer and scientist of noble lineage, who was born in Ceuta and educated in the great Caliphate city of Córdoba. Al-Idrisi's magnum opus, *Nuzhat al-mushtaq fi ikhtiraq al-afaq*, or *The Book of Roger*, is a detailed geographical text containing seventy maps that collectively offered the most accurate overall map of the medieval world, covering Europe, Asia and Africa, and played a crucial role for later explorers, cartographers and scholars. Commissioned by Roger II in 1138, the book brought together knowledge from Muslim, Byzantine and European sources. In that respect *The Book of Roger* and its esteemed author, al-Idrisi, today one of the most cited medieval Muslim geographers, epitomize the open and enlightened culture of the Arab-Norman courts in Sicily, which welcomed and actively encouraged Latin, Greek, Arabic and Hebrew intellectuals: a now Christian place that had embraced so much of the old Muslim Caliphate culture prevalent across the medieval Muslim Mediterranean in Córdoba, Seville, Kairouan, Cairo and, through Roger and his offspring, also in Christian Palermo.

8

The Last Mosque Standing

Hisn al-Hammah, Segesta and Mazara del Vallo, Sicily

For my final days in Sicily, I headed west, in search of its only confirmed historical mosque structure. This also happened to be the direction the Andalusian traveller Ibn Jubayr took at the end of his time in Siqilliya in early 1185. Ibn Jubayr doesn't mention the mosque that now sits in what is the Segesta Archaeological Park, but amazingly his route to the port town of Atrabanish (Trapani), from where he eventually left Siqilliya, passed very close by. In fact, Ibn Jubayr stopped at a spot just a few miles from the mosque to bathe in some natural thermal waters. When I had mentioned to Imam Badri that I was looking for these, he had put me in touch with Paolo, a local civil servant with a keen interest in Sicily's Islamic past and Ibn Jubayr's time on the island. Paolo, it turns out, knew exactly where these waters were, and so after a long, sweaty day traipsing through the Arab-Norman palaces of Palermo, I drove out west, along the E90 just past the town of Alqamah (Alcamo), where Ibn Jubayr spent a night, to meet Paolo and his friend Marco, a composer, near the place the Andalusian hajji called Hisn al-Hammah, known today as Calathamet. Both locals had suggested we visit the waters at night, when the crowds of tourists were gone and the intense heat of the day was no more.

'Sometimes, I come here in the winter, it is the best time, when nobody is here,' said Marco, as the three of us stepped out of Paolo's 4×4 car, having bounced our way through a field, loosely following a dirt track, before parking in a clearing. It was a beautiful warm and starry night.

'Weren't you cold?' I asked.

'No,' said Marco, 'I came in a warm coat, took it off and just stepped into the hot water, it was fine.'

We were in a field surrounded by tall grass and thick cane-like reeds. Atop the sloping hills on our left were the ruins of Calathamet, believed to be the historical 'castle called Hisn al-Hammah' – from the Arabic for baths, *hammam*, next to which Ibn Jubayr, also in the depths of winter, came upon 'many thermal springs which God throws up from the ground charged with special elements, and so hot that the body can hardly bear them'. There, 'dismounting from our animals', Ibn Jubayr and his retinue 'refreshed our bodies by bathing in it'. The castle ruins were on private land and therefore impossible to visit, but the waters of the thermal springs, where the twelfth-century Muslim traveller had bathed, remained accessible to anybody.

The small footpath we were following was getting hard to see in the inky blue of the night, as more reeds cut across our path. This was clearly a route only the locals knew. Something rustled in the tall reeds and I pointed the light on my phone towards it. Paolo and Marco hadn't noticed and kept talking. Besides, whatever it was had scampered off.

'I believe Madinah was a special place for Moslems, because of the many tombs of the saints in places like the Great Mosque, where the cathedral is now, and maybe Ibn Jubayr began to realize this,' Paolo said, referring to Palermo as simply 'The City' – *al-Madinah* – just as Ibn Jubayr often did.

'So, you think there were more holy sites like Qasr Sa'd in Palermo?'

Paolo nodded. He had a theory that built on the idea of Siqilliya being a place of ziyara and Sufism. Paolo believed Palermo was called al-Madinah as an allusion to the holy city of Madinah in Saudi Arabia. I wasn't so sure, as many medieval Muslim cities were known as Madinah by locals, simply because Madinah meant an urban centre.

The night was so warm that all three of us were already in our swimsuits. Marco and I wore colourful long swimming trunks, while Paolo wore his under his khaki trousers. He was also carrying a large bucket, a small measuring jug and a scrubbing sponge. Marco held aside some tall reeds for us to pass. As soon as we did, they sprang back obscuring the way behind us. The field looked vast in the darkness, and the noise of the crickets and grasshoppers added to the sense of being in a rural wilderness. As the path sloped gently down towards the valley floor, Paolo continued his theory on mystical Siqilliya.

'This was *the* Madinah of the West, I believe, and during Ibn Jubayr's time Siqilliya was a land of *tasawwuf* [Sufism],' said Paolo.

I nodded in agreement. Earlier he had drawn me a map. It showed several sites surrounding Palermo, in the shape of a crescent. The shape was a big clue for Paolo as Palermo was positioned in the middle, like a shining star, to resemble the medieval symbol associated with Islam – the star and crescent. Paolo claimed the dots were all holy sites where Muslim saints had been buried, and as evidence he had cited poets who had described Palermo as a 'holy town'. Paolo's knowledge of Sicily's Muslim past was impressive. Even if I didn't quite agree with all his theories, he was right about Sicily having been a special place for Sufism. Paolo had clearly been doing his homework, as it were, and without him I would not have been here, on the verge of bathing in possibly one of the very spots Ibn Jubayr had bathed. The fact that he was an everyday non-Muslim Sicilian, not an academic or a journalist, just a regular guy interested in what he believed was *his* Muslim past, was wonderfully refreshing. I had not expected to meet a Paolo in modern Sicily.

'There is the official history, written by the winners, the Christians, and the *other* history!'

The moonlight fell across Paolo's face and I could see him smiling as he made this last point.

'Can you hear that?' Marco said beaming.

I could make out flashes of reflected moonlight as water rushed past, behind long grass, off towards the right.

'That's the small river, where some of the hot water goes. We are very close.'

When the tall reeds gave way, the sight that met us was truly magical. At the end of a well-trodden path, nestled against large, sand-coloured boulders, was a pool of steaming-hot water, fenced in by carefully placed rocks on one side and huge stone slabs on the other. Two shadows to our left were sitting on beach towels, talking in low whispers, but otherwise we had the place to ourselves. Marco turned off his torch and urged me to do the same. As my eyes adjusted to the darkness – it was nearly midnight – I looked up beyond the little pool, to the cascade of mountainous silhouettes that disappeared into the dark of the night sky. Placing my bag to one side, and removing my flipflops, I slowly lowered my feet into the steaming-hot water, the high temperature catching me off guard and making me wince. But once I adjusted, the warmth combined with the cool of the evening felt delightful. Marco and Paolo were watching and grinning. Both of them soon joined me at the edge of the shallow pool. I thanked them for bringing me to such an amazing place; one that also reconnected me to the island's Muslim past. I then revealed I had also visited Sicily's only surviving hammam from the Muslim period, the tenth-century Terme Arabo-Normanne di Cefalà Diana, which sits twenty kilometres south-east of Palermo, at the foot of Mount Chiarastella.

'It's set in a nature reserve and very beautiful inside, with two iconic arches, made of red brick, that allude to the Córdoban arch,' I said.

'Is the building Muslim?' asked Marco, as he slowly scrubbed himself with the sponge.

'No,' said Paolo, before I could answer.

He had not visited the site, but his interest in Sicilian Islamic heritage meant he was aware of it.

'Is it still used?' asked Marco.

Paolo and I both shook our heads. Though I admitted I had

spent a considerable amount of time there, just like this, with my feet dangling in the much cooler waters.

'It's nothing like this,' I said.

Although founded by the Muslims, the Cefalà bath's current building dates from around 1140 and was built by the great Islamophilic ruler Roger II, who like so many of the Arab-Norman kings wrote his name in Arabic on the building.

'I followed the words all the way round. It was a bit like the Cuba,' I said, looking at Paolo, whose office was yards from William II's little palace. Paolo nodded knowingly and Marco looked astounded.

'I recognized only letters though as the script is very ancient and lots of bits are missing . . . Plus, my Arabic is awful,' I said laughing.

Apart from the band of Arabic, like the Zisa and Cuba, the bath building was a simple cube and otherwise unornamented.

'I must visit it!' Paolo said, pouring water over his head using the jug.

I took the jug from him and did the same, before wading a little way in, and lowering myself onto the soft gravelly bed and leaning back. With my entire body now submerged I looked up at the beautiful, starry night sky and over towards Paolo and Marco, who had both found their own little spot to do the same.

I stared at the rather sad-looking ruins of what was once Mount Barbaros's Friday Mosque and now Sicily's only 'mosque' with a direct link back to the island's ancient Muslims. A collection of tightly packed limestone that made up the low perimeter wall sat at the very edge of the hill known today as Mount Barbaros, the 'mountain of the Berbers', which during the mosque's lifetime might have been known as Jebel Berber. Once a large white rectangular building, measuring twenty by eleven metres, the mosque would have had a pitched terracotta-tiled roof and a small square extension bulging out of its southeasterly wall. This would have been topped by a domed hood, to signify the qibla and the mosque's

PART 2: THE CHILDREN OF AL-ANDALUS

mihrab. Now, all that remained were a few layers of bricks. Even where the villagers of Jebel Berber once placed their foreheads as they prayed all those centuries ago was covered in dry grass, as too the tell-tale bulge in the middle of the southeasterly wall. The discovery of the mihrab had been the key for archaeologists in the 1990s, who confirmed that there had been a Muslim settlement atop the hill most visitors to Segesta Archaeological Park climb, to see the spectacular Greek amphitheatre on the other side.

The remains of the only mosque believed to have been built by Sicily's historical Muslims around the twelfth century still feature the outline of its mihrab and sit inside Segesta Archaeological Park

The mosque's construction and the village's brief existence had been dated to a window – early twelfth to early thirteenth centuries – that meant it would have been standing when Ibn Jubayr came to Sicily. In fact, I could almost see the spot where I bathed the night before from the hilltop, which lay a mere six kilometres to the north-east of Jebel Berber. The Andalusian does not say anything about the route he took after leaving the springs to get to Trapani. Yet the most direct one would have seen Ibn Jubayr pass Jebel Berber, through the region known today as Calatabarbarus. Ibn Jubayr and his retinue may well have known it as Qal'at Barbariyyah ('Berber Fort'), the Arabic version of the modern name. This is because a small fort or castle once stood at the mount's highest point, next to what have now been identified as residential ruins and a cemetery. The Muslim stay here was brief, and their departure in the early part of the thirteenth century was rapid – quickly replaced by a Christian lord who took over the castle. This came right at the end of the island's Muslim presence, when the villagers of Jebel Berber were most likely shipped off to mainland Italy by Frederick II like the rest of the Muslims of north-western Sicily, following the latest Muslim uprisings.

Ibn Jubayr was privy to these tensions and describes the 'humiliation and abasement' of the island's Muslims, claiming some of the island's sheikhs had been forced to convert to Christianity by William II, the 'tyrant king'. As an example, he relates the story of the scholar Ibn Zur'ah, from Palermo, who is forced to denounce Islam and practise Christianity as one of the king's legal judges, even converting a mosque he owned into a church – though Ibn Jubayr believes he did this observing taqiyya. While in Trapani, Qa'id Abu 'l-Qasim ibn Hammud, the 'Lord of the Muslim community in this island', tells him that the king recently confiscated all his wealth and properties and placed him under house arrest, accusing the Qa'id of corresponding with the Almohad empire in North Africa. His situation had become so dire that the Qa'id revealed he 'wished to be sold (as a slave) . . . that perhaps the sale would free us'. The meeting leaves Ibn Jubayr upset and in tears. The community's desperation is laid bare further when a 'notable' local sends his son to ask a member of Ibn Jubayr's group if he would take his daughter's hand in marriage, so she can 'live in the lands of the Muslims'. The son confides that they too were looking for a way to escape the island as soon as possible. In 1189, four years after Ibn Jubayr left Siqilliya, William II died, and in the turmoil that followed, the Christians of Palermo attacked the city's Muslim quarter, which saw huge numbers of Muslims flee to the mountains, where armed militias began to organize and start to openly challenge the kingdom's Christian authorities.

PART 2: THE CHILDREN OF AL-ANDALUS

The final and complete expulsion of Muslims from the former lands of the Emirate of Siqilliya came during the reign of Frederick II, who was only three years old when he inherited the crown of Sicily, following the death of his father, the German Hohenstaufen dynasty's Henry VI, in 1197. A year later his mother died too, and for the rest of his precarious childhood Sicily was ravaged both by the civil war between the German and Sicilian-Norman factions and by the continued unrest of its Muslim populace. By the time he had retaken his father's German crown and title of Holy Roman Emperor in 1220, Frederick was facing yet another Muslim uprising. In 1219, a large and organized group had taken the bishop of Girgenti prisoner. By 1221, they numbered around 30,000 and included disgruntled Christians. Their leader was a Muhammad Ibn Abbad of the Banu Abs, who minted his own coins, called himself 'Prince of the Believers' and tried several times to recruit support from foreign Muslim rulers. The threat was deemed so serious that Frederick asked the pope to postpone the Crusade he was planning to lead the following year. Ibn Abbad and his Christian allies, William Porcus and Hugo de Fer, were caught and imprisoned in 1222, but the rebellion continued. Frederick responded by sending expeditions into the countryside, forcing the Muslims to seek refuge on higher ground, at spots like Jebel Berber, thus causing them to become divided and eventually surrender. Fearing future uprisings, Frederick took decisive action that would bring to an end any hope of *convivencia* returning to the island. The monarch transported around 16,000 Muslims and their North African co-conspirators to Lucera in Apulia and two other colonies on the Italian mainland. Two decades later when the few remaining Muslims rose up in 1243, Frederick completely extinguished the Muslim presence in Sicily – and by extension Malta and Gozo (also part of the Arab-Norman kingdom and earlier Muslim Emirate). The Holy Roman Emperor and King of Sicily, who retained close ties with Muslim rulers, nurtured intellectual relationships with Muslim scholars and shared the ruling of the Holy Land with his Muslim counterparts, was also responsible for bringing to an end over 400 years of Muslim presence in Sicily. Seven years later, when he died in 1250, Frederick was wrapped in a shroud with embroidered Arabic inscriptions and buried in the cathedral that had once been the Great Mosque of Palermo.

There's something deeply satisfying about wandering, as a Muslim, through the heart of Mazara del Vallo's North African quarter: through its narrow, winding alleys, past the brightly coloured North African-style doors and archways painted onto metal shutters. It comes from knowing that it was at this historical little fishing village with its distinct Maghrebi-medina feel that the Aghlabid commander, Ibn Furat, first landed in 827. This is where Muslim Siqilliya began and where my journey in search of it would end. Mazara – almost poetically – was also home to the largest community of Italian-Tunisians in Sicily; just like the first time around, it was here where modern Tunisian immigrants arrived when they began migrating to Italy in the 1960s.

I stopped in front of one of the few painted shutters that wasn't a doorway or an arch. It showed two medieval figures that could have been painted onto Roger II's magnificent muqarnas ceiling. They sat in flowing robes playing medieval musical instruments. One was bearded and had dark-brown skin and the other, who may have been a woman, was playing the oud, the Arab instrument that inspired the lute and, later, the modern guitar. The couple were looking into each other's eyes as two white doves played at their feet, and a river gently flowed behind them. The buildings on the opposite shore included a church, a mosque and a synagogue: a nod to the Emirate of Siqilliya's culture of three faiths.

I walked on, shaded by the narrow alleys designed to reduce exposure to the sun, just like the medinas of North Africa. After a while a small courtyard opened up, with brightly coloured doorways. One of them had a tiled depiction of the Hand of Fatima beside it, a symbol some Muslims believe brings blessings and offers protection, and is identical to the *hamsa* in Judaic culture. This one was framed in a beautiful blue and white floral pattern and featured a doe-eyed yellow gazelle and two fish in the palm of the hand. My route took me close to the town's harbour, where I came upon the Mirabilia Arab House, which had a brilliant-green wooden double door in an arabesque arch. The Arabic letters *noon* and *kaaf* were inscribed on the doors, and on the pillar to the right a series of white tiles featuring an image of the dreamy Tunisian coastal town of Sidi Bou Said. The town, popular with tourists, clings to the rocks at the very northeastern edge of Tunisia, like a blue and white mirage staring across the Mediterranean directly towards Mazara del Vallo.

Painted arches on shutters in the Muslim neighbourhood of Mazara del Vallo evoke the ancient architecture of Muslim Sicily and that of modern-day Tunisia

I pulled up a chair at a small café overlooking the estuary of the River Mazaro and ordered a coffee. Sitting outside in the warm midday sun, I watched as men crowded around a small stall next to the waterfront, where a fishing vessel was unloading its catch and selling it directly to them. There were several wooden boxes of eel-like fish, beside trays of prawn and others I could not make out. The men, mostly middle-aged and wearing Sicilian sun hats, bartered over the price.

The water gently lapped at the dockside, where small boats

bobbed up and down. Overhead a seagull cried out as it spotted leftovers, and I wondered if that was the adhan I could hear. I listened carefully. I couldn't quite believe it and strained my ears to be absolutely sure. Tunisia lay a mere 150 kilometres across the straits; that was close, but surely not close enough for me to hear the adhan over there, and certainly not this loud. Yes! That was definitely the adhan. I leapt up, leaving some euros beneath the saucer, and began running in the general direction of the muezzin's voice. I sprinted back into the medina, past the old Chiesa de San Nicolò and back through the narrow alleyways with their painted shutters. Momentarily, I stopped in front of one I hadn't seen before. It showed a dark vessel, surrounded by large waves, above it the night sky fraught with lightning: a storm. In the bottom-right corner, the cherub-like face of a tearful child whose mind's picture had also been painted of him being held in the air by his father, a red blazing sun behind them. Next to the boy's face, close to the ground, was the word 'Papa . . .' It was a powerful painting and I wanted to study it for longer, but I knew if the adhan stopped I might not find the mosque it was coming from. Could it really be? Was the adhan permitted to be called out loud here in Sicily? A woman in a white headscarf walked past holding a brown leather handbag. I listened again, and ran down a narrow alley where an old fishing net had been hung onto the wall. Up ahead, I saw a man in a Tunisian *jebba* (as the *jubba* is known locally). I tried to follow him, but when he turned the next corner, I couldn't see him any more. It really was like being in the medinas of North Africa, where people disappear into hidden alleys and invisible doorways. I came upon a halal grocery shop, and saw the bald owner standing outside. He would know where the mosque was.

'Salaams, brother, where is the mosque?' I asked in broken Arabic.

The man was leaning against a road sign, and looked me up and down.

'That way,' he said, pointing down one of the narrow alleys I was sure I had already been down. But he was right. Of course he was right. Locals are always right.

PART 2: THE CHILDREN OF AL-ANDALUS

Mazara del Vallo's only mosque had a painted archway made of wood, designed to hide the ugly building behind. Near the entrance in a large, tiled frame it said, in Arabic and English, 'Moschea Ettakwa' had been founded in 2000. I felt a little emotional as I stepped into the mosque's hallway, leaving my shoes on the shelves, to be greeted by two arches that opened up to the main prayer hall, which had a plain, deep wine-red carpet. The congregation was almost entirely North African; a couple of them were wearing jubbas, like the man I had lost in the medina. I prayed the sunnah – four rakat – of the dhuhr prayer and took a seat. A man in a stripy top began to give some kind of sermon. He quoted the Qur'an, before interpreting it. I recognized the phrases *jihad al-akbar* (the greater struggle) and *jihad al-nafs* (the struggle with the lower self). The tone was intense, but all he was really saying was that we should always try and make it to the mosque for salah. When it was finished, another man stood up and gave the iqama, at which point the imam stepped forward, a large, friendly-looking individual with a grey beard and a brown skullcap. I was urged by an elderly uncle to step forward and leave my bag against the back wall. This made me nervous, but I did as I was told, praying that nobody ran off with my passport, car keys and wallet – all inside the black rucksack. As I bowed down in prostration for the first sajdah, I caught a glimpse of the bag still against the wall, and I began to relax and enjoy the salah – the first I was able to pray in a mosque in Sicily, where the call to prayer is heard by all those living in its vicinity, just as they would have during the Emirate of Siqilliya.

The Emirate reached its zenith under a cultured Kalbid emir, Ja'far Ibn Yusuf al-Kalbi, who ruled from 998 to 1019 and had been a poet, writer, philologist and patron of the arts, sciences and literature. The Kalbids paid homage to the Shi'a Fatimid Caliphate, based in what is now Tunisia, and in spite of its majority Sunni population oversaw the longest period of stability on the island. It was also the only time a Shi'a Emirate was ever established in Europe.

His reign had been the last and only real period of stability during the island's tumultuous two centuries or so of Muslim rule, and somewhere north of here, close to Trapani, was one of his former hunting lodges. Though completely rebuilt and now a private rental property, it is one of the few tangible sites linked directly to the island's Muslim rulers outside of Palermo.

In spite of the instability during the Emirate of Siqilliya, Muslims introduced an efficient and elaborate administrative system of rule. They opened channels of trade that brought wealth and exotica to the island's shores, including foods like rice, sugar cane and, if al-Idrisi is to be believed, pasta too. They also introduced revolutionary products such as paper and cotton, through a vast and sophisticated global Muslim network that stretched as far east as China – where Muslims were trading and spreading Islam as early as 616. They improved the existing agricultural and industrial techniques to grow and increase the yield of these new foods, as well as farming and fishing techniques (especially tuna fishing). They also established refined industries, like high-quality linen and the famous Siqilliyan silk that would lay the foundations for the later Italian silk industry. They founded fabulous institutes of learning, with libraries containing more books than their Norman inheritors would have seen in the entirety of the kingdom they had left behind. They built hospitals and stunning pleasure palaces, and had harems filled with beautiful women, where the finest food was eaten and the best wine was often drunk. The Emirate's children all went to school and learned to read and write at the feet of teachers who had mastered all the sciences available to humanity. The island's population doubled, because people wanted to live in a progressive and enlightened society where living standards were among the highest in the world. Its scholars produced some of the most advanced books on medicine, philosophy and science seen in the region since antiquity; its artisans crafted fine artefacts; and its poets and musicians composed works of wonderment and romance.

The reason why this culture was so quickly established in Siqilliya is that it was the normal culture of the Mediterranean

Muslims. This culture was *the* high culture in medieval Europe, with its tone set by the tenth-century Caliphate of Córdoba. This is why, wherever the Muslims went (and, in time, the Jews and Christians who lived in their midst), they took a 'version' of that culture with them — both its tangible and its intangible aspects — one so irresistible that all those who encountered or inherited it, like the Norman rulers of Sicily, immediately embraced it. The Arab-Norman kingdom that had continued to nurture the light of that Caliphate culture came to an end with the rule of its last enlightened monarch, Frederick II, in the thirteenth century. Following a brief period of papal-backed Frankish rule after Frederick's sons failed to continue the dynasty, Sicily, its southern Italian territories and the islands of Malta and Gozo were absorbed by the Crown of Aragon at the start of the fourteenth century, which was joined by Castile following the union of the two royal houses in the fifteenth century. This Spanish period precedes rule by several monarchs originally from French and Austro-Hungarian royal houses, before Sicily became part of the Kingdom of Italy during the late nineteenth-century unification that led to the modern state.

In spite of all this, when the twentieth-century Sicilian professor of folklore Giuseppe Pitrè conducted the first scientific study of Italian culture, he was still hearing the Emirate's echoes 900 years on: in the names of Sicilian places and people; in their habits, customs, songs, music and beliefs. Pitrè saw it etched on their faces, objects, architecture and landscape: 'forgotten from the memory of average people, of all the epochs, Greek, Latin, Byzantine, etc., only the Arab remains alive, although their reign was brief and vague'. Pitrè, who was also a medical doctor, claimed that even after all those centuries of Christian rule, 'everything ancient is Saracen: monuments, hidden caches, charming treasures, mountains, farm lands, caves, abandoned ruins, and old trees, especially olive trees'.

9

Ottoman Arab Malta

Marsa, Malta

'There it is!' Ibtisam Sadegh said.

We all craned our necks to get our first glimpse of the magnificent entrance to Malta's stunning Ottoman Cemetery – the country's oldest Muslim cemetery: a solid sandstone gatehouse-like structure with integrated mosque architecture, including a small silver central dome with a crescent atop its ornate finial. This was flanked, on all four corners, by highly decorative domed faux minarets that were encased by ornate battlements along the top. Underneath, framing the *tughra* (decorative signature) of Sultan Abdulaziz, was the entrance, held up by two neoclassical pillars and a bulbous archway of vegetal patterns that had echoes of Byzantium.

Everyone stared at the spectacle in silence.

'I didn't see this the first time I came to Malta,' I finally said, 'I didn't even know it was here.'

'I've never been,' Ibtisam admitted.

Born in the tiny village of Iklin just outside Malta's capital, Valletta, Ibtisam was brought up as a Muslim by her Libyan father and Maltese convert mother, in a household that didn't eat pork or drink alcohol, and observed the Muslim festivals. Taught that there are more similarities than differences between Christianity and Islam, she was brought up to respect both faiths and recalls attending her mother's Catholic family gatherings at Christmas and Easter, and regularly flying to Libya to spend time with her father's Arab Muslim family. I came across Ibtisam after reading her deeply personal article, in *Malta Today*, called 'Growing Up Muslim in Malta. But People Still Ask, "Where are you really from?"', a headline I instantly related to. The difference was, as Ibtisam reveals in her piece, she can pass for a Maltese – I can't pass for English – at least up until she reveals her name and then the uncomfortable questions begin. The article is about those frustrations and how Ibtisam navigated her identity, while witnessing the discrimination her father endured as an Arab in Malta. What really grabbed me was just how shocked the islanders were to learn that a Muslim and an Arab could be Maltese. Given the island was once part of the Emirate of Siqilliya, it was the greatest of ironies.

These days Ibtisam is a lecturer in Law at the University of Malta as well as a practising immigration lawyer.

'The Ottoman style is so different here,' said Ibtisam's friend Jaafar Alloul, a Belgian researcher she had invited along for the day as he happened to be in Malta. Jaafar was sitting with me in the back of Ibtisam's well-loved blue VW Golf. In the front, next to Ibtisam, was her colleague from the University of Malta, an Associate Professor of Law, David Zammit, who was Catholic Maltese and very interested in the country's Muslim history.

'Yes, this is a much later style, not the classical Ottoman one,' I said.

The melancholic voice of a traditional Maltese singer emanated from David's lap, where he had a wireless speaker. Throughout the journey, as Jaafar and I had got to know each other to the backdrop of the pain and longing apparent in the songs' mostly Semitic words, some of which Jaafar and I recognized, I kept thinking how much it reminded me of Umm Kulthum, the famous classical Egyptian singer.

'What do you call this music?' I asked David, as Ibtisam turned the car off the main road and into the cemetery's car park.

'*Ghana!*'

David explained that *ghana* – essentially the Arabic word *ghena* or *ghina*, meaning richness or singing – came in two types: one was usually about a tragedy, like the one he was playing, and the other was more of a dialogue in which the *għana* was used by people to reply to each other.

'This is when Maltese language becomes the most Semitic!'

David laughed, before telling us he had come across a reference to interesting hand gestures that used to accompany the singing of *għana* 200 years ago, in particular one that resembled how Muslims started their salah: by raising both hands either side of the head.

'I remember it being called *kabeer*, and Jaafar said there is something that sounds similar in Islam.'

I listened astonished.

'The takbir!' Jaafar and I said in unison.

The woman on the speaker continued to pour her heart out to us, just as I had heard Umm Kulthum do so many times.

'It's a bit like what they say about *fado* music . . .' I said, unclipping my seatbelt.

'I was thinking the same thing,' added Jaafar.

'And classical Andalusian music, when you hear it, you can hear . . .' I began.

'It's so obvious, right?' Jaafar, who normally looked at the sociology of migration, was becoming as excited as I was. 'Because it's so dramatic, and so *deeply* from the soul!'

The thought of linking 'dramatism' to Arabs made Ibtisam howl with laughter. Her reaction reminded me of my Arab friends making fun of how dramatic their parents always were.

'It seems when the Maltese are trying to look into their souls, they become more Semitic, huh?' I asked.

'Oh yes, when we are emotional and when we are . . . erm' – David, whose English didn't roll off his tongue as easily as his Maltese, was searching for the right word – 'when we are more passionate or angry, we become very Arab!'

This made us all laugh.

I ran my hand along the smooth marble slab, following the gentle slope over the grey veins that patterned the surface, as it made its

PART 2: THE CHILDREN OF AL-ANDALUS

The stunning gate at the entrance to Malta's Ottoman Cemetery, the country's oldest recognized Muslim cemetery, built in 1874 by Sultan Abdulaziz Khan

way down towards the small dark sinkhole. Someone had left a few gold-coloured coins at one end of the funerary washing table, and I wondered if it was some strange offering to the soldiers, whose bloodied and battered bodies would have been cleaned here before being carefully wrapped in the simple white shroud all Muslims are buried in. Our first stop in Malta was the country's spectacular Ottoman Military Cemetery on Triq il-Marsa. As with most roads in Malta, the 'Marsa Road' used an abbreviation of the Arabic word for road in its name, *tariq*, which they shortened to *triq*. It was basically my name.

Built in 1874 by the Ottoman sultan Abdulaziz Khan, to replace earlier Turkish graveyards established in the wake of the famous 1565 Ottoman Siege of Malta, where Turkish slaves held captive on the island were buried, the Ottoman Military Cemetery is considered one of the finest expressions of nineteenth-century Ottoman architecture outside Turkey. I leant against the square windows crowned by green wooden arabesque onion domes, and stared out beyond the stone fountain where three slender doves were forever bathing. The aromatic hint of ripening figs delicately hung in the air. I could see one of the kindly gardeners watering the parched earth inside the two plots either side of the cemetery's central path. These contained a number of different Muslim burials, including First World War Turkish prisoners of war who had died in Malta, as well as twenty-three would-be Moroccan hajjis who perished when the SS *Sardinia* burst into flames off the coast of Malta in 1908. Both were lined by neatly manicured myrtle bushes and rows of mature olive, pine and fig trees. One of the gardeners, in a tourist sun hat, shorts and a camouflage T-shirt, was sweeping around the octagonal base of what was once another fountain in front of the cemetery's entrance. He was barefooted and beautifully framed by the arch of the monumental gate. The local architect E. L. Galizia, who built the cemetery, had been influenced by a wide range of architectural styles: his own home in nearby Valletta was dubbed 'Villa Alhambra', because of its echoes of the Nasrid Palace in Granada, Spain. The beautiful building we now stood inside had clearly been inspired by the Indian Mughal style and was more subtle than the gatehouse. It featured two silver-coloured onion domes, one above the funerary washroom and the other over its mosque.

'I read somewhere this might just be the oldest surviving mosque in Malta,' I said as the four of us walked across the connecting corridor and stepped into the room opposite. Galizia had actually made plans to integrate an octagonal-shaped purpose-built mosque at the back of the cemetery, complete with an ornately decorated dome, resembling a Fabergé egg, but this never materialized. We had entered beneath three elegant arches like those seen across the Indian subcontinent. These were mirrored by three arched windows in each of the rooms either side of the central walkway, where a large marble plaque announced the builder of the cemetery in French and beside it on smaller plaques, added later, in Turkish and English.

'I guess it is a "mosque" in the loosest sense,' Jaafar said, whose work looked at how living in Malta affected the worldview of Gulf medical students and researchers.

The mosque room was cube-shaped and mirrored the funerary washroom. Both were carpeted and had the same ornate windows and green shutters. Against the southern wall were a small set of steps that served as a minbar, and in the south-eastern corner a large white wooden square with a painted grey frame constituted the mihrab.

'Yes, it is clearly not used for daily prayers, and was probably built only for performing the *janazah* prayer in congregation,' I said.

In fact, the mosque had been used for Friday prayers and some daily prayers by the island's Muslims up until the 1970s.

David was staring at the niche with intent. A graduate of law, he was also an anthropologist. His interest in Malta's Muslim roots came from a very personal place: when he was a child, his parents had moved to Oxford, where he quickly became fluent in English, losing his Maltese along the way. When he returned, he began to relearn it and thus study its roots.

'So, tell me, David,' I began, picking up the conversation we had started in the car, 'are the Maltese Arabs, or just Europeans who happen to speak Arabic?'

His eyes lit up. The reason Maltese poetry and music tended to have a strong Arabic presence, he explained, could be down to the fact that the language's most ancient literary text – its earliest form, if you like – is a poem, *Il-Kantilena*, which is almost entirely Arabic. This fascinating fifteenth-century manuscript, attributed to the philosopher and poet Pietru Caxaro and written in Old Maltese, contained almost none of the later Romance vocabulary found in modern Maltese.

'It has I think just two Romance words!' David said, becoming animated.

We both leant against the windowsill. Ibtisam and Jaafar had wandered out to the garden and were admiring the large olive trees, where small birds perched continuing their morning song.

1. A map from a fifteenth-century copy of the great Andalusian geographer Al Idrissi's magnum opus, *Nuzhat al-mushtaq fi ikhtiraq al-afaq* or *The Book of Roger*, which he created in 1138 for the Arab-Norman King Roger II and which was considered the most accurate geographical text of the day.

2. Muslim soldiers driving out Byzantine soldiers as depicted in the twelfth-century *Madrid kylitzes*, an illuminated manuscript by John Skylitzes believed to have been produced in the Arab-Norman court in Palermo.

3. A seventh-century Sasanian-style silver dirham coin, featuring the only known depiction of the founding Umayyad Caliph, Mu'awiyah ibn Abu Sufyan, the man who brought Muslims to Europe.

4. Engraving of the famous Battle of the Masts (or Phoenix) in 655, where a fledgling Muslim navy – established by Mu'awiyah – annihilated a Byzantine fleet led by Emperor Constans II. The battle confirmed Muslims as the new Mediterranean naval superpower.

5. Mu'awiyah's naval fleet being repelled by the mysterious 'Greek Fire' at the Siege of Constantinople in 667, from the twelfth-century illuminated manuscript *Madrid Skylitzes*.

6. An astrolabe produced by the Andalusian Ibrahim ibn Sa'id al-Sahli in 1067 in Toledo, which became a major translation centre during the Christian period.

7. An imagined scene in Al Andalus where an oud player entertains an audience from the twelfth-century *Hadith Bayad wa Riyad*, a love story about an Andalusian female and a Damascene male.

8. A Jew and a Muslim play chess in thirteenth-century Al Andalus from Alfonso X of Castile, Leon and Garcia's *Libro de los Juegos*.

9. A (*circa*) sixteenth-century Latin translation of Ibn Sina's *al-Qanun fi al-tibb* or *The Canon of Medicine*, which he wrote in the eleventh century and was first translated into Latin by Gerard of Cremona in the twelfth century.

10. Teaching inside a medieval Muslim library in the *Maqama* of Hariri. The Great Mosque of Córdoba's tenth-century library was said to be home to 600,000 books and manuscripts.

11. An 1883 artist's impression of the tenth-century Córdoban physician Abu al-Qasim al-Zahrawi – considered the 'father of surgery' – tending to a patient as his assistant carries medicine, inside a medieval Muslim hospital.

12. The spectacular *muqarnas* ceiling of the Cappella Palatina – the Palace Chapel – in Palermo's Palazzo dei Normanni is considered one of the finest examples of Arab-Norman artistry. It is inscribed with white Kufic script and is a kaleidoscope of animal and human figures playing chess, juggling, wrestling and hunting.

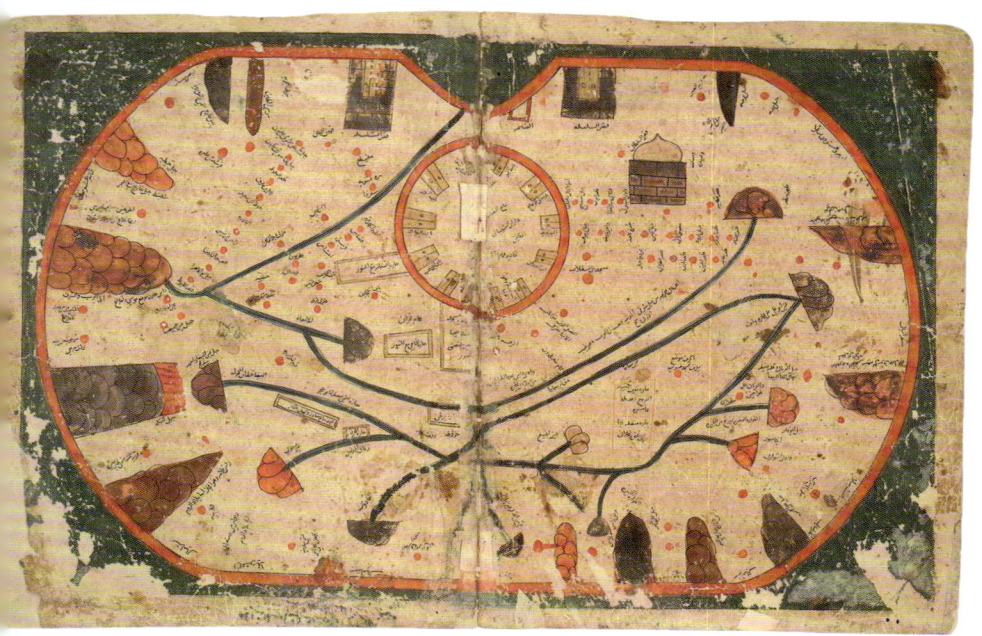

An eleventh-century map of the Emirate of Siqilliya in an anonymous Arabic manuscript called the 'Book of Curiosities'.

The Palazzo della Cuba, William II's treasure palace built in 1180 in Palermo, where Arabic Kufic script can still be seen along the upper edges.

15. Twelfth-century image of King Henry II of England, whose daughter was married to the Arab-Norman Sultan Musta'izz, or William II of Sicily. Henry famously threatened to convert to Islam if the pope did not reign in his nemesis Thomas Beckett.

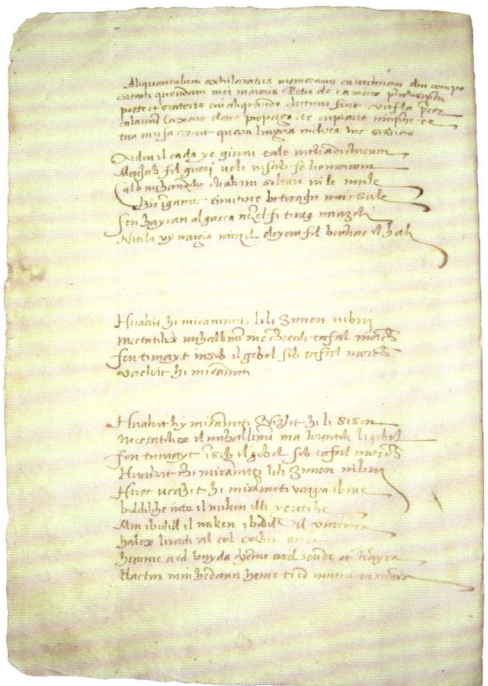

16. A copy of the fifteenth-century *Il Kantilena*, the oldest known literary text in the Maltese language. The poem, attributed to Pietru Caxaro, is written in Latin script but contains only two Romance words; the rest are of Arabic origin.

17. The fountain inside the *Salla della Fontana*, the main reception hall and best-preserved room inside al-Aziz or the Zisa, featuring classical Islamic art and engineering, completed by the Arab-Norman Sultan *Musta'izz*, or William II, in 1189.

18. Courtyard of the mosque of the University of al-Qarawiyyin in Fez, Morocco, said to have been founded as a mosque and madrasa at the end of the ninth century on the eve of the city being absorbed into the Caliphate of Córdoba.

19. One of the original mosque lamps from the mosque of the Alhambra, now on display in the Museum of Alhambra.

20. A painted scene imagining the visit of a Christian diplomat to the court of the Córdoban Caliph. The painting is on display inside the Torre de la Calahorra in Córdoba.

21. Muhammad Iqbal praying in front of the mehrab of the Mezquita in Córdoba in 1932; the first time a Muslim had done so in almost 700 years. The great mystic and poet was so moved by the experience that he wrote one of his greatest poems, called *Masjid-e-Qartiba*, while in the city.

22. The mehrab of the prayer hall inside the Palacio de la Madraza, once part of a madrasah or institute of education built by the Nasrid ruler Yusuf I in the fourteenth century, that was attached to the Great Mosque of Granada.

23. Statue of the founder of the Almohad dynasty, Abd al-Mu'min, in Nedrome, Algeria. Considered the greatest of all the Almohad Caliphs, he built some of the dynasty's greatest monuments including the Kutubiyah Mosque, the Mosque of Tinmal and the Kasbah of the Udayas, all in Morocco.

24. The foundation stone of the Maristán of Granada, built between 1365 and 1367 by the Nasrid king Muhammad V, during the Golden Age of Nasrid rule. The name *Maristan* comes from the Persian word *bimaristan*, which means 'house of the sick' and was the Muslim precursor to the modern hospital.

25. The Ben Youssef Madrasa in Marrakesh, Morocco, built in 1564–65 CE by the Saadian sultan Abdallah al-Ghalib on the site of an older one dating from the early fourteenth century.

'Around fifty years before this poem was written we see the language still being called Arabic, and by the time the poem is written, it is called Maltese,' David said.

He explained it was at this point that the idea of a 'Maltese language' was conceived; the moment the language was born.

'This Arabic is of course Siculo-Arabic, making Malta the only place in Europe where it is still spoken.'

Siculo-Arabic, as the name suggests, is Sicilian-Arabic, the ancient Arabic once spoken across the Emirate of Siqilliya of which the Maltese archipelago was historically part. Modern Maltese is over one third Siculo-Arabic; this includes the days of the week and Maltese numbers, which are almost indistinguishable from their Arabic equivalents. The rest of the Maltese language is a mix of Italian, Sicilian and English. This was the reason why I had come to Malta, because it is the only place on earth where Europeans still speak one of the continent's ancient Arabic languages.

I nodded in agreement, before adding, 'And Tunisia? I have a Tunisian brother-in-law who tells me that most Tunisians, whose Arabic has similar roots and is also influenced by Romance languages, can understand Maltese.'

'Yes, that's true!' agreed David, 'I actually went to Tunis on a scholarship around twenty years ago for six weeks . . . ah, *chismu* . . .'

'Sorry, what did you just say?' I asked, again getting quite excited.

David looked at me blankly.

'Did you just say "*chismu*" in Maltese?'

'Yes, I did.'

'This is what some of my Arab friends say when they are thinking, the equivalent of "erm" in English for us!' I blurted.

My excitement made David laugh. It was obvious this was going to happen a lot today.

'I chose to study classical Arabic, and by the end of the six weeks I could make myself understood quite well! But now I've forgotten! . . . And there was a lot of memory in Tunis of the Maltese, because the Maltese used to go to Tunis as migrants,

PART 2: THE CHILDREN OF AL-ANDALUS

and to Egypt. Throughout the nineteenth century you had a big pattern of Maltese migration to these places,' David said.

I was aware of the huge Maltese migration to Britain and other prosperous parts of Europe, but I had not known about a migration that had taken them south and east to Muslim countries.

'The person who discovered the poem, Godfrey Wettinger, was of the opinion that, like the language, Malta's modern population are also descended from Muslim Arabs.' He said the last bit with a smile. 'This theory was proposed by Joseph Brincat after he discovered the accounts of al-Himyari, a fourteenth-century Arab geographer who talks about Malta . . .'

I nodded.

'Himyari basically claimed that around the year 890 you have a fleet sailing from Sicily which takes over Malta. Now, according to older accounts there was continuity of the population, but al-Himyari says the island was laid waste and empty for almost a century.'

'So al-Himyari is suggesting Malta is populated again after *this* point?'

'Yes, that's basically Brincat's theory, which Wettinger eventually came round to . . . Brincat bases his theory partly on the idea that there were place names in Malta which were basically replicated from Sicily, a bit like you know York in England and New York . . . like Girgenti and so on,' David said.

Il Girgenti was a place in the south-west of the island with the same name as the Sicilian town of Agrigento.

'But,' added David, 'this theory is very controversial in Malta because ultimately it suggests that –'

'– everybody is of Arab Muslim ancestry!' I finished his sentence for him.

David gave me another wry smile.

'Even as late as the 1790s the Knights of the Order of St John – who ruled the island – were saying, "No, we don't want to listen to these Arabs here", because the Maltese sent a delegation to the Knights saying they needed to surrender to Napoleon, when he came here, and they . . .' David began laughing. '. . . they said, "No, we're not gonna be intimidated by these Arabs!"'

'So, as recently as two centuries ago, the Maltese were still being called Arabs?'

'Yes!'

We both laughed again. It seemed that in spite of the gargantuan effort to distance themselves from Arabic, vis-à-vis Muslim identity and ancestry, there was no denying that it ran deep in Maltese culture and explains why, even today, Maltese poets and artists retain a strong Semitic linguistic presence in their poems. When they are being at their most creative, passionate and vulnerable, the Maltese go to drink from the well of their Arabic ancestry. Our laughter was cut short by the headmistress-like voice of Ibtisam.

'So! I'm gonna manage the time!'

David and I stood up straight, like two errant students who had drifted from the main group on a school trip.

'I'm gonna need to quickly just pray in here,' I said to Ibtisam, almost half expecting her to tell me off and refuse. She smiled and nodded before heading back out to the garden, accompanied by David.

The last time I came to Malta, I hadn't even found a mosque, let alone prayed in one, and had promised myself I would correct that this time by praying in the oldest one I could find. So as Ibtisam and the others waited in the cemetery garden, I positioned myself directly in front of the mihrab and made the takbir.

Though Malta is believed to have first been inhabited around 1450 BC by the Phoenicians, who reputedly gave the island the name 'Malet' – to mean 'shelter', quite possibly because of the numerous sheltered bays it possesses – its first town is said to have been built by the Greeks, almost a thousand years later, around 404 BC, and now sits beneath Mdina. The Greeks were followed by the Carthaginians and then the Romans. According to Acts in the New Testament, this is also when St Paul is shipwrecked off the coast of Malta, around AD 58, while being transported as a prisoner to Rome. Local tradition claims this was at St Paul's Island in St Paul's

Bay, where he is met with kindness by locals who witness a miracle when St Paul survives being bitten by a viper. He then meets the island's 'prince', or leader, Publius, whose father is sick with fever and dysentery. St Paul miraculously cures him using the power of prayer. This results in Publius's conversion; he then becomes the island's first bishop, and later its first canonized saint. St Paul stays for three months, preaching the Gospel and performing miracles, and it is this incident that the Maltese believe leads to the island first adopting Christianity.

After the division of the Roman empire around 337, the Vandals took hold of Sicily and then Malta, and were followed shortly after by the Goths. When the Romans recaptured Malta, they were faced with a new threat – the Muslims. The Aghlabids arrived in approximately 869, and according to most Muslim historians, like al-Himyari, the island was completely depopulated at this point and laid waste, suggesting a break in the population from the earliest Christians to the modern ones. The archaeology for this period – which is lacking – appears to support this theory and implies that Malta was more or less empty for around a century, before Muslims began living on it from the middle of the tenth century. Prior to this it was most probably used as a 'strategic naval base', with al-Himyari saying that 'it was visited by shipbuilders, because of the abundance and tastiness of the fish around its shores, and by those who collect honey'. It is from this period that Malta becomes part of the Emirate of Siqilliya and its high Islamic culture. Muslims were also allowed to stay there, just as in Sicily, after the Normans took over the Emirate, right up until Frederick II moved them to the mainland of Italy in the middle of the thirteenth century. While physical remnants and monuments from Malta's Muslim period are long gone, the greatest legacy of the island's Islamic era remains its language, with the Maltese the last of the 'Arabic'-speaking Europeans.

The Ottoman Military Cemetery is easily the most spectacular historical Islamic monument on the island, even if most of the island's 4 per cent of Muslims have no idea it even exists. However, the monument that all Maltese Muslims *are* aware of, and the one that harboured Ibtisam's earliest memories of being part of a wider Maltese Muslim community, was the country's one and only modern mosque. Ibtisam hadn't been to the Ċentru Islamiku ta' Malta in fifteen years, and I felt honoured and excited to be going back with her after such a long time.

A sandstone rectangular building with tall, slim windows and a large grey dome, the mosque had a single minaret, featuring a muqarnas pattern, that dominated the low-rise buildings common in this little corner of eastern Malta. We pulled up in a car park overlooked by a two-storey building, and stepped out into the brilliant Maltese sunshine. I asked Ibtisam about her memories of growing up with the mosque.

'Every Saturday in my childhood, the imam's son, who is an exact replica of the imam, used to give us . . . like a class . . . He used to award us something if we learned a surah, and it was usually . . . like a calculator – it used to really help!'

All three of us listening smiled at the memory.

'I also remember coming here when I was older, my mother was with me – when a lot of women would meet up . . . it was fun. I used to enjoy it.'

'This was like a social gathering?'

'No, every week someone would give . . . like a lesson, and I remember one day I gave the lesson on the Prophet . . .' Ibtisam fell about giggling.

What she was recalling was a *halaqa*, an informal gathering or lecture based on the ancient practices observed by the Prophet's generation to share knowledge with one another, still common among Muslim communities across the world.

'Wow,' I said, 'and your mother, she embraced Islam, right?'

'Yes, she did, I mean she's not . . . like the mooost . . .' Ibtisam felt obliged to clarify her mother's level of Islamic observance.

'She embraced it mostly to marry your father, right?'

'Eh, yes, yes . . . And my mum was the first teacher hired, when the [Islamic] school opened here in the nineties!'

PART 2: THE CHILDREN OF AL-ANDALUS

'There is a school here?' I asked.

'Yes, this is a mosque and a school!'

'When you say a "school", not a madrasa?'

'No, a primary school, it is a school day so probably there are children here today.'

'In the mosque building?'

Ibtisam shook her head before pointing to the two-storey building we had passed. That was the Mariam al-Batool school, founded in the late 1990s and named after the mother of Jesus. Its name translated as the Virgin-Mary-the-Pious school.

'So you didn't go here?'

'No, I just missed it,' said Ibtisam, looking a tad disappointed.

The Mariam al-Batool primary school was a state school with an integrated Islamic curriculum – similar to 'faith schools' in England. It was opened with the support of the Libyan government, just like the mosque. Both were the result of a fascinating relationship Malta once had with the Arab nation.

'Is it true Gaddafi actually came here and opened the mosque?' I asked.

'Yes, I think he did, yes,' Ibtisam said, 'yes, when Gaddafi had very good relations with Malta, he came a few times . . . or maybe we were afraid of him, it could be either way!'

Malta had been so culturally 'eastward-facing' during this period that the country re-introduced the teaching of Arabic in state schools, which was probably the first time it had happened since the country had been part of the Emirate. I asked Ibtisam if she knew anything about this.

'Yes, the imam learned Arabic, and David – he learned Arabic at school!'

I looked at David with wide eyes.

'Yes, there was a period in the seventies when our Prime Minister was very close to Gaddafi . . . and Malta became much closer to Africa and looking towards there for cultural connections, and in that time he gave this land to the Muslim community,' explained David.

David was referring to the period immediately after Malta's independence from Britain, when Libya loaned millions of dollars to the Maltese to compensate for the loss of rental income after the British military bases were closed and Malta was reportedly turning its back on NATO and Europe to identify more with North Africa. The relationship peaked in the 1980s, when the two countries entered a 'Friendship and Cooperation Treaty', during which time Muslims, for so long framed as barbaric raiders, were framed as relatives: Arabic became a compulsory subject in secondary schools and the Libyan president, Muammar Gaddafi, who came and personally opened the mosque, claimed – like Brincat and Wettinger – that the Maltese were of Arab origin.

At the entrance to the mosque, I noted the djellabas hanging neatly on wooden hooks. We stepped onto the cool marble floor and walked towards the mosque's main hall, placing our shoes on the wooden shoe racks. Ibtisam put a headscarf around herself and approached one of the women who appeared upon hearing the double-glazed doors open. After a brief conversation in either Arabic or Maltese – I couldn't tell – Ibtisam explained that we were to wait in the mosque as the imam, who was fasting, was resting and would be made aware of our arrival. David, who had been looking distracted since we left the car, finally admitted to us and himself that he had lost his glasses. So, while he and Jaafar took Ibtisam's car back to the cemetery to try and find them, Ibtisam and I stepped into the beautiful, light, airy, domed prayer hall of the mosque that harboured so many of her childhood memories. We both sat down on the mosque's light-brown carpet, which had thick dark-brown lines where worshippers stood to pray. The interior was white, with decorative elements in a mint green, including green medallions featuring the name of Allah and Muhammad beneath the squinches that held up the large central dome. The mihrab and minbar were both made from black marble, and the minbar was topped with a gold dome.

'What inspired you to write that article?' I asked, referring to the piece she wrote for *Malta Today* that had made me contact her.

PART 2: THE CHILDREN OF AL-ANDALUS

The interior of Ċentru Islamiku, Malta's only mosque, built in 1984 and reportedly opened by the then Libyan president Muammar Gaddafi

Ibtisam explained that the article actually came from a talk she gave at a workshop, a safe space where she could speak from the heart. Her story resonated with a lot of people, and then a blog writer approached her, asking if she would write her talk up as an article.

A low hissing could be heard followed by a toxic smell that began to pervade the air. We looked around to see the woman from earlier, tracing the edge of the mosque's wall with a can of mosquito spray. As the fumes drifted towards the middle, they made us both cough.

'Their article had so many views . . .' Ibtisam covered her mouth as she spoke. 'Then *Malta Today* asked to print it! And recently, after Ramadan, a minister wrote an article . . .' Ibtisam started giggling. 'He wrote an article with the title, "Eid Mubarak Ibtisam"!'

'Sorry?' I wasn't quite sure I had heard right.

'He . . .' Ibtisam couldn't contain her laughter. 'He read the blog, and wanted to wish all the Muslims Happy Eid.'

'But why name you?'

'Because he read my article, about my experience, and . . .'

Ibtisam was really struggling to contain her laughing fit now.

I told her it was wonderful that her article had moved a government minister. In the article, Owen Bonnici, the Minister for the National Heritage, the Arts and Local Government, spoke about being deeply affected by reading of Ibtisam's traumatic experiences and described her as an 'inspiring fellow Maltese', and how he agreed with her that the Maltese 'should take pride in all Maltese history, rather than distancing ourselves from our Arabic and Islamic heritage in a desperate attempt to prove our European-ness'.

Ibtisam was still laughing, and it soon became apparent what was *really* funny.

'He was . . . like, "I've never met her", and the dean at my university was . . . like, "What do you mean? She is a lecturer at the university and you are too"!'

Now I was laughing. It was typical of a politician. Ibtisam had her finger to her nose, as she tried unsuccessfully to contain her laughter.

'It's amazing what an impact the piece has had though, right?' I said, when we had both composed ourselves again.

'Yes, because people connect with it,' Ibtisam said.

She then described some of the people who had been in touch with her, and the harrowing experiences they had shared. Like her friend Sara Ezabe, who is also Maltese-Libyan, only, unlike Ibtisam, her first name is common on the island and she wore a hijab. Ibtisam told me how Sara had been spat on for this while standing at a bus stop and how a lecturer at the University of Malta, Stephen Florian, where Sara was studying law, posted abhorrent comments about her online, describing her as a 'radical' and comparing her to 'The Mummy'. Florian, who stood as a European Parliament candidate for the country's anti-Muslim group, Ghaqda Patrijotti Maltin, resigned shortly afterwards. Florian's party made headlines back in 2014, when they handed out pork in Msida to protest against Muslims wanting to pray in the village square because they had no mosque in which to do so. At the protest, the group's leader, Alex Pisani, claimed the pork was being handed out to show solidarity with students at the local St Paul's Bay primary school, who he falsely claimed had been forbidden from eating pork because of the large number of Muslim students there. Pisani continued his scaremongering by telling the crowd that the Maltese race would become extinct due to the rate Muslims were breeding at, before describing parts of Malta as 'like Saudi Arabia' and calling for the burka to be banned. I was not at all surprised to hear this. Women in my own family had experienced the cowardly and disgusting behaviour of being spat on for what they were wearing, and across the continent the headdress of Muslim women has become an obsession, with regular debates and referendums proposed to ban it.

As we spoke, a police siren wailed somewhere in the distance and both of us wondered out loud if David had found his glasses. Ibtisam joked that he was always losing them. The woman who had been spraying the mosquito repellent returned without her spray. The imam was here.

We left the prayer hall and entered a dark corridor, passing a framed painting of the mosque with the name of the school written in English and Arabic, and a giant printed Qur'an on a large wooden bookstand. I noted it was open on the twenty-ninth surah, Surah *al-Ankabut*, or 'The Spider'.

'This was the library my mother worked in,' Ibtisam whispered as we walked into a room with wall-to-wall Arabic books on dark wooden shelves.

Sitting behind a large brown desk was a very sleepy-looking man with a friendly face in a white *thobe* (a long head-to-toe garment popularly worn by men across the Middle East). As soon as he saw Ibtisam, his eyes lit up. Originally from Palestine, the imam came to Malta in 1979 during that interesting period David had mentioned earlier.

'This is the first time Arabic was being taught since the ancient period?' I asked.

'Of course, this is a new era in the history of Malta and in the relationship with Libya and the whole Arab world.'

The imam spoke slowly, as if still waking up, but with a

warmth that reminded me of a kind uncle or grandfather. Arabic was actually taught on the island after the Muslim period briefly in 1637, when a school teaching Arabic was set up in Gozo by the Vatican's Sacred Congregation for the Propagation of the Faith. But during the 1970s Arabic became a state-endorsed language for the first time since the days of the Emirate.

The imam explained how he fell into the job when the old imam, a Syrian, was transferred to Cyprus.

'It was not planned, you see.'

I smiled.

'No, it was planned,' I said, pointing upwards.

'Planned by God . . . yes.'

The imam laughed and his eyes opened a little more.

'He married my parents!' Ibtisam said, as if suddenly remembering.

'Wow, really?'

'Yes, he did the *nikah* [Islamic marriage ceremony].'

'I'm an ooold man!' the imam said.

His warmth and humour were coming through as his tiredness receded.

'Was it a big community back then?'

'At that time, we did not fill the mosque, maybe a thousand . . . the people said, why do you need such a big mosque when you have so few people,' explained the Imam, 'now there are forty thousand of us!'

The mosque was founded in 1984 by the World Islamic Call Society (WICS) from Tripoli in Libya, in an agreement that meant the mosque and its officials had diplomatic immunity. The mosque's aim, explained the imam, was to provide services for the Muslim community of Malta and help to make the faith familiar to locals, instigating interfaith dialogue. However, Islam is not recognized by law and so the mosque, i.e. Islamic centre, does not receive any state funds and Muslims do not receive any educational, cultural or social privileges.

I asked the imam what the community considered its biggest

achievements apart from establishing the mosque and school. He told me that recently the Qur'an was translated into Maltese, modestly leaving out that he was a co-author of the translation, something Ibtisam had to point out, making the imam smile with embarrassment. The translation that the imam co-authored with the Maltese Arabist Martin Zammit was published and launched at the mosque in 2008. The imam told us another major milestone was the opening of a Muslim cemetery.

'Before that we used to bury in the Turkish cemetery in the nineties and eighties . . .'

'Really?'

I looked at Ibtisam. Neither of us was aware of this.

'We just visited it this morning.'

Civilian burials were stopped at the Ottoman cemetery around 1995 after the Turkish embassy became worried that too many burials might lead to the historical monument being changed adversely. For a while after this, the community's dead were buried in the Addolorata multi-faith cemetery. The mosque's own cemetery was opened in 2001 and sits inside a large walled area to the west of the mosque. It has a white iron gate with a large green dome at the entrance. The establishment of a mosque, school and cemetery were all positives and something Malta should be proud of, explained the imam. In that respect, Malta was clearly trying to be a tolerant and multicultural society.

'The previous prime minister, Joseph Muscat, he was proud, he said to me, "We are proud of this school,"' explained the imam, before conceding that the fact there is now a sizeable Maltese Muslim community is another reason why politicians are beginning to notice them.

'When I was young, we used to always have an iftar in the mosque, and then at some point both parties started to organize their own iftars, do you remember?' Ibtisam asked the imam.

He smiled.

'Before they do not care . . . now both parties make iftar in their headquarters.'

'Yes, for us!' Ibtisam laughed.

She explained that for the past ten years or so, both leading political parties in Malta held iftars for Muslims during Ramadan.

'We go to both of them, my parents and that. We don't support either of them, we go to meet the people,' said Ibtisam laughing, before tapping her watch subtly to remind me that my time was nearly up. We had just a day together, and quite a few places to visit, which is why Ibtisam was being so strict.

I thanked the imam and told him what a wonderful job he was doing, even if he was reluctant to take the post.

'I am the "acting" imam,' he said, making us all laugh.

10

Maimuna's Malta

Rabat and Gozo, Malta

The drive from the mosque to our lunch spot took us west towards the town of Rabat, close to the ancient capital of Mdina and the area that once formed the Roman city of Melite. The two-laned Triq Mdina was lined by pine trees leaning over a low white wall, behind which were dry farm plots. Jaafar asked me about the journeys I had been making for the book and where I was heading next. When I mentioned Portugal, David turned around.

'I was in Portugal recently,' he began, 'they were explaining to me that olive oil, they call it *zeyt*!'

'We also call it *zeyt*!' said an excited Ibtisam.

'Apparently there are nearly nineteen thousand words in Portuguese that can be traced back to Arabic roots from the Muslim period,' I explained. 'And the way it sounds when they say the original name, *Bortukal* – as if with a "B" – always tells me it must be Arab!'

The car erupted with laughter.

The traffic outside was much better now the initial morning rush was over. Earlier, a five-minute journey had taken us nearly three times as long, but now, even on the smaller roads, we were moving at a good pace.

'What you see in front of you is the city of Mdina . . . that was separated from Rabat, because in Roman times it was the city of Melite, and Arabs decided for defence purposes it is better to have a small city that is surrounded by walls, so this is actually the biggest legacy of the Arab period – apart from the Maltese language – in Malta.'

David was pointing towards a series of sand-coloured structures up on a hillside in the distance.

'How much of the wall is original?' I asked.

'Well, the original wall would be Roman, but the bit separating it from Rabat will be Arab for sure . . .'

'There are streets named –' began Ibtisam, before David jumped back in: 'There is a street named Mesquita –'

'Where surely there was once a mosque,' I said, before jokingly adding, 'and not just a place where mosquitoes used to hang out!' Ibtisam found this particular 'dad joke' hilarious.

David continued the history lesson.

'The cathedral you can see round here almost certainly was built on the site of a mosque.'

I looked up to see a vast baroque cathedral, with twin bell towers, called St Paul's Cathedral, which overlooked the Pjazza Mesquita.

'But why Mesquita?' asked Jaafar.

He had read my mind. *Mesquita* is the Spanish word for mosque.

'We have no idea,' admitted David, before adding that in the past it was actually one of the names of the noble families: 'The traditional nobility of Mdina are Spanish nobility.'

The Spanish rule of Malta began in 1530 when the island was ruled by the Knights of St John under the Spanish Crown. They fortified the island, repelling the Ottoman siege in 1565, and developed a maritime and commercial hub. Spanish influence significantly shaped Malta's cultural, architectural and religious landscape and came to an end when Napoleon invaded the island in 1798.

'There was an earthquake in the seventeenth century, and the old cathedral from the 1300s – actually it was older, it was Norman – that cathedral basically fell down, but they found built into the walls of the cathedral, they found . . .' David paused to give Ibtisam directions. '. . . built into the cathedral, they found . . .' Again David stopped to give Ibtisam further directions.

'What did they find, David . . . the mihrab?' I asked impatiently.

'No, they found a pot . . .'

David stopped to point out where to park the car. A pot felt like a bit of an anti-climax.

'Just a pot?' I asked.

'They found a pot of coins, silver and gold, some of which had been minted in Malta during the Arab period,' David said, finally completing his tantalizing anecdote.

'Oh wow, do you know where these coins are?'

'I think in the cathedral museum, but I'm not sure . . .'

'Is that where we are going?' I asked.

'No, we're gonna start off at a water source,' he replied.

Mdina's subterranean water system was installed by the Muslims, and David knew a spot where we could see some of this system. We dropped down onto a hidden little road, where the trees and bushes were overgrown and there was no pavement. It was here David asked Ibtisam to park the car. I stepped out and looked down the grey tarmac to sun-bleached fields in the distance, beyond which, rising gradually, were two- and three-storey houses.

'So where are we, David?' I asked, turning around to find he was gone.

'Come here!' came a voice from behind a large fig tree.

I looked up to see a triple-arched sandstone structure built into the hillside and obscured by overgrown foliage. Ducking beneath the fig tree's large branches, I found David's head peering out from under one of the arches where there was an unlocked green gate. As I entered, David was standing on a large stone block and pointed me towards another, indicating that I should use them as stepping stones to cross the slimy floor.

'Wow!' I said, staring into the corridor-like space where several rectangular stone troughs were lined up along the back wall with fresh water trickling into them. The floor was wet and covered in algae; some of the walls had visible cracks, but the ceiling was an impressive series of stone arches like the ribcage of a large animal.

On the back wall inside a small semicircular niche above the water troughs was a stone with a Latin inscription obscured by age and weathering.

'What is this?' I finally asked.

'A medieval washhouse,' began David, 'we are beneath Mdina. No tourists ever come here . . . As you can see, it is neglected and left to decay.'

'So, these were used until recently for public washing . . . and you believe it could have been a Muslim structure before that?' I asked, assuming that was why David had brought us here.

'I dunno, maybe originally for a hammam . . .' David said, making his way over to the trickling water, where he began washing his hands.

I snapped away with my phone. A thick lead pipe added much later could be seen going across the main space towards the entrance. The rustling of fig leaves told us Ibtisam and Jaafar had also found the entrance. Ibtisam peered in wide-eyed and astonished.

'It's amazing. I can see why you asked David to come along!' I said.

'Yes, and that's why I wanted to come along too. I knew he would show us these hidden spots!' added Jaafar.

Ibtisam was wearing white shoes and wasn't too sure about going much further than the first 'stepping stone', which she shakily negotiated. Jaafar, who was much more appropriately dressed, in jeans, a T-shirt and Birkenstock sandals, simply waded across the watery floor.

'It would be wonderful if someone could interpret this space,' said David, staring at the crumbling brickwork of the wash basins.

'So, David, you think the spring these waters come from was originally harnessed by the Muslims?'

'And the channels, definitely!' said David, raising both arms and moving them up and down to indicate a channel-like structure. 'No doubt even the name Ghain Hammet, which means Ghain Muhammad.'

PART 2: THE CHILDREN OF AL-ANDALUS

It was true that *ghain* was essentially the word *ain* in Arabic, which means 'spring', but as this was also a Maltese word used locally for springs, it did not mean that the original spring was named by the Muslims. David's theory about the name was also interesting. Some sources suggest 'hammet' was a take on hammam, which actually lent itself better to his theory that it was a public Muslim bathhouse. The current structure is said to date from the seventeenth century and was reputedly built by the Knights of St John. There were bathhouses like this all over Malta, and the oldest was l-Għajn il-Kbira, in Fontana, on the island of Gozo, which translates as 'the Great Spring' and dates back to 1373, a mere century or so after Maltese Muslims were permanently expelled (or converted to Christianity) by Frederick II.

'This is where the Prime Minister brought Angela Merkel!' announced Ibtisam, as we stepped into Is-Serkin, a tiny traditional Maltese *pastizzi* bar in the middle of Rabat, the small town founded by the Muslims next to the ancient capital, Mdina. Both names are from Arabic words: a ribat is a fortification, while Mdina comes from medina. I looked around at the white-tiled walls of the eatery where two large gold frames contained a series of photos showing *serkin* jockeys celebrating wins; a serkin was a small chariot pulled by a horse during a race. In its early days, the bar was very popular with people who drove serkins, which is how it got its name. Next to the frames was the mouth of a huge metal oven where the famous *pastizzi* – filled diamond-shaped filo pastries – were cooked. The bar's counter had a large glass cabinet where *ftiras* – stuffed bagel-like sourdough rolls – were displayed. On top of this was a huge silver cup, most likely awarded at a serkin race, and underneath it the Maltese word for bread, *hobz*, just two letters away from the Arabic, *khubz*. A large wooden beam above the counter hinted at the building's traditional architecture. Merkel wasn't the only world leader treated to the local street food delicacies at Is-Serkin: the prime ministers of Belgium, Luxembourg and Slovenia have all wandered into the humble eatery, which used to be open twenty-four hours to serve soldiers, farmers and, later, those stumbling out of bars and clubs. The soldiers were British ones stationed in nearby Mtarfa during the world wars. Most of them hailed from Crystal Palace in South London, which is how the Is-Serkin got its nickname, 'the Crystal Palace'.

'My Maltese grandfather was also a champion of serkin when he was younger,' said Ibtisam, as we sat down at the small collection of simple tables and chairs.

'And once he was arrested!' she laughed.

'What?' asked Jaafar, handing me a bottle of Kinnie, a traditional Maltese drink. I looked at the label, which said it was a classic orange flavour with aromatic herbs.

'In Gozo actually, where we are going,' continued Ibtisam, 'because there was a race with . . . erm, what do you call it?' Ibtisam turned to David for help, telling him the Maltese word she was struggling to translate.

'With mules!' said David.

'Like donkeys?' I asked

'Yes, and he was arrested because he pinched it to run faster!' Ibtisam fell about in fits of laughter.

I undid the bottle of Kinnie and took a sip of the caramel-coloured liquid.

'Ooh, that's bitter . . . do they use bitter oranges?'

'No, just normal oranges, no?' Ibtisam asked.

'Yes, normal oranges,' David confirmed.

'It tastes like bitter tea,' I said, as Jaafar brought over our lunch: a couple of *pastizzi*, several *ftiras* and Maltese biscotti of some kind. I began with a slice of the *pastizzi* the bar is famous for, stuffed with ricotta cheese.

'Hmm, interesting.'

'The ricotta cheese inside is washed in sea water!' David said.

I decided to bite into the *ftira* next, which looked far more appetizing: a crispy bagel-like sourdough roll filled with tuna, mint, onion, olives, beans, tomato paste and capers.

'Mmmm, that's good!' I exclaimed. 'Very filling.'

PART 2: THE CHILDREN OF AL-ANDALUS

David and Ibtisam were both nodding in agreement. Ibtisam urged me to try a more recent spin on the *ftira*, nudging a chopped segment of it towards me. I grabbed it and took a bite: the crispy crust gave way to the soft sourdough before suddenly my mouth was filled with a warm and familiar flavour – a very British one, even.

'Ooh, what's going on in here?'

David grinned at me.

'Haha, that's a recent innovation!' Ibtisam said.

'About four years ago, they started putting this inside it . . .' began David, who isn't overly keen on the innovation.

'But what is the sauce?' I asked.

'Some kind of curry sauce,' Ibtisam said.

'Aah, yes! That's what it is, there's definitely curry in here . . . mmm, that's nice.'

'You like it?' asked Jaafar.

I nodded.

The name *ftira* comes from the Arabic for unleavened bread, *fatir*, and the popular sourdough bread was placed on the UNESCO Intangible Cultural Heritage list in 2020. Though no other link to the Muslim past has been made for it, a number of traditional Maltese dishes bear a striking resemblance to those eaten across the Muslim world, especially in the Levant and North Africa. These include the popular soup dish *kusku* and the broadbean-based *bigilla*, which resembles *ful* dishes across the Middle East, and is also eaten by dipping bread into it.

We had come to Rabat for more than just David's hidden fountain and Is-Serkin's famous *ftira*. The bar was flanked on one side by the hidden fountain and on the other by Pjazza and Triq Mesquita, just beyond the Mdina walls. Whether the piazza and road were named after a long-gone mosque or a noble medieval Spanish family (who surely had a connection to a mosque at some point), by Maltese standards, this was an area with significant Muslim heritage, and our next stop offered irrefutable evidence of this. Unlike the Emirate of Siqilliya's mainland, the islands of Malta and

Gozo – almost 100 kilometres from Sicily – were isolated from the heart of the Emirate and this has meant sources and accounts of Muslim Malta are scarce, with few of the famous Muslim travellers who visited the mainland ever coming out to its smaller archipelago. Throw into this the neglect and systematic eradication of the island's Muslim history for the past seven centuries, and you really are up against it.

The Domvs Romana became Malta's premier Roman museum after a number of well-preserved Hellenistic-style mosaics were discovered by accident on the site in 1881, during a landscaping project. Plans were drawn up immediately to build a museum around the peristyle of the original Roman house, which is believed to have been built at the beginning of the first century BC and became the home of other Roman artefacts found across the island. When the Muslims established Rabat, the area in and around the Roman house – sitting at the very edge of Mdina and Rabat – became a vast cemetery, and excavations have revealed nearly 250 Muslim graves.

We walked over to the green railings that surrounded the neo-classical facade of the Domvs Romana to find two young archaeologists, hard at work inside a trench that had been dug near the entrance to the museum. They both spoke excellent English, and when we enquired about what they were looking for, the answer left us flabbergasted.

'We're actually looking for a mass Muslim grave,' said the girl, who had bright-blue hair.

She stood in the three-foot-deep trench holding something that resembled a pendulum, with a silver triangular instrument at the end. Her colleague sat on a camping chair at the edge of the excavation, holding a clipboard, his big safari hat obscuring his face. When I asked why Muslims would have been buried in a mass grave, the young archaeologist on the camping chair explained that they hadn't. It was where they were unceremoniously dumped when their graves were being excavated. The initial discovery of a Muslim cemetery was not very exciting for

PART 2: THE CHILDREN OF AL-ANDALUS

European archaeologists during the nineteenth century, when neoclassicism was all the rage, and everyone was desperate to find their own tangible links to that imagined Graeco-Roman period. Nobody, certainly not those who viewed Muslims as the barbaric 'other', was interested in finding Muslim heritage in the ground. As a result, the grave excavations, carried out at a time when archaeology was in its infancy on the island, were not really done properly or ethically. The leading archaeologist of the day, the much lauded Sir Themistocles Zammit, is believed to have dumped a host of Muslim remains in one large mass grave, somewhere underneath where we were standing. Their search had led them to also dig a trench by the side of the museum building. We all listened with our mouths open. I then turned to David in jest.

'A relative of yours?' I asked.

'A very, very distant relative . . . very distant!' David joked, as we headed into the small museum.

Zammit wasn't actually a trained archaeologist and only entered the field when he was chosen to curate the archaeological collection at the University of Malta, and yet he is remembered fondly in Maltese history as being a founding father of Maltese archaeology. His own education was in medicine in the field of bacteriology, and he is credited with discovering the cause of undulant fever.

'Archaeology was more his hobby and I think then it became his full-time job . . . It was a different time, and I think people like Zammit might have meant well, but they didn't always follow the rules,' David said.

We paid for our tickets and entered the museum, where we were greeted by a stunning floor mosaic of a large geometric maze-like pattern with a central framed motif of two doves drinking at a bird fountain – one of the most famous images of antiquity – known as the 'drinking doves', which had clearly inspired the fountain in the Ottoman cemetery.

Ibtisam had found the display on the Muslim burials. It featured a series of partially recovered tombstones with Arabic inscriptions in various styles and scripts, beside a reconstructed grave with a skeleton in it.

'Do you think they're real bones?' asked Ibtisam.

'No, they will be replicas . . . that would be extremely disrespectful,' I said, as we stared inside the stone rectangular grave where an entire human skeleton lay atop a bed of gravel. The stone box was partially covered to show how the grave might have been encased. I read the sign directly above, which featured black-and-white photos from the original excavations towards the end of the nineteenth century, as well as pictures of Temi Zemmit's actual notebook, where he had sketched some of the positions of the occupants of the graves. The majority of these, said the sign, were oriented east–west with the heads positioned to face south – towards Makkah. Zammit and his team had discovered at least six types of graves, with the most common being the 'pit graves' – simple holes dug in the ground – and 'cist graves', where stone was reused to build the grave, like the one on display. The sign went on to explain that most of the tombstones discovered displayed Qur'anic verses written in the classical Kufic style of script, and the only artefact discovered in an Islamic grave was a simple solid-silver ring, also inscribed with Kufic script. The text was accompanied by a diagram showing where the Muslim graves had been located. The largest concentration was behind the museum building, where a small balcony had been installed for visitors to look out over the area that was once Rabat's Muslim cemetery. I walked through the museum to the balcony and stopped in the Maltese sunshine, staring over the mishmash of large stone slabs and uneven earth squeezed in between two modern roads, which no doubt had cut through the original Muslim cemetery. I wondered if due diligence had been observed during the construction of the roads, as I stood for a while and stared out over the cemetery before going back in to meet the rest of the guys.

That evening, I visited the museum's website and looked at the frequently asked questions, one of which was Ibtisam's question from earlier: 'Are the displayed items (including the skeleton from the Saracenic cemetery) original?' I clicked the arrow to reveal the museum's response. It said 'yes'.

Malta's greatest historical artefact from its Muslim period is a tombstone. I first saw the beautiful marble 'Maimuna Stone' online shortly after returning from a family holiday to the island. It is the only Islamic funerary stone in Malta that remains fully intact and the only one to offer a date. Reportedly found in Gozo, the Maimuna Stone belonged to a woman called Maimuna who died on Thursday the 16th of the Islamic month of *Sha'ban* in the year 569 AH, which equates to 21 March 1174 in the Gregorian calendar, almost a century after the Norman invasion of Muslim Malta. The stone is kept in the Gozo Museum of Archaeology on Malta's second largest island, Gozo, which has historically been linked with ancient myths such as that of the nymph Calypso in Homer's *Odyssey*, and like Malta has seen a succession of rulers, from the Phoenicians, Romans, Muslims and the Knights of St John to the British Empire.

Having crossed over by ferry in thirty minutes, we parked the car outside the sand-coloured walls of the island's main citadel and went straight to the museum, which is housed inside the walls of the fifteenth-century fort in an old town house and is home to relics stretching back 5,000 years. None of these interested us though.

'So, it's called the Maimuna Stone?' asked Jaafar as we headed downstairs, having briefly admired some of the museum's other treasures.

'Yes, because that was her name . . . It was *her* tombstone,' David explained.

'There she is!' I announced excitedly, catching a glimpse of the famous stone, where it sat encased in Perspex on a large black plinth, which raised its mesmeric facade to eye level. One Maltese writer had described the Maimuna Stone as the museum's 'pride and joy'. I looked around the small room we had descended several flights to reach: along the tops of the walls was a timeline detailing the dates of the Christian and Muslim periods; the room was filled with other artefacts dating from those Christian eras, including a number of large stones carved with decorative crucifixes and Christian iconography. Each item was brought to life with large prints of medieval tapestries, historical photos and litho prints, as well as Maltese and English text, but there was nothing to suggest the Maimuna Stone was considered any more special than the other items in the room.

'Now, this stone has kind of a long history,' began David, reassuming his role as tour historian. 'There was a period when it was built into a house in Valletta, and a period when it was apparently used as an anchor.'

'Anchor?' I asked. 'Like, for a boat?'

'Yes.'

'Wow, I did not know that!'

'So, it's been dislocated big time. On the other hand, it's true that here on Gozo there exists a field called Ta' Majmuna, so that might be where it was found,' David explained.

The Maimuna Stone had the most arresting of designs: every inch was covered in exquisitely carved Arabic that appeared to dance around a near-invisible and delicate arabesque frame woven into the design. The effect was dizzying, making it impossible to know where to look or how even to start reading the Kufic script. I wandered around the back of the plinth, where the Perspex didn't reach as high. The marble was plain on this side, except for a square hole once used to fix it in place for its original purpose – or maybe, as David believed, as an anchor – and towards the bottom there was a carved rose-like relief that hinted at the stone's Roman origins. As David had said, there was very little concrete evidence about the stone and its origins, except for the toponymic link to the place called Ta' Majmuna, near Xewkija, where the stone is said to have been found. It first became known in the late eighteenth century, but it wasn't until the following century that its extensive script was translated, making it immediately apparent that it was not only the work of a highly skilled stonemason, but also a highly competent wordsmith, maybe even a poet. In fact, such was the poetic beauty of the stone's epigraph that when the great Italian composer Ottorino Respighi visited it in 1933, he instantly fell in love with the words and took them back to Italy, intending to set them to music. Sadly, Respighi died shortly after his visit to Malta, and this never happened. The stone's central inscriptions – within the frame of the arabesque – is where we learn who Maimuna is, through her name, which, as with most Arabic names, includes that of her father and grandfather. This sits alongside words glorifying God and His messenger, but it is the words around the edges of the tombstone that so moved Respighi. David began reading them out loud.

We all fell silent.

'Look around you! Is there anything everlasting on earth? Anything that repels or casts a spell on death? Death stole me from a palace and, alas, neither doors nor bolts could save me. All I did in my lifetime remains, and shall be reckoned . . .' David paused.

We all stayed silent.

'Oh, he who looks upon this tomb! I am already consumed inside it, and dust has settled on my eyes. On my couch in my abode there is nothing but tears, and what is to happen at my resurrection when I shall appear before my Creator? Oh, my brother, be wise and repent.'

It was easy to see why, like Respighi, David was also moved by the words.

'It's so wise . . . It's like a wake-up . . . It's . . . it's a mirror, it's a mirror asking us to wake up,' Jaafar said, slowly processing his thoughts as he spoke.

'It's nice, I like that,' he added, in a more measured tone.

David, Ibtisam and I just stood and stared at the Arabic inscriptions.

'I was wondering, how far is Sicily from Malta?' Jaafar asked.

'Sixty miles,' replied David without looking away from the stone.

'It is so close,' I said, 'that the snack trolley on the plane didn't even make it to my seat before we started the descent for landing!'

This made Jaafar and Ibtisam laugh. David didn't – he was still staring at the tombstone intently. The Maimuna Stone's sophisticated poetry, combined with the skill of the craftsmen and the expense necessary to produce it, made it clear Maimuna was of high stock and that Malta had once been home to a cultured and learned Muslim class, just like that across the water in Sicily. I read Maimuna's full name again: Maimuna, daughter of Hassan ibn Ali al-Hudali, called Ibn as-Susi.

'I was looking into her family name's origins, and found suggestions that it could go back to a tribe from the Hejaz,' I said.

'I see,' David said, the new information finally grabbing his attention, 'and the Hejaz would be in . . .?'

'In Saudi Arabia, where Makkah and Madinah are . . . And this was quite a famous tribe, of scholars and poets,' I continued, divulging more of what I had discovered about Maimuna's potential ancestral tribe.

'There's a lot of knowledge about Muslim Malta, I'm sure, preserved somewhere in the Muslim world, that we don't know about,' David said.

According to her name, Maimuna's paternal grandfather, 'al-Hudali', was from the very noble Arab tribe of Banu Hudhayl, famous throughout Islamic history for producing great poets and intellectuals. Although its descendants now lived across the globe, the tribe had originated in the extremely holy Hejaz region of Saudi Arabia, and was there during the seventh century, which meant some of Maimuna's ancestors would have personally known the Prophet Muhammad. This included the seventh-century poet Abu Dhu'ayb al-Hudhali, and the great *mufassir* (exegete) of the Qur'an and Companion of the Prophet, Abd Allah Ibn Mas'ud. This was the real magic of Maimuna's Stone and what had attracted me to the stunning tombstone from the moment I had first laid eyes on it, albeit online: the tantalizing glimpses it offered into that long-forgotten and little-known Maltese Muslim society. The stone allowed us to piece together a picture of who Maimuna might have been, and the highly cultured society she belonged to. Maimuna's name also told us that her father had been known as Ibn as-Susi, which just happens to be what the near-contemporary Maltese poet Uthman Ibn Abdu'r-Rahman, who saw out his days in Palermo, had been known as. The only poem to come down to us by Ibn as-Susi is a melancholic one about loss. Living in an age immediately after Muslim Sicily and Malta (and Gozo) had fallen under Christian rule, Ibn as-Susi might well have been alluding to *that* loss in his poem. His father, Abdu'r-Rahman Ibn Ramadan, had taught young Ibn as-Susi humanities when he was a child in Malta, and was also a poet living in Sicily. Ibn Ramadan was nicknamed *al-Qadi*, which is a scholar of jurisprudence and an expert on Islamic theology – someone who normally sits as the religious head of a community. In other words, he would have been both highly educated and revered. It is therefore likely Ibn Ramadan was an important person – maybe even an actual qadi – in his native Malta. The combination of what we know of Maimuna's ancestral family and this group of contemporaneous poets and theologians offered a fascinating picture of medieval Muslim Maltese society, but it didn't come as a surprise, given our knowledge of medieval Muslim culture across the Mediterranean. Just as it was on the mainland, the little islands of the Emirate of Siqilliya had been sophisticated, cultured places able to nurture and produce polymaths like those found across the waters in Bal'harm. What makes this image of Maltese Muslims even more interesting is the fact that many historians believe the Muslim family name 'Ibn Ramadan' could well be what became the medieval Christian family name 'Randan' – after all, *Randan* is the Maltese word for Lent, the festival of fasting; the Islamic equivalent of which is of course Ramadan. In the same way, the word for Easter, *Għid*, has been taken from *Eid*, the Muslim name for the festivals that celebrate the end of Ramadan and the feast of sacrifice during the month of Hajj. Another early Maltese Muslim poet whose descendants may have also converted to Christianity and retained their original name is Abd Allah Ibn al-Samti al-Maliti, whose family name – the al-Maliti is an obvious reference to his origins – 'al-Samti' is said to be the source of the Maltese surname 'Samut'.

'This is another stone they found.' David was now pointing to a much smaller stone next to Maimuna's, which resembled the long, thin, triangular tombstones we had seen in the Domvs Romana earlier. The stone had Kufic inscriptions etched into all the visible facades, but none as decorative or sophisticated as the delicate lettering on the Maimuna Stone.

'This is from the Qur'an, no?' asked David, after reading out loud the Maltese translation of the inscriptions, possibly forgetting that I didn't understand what he had read. I read the English translation of the Maltese translation; something had clearly been lost in between, as it took me a while to realize I was indeed reading the Qur'an, and verses that were highly familiar to me in their original Arabic.

'This is the verse designed to negate the story of Jesus . . . you know, "he does not beget, nor is he begotten,"' I finally said.

Jaafar and Ibtisam also began reading the words.

The stone had been inscribed with verses from the Qur'an, from two different chapters – one of them, the extremely revered Surah *al-Ikhlas*, the 112th chapter in the Qur'an, in its entirety. The name *al-Ikhlas* translates as 'the purity' and is widely considered one of the most important chapters in the holy book, with several hadiths equating its significance to 'one third' of the Qur'an in spite of its being one of the shortest surahs. The reverence for *al-Ikhlas* was mostly due to its focus on God's oneness – tawheed in Arabic – which is seen as the key distinguishing feature of Islam when compared to Christianity and its concept of the Trinity. This is made explicit in *al-Ikhlas* by verses overtly denouncing the idea of God having children – a direct rejection of the Christian claim that Jesus is the son of God. For Muslims, Jesus is a mortal and a prophet.

'It might also be symptomatic of the fact they were living among Christians,' I suggested.

'Aah,' Ibtisam said, smiling.

Tentatively dated to 1155/6, when the Norman invasion of Malta and Gozo had been completed and there was a strong possibility that Christians were again living on the island, the

PART 2: THE CHILDREN OF AL-ANDALUS

tombstone's discovery in 1901 in nearby Savina Square suggests there was once a cemetery outside the walls of the medieval town. I now read the second set of verses, which came after a few details about the deceased, whose name had been lost, but we knew they had been considered deeply pious by their community as they were referred to as 'the holy . . .' The stone also revealed that they had died on a Wednesday and were buried the next day, but not which month or year this happened in. The second set of verses had been taken from the same chapter as the verses I had seen carved on the pillar outside Palermo Cathedral believed to have once belonged to the Great Mosque of Bal'harm, Surah *al-A'raf* – 'The Heights'. In fact, they were the exact same verses and I wondered why they had been chosen for the tombstone; whether it was mere coincidence or there was another reason, given the mosque's significance to the then citizens of the Arab-Norman kingdom.

'And, where was it found?' asked Jaafar, examining the words again.

'At the foot of a church,' I replied.

'A church?'

'In Savina Square in Rabat,' David said.

'*Ta'gmiel* . . .' said Ibtisam, before repeating in English, though I had understood the Arabic word for beautiful in her Maltese, 'it's really beautiful . . .' Her words trailed off as she stared intently at the stone.

Before the trip, Ibtisam had admitted to me that many of the places we would visit and the relics we would seek out she had never herself seen before. It was why she had brought along her infectiously enthusiastic and knowledgeable friend, David. I had learned so much from them both and felt truly privileged and honoured that Ibtisam had allowed those moments to also be a part of my journey.

'It was found when they tore down the chapel . . . I'm pretty sure many of the old chapels were built on Islamic spaces,' David said, cutting through the silence.

'Yep . . .' I nodded, as we all continued to stare at the two stones in silence for a little longer.

11

Looking for the Moorish Maiden

Sintra, Portugal

Driving to Sintra from Lisbon feels like going from one neighbourhood of Portugal's capital to another. No sooner have you left the tall tower blocks of the residential greater Lisbon area, along the busy A37 highway, than the lush green hills of Sintra begin to come into view, topped with silhouettes of fairytale castles, where once upon a time the city's royals and aristocracy retired in the warmer months.

Sintra has a rich history dating back to prehistoric times, with evidence of early human settlement. Its popularity with Portuguese high society led to the construction of magnificent palaces, many inspired by the Muslim culture they were replacing, such as the Pena Palace and the National Palace of Sintra. It first became popular during the country's Muslim period in the eighth century, when a huge castle known today simply as 'the Moorish Castle' was built there – Portugal's largest surviving Muslim monument. Sintra's verdant landscapes and romantic architecture have inspired writers and artists through the ages, including Lord Byron, who dubbed it 'glorious Eden', which has helped the area become recognized as a UNESCO World Heritage Site.

Very few people got off at my stop, most making straight for the Pena Palace, which encapsulates the romantic reimagining of Iberian Muslim culture during the nineteenth century. A wild mishmash of gothic and Islamic architectural influences from across the globe, including North Africa, the Middle East and even Mughal India, Pena Palace is the pin-up palace seen on the front of Sintra's tourism brochures and many an Instagram shot. It was the palace that first captured my imagination when I picked up a book on Islamic art in Portugal, romantically titled *In the Lands of the Enchanted Moorish Maiden*, written by, among others, the great 'guru' of Portuguese Islamic history, Cláudio Torres. The book's cover features the palace's iconic bright-yellow Mughal-style dome at the top of a faux minaret on the edge of a roof terrace with the green treetops of the park behind, and the Atlantic plains disappearing into the horizon. In the book, as if echoing Sicily's Giuseppe Pitrè, Torres claims Muslims 'continue to inhabit the dream-filled nights of popular romances' in Portugal, where 'all that is mysterious and inexplicable' comes from the Muslims. All over Portugal, but especially in the south, legends, myths and stories about the Moorish maiden continue to dominate folklore and the romantic imagination. In Sintra alone, there are at least four or five such legends. Torres tells us about one, which claims that on certain moonlit nights, if you wander through the wooded mountains of Sintra, you might just encounter a 'beautiful maiden dressed in white' emerging from a rock to fill her water pot at a spring of cool fresh water. Torres ends the legend by telling us that when the Moorish maiden passes you, in the silence of the night you will hear her 'doleful' mourning for a 'time that will never again return'. Most of the other legends about the fabled Moorish maiden or princess which exoticize or fetishize her also position her as a helpless object of Christian desire, yet Torres chose to retell the legend that intimates regret and a sense of what might have been.

I had visited Pena Palace many times before and wanted to start this trip at Portugal's largest surviving Muslim monument, known locally as the Castelo dos Mouros. The fortress is a formidable structure dating back to the eighth century, when it was built by subjects of the Syrian Umayyad Caliphate, which by then had control of almost the entire Iberian Peninsula and much of what is modern-day Portugal. Back then it was known as Gharb al-Andalus or simply al-Gharb, which meant 'west of al-Andalus', historical al-Andalus being what is today mostly southern Spain. It is from these names we get the modern regional ones of the 'Algarve' in Portugal and 'Andalusia' in Spain. Strategically situated atop a high hill, the castle protected the town of Sintra and, more importantly, al-Ishbun – modern Lisbon – which the Umayyads took between 714 and 716. It offered panoramic views of Sintra and the Atlantic Ocean, and for four centuries a flourishing Muslim community lived in the castle's immediate vicinity, while al-Ishbun's great and good built stunning summer residences in the surrounding green hills.

The outer walls of the eighth-century Castelo dos Mouros in Sintra, Portugal's largest Muslim monument

The Christian conquest of the castle took place in 1147, when forces led by King Afonso Henriques I of Portugal arrived having already taken al-Ishbun. The fall of the regional capital saw the inhabitants of the castle surrender without a fight. By then Gharb al-Andalus had already enjoyed three centuries of stability and high culture under the Umayyads, especially the local Iberian Umayyads, who arrived to set up the Emirate of Córdoba in al-Andalus in the middle of the eighth century. This evolved into the Caliphate of Córdoba, which lasted until the early eleventh century. Following the collapse of the Caliphate, al-Gharb was ruled for another century or so by different smaller Muslim *taifa* kingdoms, and this continued in the south of al-Gharb long after Afonso's capture of al-Ishbun. Thus, by the time the Kingdom of Portugal took the territories we consider Portugal today, the Muslim presence had lasted over five centuries and, as with Sicily and Malta, changed Portugal for ever.

Following its capture, the Christians reinforced the Muslim castle in Sintra and continued using it as a key military stronghold and lookout point. However, over time it began to lose its significance and slowly fell into disrepair, before being abandoned in the sixteenth century. It was restored to its current state in the nineteenth century by King Ferdinand II, who added romantic and neo-*mudéjar* (art and architecture by Christians inspired by al-Andalus) elements to its structure. Today the castle's winding stone walls, battlements and towers provide a fascinating glimpse into medieval Muslim military architecture, while the luxuriant surrounding vegetation and breathtaking vistas create an enchanting historical site that blends seamlessly with the natural landscape.

I took off my hat and held it in front of me; the Canadian-Chinese woman clicked away on my camera phone as the large green flag flapped furiously above my head, battered by the mountain winds. She showed me her handiwork. I cupped my hand over the phone screen to stop the glare of the brilliant sun and noticed that she had cropped the flag from the picture.

'Could you try to get the flag in the shot?' I asked. The kindly lady, squinting in the sunshine, nodded.

I had picked my photographer carefully. Standing on one of the central bastions along the castle's most impressive remnant of the north-western wall, I had noticed the lady nursing a sore knee as she waited for her family to return from walking the entire length of the wall, which had been re-created combining the ancient battlements, parapets and steps. The woman handed me the phone again. She had taken six shots, including one with the flag fully unfurled to reveal the name 'Sintra' in Arabic. I smiled and thanked her, before stepping out of the way so that a young South Asian boy and his father could do the same. In total there are six bastions, and having walked the entire length of them I had returned to stop at the only one that alluded to the castle's Muslim roots. Every other bastion carried a different version of the Kingdom of Portugal's national flag, demonstrating its evolution through the ages. The bastion looked down on to the Arms Square, the largest area of the castle, remodelled by Dom Fernando II into an idyllic setting for reflection and contemplation, bordered by huge boulders and thick greenery. I watched as a woman in a yellow jumpsuit set up her camera phone on its stand and proceeded to pose in a host of different ways in front of one of the castle's neo-*mudéjar* features, a blind door in a horseshoe arch. The number of tourists was growing now, and with no protective barrier on the inside of the wall's walkway, just a low battlement stopping people falling to a certain death, many looked increasingly nervous as they negotiated the narrow ramparts. A South-East Asian woman stood paralysed, unable to continue past the lowest battlements, the heavy winds adding to her sense of impending doom. Her husband, after attempting to cajole her, gave up and walked off. Just then a bubbly black American lady coming in the opposite direction offered to walk her across.

'I get it! This is a scary walk!' she said in a strong Southern accent, taking the petrified lady by the hand.

I had earlier been similarly nervous myself walking the path, which at its highest point looms above the tops of the surrounding trees. This is where the Alcáçova, which incorporated the castle's original keep, used to be and where the most important members of the Muslim military community would stay. The views from the Alcáçova were truly something else; from the sheer lush hillside the castle perched upon, I stared over all the way to Lisbon, which sprawled out in front of us, like an image on a satellite map. It was easy to see why the Muslims had picked this hill: with nothing to block the views to the capital, al-Ishbun, if an attack was imminent the watchers would have lit flames to raise the alarm, knowing they would easily be seen by the military in the capital city.

Before I left the Moorish castle, I stopped near the entrance to visit its Interpretation Centre inside the Church of São Pedro de Canaferrim, Sintra's very first parish church, where some of the artefacts dug up at the ancient fortress are on display. The cool building was dimly lit to protect the ancient finds, which were mostly inside large glass cabinets. I was alone, except for the odd tourist stumbling in before quickly leaving, uninspired by the displays. I sought out the scant finds from the Muslim period on display, the largest and most complete of which was a granite millstone dating from the tenth to twelfth centuries. Inside the glass displays were shards of a decorated jar, several near-complete oil lamps, a number of highly decorated ivory plates – some featuring ancient Kufic inscriptions – and pieces used to play board games such as dice made from bone. It was easy to see why no one really lingered.

I left the Moorish castle along a stunning stone path that wound its way around the edge of the hillside, canopied by cypress and hazel trees. The path occasionally gave way to spectacular as it wrapped itself around the south-eastern slope of the hill, where the Muslims of Sintra once lived. I stopped to examine a few of the surviving remains of the foundations of their homes, where they might have once sat using those oil lamps at night and played with those dice. The area was later used as a cemetery by the Christians. There were also large holes in the ground, which used to be silos for storing grains and legumes – a storage method the Muslims introduced across al-Gharb and al-Andalus.

After leaving the castle area, I wandered west along Estrada da Pena, in search of the Pena Palace Lakes, created by Dom Fernando in 1836 when he constructed the Parque de Aclimação Florestal, or the Forest Climate Park, a pleasure garden of lakes that cascades gently down the western hillside upon which his flamboyant Pena Palace sits. I entered to be greeted by a picture of serenity. A stone-built castle folly sat in the middle of a small man-made lake, resembling a miniature Rapunzel's tower. Amorous couples wandered around the edges holding hands, past blooming flowers of reds, yellows and oranges, and walls built with ancient stone. Overhead, the sun winked through the green foliage that offered a cooling canopy of shade. I continued along the cobblestone path, past a second castle folly serving as a duck house, up beyond a large bronze medallion with a relief portrait of Dom Fernando, complete with a KFC Colonel moustache, above the name of the park. From there I could see the Fonte in the distance, its large round dome topped with a crescent finial, peering from behind thick foliage. The dome had a ring of delicately carved naskh Arabic script and sat atop an octagonal structure elongated by tall arched openings on three sides that resembled monastic windows. The entire structure was covered in blue tiles patterned with the geometric star synonymous with medieval Islamic architecture. Dom Fernando's fountain looked more like the *türbesi* and mini-mosques I had seen in Cyprus than a fountain. From every angle, the Fonte resembled a religious Muslim monument. It was only when I stepped into the cool interior, past green iron gates topped with elegant crescents, and heard the gentle sound of trickling water, that it became apparent this was no mausoleum, nor a place of worship. It was in fact an elaborate house for a tiny bird fountain. The water fell into a modest stone basin, decorated with an oyster-like pattern, and flanked by two stone benches. The interior was also covered in tiles, making it extremely cool.

Designed by Baron Wilhelm Ludwig von Eschwege, the German architect for the whole palace, the fountain was built in 1840 by the architect João Henriques and is the most intriguing of all the Pena Palace's structures. While there were more impressive *mudéjar* features up on the hill, such as the imposing horseshoe-arched gate at the beginning of the palace grounds that could have stood at the entrance to a medina in Meknes or Fez, or the aforementioned yellow neo-Mughal dome, only the fountain contained Arabic inscriptions, and just like those on the monuments of Sicily's William I, William II and Roger II, they offer us a glimpse into the mind of Dom Fernando and his sense of self-image.

PART 2: THE CHILDREN OF AL-ANDALUS

'Sultan Manuel built this blessed chapel in the name of our Lady Maria Pena, in the year 1503, in commemoration of the safe return of Vasco da Gama from the discovery of the lands and countries that he did find, these being the Cape of Good Hope, India and others. Thus did His Highness Sultan Ferdinand (Dom Fernando) the Second, husband of Her Majesty Maria II, build this in the magnificent royal fashion in the year 1840.'

Like the Christian sultans of Siqilliya, Dom Fernando saw himself and his sixteenth-century predecessor who built the original convent where his palace now stood as akin to the fabled sultans of Islam. No doubt, this was mere play and folly in an age when neo-Islamic architecture was all the rage, and an imagined Muslim culture was heavily romanticized, or as the twentieth-century thinker Edward Said might have put it: exoticized, fetishized and 'othered' by the colonial classes of Europe, building on their earlier medieval repulsion. The nineteenth century was when Washington Irving published his seminal *The Alhambra* (later retitled as *Tales of the Alhambra*), to firmly put the fabled palace in Granada, Spain, into the European romantic imagination and inspire a thousand fictions about medieval European Muslims and the palace-city. It was the century in which Sir Richard Burton published his translations (arguably, rather interpretations) of the *One Thousand and One Nights* and *The Perfumed Garden of Sensual Delight*, the latter dubbed the Arabic *Kama Sutra*. The widespread popularity of such books on Muslim culture helped to embellish and fetishize further the image of Muslims as both the terrifying and the exotic other.

I sat down on one of the benches opposite, each flanked by a spider plant sprouting from a concrete plant pot featuring faux Arabic inscriptions around the upper rim, mimicking the real Arabic on the Fonte's dome. The perspective from the bench allowed the majesty of the monument to be fully appreciated, and the more I stared at it, the more familiar it became. As well as the crescent-topped dome and Arabic inscriptions, tiles featured the famous 'Moorish star' – the evolutionary bridge from the classical Islamic tile to the *azulejo* synonymous with Portugal – that created a mesmerizing and dizzying geometric pattern, inspired by God's infinite nature. Then there was the architectural symmetry and use of flowing water inside a building, as I had seen at the Zisa. Even the painting of the crescent-topped rails in green – the Prophet's colour – were all redolent of the region's classical Islamic influence.

The bird fountain in the Pena Palace gardens at Sintra, built in the *mudéjar* style, featuring Islamic motifs and Arabic inscriptions by 'Sultan' Ferdinand II in 1860

A small English family came over to the fountain, on their walk through the gardens.

'What is that?' asked the son, who was lanky and resembled a young Andy Murray.

'Built by the Moors probably,' said his older sister, her hands on her hips as she stared up at the Fonte.

'Who were the Moors?' asked young Andy Murray.

'They were an ancient Muslim tribe that invaded Europe . . . It's very beautiful,' chimed in Dad, who was dressed in classic middle-aged, middle-class attire: chinos and a polo shirt.

All four of them walked into the fountain building, where the conversation continued.

'How do you know which way is Mecca?' asked the boy, after a quick look around.

'It's not a mosque,' said his sister, dismissively.

Mum and Dad said nothing as they looked around.

'Really?' he asked, pointing out the dome and little crescents on the gate.

'Hmm . . .'

His sister's earlier confidence had now been knocked. She looked around and up at the dome with greater scrutiny.

'Could be . . . Maybe they built it to pray in and the Portuguese changed it?' she finally said.

It was the same crescent-topped railing as the Fonte that first caught my eye. A large overgrown bush and two large pines made it impossible to see much from the ground, so I crossed the road and climbed up onto the baroque stairs of the Regaleira Palace. The vantage point allowed me to see the Córdoban arches, though the central three were obscured by large cement blocks weighing down a construction crane. In total there were five arches, all nineteenth-century reimaginings of the famous arches inside the Great Caliphate Mosque of eighth-century Córdoba. The building was in a bad state: most of the paint had peeled away and small bits of masonry lay on the floor, yet I could still make out Arabic written in white inside a decorative blue frame, beneath the middle arches. I took a picture and zoomed into the Arabic lettering on my phone, nearly falling off the step I was standing on.

'*Wa la ghaliba illa-llah.*'

The words translate as 'There is no victor except Allah', the motto of the emirs of Granada, the Nasrids who ruled parts of southern Spain from the thirteenth to the fifteenth century. It was a phrase I had seen engraved on the Alhambra's walls over and over again. In re-creating the arches from Córdoba and the motto of the Nasrids, it was a romantic homage to the most enlightened period of Muslim Iberia: from Córdoba to Granada, where it came to an end.

I watched as a smartly dressed man in moccasins directed some labourers through a gate to the left of the building. I walked down and introduced myself. Amazingly, he turned out to be the new owner, though I didn't catch his name. He was trying to restore it.

'It's been abandoned since the 1970s . . . It's a listed building, but lots of the inside parts were wood and destroyed by termites,' he said in an accent I couldn't place.

The man, who had short mousey-brown hair, explained that the house was called the Quinta do Relógio and had reputedly been constructed by the nineteenth-century Portuguese slave trader Manuel Pinto da Fonseca, who commissioned the architect António Tomás da Fonseca to design and build it for him. In 1997, the Relógio was classified a property of public interest and included in the UNESCO World Heritage Site of Sintra, and in 2010 Sintra City Council tried to buy it for 6.75 million euros, but the deal never materialized. A decade later, rumours were rife that the Queen of Pop, Madonna, had bought it for her family for 9 million dollars, but this turned out to be nonsense.

'It is an interesting building, and it's very close to the centre,' said the man, when I asked what prompted his family to purchase it. It turns out they used to come to Sintra in his youth. He had also spent time in London, studying at the American International School and briefly at King's College.

'And will you be keeping the building open to the public?' I asked.

'For now, it is being restored as a private house, but the gardens, we are thinking to open for the public,' he said, adding that he hoped the works would be complete in two or three years.

I later looked the building up online and found an 1864 etching, a mere four years after it had been completed. Three spectacular Umayyad-style horseshoe arches rise up in front of a round fountain, which is flanked by two young pine trees in a manicured grassy courtyard. On either side of the central feature are two more modest arches, also decorated with the Umayyad red and white stripes, as too the walls of the monument's facade. Above the grandest arches, running along the top of the building, are battlements, and beneath these, set slightly back, are three smaller arches, above which is the Nasrid motto.

The Romantic neo-Muslim (also neo-Moorish and neo-Saracenic) trend also made its way to Britain. Several such buildings were neo-Mughal in style because of Britain's rule over and thereby romanticizing of India, including the Royal and Western pavilions in Brighton, Sezincote House in Gloucestershire and, most notably, north-western Europe's first purpose-built mosque, the Shah Jahan Mosque in Woking, Surrey. Examples of neo-Moorish architecture, like Leighton's Arab Hall, were also popular, two of the most famous being the Alhambra Room in the Rhinefield House Hotel, a former stately home in the New Forest, and the Arab Room in Cardiff Castle.

12

Rediscovering al-Gharb al-Andalus

Mértola, Portugal

'Look this is . . . eh . . . eh . . . a replica of a big piece in the museum.' The grey-haired Manuel Passinhas da Palma was peering over his thick-rimmed black spectacles and pointing to four enormous tiles placed at the edge of a large brick wall in the centre of the small Portuguese town of Mértola, two above and two below. The pattern on them was unmistakably Islamic, and it ran horizontally repeating across the tiles. There were vegetal patterns, arabesque arches, the geometric stars synonymous with Islamic art, and along the upper edge a series of Arabic letters I could not decipher. The way they were positioned close to the top reminded me of how Sultan William II had inscribed the top of the Zisa and the Cuba in Palermo. They were on the corner of a historical wall that jutted out from a small café, right in the centre of town, called Guadiana – after the town's river. White bistro chairs and tables stood scattered beneath it, where a handful of early-morning tourists were enjoying their coffee. One of them, a woman in black Chanel sunglasses, was admiring a traditional-looking bicycle that had been painted white and stood on two thick integrated stands as a permanent advert for 'ecoland e-bike tours'. A bike with an electric motor would be essential in exploring Mértola, which cascaded down the hilly south-western bank of the River Guadiana's valley. Like so many Iberian rivers, the name Guadiana has Muslim ancestry, with the 'Guadi' a direct adaptation of the Arabic word for river-valley, *wadi*. The Ana on the other hand is said to be a leftover from the Roman name, Flumen Anas.

'It is from the festival . . . eh . . . eh . . .' Manuel was struggling to find the words. 'We'll see!' he finally said.

Warm and friendly, Manuel was speaking in his fourth language, and when I first shook his hand, he had asked if I spoke Portuguese, Spanish or French. Much to his dismay I did not and apologized. Manuel also apologized because he only spoke a 'little English', which made me feel worse, but also a little relieved, as we had planned to spend the whole day together, and I wasn't sure my phone's translation app was going to quite cut it.

'I came to Mértola in 1982 but the first discovery was made in 1976,' Manuel said, as we headed past the giant tiles towards the town's low snow-white perimeter wall. Here the footpath began to steadily decline, offering my first glimpse of the Guadiana's valley, which had been so crucial to Mértola's fascinating Muslim past.

Like the rest of Portugal, Islam came to Mértola when forces loyal to the Umayyad Caliphate founded by Mu'awiyah in Syria conquered the Iberian Peninsula by defeating the local Christian Visigoth rulers in the early eighth century. Al-Gharb al-Andalus – Muslim Portugal – was then absorbed into the Umayyad Emirate of Córdoba, which was founded in 756 and evolved into the Caliphate of Córdoba, ushering in an enlightened period of high culture and coexistence. Even after Umayyad rule collapsed in the early eleventh century, much of Portugal, including Mértola, remained Muslim, so that by the time the Christian King Sancho II took the town in 1238, Mértola had been Muslim for over 500 years.

The emerald-green water of the river, flanked by tufts of green trees on either side, snaked its way along the valley floor, resembling a large serpent disappearing into the hilly interior. The other way, the valley widened, and the Ponte de Mértola, an ugly grey concrete bridge that brings the N265 highway into the town, jarred against the beautiful white terracotta-roofed houses cascading down both banks of the river.

The story of how Mértola rediscovered its Islamic history is now almost legendary. According to that legend, it begins with children kicking up some red ceramics on top of one of the local hills. When these were brought to Mértola council's attention, it sparked a movement that would completely alter the face of the town for ever, in terms both of its future and of what it thought was its past. Mértola reached out to the now legendary Cláudio Torres – Manuel's 'guru' – at the time a young lecturer of medieval history in the capital, Lisbon. Torres put together a task force made up of members of his faculty at the University of Lisbon and an army of volunteers who set up a research camp in the town that has never really gone away. The work by Torres and his team would unveil a rich Muslim history that suggested Mértola was once a highly cultured thriving Muslim port of trade, art and intellectual activity. The timing of the discovery was key, just three years after the Carnation Revolution toppled the strict regime, Estado Novo, founded by António de Oliveira Salazar, which promoted a nationalist narrative centred on an anti-Muslim, Catholic identity.

'Wow!' I said, stopping us both in our tracks and pulling out my phone to photograph a once beautiful arabesque brick doorway. It was embedded into the snow-white wall of one of the low-rise terraced houses that overlooked the cobblestone path.

'I excavate that!' Manuel said, grinning from ear to ear.

'What? . . . You did?'

'Yeah, I and . . . eh . . . other guy.'

'So, what is this, an Islamic door entrance?' I asked.

'Eh, no, no, no! . . . It's erm . . .'

I waited for Manuel to find the words.

'It's erm, fifteen . . .'

'Ah okay . . . so later than the Muslim period,' I said, sounding a little disappointed.

'Later . . . but . . .' began Manuel, who was originally from the town of Beja, to the south, but had spent his entire adult life excavating Mértola's Muslim past.

'The traditional techniques . . . is the traditional techniques . . . er . . .' Manuel was again struggling to find the words. I offered my thoughts.

'Like *mudéjar*?'

'Yes! Like the *mudéjar*!'

We were on our way to meet the Vice-President of the Mértola Municipality's Cultural Department, Rosinda Pimenta, and stopped in front of a white-and-blue-tiled building with two dark double doors. After walking through them, we found ourselves in a beautiful inner courtyard, in the style of a North African riadh, complete with a central fountain covered in mosaics and surrounded by large potted greenery. The arched arcade around the edges was coloured in that wonderful baby blue seen across the Mediterranean. I sat on a chair at a patio table beneath a retractable linen awning.

Rosinda had been working in Mértola since 2007 and became the department's vice-president ten years later. She spoke perfect English and arrived dressed in a pair of casual jeans, a loose green floral top and what looked to be a set of *tasbiyyah* wooden beads around her neck, complete with a tassel. After telling her about my work, and the journey that had brought me to Mértola, I asked her about the beads.

'I bought it in the festival,' Rosinda said.

'They're the Islamic ones, right? . . . so, these are the tasbiyyah, because I can see they've been split with the gold in thirty-three . . .'

Rosinda smiled.

'Yes, I buy a piece every year from the same seller!'

It was Rosinda's department that oversaw Mértola's flagship event to celebrate its Muslim heritage, called the Islamic Festival of Mértola. There have always been festivals about 'Islam' in Portugal just as in Spain, but historically these celebrated the Christian victories that made up Portugal's own Reconquest narrative, which began when the founder of the Kingdom of Portugal, Afonso Henriques I, also known as 'O Conquistador' – the Conqueror – won two decisive battles: the Battle of Ourique in 1139 against the Almoravids, who were at the time the Muslim rulers of the former Caliphate lands across Iberia, and, with a little help from Crusaders headed to the Second Crusade, the battle for the country's capital, Lisbon, in 1147. In between, Afonso also defeated his cousin Alfonso VII of León to secure his new kingdom's independence. The festivals, held in Portugal and Spain for almost eight centuries, helped to construct the image of the murderous, barbaric and sexually depraved 'Moor', or Muslim, and sat at the tip of a huge iceberg. In some of the earliest poetry written in Portuguese in the *Cantigas d'escarnho e de mal dizer*, Moors are depicted as predatory sexual deviants, frequently engaged in fornication and sodomy; meanwhile Muslim converts to Christianity and even those merely resembling Muslims are consistently ridiculed. In the *Livro de linhagens* (Book of Lineages), considered a landmark of Portuguese literature, the fourteenth-century author Pedro Afonso, the Count of Barcelos, constructs an anti-Muslim Portuguese history, in which the Moor is nothing more than a subject of reconquest. These tropes were repeated throughout Christian Portuguese history, continued under Salazar when school textbooks – which might well have been read by Rosinda and Manuel – still depicted the Moors as 'foreign enemies' of the 'fatherland' and 'Christian faith'. Some of these books remained unrevised and were still in use in schools as late as the 1990s. In fact, even today, students are required to read *The Lusiads*, a sixteenth-century epic poem by the Portuguese poet Luís Vaz de Camões that celebrates the glories of Portugal's Christian kingdom while demonizing its Muslims. All of this has helped to construct a nation-forming narrative where, as one Muslim-Portuguese scholar put it, 'the making of Portugal is literally the erasure of Islam'.

'They are based on folklore,' Rosinda explained, referring to the historical festivals.

'They are more medieval . . . history,' added Manuel.

I could see they were both uncomfortable with these festivals, which are less and less common across Portugal these days.

'In the Islamic Festival of Mértola, it kind of transports Mértola to a parallel universe . . . a cosmopolitan Islamic Mértola that happens in the present and it's not like a re-creation of the past,' Rosinda explained, 'we create a medina, a souk, we have artisans . . .'

'And the artisans come from . . . ?'

'From everywhere . . . some from North Africa and some from the Islamic community in Spain.'

'And . . . and here in Portugal,' added Manuel 'and many, many sellers come here.'

The festival is biennial and was first held in 2001 as the Festival Islamico and was Mértola's way of saying, we are actually quite proud of our Islamic heritage, and we wish to celebrate it. The shift in attitude towards Portugal's Muslim past by the likes of Manuel and Rosinda began after the discoveries in the 1970s.

'Why were the discoveries in the seventies so important?'

'For Mértola or Portugal?' Rosinda asked.

'For both.'

'Well, it brought knowledge of this period of history,' began Rosinda, 'and I think the main thing is that this group of archaeologists and historians were dedicated to that period. Until then, it was some isolated ones, and so with that and the . . . abundance of archaeological remains, that was easier. We had a lot of people studying that and it gave a different perspective of the Islamic period. So, it was not just a page in your history book, it was much more than that.'

'This is very important,' chipped in Manuel, who had been nodding along as Rosinda explained.

I could tell he was itching to interject and his lack of language skills was frustrating him.

'So, it was five hundred years of knowledge, development, commerce, culture . . . eh . . . and that's what Mértola meant to the Islamic people,' continued Rosinda.

From the quintessentially Portuguese azulejo tile – derived from *al-zillij* – to the Portuguese language (almost 19,000 words with Arabic roots), and the ruins of former *qusur* (castles) found all over the south in towns once called al-Buhera (Albufeira), Faraon (Faro) and Shilb (Silves), and a hundred other names I had driven past on my way here – Alvares, Algodor, Albernoa, Aljustrel, Algalé – 'Islam is in Portugal's soul', as the country's president, Marcelo Rebelo de Sousa, declared at the recent fiftieth-anniversary commemorations of the Central Mosque of Lisbon. It is there in the poetry, carpet weaving, music, architecture, science and 'explorations' – explorers such as Vasco da Gama relied heavily on cartography, maps and navigational tools developed by Muslim geographers that came before them. There would have been no Age of Discovery without the Portuguese-invented mariner's astrolabe, which was modelled on the conventional astrolabe brought to the peninsula by the Muslims. Islam is even in the Portuguese blood, with a recent study revealing one third of Iberians have Jewish or Muslim ancestry, which might just explain why the Portuguese hope for something by saying *oxalá* (pronounced 'oshala') and the Spanish by saying *ojalá* (pronounced 'ohhala'), the way Muslims hope for something by saying *insh'Allah* – if God wills.

'Do you feel like the discovery inspired more interest in this? Because it sounds like before that, there wasn't any,' I asked.

'There was no interest . . . There was this intention . . . like other European countries.' Rosinda, who was also probably speaking in her third or fourth language, was understandably being careful in choosing her words.

'They didn't want this history to be known and there was always the prevalence and dominance of the Christian period. Also of the Roman period, and they are all very European!'

'Yes,' agreed Manuel.

'So, what this brought was the knowledge of this society, that it was open . . . and . . . and inclusive, because that's what the remains show. The archaeological remains show connections with the Christians, the Muslims and the Jewish people. You could see that the three cultures co-existed, we don't know exactly how, but we know they were here. Also, maybe because we are in a place of trade, with the port. There is also a sense of being practical and pragmatic . . .' explained Rosinda.

'So, it's not super romantic and everybody here is the best of friends, but they are finding a way to co-exist,' I said, reading between Rosinda's lines.

'Yes,' she agreed.

Manuel was continuing to nod away.

'And that's what Mértola brought,' she added.

Rosinda explained how Torres and his team effectively lived here, creating a research centre in Mértola, to study not just the Muslim period but also other periods of Mértola's history. But Rosinda and Manuel were in no doubt about which period had the most profound impact on Portugal's understanding of its national narrative.

'Yes, the Islamic period of Mértola changed the national narrative the most, because it was the least known.'

'We have, we have the . . . the centre of knowledge, we have Córdoba, Granada, Seville in al-Andalus . . . and then here in Gharb al-Andalus' – Manuel used Portugal's Islamic name – 'we have other centres, little centres! You have two . . . two different worlds in some different kinds to . . . they have different ways. The introduction of some techniques from the big centres of knowledge give us some knowledge to export all of Gharb al-Andalus, this is the knowledge in several centres.' Manuel was struggling to find the words in English, but I understood what he was trying to say.

'In agricultures, education, academia, science . . . in everything!' he said, throwing his hands up. 'For other way, we have the claim of the Christians . . . the kings that came from France.'

'The Franks, from the North?' I asked, making sure I understood that we were talking about the same people.

'The Franks! From the North,' agreed Manuel, before adding, much to my surprise, 'the barbarians!'

'*They* are the barbarians?' I asked, laughing, for I had not heard the Franks described this way by non-Muslim Europeans before. 'Normally in Europe's history, it is the Muslims that are the barbarians,' I said, asking Manuel to explain.

'Because . . . They want, they want . . . the lands and they want to expand; they don't want to build civilization or culture . . .' It was Rosinda's turn to interject and Manuel was in agreement.

This was a fascinating turn-up for me, to be sitting here with two non-Muslim Portuguese people, both professionals working on the country's heritage, telling me that, actually, the historical Christian 'saviours' and 'heroes' of Iberia were the real barbarians.

The Umayyad-led conquest of Iberia saw Muslims entering Gaul within two decades of the start of their campaigns on mainland Europe in 711. After taking Septimania, which they renamed Arbunah (hence the name Narbonne), they continued through Aquitaine and, according to some reports, got as far as the outskirts of Paris before the rapidity of their expansion alarmed the Franks into taking serious action. The lack of resistance along the way – as with Iberia – has been put down to locals welcoming the Muslims in the hope of being liberated from the oppressive feudal system of governance in the region. The two sides met at the decisive Battle of Tours (or Poitiers) about 150 miles south-west of Paris. The Muslim army was led by the Umayyad governor, Abd al-Rahman al-Ghafiqi, who had also taken Bordeaux, and the Christians were led by the mayor of the Frankish court, Charles Martel. Martel's victory at Tours has been lauded throughout European history as the moment the continent was saved from the 'marauding' Muslims. The Muslims would remain in southern France for another forty years or so until Martel's son Pepin the Short took Narbonne in 759. Pepin also went on to found the Carolingian dynasty as its first king. The defeat took place at a time of serious uncertainty among the Muslims, with a successful coup against the Caliphate by the Abbasids in 750 almost wiping out the Umayyads in Syria. Although one of them survived and managed to found a small Emirate in Córdoba six years later, he was yet to really consolidate his power in the region, so it was no surprise that the Muslims retreated back to their central Iberian strongholds, halting any further expansion northwards. The pause allowed Martel's grandson Charlemagne to extend Frankish influence into the north of the peninsula, creating the Hispanic March, a defensive buffer zone that split the remaining sliver of Christian northern Iberia from the large Umayyad territories in the south. Frankish society at this time was agrarian, centred largely on self-sufficient manors producing goods and crafts. Land inheritance was a particularly sensitive issue in Frankish society, as a person's political and social standing was closely linked to the amount of land they possessed. The inheritance system directly influenced a Frank's status, as it was determined by the size and wealth of their landholdings. Urban life was minimal, with 'cities' resembling fortified towns. Trade was limited to local exchanges. The Franks adopted Christianity in the late fifth century and were hostile to Jews. In 629, King Dagobert ordered all Jews to be baptized or face expulsion. The Franks also had a history of being intolerant of other Christian sects, often imposing by force their papal-approved version on those around them. It was therefore inevitable that after Charlemagne was crowned Holy Roman Emperor, the Franks did the same in northern Iberia and the region transitioned from observing Visigothic rites to Roman Christian rites. To facilitate this, Frankish clergy and monks – arriving from a religious culture of intolerance – reorganized northern-Iberian monastic and church life to resemble that of their homelands.

Rosinda and Manuel believed the Franks had only been interested in territorial gain, while the Muslims arrived with the most advanced culture Europe had witnessed since antiquity. They would go on to turn the small towns of Iberia, like Córdoba, Seville and Lisbon, into the largest and most enlightened urban centres on the continent: places through which international trade flowed, home to hospitals, public baths and institutions of learning that saw locals engaging with the latest and most revolutionary ideas in science, medicine, architecture, engineering, the arts, literature and philosophy. These would be home to societies where Europe's existing Jews and Christians (of all sects) would flourish. The Muslims, as Rosinda and Manuel knew only too well, far from being the 'barbarians' popular Portuguese (and Western) history will have you believe, would in effect give birth to Europe's first *real* Renaissance since the classical period; one that would lay the foundations for the much-lauded later Christian Renaissance.

Manuel explained how modern politics had affected the writing of this history in Portugal; how certain political leaders were close to the church – a reference to Salazar's regime – and this is why Portugal's Islamic history is the most badly understood of all the country's histories, as well as some other worrying tendencies.

'Do you know . . . erm . . . eh . . . what the archaeologs from the . . . the . . . who research the Roman levels do from the . . . huh' – Manuel laughed – 'Islamic levels?'

I shook my head.

'They throw . . . with the machines . . . and go out . . .'

I didn't quite understand what he was saying, and asked him to clarify.

'So, they destroyed it?'

'Destroyed it,' nodded Manuel.

What is left, he explained, are just scraps that explain very little. I was shocked but not surprised to hear this. I had come across example after example of efforts to erase Europe's Muslim past. I had seen it in the tit-for-tat destruction by Greeks in the south of Cyprus. I had come across it on a grosser scale, while writing my previous book, in places like Albania, by the country's communist dictator Enver Hoxha, and in Bosnia and Herzegovina when Serb and Croat forces targeted Muslim monuments like the Mostar Bridge in 1993.

The two examples of historical 'archaeologists' taking part in this, first in Malta and now here, added another layer – to use Manuel's phrase. It proved that during Europe's effort to reimagine itself in a neoclassical mould, when archaeologists went digging for evidence to support this, those 'layers' that didn't fit this narrative, or were still despised – like Europe's Muslim period – were unceremoniously done away with. I wondered how much had been lost in this way. It was yet another reason why so little of the Islamic history of Europe was decipherable.

'They don't read . . .' began Manuel, who had become very animated, even angry, as he spoke about this. Rosinda interjected again.

'The Roman . . . the Roman archaeology is much more . . .'

'Valuable?' I asked.

'More monumental . . .'

'Aah, more spectacular?'

Rosinda nodded. 'More spectacular, more monumental, ornamental . . .'

She explained that, while there are some monumental Islamic remains in Sintra, Portugal did not have the monumental architecture of, say, Granada or Córdoba in Spain. I agreed, but also now wondered if once upon a time it did.

'In here, in Portugal, you would have the Mezquita here . . . as a small remain, but very, very much transformed, so you have an archaeology that is of the day-by-day routine. It's not monumental,' Rosinda said, before conceding that ultimately Portugal's national history is built upon a narrative of conquering the Muslims. As in Cyprus, Sicily and Malta, and so many other European nations, the Portuguese identity was constructed in opposition to and in fear and hatred of Islam. In that respect, Islamophobia was part of the historical DNA. Rosinda was being more measured than I suspected Manuel would have been – after all, he went into the trenches, literally: someone who excavated and reconstructed the artefacts. He saw what was in the ground and was more likely to appreciate what might have been destroyed. It made me wonder what great Islamic monuments in Portugal had been destroyed and removed from the face of history and from memory. Portugal's Islamic history was traditionally not preserved, respected or valued. It was seen as the history of the enemy, which explains why there was so little regard for it, and why its destruction would have once been so widespread.

'They're not going to champion the loser . . .' explained Rosinda.

'It's a classic case of the winner writes the history,' I said.

'Yeah, yeah!' Manuel was again very animated, tapping the table in agreement.

Rosinda continued to explain how the work done in Mértola had begun to change that. The work done there since the 1970s, unearthing the town's Islamic and other histories, was educating the Portuguese about this overlooked and neglected heritage. In Mértola, they had set up fourteen 'museums' that made up the 'Museum of Mértola' – a kind of trail of mini-'museums' – covering all the diverse history and heritage of the town. Eleven of these were in the town and three outside. This, along with the Islamic festival, was making the town's Islamic history more visible and accessible. But not everyone was happy about this, explained Rosinda.

'Especially after the appearance of Daesh and lots of people from Europe going to Syria, if we went to places to promote the festival, people would say to us: "Why are you doing this?", and we would say, we are communicating that Islamic culture is not what you think . . . as well as the Christians are not the Inquisition, you know?' Rosinda laughed.

Manuel tapped the table in agreement again. Rosinda explained that the name also bothered people. I was not surprised they faced challenges. Launched in the same year as the 9/11 attacks in New York, which unleashed a global wave of Islamophobic attacks, the festival was always going to be up against it, but I admired what Rosinda, Manuel and their team were trying to do. This was not the nineteenth-century romanticism of Dom Fernando and Manuel Pinto da Fonseca: this was grounded in reality because it began with an admission that traditional Portuguese history is founded upon Islamophobia.

13

The Christians Who Pray towards Makkah

Mértola, Portugal

When the Islamic Art Museum of Mértola was opened in December 2001, three months after 9/11, it was the first museum to open in Portugal exclusively dedicated to the country's Muslim past. Curated by Cláudio Torres and his colleague Santiago Macias, the museum sits in a beautiful eighteenth-century building that was once a royal storehouse, at the very south-western edge of Mértola. The collection covers the town's Islamic period between the ninth and thirteenth centuries and is home to a host of items that have inspired patterns and murals I had seen scattered across the town.

We were greeted by Susana Gómez Martínez, a professor of medieval history and archaeology, who had agreed to give us a brief tour of the key objects in the small museum. One of the first she stopped in front of was a beautiful ceramic bowl of faded green with sand-coloured vegetal patterns that framed a large bird in the middle.

'This is very unusual,' I said.

'No, not for this period . . . there are ideas that this symbol is to remember a legend about the Caliph al-Mu'min, and a bird,' explained Susana, who was of late middle age and wore a polka-dotted grey blouse and navy-blue shorts.

The Caliph in question was Abd al-Mu'min, one of the

greatest 'caliphs' of the Almohad empire (or Caliphate), which ruled Mértola between 1151 and 1250 – the longest of any Muslim dynasty after the collapse of the Caliphate of Córdoba in the eleventh century. Al-Mu'min, who reigned for twelve of those years, was the founder of the Almohads' Mu'minid dynasty. Their use of the terms 'caliph' and 'caliphate' did not constitute any claims to global Muslim supremacy. It was during al-Mu'min's reign that the Almohads came out of North Africa and took over al-Andalus from the Almoravids – also from North Africa – who had first stepped into the vacuum left behind by the Caliphate in 1086, when, panicked by the fall of Muslim Toledo in 1085, the Muslim taifa rulers led by Seville's Abbadids had sent an SOS to their co-religionists in North Africa. Both the Almoravid and the Almohad reunification of the former Caliphate lands began with periods of conservatism and, in some cases, intolerance, before slowly developing into cultures which resembled that of the Caliphate they had initially despised as too decadent and lacking in piety. Each one went on to produce its own distinct culture, architectural style and body of intellectual work. Al-Mu'min, whose name means 'the Believer', helped to define the Almohad architectural and artistic style by building some of its greatest monuments, including the Kutubiyah Mosque, the Mosque of Tinmal and the Kasbah of the Udayas, all in Morocco.

'Wow, these are really impressive,' I said as we approached several large 'winged' ceramic glazed jars.

'You remember I showed you the tiles on the wall?' Manuel asked.

'Yes, yes! So this was the inspiration,' I said excitedly.

Manuel nodded.

Each jar was about the height of a small child, but much wider. Starting from the thick neck, every inch of the green glaze was covered in beautiful, almost rhythmic patterns, just as I had seen in giant form beside the Guadiana café. There were rows of classical Kufic Arabic above thin rows of delicate vegetal patterns that sat above mosaic ones. The largest motifs were of the classic horseshoe arch synonymous with the Umayyads, which ran around the most bulbous part of the jar and were the most visible when the jar was on its stand. The glaze had almost disappeared on even the most complete jars. All had large cracks going through them and many had plain segments that had been positioned to help reconstruct the jar. The arches were modelled on those once in the town's mosque, now the Church of Our Lady of the Annunciation. The museum had a small white model of what the mosque might have looked like: a plain white rectangular building with a low-pitched terracotta-tiled roof and a white square minaret that resembled those I had seen across North Africa.

The next few items finally introduced me to Mértolan Muslims, individuals who would have prayed in the mosque and known for certain what it looked like. Ishaq Ibn Faras al-Ansari had died towards the end of Rajab in 346 AH (approximately AD 957). His tombstone was a badly weathered rectangular stone with faded Kufic Arabic etched into it. Beneath Ishaq's name, after an affirmation of God and his Prophet, there was a reminder that every human being would be resurrected, using verse seven from Surah *al-Hajj* in the Qur'an. There was no other detail about Ishaq, but his surname, al-Ansari, suggested Ishaq's family traced its lineage back to some of the most noble Muslims in Islamic history, the 'Ansar', which meant the 'Helpers' or 'those who brought victory', and was a name reserved for the inhabitants of Madinah in Saudi Arabia, who helped the Prophet Muhammad and his followers by taking them in after they had been exiled from Makkah. The title was given to them personally by the Prophet Muhammad and it is from the moment they took in the refugee Prophet, in the year 622, that the Islamic calendar begins, for this is the period *Anno Hegirae*, which means 'after the migration'. These now legendary first generations of Muslims from the tribes of Khazraj and Aus took part in a number of battles alongside the Prophet and are considered a cornerstone of the very first Islamic community in Madinah.

The next tombstone dated from a much later period, 598 AH, or AD 1202. It was much more elaborately inscribed with raised thick Arabic inscriptions in lettering closer to the naskh style. It had once stood above the grave of one of Mértola's most respected Muslims, as he had been buried with the title 'sheikh', reserved for respected, knowledgeable or deeply spiritual individuals in the community. Abu Bakr Yahya ibn Abd Allah Ibn al-Huwari had died on a Wednesday in the month of Dhu al-Hijjah. There was a third tombstone, but it had only survived in part, and was easily the most decorative and elaborate with parts of an arabesque arch like the one on Maimuna's headstone in Malta. No name or details of the deceased were on the section that had survived; the only words that could be deciphered were verses from the Qur'an, including verses from Surah *Luqman* and Surah *al-Baqarah*.

'We only have a few of these tombstones,' Susana said, watching me examine the etchings on the stones.

'Yes, they are often used as building material,' I said.

Susana nodded in agreement.

'And here we have the most important pieces of the museum!' she said with a degree of triumph in her voice.

I stared into the tall glass cabinet where a glazed bowl with a familiar scene sat.

'For us it's very special because it is the symbol of our institution!' Susana said. 'It is a ceramic from the end of the tenth century, inspired by the African style but made in al-Andalus.'

'And what are the animals?'

'We think it is an antelope, a wolf and a falcon.'

The chipped ceramic glazed bowl had once been green and was encircled by a simple arched pattern. Each animal had been painted in a primitive style using lines and cross-hatching. The antelope was the largest, and stood at the front, its horns almost piercing the neck of the low-flying falcon, while the wolf appeared to be riding atop the antelope. I had seen it on a number of large signs announcing Mértola as an archaeological park on my drive into the town, and on a mural – painted by Manuel – near the middle of town, complete with imagined colours in the wings of the falcon and

PART 2: THE CHILDREN OF AL-ANDALUS

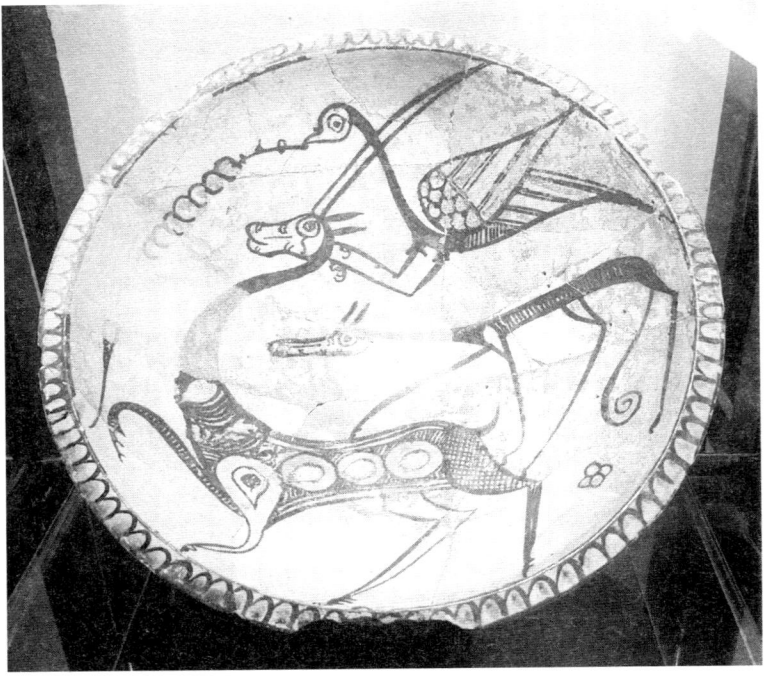

A tenth-century ceramic bowl discovered in Mértola believed to feature an antelope, a wolf and a falcon – now the symbol of Mértola's archaeological park

bodies of the animals. I had spent quite some time staring at it, assuming the image had been inspired by a non-Islamic artefact.

'This is another one that is the symbol of the association for the protection of the region of Mértola.'

Susana was now pointing to an adjacent bowl of equal size, with a star-like pattern around the edges in a faded yellow. In the middle, painted in a very different style, was another animal, which was fuller and more anatomically correct.

'We think this is also an antelope,' Susana said.

'Or a gazelle,' chipped in Manuel, pointing to the neck.

We passed the keys to Muslim houses that no longer existed, wedding jewellery for weddings that have long been forgotten, dice for games that will never be played again, and even a tiny *khamsa* amulet that now protects nobody.

The last item we saw was very special to Manuel and Susana, as they had worked on it together. Susana had researched it and Manuel had restored it. This was a beautiful twin-handled glazed water vessel from the twelfth century. It was decorated with exquisite floral patterns and Arabic cursive script, but had so many cracks it resembled a 3D jigsaw puzzle.

'This was created somewhere in the peninsula, and something similar was created in the east . . . but here in this peninsula, this type of vase first appears around the eleventh century,' Susana explained.

'And what was its use?'

'We think there was maybe a filter inside, so maybe for rose water, medicine . . . or some kind of infusion.'

'How long did it take to re-create it?' I asked them both, looking at the tiny fragments and imagining trying to put it together myself.

'From 1980 . . . '90 . . . no! 1984 . . . and I finished it in 1998.'

Fourteen years. It had taken Manuel and Susana almost a decade and a half to painstakingly reconstruct this piece of Portugal's Muslim heritage, heritage their forefathers had cared little for, and may well have swept aside in their search for the classical Graeco-Roman – but not Manuel and Susana. Being in their company, like that of Paolo in Sicily and David in Malta, was showing me there was real hope. I was learning more and more on this journey that some of Europe's non-Muslims do care about the continent's Islamic heritage. In the case of Manuel and his colleagues, often very deeply.

'When the Christians came, they move . . . the hal – . . . altar?'

Manuel looked to me for confirmation he had picked the right word.

'They moved it that way' – he pointed towards the back of the church, opposite the current south-east-facing altar – 'and the people from Mértola request the king for the . . . the altar to be put back here . . .'

'. . . because this is the direction they had *always* prayed.' I smiled as I finished the sentence for Manuel, who was also smiling.

PART 2: THE CHILDREN OF AL-ANDALUS

Manuel Passinhas da Palma and Professor Susana Gómez Martínez stand proudly in front of a twelfth-century Muslim water vessel – one of the items they worked on together now on display inside the Islamic Art Museum of Mértola

'. . . In the place of the old Qur'an.'
'The Qibla?'
'They talk about the Qur'an.'
'But this direction is called Qibla.'
'In the old language: "we want to put in the place of the old Qur'an".' Manuel mimed the act of writing as he said this to make clear the use of 'old Qur'an' is what is written in the historical documents. This was the request the people of Mértola made to the king, and the king agreed the altar should point that way, which was in fact the direction of Makkah.
'The king said, "Yes, change it"!'
Manuel was telling me the story of how Mértola became the place where its Christians prayed towards Makkah. We were standing in front of Portugal's only historical mihrab, discovered behind the altar of the Church of Our Lady of the Anunciation in the 1940s when workmen removed the old wooden altar to find four delicate arches set within a large niche. The careful design, the faded patterns above, and the scant remnants of slim plaster pillars that once held up the arches, all pointed

to one thing: this had once been the Great Jamme Masjid of Mértola. Very little is actually known about the mosque and even the dating of its foundation to the twelfth century is based on stylistic comparisons with the Tinmal Mosque in Morocco, which has a square minaret, similar to the one believed to have once been attached to the mosque, as well as similar horseshoe-arched entrances within decorative frames called *alfiz*. This is why the construction date has been placed within Mértola's Almohad period.

Manuel and I were now standing where the first row of worshippers would have lined up, where Ishaq and Sheikh Abu Bakr would have stood during their lifetimes, or maybe the sheikh would have been in the niche, leading the prayer. I looked up at the white baby Jesus, a small loincloth around his waist and a silver crown with a cross on his head. His mother, as always, was covered head to toe and wore the 'hijab' common among the pre-Islamic women of the Middle East, and later among the Christian women in places like Portugal. In her hand was a bunch of grapes – a reference to the Eucharist and Jesus's role as the redeemer. The mosque's marble pillars had each been visibly extended in height from their original size, a telltale sliver of connecting cement three quarters of the way up the giveaway. The pillars were perfectly aligned so the wooden pews lined up where the Muslims would have stood in salah, facing south-east towards Makkah.

'Are there other clues?' I asked Manuel.

'Yes,' he said loudly, his voice bouncing off the cold terracotta floor tiles.

Manuel and I left the altar area and walked past the wooden pews. The church interior was a cool relief from the blazing August sun outside, and I wondered if it would have felt warmer as a mosque with woven mats and rugs spread out across the floor, and the numerous arches open to the elements, as the model in the museum had suggested. This would have allowed air to flow through as well as flooding the interior with light, taking away the gloom that now pervaded it. Manuel led me towards the northern wall of the church, where he lifted a red cordon to allow us into a private prayer space.

'Here we have two doors in arch . . . two Islamic doors,' Manuel said, stepping into the room, turning around, and using both his hands to make the shape of an arch as he pointed towards the doorway we had just walked through. He then pointed to another beside it. Both had large double wooden doors flanking the arch and obscuring the original Islamic design; the same one I had seen on the outer walls of the mosque model in the museum and on the large winged jars.

'One more!' Manuel said, leading me out through the back of the church and another set of double doors, which upon opening immediately revealed the curvature of the Islamic brick arch. This was the most photogenic of all three of the church's arches. The main arch had the iconic intermittent red bricks fanning out across its curvature in the style of the Umayyad arch, first seen in the great mosque in Damascus, then re-created and copied across Umayyad territories, to become a kind of insignia of the Caliphate culture. The entire structure had been exposed from the white rendering covering the rest of the walls to reveal thin bricks in its construction. I photographed it in portrait form and with its small green and beige doormat, noting how much it resembled the entrances of hundreds of mosques I had stepped through. Inspired by the Umayyad mosque design, it was *the* archetypal mosque doorway.

'Is the minaret – I mean, bell tower – also the original minaret?' I asked Manuel, as we began to wander around the side of the church.

'No, it was on that side.' Manuel was pointing towards the north-western wall of the church, the opposite side to where the current bell tower and mihrab were.

'So this is a new bell tower?'

'Yes.'

Before we left the church, Manuel showed me the small

museum that had been set up around parts of the foundations of the church. Here signs theorized that the original Roman temple may have been dedicated to an emperor.

'We don't know! . . . We don't know nothing about this!' he laughed when I asked him his thoughts on the theory, which claimed the temple was Christianized around the sixth century. Evidence of this had been found in the shape of an altar stone with a cross carved on it, as well as a few other smaller artefacts that included a series of glazed tiles, among them fragments of obviously Islamic geometric tiles. Before we left the vicinity of the church, Manuel stopped me and pointed to the large open area near the entrance of the church. This, he explained, is where Islamic prayers were held during the festival. I nodded, recalling the videos of the festival I had watched before my trip. It showed a large group of men prostrating in the direction of the altar in neat rows, just as the sun was setting.

'Did anyone complain about Muslims praying here again?' I asked Manuel.

'When they did, the Muslims said, "You have the mosque five hundred years, we have it only for one day!"'

This made us both laugh.

'So *this* is called the Bairro Islâmico!' I read the large sign at the entrance of the archaeological park behind the church. 'What does that mean?'

'The Islamic quarter,' said Manuel.

We stood in the shade of a large tree as I assessed the scene before me: a multitude of excavated domestic foundations lay below ground level, hemmed in by a fort-like wall and a series of light metal walkways to allow visitors a glimpse into the ruins. I had seen similar ruins but on a smaller scale around St George's Castle in Lisbon on my last visit. That castle, like the one in Mértola, had also been built by Muslims, but almost nothing from the Muslim period had survived, except the foundations of a few of their homes.

'We can see houses, a central patio and each house . . . eh . . . has a central patio, and all the rooms around it.'

Manuel was pointing to one of the ruins, where the dilapidated remnants of a small square patio could be seen with the remains of tiny rooms around it.

'Like the riadhs in Morocco?'

'Yes! . . . Like the mosque, here we have levels.'

Manuel explained that the Muslim dwellings were built upon Roman ruins, and then later the site became a Christian cemetery, just like the Muslim dwellings in Sintra.

'This was a special place, next to the temple, mosque, church, the castle . . . the high point.' Manuel reeled off the reasons for the busy nature of the site. Somewhere close by a cock crowed, and we could hear children playing in a garden. We passed a pile of millstones on wooden pallets, as if drying in the sun; beside them were a number of bricks and stone construction material piled up.

'So these are things the archaeologists have put here?'

'Yeah . . . this is also for grain,' said Manuel, pointing to a large oval-shaped stone structure with a hole in the top.

The finds had been laid out beneath a large pine tree in which a pigeon could be heard cooing.

'Look, there is a canal in the patio there.'

Manuel stopped where the path overlooked the ruins of a central patio of what had been a large house. In the middle, framed by a square of tiles, was a cavity, with a visible small channel disappearing underneath the house. The Muslims had installed an underground drainage system adapting some of the existing Roman structures, explained Manuel.

'When it rained in the courtyard, the water went out . . . And you can see the little rooms around it.'

Manuel, who had worked on the site since 1977, explained which rooms were used for what. He pointed to a large space, which had a smaller rectangular structure, and said this was the sleeping quarters, and that the structure at one end had been the marital space, separated by a curtain.

'We found a little piece, like an S to suspend the curtain.'
'And how long does the work take?'
'One house can take five, six years to excavate.'

As Manuel showed me house after house, pointing out where the cooking area was, where the large decorated amphoras we had seen in the museum would have been kept, where the latrine was and which parts were the streets, he also told me about the finds that helped them understand the purpose of each space. A fragment of an amphora here, the remains of a large washbasin there. As he spoke, bringing the ruins to life, I tried to imagine where Ishaq and Abu Bakr might have lived. I saw them sitting with their families to eat. I imagined Abu Bakr, the 'sheikh', teaching the young children of the neighbourhood, either at his house or leading them towards the mosque.

Manuel and I ended our tour of Mértola, high up above the town, in the shade of the Castelo de Mértola, beside a beautiful bronze statue of one of Mértola's most famous Muslim rulers, Abu 'l-Qasim Ahmad Ibn al-Husayn Ibn Qasi, a prominent Sufi and skilled leader and founder of the Qasid dynasty, which briefly ruled Mértola. His statue was surprisingly dignified. It presented Ibn Qasi astride a noble steed, dressed in military attire, as befitting a medieval Muslim leader but not in a clichéd or aggressive pose.

'We have 80,000 people come to the festival in a good year,' Manuel said, as we watched a young Portuguese brother and sister, both dressed in bright summer colours, climb onto Ibn Qasi's stone plinth to pose for a photo for their mother. As she assessed the picture, the children tried to climb onto Ibn Qasi's horse. Suddenly noticing this, the mother scolded them and asked them to get down immediately, before looking over at us apologetically. Manuel smiled. The statue occupied a prominent spot, close to the path that led to the entrance of the castle, and at the edge of a precipice directly overlooking the old Islamic quarter and the mosque Ibn Qasi would have prayed in many times. It was a spot that had offered Ibn Qasi stunning vistas over Mértola and the Guadiana, and felt like a fitting tribute for a through-and-through native of Gharb al-Andalus. Ibn Qasi had been born in Silves, an hour and a half's drive south-west of Mértola, close to the coastline, and was known as *rumi al-asl* by his peers, to mean 'originally of Europe' or someone whose blood is Iberian (Rum in Islamic antiquity referred to the Roman territories). Known for his leadership of the Muridun movement – from the Sufi term for 'student', murid – a Sufi-inspired movement that sought to challenge the political and social order of the time, he stood up to the might of the Almoravids in 1144 and formed an alliance with Afonso I to briefly hold sway over his own semi-autonomous kingdom in what is today the Algarve region, with Silves as his capital. His efforts to implement Sufi principles in governance and his alliances with Christian and Muslim rulers alike highlight how complex and multifaceted he was. Much like Mértola's history.

'The artist is from Romania,' Manuel said, as I admired the statue.

'Do you feel like your ancestors were Muslims, or do you believe there were the Muslims and then your ancestors came along?'

A statue of Abu 'l-Qasim Ahmad Ibn al-Husayn Ibn Qasi, the twelfth-century Muslim ruler of Mértola, sits high above the town next to the Castelo de Mértola

'I feel like my ancestors were Muslim, yes,' Manuel replied, once he fully understood the question, adding, 'I did some research, at some big archives, and I discover a document which talks about my name, it is unusual.'

'Really?'

'Passinhas . . . I discovered two Passinhas were Jewish; the Church, the Christians, the Inquisition take them to court and accuse them to be Jewish.'

'So your roots are potentially Jewish.'

'On one side. We don't know . . . Jewish!' Manuel laughed.

PART 3

Europe's Caliphate Culture

14

The Caliphate Palace-City

Córdoba, Spain

We all let out a huge sigh of relief as the friendly bus driver finally pulled up in the car park for Madinah az-Zahra, the only part of the visit tonight that we would need to pay for. A three-euro bus fare is all that is needed to visit the archaeological ruins in the cool of the Spanish night. With the site's museum – which also acts as the visitor centre – closed and nothing to tell us what we should do on a night visit to the fabled Umayyad palace-city, before the bus arrived the crowd of mostly white Spanish tourists and I had been anxiously waiting for fifteen minutes or so wondering what the protocol was. Now, as the bus slowly wound its way up towards the mountains silhouetted by the last embers of twilight, the distant lights of the Caliphate city of Córdoba to our right, I could finally see the eerie ruins coming slowly into view: the ghostly glimpse of a half-arch here, the faint outline of a classical pillar there. I had chosen to visit Madinah az-Zahra at night because on my previous daytime visits I had nearly melted in the open plain of ruins that cascaded down the side of a scorched hill with no shade. I had struggled to make sense of the piled-up stone bricks, smashed pillars and traces of ornamentation: the result of Almoravid zeal and later Christian, Spanish negligence. The ruins had lain for centuries either buried beneath the earth that accumulated near the foot of the hills of the Sierra Morena or had been hauled away and reused for construction by locals. What was left of Madinah az-Zahra lay dormant and ignored by Spanish culture until the mid nineteenth century. The hold-up after this was a combination of land disputes and the usual civic bureaucracy, with excavations finally beginning in 1911.

Madinah az-Zahra sits a mere six kilometres to the west of the Caliphate capital, in a spectacular spot where the mountains of Córdoba meet the Great River Valley, or Wadi al-Kabir (today's Guadalquivir). Its construction in 936 was an announcement that Europe's first and only Caliphate had arrived. It had taken eight generations for the Umayyads to reinvent themselves as caliphs in Iberia after almost every member of the family had been massacred in 750 in an ambush in Damascus by the incoming Abbasids, who now ruled from their brand-new capital of Baghdad. One survivor was Abdu'r Rahman I – the legitimate heir – who escaped to the Maghreb to regroup before gathering enough local support to make his way across to southern Iberia six years after the murders. The memory of his family, under whom the peninsula had first become Muslim, helped the young prince quickly install himself as a local emir and found the Umayyad Emirate of Córdoba around 756. Over the next two centuries, his children and grandchildren would rapidly bring most of the Iberian Peninsula, barring the north, under the Emirate's sway. Thus by the time his namesake, Abdu'r Rahman III, declared himself Caliph of the Muslim world on 16 January 929, it would have felt particularly satisfying and like a destiny fulfilled. Descended from a long line of European mothers and grandmothers, the Arab, Hispano-Basque Abdu'r Rahman looked so Northern European, with his white skin, blue eyes and reddish-blonde hair, that legend has it he dyed his hair black to try and look more Arab. A short, handsome man, Abdu'r Rahman was a tolerant and pragmatic ruler, whose father, Muhammad, was murdered by his uncle when he was just a baby. In spite of the many uncles being available to take the throne, Abdu'r Rahman's grandfather, Abd Allah, picked him. The old man had a deep affection for the fatherless boy, raised by his aunts in the palace harem, and would often let him sit on the imperial throne. It was an inspired choice. Inheriting a highly reduced realm at the age of twenty-one in 912, the ruthlessly ambitious Abdu'r Rahman immediately set about campaigning to secure and expand the frontiers of his empire. Defeating and creating alliances with Christian and Muslim rulers, he also faced the significant challenge of the Fatimid Caliphate, which — announced three years before — had been advancing towards Iberia via Sicily and Ifriqiya. The Shi'a Fatimids, named after the Prophet's daughter Fatima, from whom they claimed direct descent, did not recognize the Sunni Umayyads or the Abbasids as legitimate rulers of Islam, and after taking over former Aghlabid territories, including the Emirate of Siqilliya, were now on their rival's doorstep. Thus in the early tenth century, the Islamic world had three Caliphates, and all three built new capitals to announce themselves; the Abbasids built Baghdad, the Fatimids built al-Mahdiyya (Mahdia, Tunisia) and Abdu'r Rahman III, who loved the arts and culture and was a great patron of architecture, built Madinah az-Zahra. Like any good Caliph, Abdu'r Rahman knew the only way to *really* announce yourself as a ruler of Islam was to build a magnificent new Caliphate capital.

Stretching for seven miles at a time when London and Paris were less than one square mile in size, Madinah az-Zahra — dubbed the Versailles of Córdoba by modern historians — was minting its own money within a decade of completion and featured stunning landscaped gardens, artificial lakes, grand fountains, streets with lighting, a spectacular mosque, baths in every quarter, libraries, schools and palaces built in such magnificence that when foreign delegates entered, they were spellbound and bedazzled. Al-Maqqari, the sixteenth-century Muslim historian of al-Andalus, tells us 'travellers from distant lands, men of all ranks and professions in life, following various religions, princes, ambassadors, merchants, pilgrims, theologians, and poets . . . all agreed that they had never seen in the course of their travels anything that could be compared to it'.

The silence was deafening. I had expected to hear the chirping of crickets, grasshoppers and other insects as I stood beneath one of the giant horseshoe arches in front of the Great Portico and Parade Ground at the foot of the ruins of the palace-city. But there was nothing, just silence, occasionally broken by a faint conversation taking place in some corner of the vast grounds. The voices drifted over like ghostly echoes, adding to the eeriness of a place lit up by carefully positioned uplighting, leaving many corners pitch black. I had left the crowd from the bus at the top of the ruins, next to the small visitor centre where a tiny exhibition showed the kind of artefacts excavated here and on display in the closed museum. The majority of the visitors had arrived for a performance in Spanish about the Caliphate for which I had tried and failed to get a ticket, so I decided to wander down through the ruins – nearly tripping and injuring myself on more than one occasion – all the way to what was once the front of the complex, where visitors would have stood in awe at the spectacular Bab al-Sudda, or Gate of the Threshold. Featuring no less than fourteen giant arches and a central gate with a balcony above, this was the 'symbolic and ceremonial entrance' that once ran along the road that led all the way to the city of Córdoba. The arcade's huge red and white horseshoe arches had but one purpose, to impress. At one point, Abdu'r Rahman III apparently had the entire four miles of road from Córdoba to the new city lined with soldiers to receive a foreign delegation, of which he received many here from Byzantium, Castile, Catalonia and Germany. At the grand arched gates, they were received by his attendants, all in stunning livery. The visitors might have then watched a military exercise or a recitation composed for the occasion by one of the talented court poets, before being presented with rare and valuable books, luxurious clothes and fabrics, or even an exotic animal as gifts in the large square known today as Plaza de Armas, but probably referred to as a *mechouar* – the large open courtyards still seen at the front or within palaces in the Maghreb.

In the dim light of nightfall, I stood in the former mechouar, taking a few steps back to admire the four surviving arches, complete with the iconic red and white stripes synonymous with the Umayyad arch, hauntingly lit up with uplights positioned to accentuate their size and magnitude. It was at that moment I noticed the two shadowy figures of Robin and Miguel emerging from behind the pillars of one of the arches.

'Do you know how to get to the Salon?' I asked, hoping one of them spoke English.

'The Salon?' asked Robin, in perfect English, much to my relief.

'Yes, that building over there.' I pointed to the only near-complete monument in the entire complex. 'That's called the Salon of Abdu'r Rahman III, and I can't see how to get there.'

'Ah, there's a gate in the front of that, but it's under construction at the moment. You can't go there right now,' Robin explained.

'Oh no! Really?'

Robin nodded.

I was gutted.

Every single time I had visited the site, the Salon had been closed, and I had been hoping tonight that was going to change. Less than 10 per cent of the actual city has been excavated. The efforts since 1911 have been slow and laboured, with the Salon one of the few structures still standing, and believed to have once housed the most ostentatious of the palace features: a mammoth bowl of mercury, so finely balanced that when it was gently rocked, sunlight bounced off the liquid element, throwing shards of light onto the walls to enthral, impress and awe those awaiting the Caliph. Another such feature, brought back from Constantinople by one of Abdu'r Rahman's Christian diplomats, Recemundo, the Bishop of Elvira, known as *Rabi ibn Zayd* in Arabic, was a green onyx fountain adorned with human figures. It is also said that some of the palace halls were made from mesmerizing sheets of crystal and others from thin, translucent sheets of marble. No expense was spared in the new Caliph's capital, reportedly built by 10,000 workers, who used 3,400 marble columns and materials as luxuriously varied as gold, silver, ivory, ebony and alabaster. It was like nothing ever seen in Europe, not even in antiquity.

I thanked Robin for her information and seeing how young

they looked – early twenties – asked what had brought them to the ruins late at night.

'He lives here . . . We live here and I've never been.'

'You both live here, in Córdoba?' I asked.

'Not in Córdoba, in a village about thirty minutes away.'

Robin explained that Miguel was a local Andalusian and they had met when Robin's family moved from the Netherlands to the Andalusian countryside after her mother found a farmhouse on Facebook that she really liked and turned it into a B&B. The move hadn't been easy though, as they arrived just before Covid to find themselves in rural Spain, detached from the closest village, where everyone spoke Spanish and they didn't.

'The first year or so was very hard, I had no friends here and it was very lonely . . .'

Robin explained that she was now learning Spanish, which is why she was translating for Miguel, who didn't speak English. We were now wandering through the upper gardens, where a cool breeze rustled the leaves of the small trees, and in the distance a couple of dogs could be heard barking. I asked Robin if she had visited the Mezquita, and what she thought. She had been twice, she said, and was impressed: the tombs, the ancient bibles. But what did she make of the Islamic parts?

'Most of the arches are like this,' said Robin, pointing to a series of three Umayyad arches that had been reconstructed in what was called the House of Ja'far, home to some of the most ornate decorations of all the residential dwellings in Madinah az-Zahra. This gave rise to the hypothesis that it was where one of the later caliphs' *hajib* – court chamberlain – Ja'far might have lived.

'And on the walls, there are still Islamic inscriptions.'

'And Miguel, what does he make of the idea that Spain was ruled by Muslims and had a Caliph?' I asked.

'I mean, I've tried to talk to him about a few things to do with Islam, but he does not really understand Islam,' said Robin, not asking Miguel the question I had asked.

'There's also not much around here, there's history but not a lot of Muslims, whereas in the Netherlands there is a lot, so I'm used to it,' continued Robin. 'I think we have one Muslim family in our village, and they own the kebab shop!'

She laughed.

Interestingly, Spain and the Netherlands have a very similar percentage of Muslims: 4 and 5 per cent respectively, with the Netherlands just edging it. But being a much smaller country, with a population density more than four times that of Spain, encountering Muslims, even in rural Netherlands, is far more likely than in Spain. This exposure – Robin had lots of Muslim friends and had recently dated a Muslim Lebanese guy – meant she was far more familiar with the religion.

'I was talking to him about all these things, like halal meat, and he was like, "What is that?"' she laughed.

'What's really crazy,' I said, when we had both stopped chuckling, 'is he lives right next to one of the most important Islamic sites in Europe.'

Robin nodded.

'Which way do you go?' I asked, staring at several arrows pointing in different directions.

'Don't worry, he knows, he's been many times,' said Robin, following Miguel, who, seeing the confusion on my face, urged us to follow him along the ruins of a street where, once upon a time, according to al-Maqqari, the 'throng of soldiers, pages, eunuchs and slaves, of all nations and religions, sumptuously attired in robes of silk and brocade', or 'the crowds of judges, *katibs* [scribes], theologians and poets' would have wandered 'with becoming gravity'.

'Have you been before?' I asked Robin.

'Here? No, I've not been to many of the places in Córdoba so he's taking me around.'

'Wonderful . . . does Miguel know much about the history of this place?'

Robin used her Spanish to ask Miguel, who looked a little sheepish before responding.

'No, he doesn't,' translated Robin, laughing as she did.

We were now in the ruins of the royal kitchen, and when we read the sign that told us this, all three of us moaned about feeling hungry. Like myself, Robin and Miguel had rushed to get here, and their last meal had been late in the afternoon.

It wasn't just the sciences, philosophy and medicine that the Umayyads changed for ever across Europe. They also changed music, fashion and culinary etiquette, with many of the innovations introduced to Córdoban culture by a fascinating figure called Abu al-Hasan Ali ibn Nafi, better known as Ziryab – the blackbird – who arrived, like a modern-day rockstar, brimming with ideas about the latest music, fashion and food trends from the Abbasid court in Baghdad around 822 to completely revolutionize Córdoba. Ziryab introduced eating etiquette, doing away with serving everything all at once on plain tables – as was the habit – and suggesting courses, served in a set order on tables dressed in beautiful leather covers, to be eaten with cutlery, and drink to be drunk from crystal goblets as opposed to metal ones. The meals began with a soup and ended with a sweet, with fish, meats and chicken or fowl courses accompanied by vegetables like asparagus making up the main meal in the middle – still the convention across Europe today. Ziryab, who is said to have acquired his nickname because of the colour of his skin, and the sweetness of his character and voice, had been trained by the best musical masters in the Abbasid capital, and founded his own school of music in Córdoba, where he taught boys and girls using innovative training techniques. He improved the oud (lute) by adding another pair of strings to give it greater range and delicacy, and would pluck it using the sharpened talon of an eagle, as opposed to a wooden pick, giving it heightened sensitivity, or, as some historians have suggested, a 'soul'. Ziryab is considered one of the founders of classical Andalusian music, having established the rules for the *nuba*, or *maluf* as it is known across North Africa. This important Arab musical form later became popular among Iberia's Christians and thus influenced troubadours, minstrels and medieval European music. Ziryab, whose relationship with Abdu'r Rahman II was so close that he began serving him as a kind of minister of culture, also introduced the concept of seasonal fashion and dressing differently according to the weather, like brightly coloured cotton shirts and blouses in spring and fur-lined long cloaks in winter. He encouraged better oral hygiene by bringing over deodorants and toothpaste. The historian al-Maqqari tells us that when Ziryab came to al-Andalus, the men and women would wear their hair long and parted down the middle, whereas he wore his hair short with a fringe, which quickly became all the rage, as did the shaving of men's faces and the shaping of eyebrows. He also encouraged washing hair with salt and fragrant oils to improve its condition, and it is around this time that beauty parlours first appear in the city. The story of the celebrity-like Ziryab represents how Muslim culture also revolutionized Europe domestically and socially. Al-Maqqari said of the talented polymath: no one before or after Ziryab was more 'loved or admired'.

'That's one thing I really miss about the Netherlands: all the amazing food from around the world.'

Rural Spain was not renowned for its diverse cuisine, something Robin had learned very quickly.

'Like, I want *roti*!' she laughed, explaining how she had been craving the South Asian Caribbean street food made popular in the Netherlands by migrants from Suriname, a former Dutch colony in the West Indies.

'I can't even buy the ingredients to make it here.'

I suggested the best bet would probably be in Granada, home to the largest Muslim population in Spain.

'I did not know that.'

'Yes, and it is also home to the first purpose-built mosque since the expulsion,' I added, repeating a myth I had first heard almost two decades ago, before realizing.

'No, actually, that's wrong, because the first purpose-built mosque is right here in Córdoba. Does Miguel know that Franco built a mosque, and it is here?'

PART 3: EUROPE'S CALIPHATE CULTURE

The al-Morabito mosque in the north of the city was built by the country's fascist dictator, Franco, for his little-known Muslim unit the *Guardia Mora,* or Moorish Guard, after the Spanish Civil War in the 1930s. The *Guardia Mora* emerged from Spain's Army of Africa: a field army made up of predominantly Muslim Moroccan troops established in the early twentieth century when parts of northern Morocco were under Spanish colonial rule. Considered the army's toughest troops, they were employed by the Nationalists in the fight against the Republicans and are credited for Franco's rapid advance through the country. After the war they served as mounted guards, performing mostly ceremonial and escort roles, and were given quarters at the Royal Palace of El Pardo when Franco moved his official residence to Madrid. The unit was disbanded when Morocco gained its independence in 1956.

I pulled up a picture of the mosque on my phone and showed it to Miguel. He looked blankly at the modest whitewashed square building, obscured by large palm trees. The mosque had the Caliphate's signature horseshoe-arch entrance and was topped by a small green dome. I zoomed in to show him these details and suddenly his eyes lit up.

'*Si, si!*' he said excitedly, before telling Robin that he knew the building but he hadn't known it was a mosque.

Córdoba today has a Muslim population of less than 0.2 per cent, and the mosque is located 2.5 kilometres north of Abdu'r Rahman's historical Mezquita in a nondescript green square called Jardines de le Marced. Every time I have prayed there, it has been in a congregation numbering no more than four or five people. The al-Morabito mosque was on none of the tourist trails and visited by none of the guides. The first mosque built in Spain since the Inquisition just wasn't that important. With neither Córdoba nor Spain making a fuss about a monument that to Miguel was indistinguishable from any other historical building featuring the iconic Caliphate signature horseshoe arch, I wasn't surprised he didn't know it was a mosque. Like the geometric 'Moorish' star pattern we now see across the Muslim world in mosques from London to Indonesia, the arch was also intrinsically Iberian. So much of what I saw as Islamic architecture, Miguel simply saw as his very own, Andalusian, culture. I was warmed by this but also saddened that he was embracing it as something disconnected from his Muslim heritage.

We passed some security guards who did their best not to look bored; one or two had been sneakily scrolling their phones and quickly pushed them back into their pockets when they saw us approaching. We all agreed it couldn't be much fun standing around in semi-darkness late into the evening while a handful of tourists milled around, tripping over ancient tree roots and ruins as they tried to work out which direction they were meant to go in. We could hear a bit of a commotion and looked up to see a figure dressed as one of the caliphs high up in a part of the ruins, addressing an audience in Spanish in a booming voice.

'I think he's meant to be Abdu'r Rahman III,' I said, as we craned our necks to see what appeared to be the end of the performance, in which the Caliph, in glamorous robes and a turban, swooshed this way, then that, before the audience clapped enthusiastically.

'It's weird that they just forgot about this place!' Robin said, as we continued to follow the arrows.

In truth, it wasn't actually that unusual – it had happened all over the world, from Angkor Wat in Cambodia to the lost Mayan cities of Central America, and often, as well as being neglected, the ancient cities were looted for building materials. Started by Abdu'r Rahman III and finished during the reign of his son, al-Hakam II, Madinah az-Zahra lasted a mere seventy-four years before it was razed to the ground in 1009 during the Caliphate's *fitna*, or civil war. Al-Hakam II was succeeded by his only son, the eleven-year-old Hisham II, which saw his top adviser and the Caliph's chamberlain, Muhammad ibn Abdullah ibn Abu Amir, better known as al-Mansur – the Victorious – grab power to become the *de facto* ruler. Al-Mansur's 'reign' was the start of a period of bitter rivalry and in-fighting that would tear the Caliphate asunder as Umayyads and chamberlains fought for control of the crumbling polity, while also contending with claimants from North Africa. Between 976, when al-Hakam II died, and the overthrow of the last Umayyad Caliph, Hisham III in 1031, no fewer than seven Umayyad and five Hammudid – a North African Arab dynasty – caliphs tried and failed to hold on to the reins of Europe's first and only Caliphate.

When it was dismantled, by Berber mercenaries brought over from North Africa by al-Mansur, the job was comprehensive. Parts of the palace and the city have been found all over Spain and even as far away as Rabat in Morocco. When Córdoba fell two centuries later, the Christians used Madinah az-Zahra and what remained as a quarry for sourcing building material right up to the nineteenth century.

'There are probably houses all around here with bits of Madinah az-Zahra in their walls,' I said, 'You should check yours!'

This made Robin laugh.

The climb was steeper now, as we entered the last sections of the ruins, leading us back up to the visitor centre and the bus stop. My breathing was noticeably heavier, while Robin and Miguel, both at most half my age, took the steep steps in their stride. As we got close to the entrance, Miguel spotted the bus, and the three of us made a sprint for it. Missing it would mean sitting around waiting for anything up to thirty minutes for the next one.

'Whoever gets there first, tell them to wait,' I said, knowing full well it was not going to be me.

Fortunately, the bus driver was the same friendly one that had brought us up earlier and took pity on my overweight, middle-aged self, waiting until I got through the double doors, before shutting them behind me.

For most historians of al-Andalus, the end of Madinah az-Zahra, in 1009, was *really* the end of the Caliphate, for this was when the unity of al-Andalus disintegrated and we enter what is known as the period of the taifas, or 'parties', with around thirty separate political units emerging. These taifas were split broadly into those controlled by Berbers, Slavs and Andalusians (Muslims of Arab and Iberian stock). The Berbers controlled much of the south coast from the Guadalquivir to Granada, with the most prominent dynasty there being the Zirids; the Slavs took coastal towns in the east like Almería and Valencia; while the strongest Andalusian power was in Seville, under the Abbadids, who controlled the territories to the west and south-west, including parts of the al-Gharb, and in time Córdoba too. While this disintegration was welcomed by the Christian rulers in the north, who no longer had to pay tribute to the Caliph and could themselves now demand tribute from the Muslim taifas, the collapse of the Caliphate did not mean the end of the Caliphate culture. The memory of that great united Umayyad rule, its enlightened culture and its palatial city remained strong among the rulers of the new taifas. Inspired by this memory, many of them would try to recreate similarly brilliant versions of that culture — with varying degrees of success — in the following centuries while facing the growing Christian power and pressure from the north. Thus Madinah az-Zahra's architectural style, including the iconic Umayyad arch — the Caliphate insignia — would still be transported across al-Andalus and to places like Sicily, Malta and the Maghreb; something that continues right up to the present day.

15

The Caliphate's Jews

Córdoba, Spain

When Dom Fernando was calling himself a sultan and constructing his Muslim-inspired palace in Sintra; when Leighton was modelling his Arab Hall on Palermo's al-Aziz; and when Mrs Mable Walker-Munro of Rhinefield House brought architects over from Spain to build her husband's Alhambra smoking room, there was another nineteenth-century Romanticism vogue that rarely gets a mention, and this was the sudden surge of neo-Moorish synagogues and edifices, constructed across Europe by wealthy Jews who, after centuries of constant persecution, genocide and pogroms, felt safe enough in a post-Enlightenment Europe to express themselves. This expression was also the communication of a memory, passed down to them through the centuries, a memory of the last time Europe's Jews felt safe enough to build and express themselves in this way, a memory of a Golden Age.

Sebastián de la Obra leant on the wooden chair, his round white moustachioed face a picture of concentration, his eyes closed behind his round spectacles, as he sang with a voice far too gentle for a man of his size. His young companion, Alex – a volunteer at Casa de Sefarad – stood beside him, hands clasped in front of his wrinkled blue-flannel shirt. The duo sang a traditional Sephardic song; I did not understand the words, yet the mournful melody reminded me of David's *ghana*, the *fado* of Portugal, and the classical Andalusi music of Spain and North Africa. To my left, a South-East Asian woman in dark clothes and a bumbag leant against her husband; her eyes closed as he wrapped his arm tenderly around her, both lost in the moving performance. Climbing up the side of a pillar in the courtyard were fragrant jasmine flowers that reached the floor above, where another couple were leaning on the wooden balcony watching the performance. In total there were about ten of us, and when the singing finished, we all clapped enthusiastically. Sebastián walked straight over to me. I thanked him for a wonderful performance and he smiled, urging me to follow him. Dressed in a pair of chinos and a pristine white shirt, Sebastián had a bald head with white hair at the back and sides, reminding me of an old university professor. We went upstairs and into a room marked 'private' with floor-to-ceiling bookshelves filled with titles on the Sephardim, all neatly organized into subjects and topics. There were entire shelves dedicated to famous Sephardic Jews of the Middle Ages like Judah haLevi and Abraham ibn Ezra, while the Córdoban Maimonides – the most famous Sephardic Jew – had several shelves to himself. Other labels included 'Diaspora' and 'Judeoconversos' – the former referring to where the Sephardim now live, following their expulsion from

Sebastián de la Obra, founder of Casa de Sefarad, sings a traditional Sephardic song with a colleague in the courtyard of his museum

Iberia over 500 years ago, and the latter about those who stayed and were forced to convert to Christianity. In the middle of the room were three simple brown tables and chairs, set up for readers of the private collection.

Sebastián urged me to sit at one of them where a book holder had two titles resting on it, *The Woman Who Defied Kings: The Life and Times of Doña Gracia Nasi*, about the medieval world's first female banker — a *converso* (forced convert) who saved hundreds of other *conversos* from the Inquisition and later became one of the most important bankers for the Ottoman sultan Suleiman the Magnificent. The other was called *Maimonide-Averroès: une correspondance rêvée*, a French book that imagines a correspondence between Córdoba's two most famous Jewish and Muslim philosophers, Musa ibn Maimon and Ibn Rushd. There was a knock at the door and Ramón, our translator, walked in. He was much younger than Sebastián and had a ponytail and box beard. He also wore round spectacles.

'You have such an impressive collection,' I said to Sebastián via Ramón.

Sebastián explained that his collection was open to researchers and writers. He asked whether I was one. I explained the journey I was on.

'Are you writing a *rihla*?' Sebastián used the classical Arabic term for the genre of travel writing. We all laughed.

A retired archivist, Sebastián was born in Granada and lived for many years in Seville. I wanted to know what he was doing here in Córdoba running a museum dedicated to the memory of Iberian Jews.

'Are you Jewish?'

'Who knows?' came Sebastián's cryptic reply, before he added, 'But I now devote my life to recovering the Jewish memory in Spain.'

'Why?'

'I believe this country has a very strong debt towards the minorities . . . the black population, a debt towards the Gypsy minority. a debt towards the Hispano-Muslim memory, and a huge debt towards the Jewish memory.'

Sebastián spoke slowly and deliberately – maybe to ensure nothing was lost in translation, but I also got the impression that he wanted to be clear about his motivations. He believed Spain had a debt that needed to be repaid, and through his museum he was trying to do that: a project he began in Seville, but always knew belonged in Córdoba.

'The whole time I was aware *this* city, this quarter – the Jewish Quarter – with the synagogue across the road, the statues of Maimonides and Ibn Rushd, was the real home of Sefarad,' explained Sebastián, as he lit a cigarette.

The house his museum sits inside dates from the fourteenth century in what became the Jewish Quarter after the Christian conquest of Córdoba in 1236. Before that, during the Caliphate, the Jews lived independently outside the city walls in their own area to the north and were considered citizens with their own rights, albeit as tax-paying *dhimmi* – protected people.

'So this is not where Maimonides would have lived?' I asked.

'No,' Sebastián replied.

'What about Ibn Rushd?'

The area we were in was originally part of the Muslim medina, explained Sebastián, but who lived where was impossible to ascertain. Maimonides and Ibn Rushd were contemporaries who lived in twelfth-century Córdoba, and although Ibn Rushd would have regularly prayed at the Mezquita in the centre of the city, Maimonides would not have worshipped in its only surviving historic synagogue, across the road, as it was built in 1315, during the later Christian period.

'They read each other's works, had admiration for one another. They were both doctors and represented humanism within the Muslim and Jewish traditions, and were rejected by their orthodoxy, persecuted by their own rulers and their enemies!' Sebastián said in his pointed, deliberate style. 'It was through them, especially

Ibn Rushd, that Aristotelianism arrives to the Christian world and makes possible the Renaissance!'

Sebastián had been born in Granada, a city known as 'Granada of the Jews', so I asked why he did not create his Casa de Sefarad there.

'Because Córdoba *is* the place . . .' he began, rubbing his hairless chin, 'there is a huge memory in Granada, but the Granada of the Jews is completely gone! There is now a nineteenth-century modern neighbourhood where the Jewish Quarter used to be. There's nothing like here. This is like a "mother" Jewish Quarter and was well preserved because it was created after the Muslim period.'

Sebastián grew up in a Catholic household like most Spaniards of his generation, but was now agnostic. I wanted to know what it was like growing up in a city with the Alhambra, did he have any memories of it? A mischievous glint came to Sebastián's eyes.

'When I was young one of my favourite things to do with my friends was to sneak into the Alhambra and go swimming in the pools.'

'What?' I shrieked in astonishment.

'Yes, we used to get chased by the guards.' Sebastián laughed out loud as he recalled the fond memory.

'I think you have just become my hero!' I said, picturing a young Sebastián and his mates divebombing into the famous pool in the Alhambra's Court of the Myrtles, before being chased by an overweight – a prerequisite for the job – security guard. When we all stopped laughing, I asked again why he was running a Jewish Museum.

'Over the past five hundred years, Spanish history has denied the Jewish elements, the Muslim elements, the Gypsy elements, the black elements . . . Everything was Christian,' said Sebastián.

He believed that, over the last century, the Muslim and Gypsy memory had been recovered, mainly for commercial interests, but the Jewish one had been neglected. Ramón didn't quite agree and felt there was sincere interest in all three memories, albeit by a minority.

'In this process, the Jewish memory has a challenge – no Alhambra, no Mezquita.'

Sebastián's words reminded me of what Rosinda had said about Muslim heritage in Portugal, but I wasn't so sure.

'There is not even a Jewish minority existing in Spain, like the Gypsy one with flamenco, it is something intellectual, something you cannot touch, you cannot see, so that makes it even harder.'

It was true that Córdoba had just the one surviving synagogue, and Granada had none, but the city of Toledo boasted two magnificent Sephardic synagogues and had also become a site of mass Jewish pilgrimage.

Sebastián and Ramón believed that in recent decades the pendulum of interest had swung too far in the other direction and a romantic myth about al-Andalus had taken root. They explained that many visitors to the museum arrived with this fiction in their minds, as if that period – dubbed a Jewish Golden Age – were some kind of Utopia.

Towards the end of the ninth century, just as the Emirate of Córdoba was gaining in confidence, so too was its Arabized Jewish community. Having spent almost two centuries under Muslim rule, they not only felt safe and secure in a way they had not experienced before in Europe, but in the Arabs they also found their Semitic and, thus, poetic brethren. The constant exposure to classical Arabic poetry began to chime with the Jewish youth of Córdoba, who started to experiment and push the hitherto limited boundaries of their own Hebrew poetic tradition. They introduced Arabic rhymes and metres to their verse, something only possible because the two Semitic languages were relatives. Arab forms like the *muwashshah* and *zajal* completely revolutionized Hebrew poetry, both secular and religious, mirroring their Arab counterparts. Soon Jews across the city and al-Andalus began creating Hebrew verses on themes of love, exile, friendship, youth and drinking. So much so that visitors to the city in the tenth century might walk past a hidden courtyard in the city's Jewish quarter and hear Sephardic men reciting their verses: sometimes in a multitude of tongues (Arabic, Hebrew and Romance), or maybe while sitting along the banks of the Wadi al-Kabir or near one of the city's stunning fountains strumming an oud as they put the words to music. These verses were then repeated at courts, soirées and parties as a class of professional Jewish poets emerged unlike any other in Jewish history. These innovations saw the Sephardim effectively lay the foundations for the eventual resurrection of Hebrew as a spoken language. Until the Jewish Renaissance of Sephardim, Hebrew had been limited to scripture and worship for centuries. While the Jewish Renaissance of Iberia gave birth to many things for the Sephardim, the fact that it is also the Golden Age of Hebrew poetry might explain why it is so often romanticized.

I explained that some Muslims coming to visit the Alhambra and the Mezquita were also susceptible to this, but not all.

'Many people still don't know this history. Maybe it's visible in Spain for people like yourselves, but I travel all over the Muslim world, and many Muslims know nothing about this heritage, they wouldn't even be able to tell you who Abdu'r Rahman the First was,' I said, adding, 'It's even worse in Western Europe, the non-Muslims, most of them think Muslims arrived in Europe "yesterday", as immigrants.'

'I always tell people the main difference between medieval Christian and medieval Muslim society is that Islam from the beginning recognized the truth of the Torah and the Gospels . . . allowed [them] to exist, and to pray, that give you a little space. In the Christian space, in the Christian religion, not only for their religions, among Christian sects, there is intolerance because it is *the* Truth or nothing!' Ramón said, returning to the conversation about coexistence.

'Yes, *ahl al-kitab*,' I said, using the Arabic term to mean the 'people of The Book', who in the Qur'an are identified as followers of the Torah and the Gospels.

We agreed that's what made the Caliphate culture so special: the fact that it facilitated the Sephardic Jewish Renaissance and Golden Age; one that allowed great Jewish intellectuals, poets, writers and musicians to thrive as never before. Like Hebrew poetry,

Jewish philosophy also benefited immensely from its encounter with Islamic culture. This was down to the fact that every Sephardic Jew during this period was fluent in Arabic and therefore also had access to the huge body of ancient Greek works brought over from the East originally translated into Arabic, and thus exposed to a whole new body of philosophical literature, argumentation and theological language. This allowed them to consider old religious questions in new ways, unpick the seeming contradictions in scripture and contemplate the meaning of anthropomorphic references to God. Many of the Jewish philosophers of this period, like Solomon ibn Gabirol and Judah haLevi, often straddled both disciplines as poet-philosophers.

'Romanticism aside, they were clearly not *just* tolerated, they were able to flourish,' I said.

'Yes, but when the Muslim power is established here, the Jews are already here and they had suffered a lot under the previous regime of the Visigoths,' added Sebastián, 'to them the Muslims were not an invading enemy, but a saving force . . .'

'They were welcomed,' I added.

One of the most overlooked and denied aspects of the Muslim 'invasion' of al-Andalus by Tariq Ibn Ziyad and his (largely) Berber troops in 711 is the role of the Sephardim. In fact, some Jewish historians claim Tariq's troops also included Berber Jews, and that prior to the Muslim conquest the horribly oppressed Sephardic Jews had attempted to overthrow the Visigoths themselves, with many frequently migrating to North Africa to flee the persecution. Some have gone as far as to suggest that the Sephardim planned the conquest alongside the Muslims. What is certain is that everyone has marvelled at the speed with which the Muslims took over the former Visigothic territories. For many historians this is irrefutable evidence they had assistance from 'inside'. This theory is supported by the fact that often when Tariq and his army took a city, they felt secure in entrusting it to the local Jews – or those they brought in – who watched over the newly conquered territory, so they could move on to the next city or town. Such was the case with all four of the major Muslim towns of Seville, Córdoba, Granada and Toledo. Al-Maqqari says that after capturing Córdoba, Tariq's commander, Mugheyth ar-Rumi, 'assembled all the Jews in the city, and left them in charge of it' and that it was the same for Granada. In fact, claims the Muslim historian, 'this practice became almost general in the succeeding years; for whenever the Muslims conquered a town, it was left in the custody of Jews, with only a few Muslims'. It is therefore almost certain that whether it was a purely Muslim or mixed army that arrived on the shores of Iberia, ready to oust the Visigoths, the Jews at the very least saw this as a *most* welcome development. They would have known from their brethren the Sephardim in the newly conquered Muslim lands of North Africa that their lot under Muslim rule would be significantly improved.

'Yes, the small bourgeoisie of Granada, Córdoba and Seville – doctors, artisans, etc. – are Jews, and when the Muslims arrive this Jewish community becomes auxiliary – accomplices and helpers of this conquest,' agreed Sebastián, adding, 'The Caliphate lasted only one hundred years and it was during its period of political stability that Jewish minority gets power and influence'.

'Through people like Hasdai,' I added, referring to the tenth-century Jewish polymath of Córdoba, Hasdai ibn Shaprut.

Known as the *nasi* – Prince of the Jews – a title he was afforded after impressing Caliph Abdu'r Rahman III with his discoveries of antidotes to poison, Ibn Shaprut joined the royal court as a physician before rising up through the ranks. Learned in Hebrew, Latin and Arabic, he became one of the Caliph's most trusted diplomats and translators, playing a key role in diplomatic exchanges with rulers such as the Byzantine Emperor Constantine VII. Originally from the city of Jaén, Ibn Shaprut was the son of a wealthy Jew who had patronized Jewish scholars and paid for the construction of synagogues. This philanthropic trait and sense of communal responsibility were also strong in Ibn Shaprut, who used his position to help Jews not just in Iberia – as a patron and religious scholar – but also abroad, especially the ones facing persecution. For example, when the Byzantine Emperor Romanus I Lekapenos introduced anti-Jewish measures across his realms, Hasdai wrote to his wife, Helena, in 948, using the Caliph's diplomatic envoy and asked her to relieve his co-religionists of the oppressive laws, while reminding the empress that his own Muslim ruler was highly tolerant of her fellow Christians in al-Andalus. In another instance, which reinforces Manuel's 'barbaric' assertions about the Franks, Ibn Shaprut wrote to defend the Jews of Toulouse against a humiliating local tradition. Every year on Easter Eve, the town's Jews were commanded to arrive at the gates of its cathedral with thirty pounds of wax to be used for church candles. Upon handing this donation over to the bishop, they would each be promptly slapped as hard as possible by him. It is not clear if Hasdai was successful in defending the humiliated Jews, but the fact that the Sephardim had their very own 'Prince', one with the political leverage of a Caliph, was not only a cause célèbre but essential for the manifestation of a Jewish Renaissance.

'That situation then survives into the taifa kingdoms. Especially in Granada, where there is a moment for about fifty years when a group of Jews have so much political power and influence, because of the Emir's reliance on them, that they are the *real* rulers of the Emirate, and we see a backlash, a pogrom by the Muslims, and this is the beginning of the decline of the Jewish communities in Muslim Spain . . . but there is no denying that the Golden Age of Spanish Judaism is under al-Andalus rule and it's to do with that stability,' Sebastián said.

The Jewish Golden Age of Sephardim was a period of extraordinary cultural, intellectual and economic flourishing for the Jewish community of Muslim Iberia. Spanning roughly the tenth to the twelfth centuries, it is often split into two distinct zeniths. The first was during the Caliphate of Córdoba, which produced luminous polymaths like Hasdai Ibn Shaprut, Rabbi Musa ibn Maimun – Maimonides, the Aristotelian philosopher and physician Judah haLevi, neo-Platonic philosopher and poet Solomon ibn Gabirol – all of whom produced literary masterpieces still celebrated today. The second zenith is under the Zirid and Nasrid rulers of Granada, when figures such as Samuel ibn Naghrillah (Shmuel Hanagid), who served as both a vizier and a military commander, and his son Joseph ibn Naghrillah not only held high political positions but also contributed to the vibrancy of Jewish scholarly and literary life. The two zeniths are most poetically described by the great twelfth-century Sephardic historian, philosopher and martyr, Abraham Ibn Daud: 'in the days of Hasdai the Nasi they began to chirp, and in the days of Samuel the Nagid they sang out loud'.

Even in the periods around these zeniths, the Jewish community of Iberia flourished and was able to actively participate in aspects of social, political and economic life it had previously been excluded from. As a result prominent Jewish figures took up influential positions as court physicians, diplomats and advisers, and Jewish communities thrived economically, benefiting from trade and commerce, facilitated by their integration into the broader Islamic commonwealth. This era of prosperity and intellectual achievement left an enduring legacy that influenced subsequent Jewish generations and helped shape the cultural and intellectual landscape of medieval Europe, for during this Golden Age in Iberia, just as in Sicily, Jewish scholars and thinkers were instrumental in the transmission and development of knowledge to Christian Europe, with the likes of Hasdai playing a pivotal role in translating important medical and scientific texts into Latin and Hebrew.

We had been speaking for almost an hour, and I was yet to visit the museum. So I asked what they thought of the decision by Portugal and Spain to offer citizenship to historical Sephardic Jews, in an attempt to 'heal centuries-old wounds' – the guilt Sebastián also felt – and why the 'wounds' of the Iberian Muslims were overlooked.

Sebastián picked up another cigarette and Ramón opened another window, bringing the noise from the street into the room. After pointing out that he had previously campaigned for the plight of the *moriscos* – Muslims forcibly converted to Christianity and expelled in the sixteenth century – to be recognized, Sebastián first suggested the Sephardic identity was more distinct: they had retained many traditions and even the Ladino language, and kept their genealogy alive.

'For them it is a pillar of this memory,' he said.

I understood and had read about how obsessive the Sephardim in exile had been about their roots and traditions, but I also knew just how obsessive Arabs were about *their* ancestry – a Semitic trait – and felt tracing their Iberian lineage would not be too difficult either.

'*Si, si, si!*' agreed Sebastián.

For him, though, the tradition was much bigger among the Sephardim, but he agreed the offer of Iberian citizenship should be a right for the *moriscos* too.

Ramón and I felt other factors were at play. I believed it was to do with the Islamophobia intrinsic to the historical European psyche, while Ramón felt it was about the popular image of the Jewish and Muslim migrant, suggesting that if *moriscos* were all Gulf sheikhs – who would not be a drain on the economy – there would be no problems.

'The image we have in the West today of Islam is split into two parts: we have poor immigrants, possible terrorists, and then rich people that can buy a football team that are not terrorists!' he said.

I laughed at how succinct and accurate his summary was. Sebastián conceded that the origin of the law was to appease the Jewish sentiment, then glanced at his watch. The expulsion of the *moriscos* was about expelling the defeated 'enemy' (they are not us), he explained. Whereas there was never a war against the Jews and so they were part of us. I again hear 'guilt', and then the church bells from the former minaret of the Great Mosque of Córdoba telling me it is time to leave.

After thanking Sebastián, Ramón and I stepped outside, and he offered to give me a quick tour upstairs before leaving me to explore the rest myself. We started in a room with dark-green walls, and a number of Sephardic artefacts in small red display cases, with several foldable chairs underneath ready for sitting on.

'The synagogue is across the street, but this is also the synagogue,' Ramón said.

I looked at him blankly.

He explained how they have an actual 'Sefer Torah', a gift from the Jewish community of Marrakech, right here, making it a functioning synagogue that can be used by anyone outside the museum's opening hours.

The ornate architecture of Córdoba's La Sinagoga resembles that seen in the Alhambra. Built in 1315, the synagogue was forgotten for centuries and only rediscovered by chance in 1884

We wandered into another room.

'The most important room for me, the Inquisition room. Here we have all the Inquisition victims in Córdoba . . . *moriscos* and some Protestants, but ninety-five per cent were crypto-Jews.'

The room, Ramón explained, makes clear the central role the Inquisition played in the construction of the Spanish identity.

'The Inquisition *is* the first common institution we have in Spain. Spain has been built around the idea that Spanish means Catholic and —'

'And anti-Muslim, anti-Jewish!' I interjected.

'I would even say anti-Jewish more than anti-Muslim,' Ramón said.

Ramón believed this was down to an ancient dislike for Jews by Christians because they had not accepted Christ as the Messiah, whereas the Muslim challenge was a political one. Again, I wasn't so sure, but then I wasn't Jewish and clearly felt the anti-Muslim sentiments more acutely.

'I think maybe equal . . . when you look at Matamoros,' I said.

Ramón paused, either because he had forgotten about this key figure of Spanish Catholicism — someone whose entire identity is constructed around killing Muslims. 'Matamoros' literally means 'Moor slayer', i.e. 'Muslim killer'.

'Yes, but that is ahh . . . eh . . . a military challenge,' he finally said, somewhat hesitantly, making me wonder how carefully he had considered the implications of an actual Companion of Christ being reframed as a 'Muslim killer' by the medieval Spanish Catholic Church.

Matamoros was the nickname given to Spain's patron saint, Saint James — one of Jesus's twelve Apostles — whose remains, according to legend, were brought in a stone boat from the Holy Land to Galicia, in north-west Spain, a century after Muslims had conquered almost all Iberia. He was dubbed Santiago Matamoros — 'Saint James the Moor Slayer' — for miraculously appearing in the mythical Battle of Clavijo, where he arrived on the back of a white horse complete with banner to help the Christians defeat the Muslims. The mythology of this cult, conceived towards the end of the twelfth century — four centuries after the made-up battle was supposed to have taken place — was also the first time another powerful Islamophobic myth appears in

Spanish Catholic lore. This is the Tribute of 100 Virgins the King of Asturias was forced to send to the Umayyad rulers every year: fifty of noble blood and fifty of common lineage. Both Matamoros and the Tribute of 100 Virgins are complete fabrications: one depicts the Muslims as barbaric and only worthy of slaughter and the other sees them as licentious sexual predators – a dual slur repeated throughout European history and still popular in tabloids across the continent today. Matamoros was successfully touted as the patron saint of Spain in the seventeenth century; by then the two myths had become central pillars of the *Reconquista* narrative and remain powerful in the Spanish national cultural memory. Matamoros is also a popular surname among Latin communities across the globe, as too Matajudios (Jew killer), albeit to a lesser degree.

'Religion became the glue for this country. All foreign policy would be based on ideological religious lines,' Ramón explained.

I nodded in agreement.

My time with Ramón was up, and after a quick explanation of the layout downstairs as we both descended, we shook hands and said goodbye.

I wandered through an exhibit about the traditional Sephardic kitchen, before meeting in another room some famous Sephardic women, like Emma Lazarus, the nineteenth-century American poet who helped Jewish refugees fleeing pogroms in Eastern Europe. It was in this room that I met Susan, a middle-aged American woman from Detroit.

'What brings you here, the rain?' I said, mocking the unusual Córdoban weather we were experiencing.

Susan laughed, before telling me in a thick American accent that her husband's family are Spanish and they were here for a wedding.

'Hey,' said a tall clean-shaven man wearing a T-shirt with a print of what appeared to be Van Gogh's famous *Starry Night*, but with the silhouette of the cypress tree replaced by Seville's Giralda bell tower. I shook Antonio's hand and tried not to wince as he squeezed mine to within an inch of its life.

'So,' continued Susan, 'we used to live here and were on our way up to Madrid and –'

'You used to live in Córdoba?'

'No, Madrid,' said Antonio.

'We always wanted to visit and never did . . . I mean, I'm Jewish, so I already know all this horrible history,' Susan said.

'You're Sephardic?'

'No, Ashkenazi . . . but Antonio thinks he was Sephardic at one point.'

I turned to her husband.

'Really?'

'Yeah . . .'

Antonio explained that the toponomy of his surname came from a word that meant 'cherry tree' and that his family had traced it all the way back to the Inquisition, when there is a gap and a link to the *marrano* – crypto-Jewish – community, but establishing the strength of the link required more research. I asked the obvious.

'Have you ever considered a DNA test or anything?'

'No, no.' Antonio shook his head emphatically.

'He won't,' Susan said, 'he's afraid people are gonna use it against him.'

I looked at them both, not quite sure what that meant.

'There's no telling this is not gonna happen again,' Antonio said grimly.

I agreed with him on that front. We all felt the direction of global politics and the rise in xenophobia in our respective countries suggested a repeat of something like this might not be as impossible as once imagined.

'Given your potential roots and your wife being Jewish, this must be very emotional for you?'

'It is . . . it is quite emotional . . .' Antonio said, looking away.

'Yes,' said Susan in a solemn tone.

We walked out of the room about Sephardic women in silence. I waited for them to speak, and eventually Susan began telling me how this was their first trip away together since having children. The children were now in their twenties.

'You remember I said it could happen again?' Antonio was standing in front of a glass cabinet, his face even more solemn than earlier. The cabinet contained a facsimile of the Sarajevo Haggadah. Above it on two blue tapestries was the amazing story of how a Bosnian Muslim scholar, Derviš Korkut, had saved the priceless scripture from the clutches of the Nazis in 1941, and how Korkut and his wife had also saved a Sephardic Jewish girl called Mira Papo by disguising her as a Muslim girl, Amina. I knew the story well, and that Korkut was posthumously honoured by Yad Vashem in Jerusalem – the World Holocaust Remembrance Center. In the final paragraph, the tapestry revealed the story had come full circle during the 1990s Balkan Wars when Serbian forces were ethnically cleansing Muslims in Kosovo, where Korkut's daughter and her family lived. Upon presenting the letter they had received from Yad Vashem, they were offered refuge in Israel, where they were greeted by Papo's son.

I told Antonio and Susan that I had written about Korkut in my previous book, and explained that one of the reasons Sephardim survived in Europe was that when the Catholic Monarchs were forcibly converting, killing or expelling the Jews during the fifteenth and sixteenth centuries, the Ottoman Empire welcomed them with open arms. In fact, Sultan Bayezid II reportedly sent an entire naval fleet to pick up the Jewish refugees and resettled them across Ottoman territories. This was at a time when virtually nowhere else in Europe was safe for Jews, barring isolated parts of Italy and Germany.

As if echoing Ibn Daud's sentiments of Renaissance-era Sephardim, a German Rabbi, Isaac Zarfati, who had migrated to Adrianople (Edirne), wrote a letter to his Ashkenazi brethren, in which he begged them to leave anti-Semitic (Western) Europe, that 'Turkey is a land where nothing is lacking, and where, if you will, all shall yet be well with you . . . Here every man may dwell at peace under his own vine and fig tree.'

Thus, over the course of Europe's Muslim history, from the eighth century, when Muslims established the first European Emirate in Iberia, right up until the collapse of the Ottoman Empire in 1922, the safest places in Europe for the continent's most persecuted religious community, the Jews, were usually in Muslim Europe.

After bidding farewell to my American friends, I passed a display on my way out of the museum called 'Genealogy of Persecution', which had three phrases mapping the treatment of Jews in Europe on it: 'you cannot live among us as Jews' (Europe, fifth century); 'you cannot live among us' (Spain, fifteenth century); 'you cannot live' (Europe, twentieth century). The interpretation of Europe's Jewish history on display summed it all up. Entirely Christian-centric, it completely neglected the Sephardic experience in Muslim Europe, which was astonishing given that that was exactly the culture the museum was celebrating. I made a mental note to ask Sebastián to add one more sentence: 'you are the honoured people of The Book' (Muslim Europe, eighth to twentieth centuries).

Every time I have stepped into the small La Sinagoga, Córdoba's only ancient Sephardic synagogue, I have been overcome by the same sensation: that I could just as easily have been standing in the Hall of the Ambassadors inside the Alhambra's Nasrid Palace. The synagogue is modest in size, hinting at the possibility that it was a private family one. The upper walls are covered with the same stunning geometric star-like motifs, synonymous with the Nasrid Palace in Granada: the same vegetal patterns and the iconic muqarnas archways. The only difference is that whereas the Nasrid's inscribed verses are from the Qur'an or Arabic poetry in stylized Kufic or naskh script, here they are words from the Torah in Hebrew.

Built in the Jewish year 5075 – AD 1315 – the synagogue became the St Quiteria hospital for sufferers from rabies after the Jewish expulsion. In 1588 it became the property of a shoemakers' corporation, which turned it into a small chapel, with the discovery of its original purpose only made in 1884, when part of the mortared walls fell down to reveal the stunning plasterwork behind. The building was declared a national monument the following year, when restoration work began.

I craned my neck along with half a dozen others to stare up at the beautifully framed women's balcony above the entrance to the main worship space. It really was uncanny how much the design resembled the Nasrid Palace. As I stared, a memory from my last visit to the synagogue with Swiss friends, a couple who were both retired radio journalists, came back to me.

'They were the same people!' joked my friend, Felix Schneider.

'It looks like the style you see all over Morocco,' Gabriella Kagi had said upon seeing the mesmeric artistry of the synagogue.

I could see why the Moroccan Sephardim gifted Sebastián a Torah to create a living synagogue so close by. Even as a Muslim, this felt a familiar and welcoming space; I can only imagine just how it would have felt to them. Every single one of the four walls had Hebrew script – mostly words from the Book of Psalms. I stood in front of the east wall, equivalent to the Muslim mihrab, and the direction of Jewish prayer towards Jerusalem – a direction Muslims shared with them for the first fourteen years – where, on a tall dark cube-like plinth, there sat a gold menorah, the only item in the entire structure. The east wall also revealed that the builder of the synagogue was a Yishaq Moheb, son of Efraim Wadawa. Although it was no longer a functioning synagogue, a Jewish service was held here, for the first time since the expulsion, in 1935 to mark the 800th birthday of Maimonides. The event saw the renaming of the square the synagogue is in as Tiberias Square – the city where the great polymath is buried. With little else to do in the tiny space measuring 6.5 by 7 metres, and the number of visitors growing, I decided it was time to go and quickly say hello to him.

I turned right out of the synagogue and headed south into the small adjacent square, where atop a sandstone plinth – wearing long flowing robes and a turban, a book in his right hand – sat Maimonides. Like Córdoba's synagogue, he was dressed in 'Islamic attire' and looked every bit an al-Andalusian. Even the inscription on the plinth was in Arabic – the language he wrote most of his work in – just beneath his pointed left shoe, worn and whitened from decades of being rubbed by tourists for good luck.

The statue of the twelfth-century Córdoban rabbi Musa ibn Maimun, or Maimonides, near the synagogue of Córdoba

16

The Caliphate Mosque

Córdoba, Spain

I could see Youssef squinting in the early morning sun, the light bouncing off his thin-rimmed glasses and through his curly black beard. He had his head tilted back as he tried to decipher the Arabic on the exterior wall of Europe's one and only Caliphate Mosque, Córdoba's Mezquita-Catedral. The ancient Arabic could barely be seen around the inner semi-circle of the iconic red and white Umayyad horseshoe arch of what was once one of the many gates into the mosque's Courtyard of the Oranges. I had met Youssef the day before while we were listening to classical Andalusian music inside the Torre de la Calahorra's Museo Vivo de al-Andaluz, or Living Museum of al-Andalus. Youssef had told me the music had the same rhythms as that which he listened to in Morocco.

'We actually call it Andalus music,' he had said, before explaining that the music remains very popular in Fez, the artistic and intellectual capital of his country, and home to what many believe is the oldest university or higher-learning institute in the world, the University of al-Qarawiyyin, said to have been founded as a mosque and madrasa at the end of the ninth century by Fátima bint Muhammad al-Fihriya al-Qurashiyya, just before the city and other parts of northern Morocco became absorbed into the Caliphate of Córdoba at its zenith under Abdu'r Rahman III. During this time the Caliph sponsored the building of the mosque's minaret, along with the minaret of the nearby Jama'a al-Andalusiyyin, or the Andalusian Mosque, believed to have been founded by Fatima's sister, Maryam. The University of al-Qarawiyyin's alumni also point to strong ties with al-Andalus; among them are the great geographer Ibn Khaldun, who spent time at the court of the Nasrids of Granada, the mystic Ibn Arabi of Murcia, the historian al-Maqqari and even the Córdoban Jewish philosopher Maimonides. It was amazing to realize that while other visitors as well as me had imagined we were listening to the music of a distant European past, Youssef was listening to his living ancestral music, still played across the Maghreb today.

The Torre de la Calahorra, which sits on the other side of the Guadalquivir with spectacular views towards the Mezquita and old Córdoba, was originally built by the Almohads as a watchtower to protect the bridge it overlooks but is now an interpretation centre for medieval al-Andalus. Each floor evokes a different aspect of the culture and society that existed under the emirs and caliphs of Córdoba, which at times fall foul of the romanticism Sebastián and Ramón had alluded to. Youssef, who is doing a Master's degree in Cologne, is from Tangier, one of the places the Iberian Muslims and later the *moriscos* ended up in. Morocco as a whole is often viewed as the inheritor of that Muslim culture, especially its art, architecture and music. I had asked Youssef what it felt like seeing the exhibition inside the Torre.

'I feel like I'm in Morocco!' Youssef said, before adding, 'It was the same when I went to Granada: it was like I am in Fez or Marrakech. Same art, same architecture . . . I feel like it is part of Morocco, like it is more Moroccan than Spanish.'

Wandering around the Torre's exhibits alongside a modern-day 'Moor', someone whose ancestors may well have come from Iberia and would have certainly lived among those who did, had been fascinating. We had begun the tour by listening to the wisdom of four great Andalusians, the mystic Ibn Arabi, the great philosophers Ibn Rushd and Maimonides, and the thirteenth-century translation king, Alfonso X of Castile and León. They had been created as slightly eerie animatronic figurines who came to life one by one.

A young Ibn Arabi's mystical insight momentarily stumps the great philosophical mind of Ibn Rushd – a nod to a famous meeting between the two great Andalusians. Ibn Arabi, who is considered one of the greatest mystics to have ever lived, was still a 'beardless youth' when the great philosopher asked to meet him. What followed was a fascinatingly bizarre interaction few people understand and hints at the elevated plane the two minds manoeuvred on.

'Yes,' said Ibn Rushd, greeting Ibn Arabi with a smile as he noted the young mystic had understood.

'No,' Ibn Arabi said.

This caused the great philosopher to retreat a little, and his colour changed.

'What solution have you found as a result of mystical illumination and divine inspiration?' Ibn Rushd asked, before adding, 'Does it coincide with what is arrived at by speculative thought?'

'Yes and no,' Ibn Arabi replied.

He then explained what he meant.

'Between the Yea and the Nay the spirits take their flight beyond matter, and the necks detach themselves from their bodies.'

The explanation made Ibn Rushd turn pale and tremble with

The statue of Ibn Rushd, the great twelfth-century Córdoban philosopher and physician known as Averroes in the West, outside the medieval gates of Córdoba

fear, muttering, '*La hawla wa la quwwata illa billah.*' This means, 'There is no power save from God', something all Muslims recite when experiencing extreme fear, and told Ibn Arabi that the great philosopher had understood the allusion.

We had also heard how Maimonides experienced both enlightened and conservative aspects of medieval Muslim culture after the 'second Moses' – as he is known to many Jews – was forced to flee his birthplace for Fez, when the (initially) intolerant Almohads arrived. Finally, we heard how Alfonso X, known as 'The Wise', replicated what he knew to have taken place in Umayyad Córdoba, (Muslim and Arab-Norman) Palermo and Abbasid Baghdad, by establishing the Toledo School of Translators. Employing numerous translators, Alfonso made the works of classical Greek authors and Muslim intellectuals (both local and from the East), like Plato, Aristotle, Ptolemy, al-Kindi and, of course, Ibn Rushd, available to the rest of Christian Europe – something he was doing in tandem with Frederick II to pave the way for the future Christian Renaissance.

We critiqued the imagined scenes of Muslim Córdoban life; appreciated just how far ahead medieval Muslim minds like Albucasis were; laughed at the exoticizing of Muslim women; peered through the forest of pillars of the scaled model of the Mezquita at its peak; and saw how worshippers might have sat in the synagogue – all to a backdrop of classical Andalusian music.

It had been a real privilege to hang out with someone who felt a direct and unbroken connection to the heritage we were seeing, and so I asked Youssef to join me for a visit to the Mezquita as well.

When the Pakistani scholar and poet Muhammad Iqbal visited the Mezquita in 1932, he became the first Muslim in almost 700 years to pray in the iconic Mezquita-Catedral. Black-and-white photos show a 55-year-old moustachioed Iqbal kneeling on a patterned prayer mat and wearing a fez hat in front of the mosque's glorious mihrab. In another picture he is standing beneath its horseshoe arch looking pensive as he leans on his walking stick. It was an emotional and powerful visit for the ageing Muslim polymath, who became so overwhelmed by the magnitude and

PART 3: EUROPE'S CALIPHATE CULTURE

Restored outer walls of Europe's one and only Caliphate Mosque, Córdoba's Mezquita-Catedral, where Muslims began praying from the early eighth century

significance of Europe's first great mosque – its only Caliphate mosque – and the culture and society it once served that it inspired him to pen one of his greatest poems, *Masjid-e-Qartiba*, an elegant meditation on love using the mosque as an object of that love. In the poem, considered a masterpiece, he says the 'Haram' of Córdoba owes its existence to Love. By using the term 'haram', Iqbal was elevating the Great Mosque to the realms of Masjid al-Aqsa in Jerusalem, Masjid an-Nabawi in Madinah and the Masjid al-Haram in Makkah: in doing so he might well be accused of being drunk on his 'love' for the Mezquita-Catedral, maybe even blaspheming for equating it – like the Cypriots and Hala Sultan – with the three holiest mosques in Islam, each with an explicit link to the Prophet Muhammad and the founding narrative of the faith. But these were words of a great intellect, who had the soul of a great poet. I had visited Córdoba so many times in the past, armed with all the literary outpourings Western writers had to offer, from travel narratives by Jason Webster to histories written by W. Montgomery Watt and John Gill, but none of them understood what it meant to step into this space as a Muslim. How could they? Only the words of Iqbal came close.

As we entered the Courtyard of the Oranges, to our right was the mosque's minaret, now the church's bell tower, from which the ninth-century local polymath Abbas ibn Firnas first launched himself in an attempt to fly using a kind of primitive hang-glider. The experiment failed, and somehow Ibn Firnas walked away unscathed. Known in the Latin world as Armen Firman, Ibn Firnas would eventually achieve flight, at the ripe old age of seventy, when dressed in a bird-like suit, made from silk and eagle feathers, he would fly for around ten minutes from the top of a hill, close to Abdu'r Rahman I's summer palace, ar-Rusafa, to the north-west of the city. Born in about 810, Ibn Firnas was a typical Córdoban who was also a poet, astrologer, musician, astronomer and engineer, and almost certainly the first human being to experience flight, more than 600 years before the Renaissance man Leonardo da Vinci merely drew a similar contraption in his famous notebook, and over a thousand years before the Wright brothers took to the air. Ibn Firnas also invented a technique for making colourless glass, a number of glass planispheres, corrective lenses, a kind of primitive metronome, a water clock and a process for cutting rock crystal. Had he been born 500 years later a Christian in Spain, he might also have been revered today as a Renaissance man.

Approaching the entrance to the Mezquita, I told Youssef about my experience on a previous visit, with a group of childhood friends from the East End of London, all of South Asian descent and all visibly Muslim.

'The security guard looked a little panicked when he saw us walking up to the entrance,' I said, making Youssef laugh.

'How many of you were there?' he asked.

'There were five of us.'

'Only five? And he was scared?!'

'Look around, how many of us are here . . .' I said, pointing to the handful of late-middle-aged white tourists milling around beneath the orange trees, each planted in its own neat little circular bed, and linked to others via smart irrigation channels. Like us, they had read their guidebook and picked up on the tip to save money by entering the Mezquita free of charge before morning mass.

'He kept telling us we couldn't pray in there. We told him we didn't intend to,' I said, 'but it was like he didn't believe us and kept repeating his point, and wouldn't let us pass until one of my more conservative friends got a tad agitated and said, "We don't pray in churches!"'

'What did he say?'

'"Okay!" I think he was happy we considered it a church and not a mosque,' I laughed.

Youssef shook his head in dismay. We were now near the front of the queue.

'Musulmano?' asked the security guard as soon he caught sight of us.

I ignored him and smiled at Youssef.

'Muslim?' he said, assuming my silence suggested I didn't know what 'Musulmano' meant.

'Yes,' I replied in the same tone I use when running out of patience with my five-year-old.

Youssef and I both knew exactly what was coming. The security guard peered over his glasses to make sure there was eye contact.

'No pray here, no pray inside!' he said.

This was a very different welcome to the one Muhammad Iqbal received. Somehow the Indo-Pakistani mystic had convinced the authorities to let him pray in there. Things had changed a lot since the 1930s.

With only fifty minutes left before the start of morning mass, I took Youssef straight to the Mezquita's *pièce de résistance*.

'This . . .' I said, pausing for dramatic effect, and waiting until

26. One of the stone lions that stood in the courtyard of the fourteenth-century Maristán of Granada, now kept in the Museum of Alhambra.

27. The mihrab of the Almohad's Tinmal Mosque in Tinmel, Morocco, framed by the dynasty's distinct muqarnas-style arch, which are seen in historic monuments across Iberia and North Africa today.

28. The minbar of the Kutubiyya Mosque in Marrakech, Morocco, was produced in Córdoba, Spain, in the early twelfth century by the Almoravid amir Ali ibn Yusuf.

29. Close-up of an Almohad manuscript page featuring geometric motifs and gold decoration like that seen in the architecture of Al Andalus.

30. A detailed nineteenth-century engraving of a mass burning of heretics (Muslims and Jews) at the stake by the Spanish Inquisition.

31. Nineteenth-century British artist Edward Long's painting 'The Moorish Proselytes of Archbishop Ximenes', illustrating forced conversions of Muslims during the Inquisition.

32. An artist's impression of the horror of expulsion: a figure of terror in the sky atop a fire breathing beast drives the Jews (silhouetted figures at the bottom) from their houses as they are set alight in the background.

33. A seventeenth-century painting of Spain's patron saint, Saint James, dubbed Santiago Matamoros – 'Saint James the Moor Slayer' – for miraculously appearing in the mythical Battle of Clavijo on a white horse to defeat the Muslims. The mythology of this anti-Muslim cult, conceived four centuries after the made-up battle, became central to the Reconquest narrative and the medieval Spanish identity.

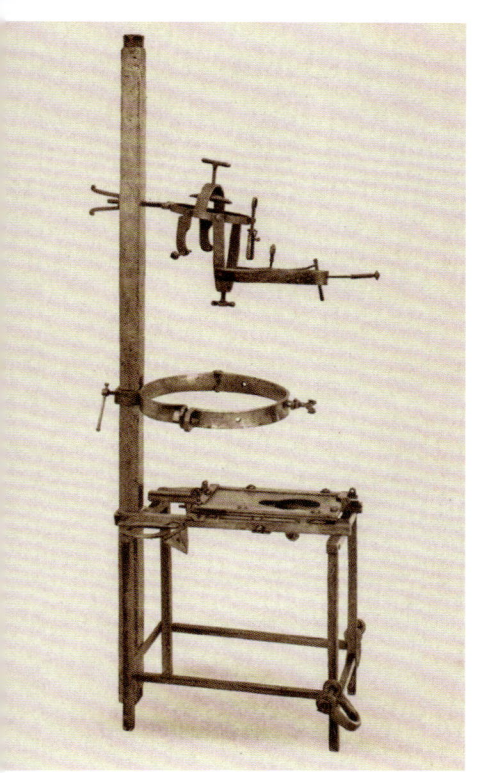

34. Picture of an authentic torture chair used during the Spanish Inquisition to extract confessions or inflict punishment on suspected crypto Jews and Muslims.

35. Poster for *Le Tribut de Zamora* (1881), an opera set in Moorish Spain based on the made-up narrative of forced virgin female tributes paid to Muslim rulers – part of Iberia's Reconquest narrative which quickly became accepted as factual.

36. A dramatic Serbian nineteenth-century Romantic-era oil painting by Adam Stefanović, showing Prince Lazar's fall and the battlefield carnage during the 1389 Battle of Kosovo, which saw the Ottomans begin their presence in modern-day Europe.

37. An 1877 wood engraving published in *Frank Leslie's Illustrated Newspaper* of a service at the Ahrida Synagogue during the Russo-Turkish War. Figures are shown praying beneath Ottoman banners – symbolizing Jewish loyalty to the empire.

38. A richly coloured sixteenth-century miniature from Lokman's *Hünername* depicts Miloš Obilić – a mythical anti-Muslim Balkan figure – assassinating Sultan Murad I at the 1389 Battle of Kosovo.

39. Eighteenth century Jewish woman's attire in Ottoman lands, where many of the Sephardic Jews expelled from Iberia were welcomed after the fifteenth century.

40. A synagogue scene from the fourteenth-century Sarajevo Haggadah, believed to have come from Iberia with Sephardic Jews. It was saved twice by Bosnian Muslims and is now displayed at the National Museum of Bosnia and Herzegovina in Sarajevo.

41. The tomb of Ottoman Sultan Murad I, nicknamed Hüdavendigâr, meaning the 'God-liked one', on the site of the fourteenth-century Battle of Kosovo near Pristina, the capital of the Republic of Kosovo.

42. A young King Charles III wearing Islamic attire on one of his many visits to an Islamic centre in Britain as the Prince of Wales.

43. Painting of the ambassador of the Saadi sultan Abu al-Abbas Ahmad al-Mansur – believed to be the earliest painting of a Muslim ever made in England – who arrived in London in 1600 to try and conclude an alliance that would have seen England help the Muslims retake Spain from the Catholics.

44. The eighth-century dinar of King Offa, the King of Mercia, one of the largest Anglo-Saxon kingdoms in what is now Britain, featuring the Islamic declaration of faith. Minted in 774, it features the Islamic declaration of faith and the Latin words *Offa Rex* and offers a tantalizing link between the ancient British Isles and the Islamic world.

45. King Charles III alongside Professor Keith Critchlow – who introduced the young King to Islamic art and architecture and Sufism – admiring central Asian Islamic art and architecture.

46. A fourteenth-century miniature of King John I of England, who like his father Henry II threatened the pope with conversion to Islam by reportedly trying to forge an alliance with the Almohad Caliph Muhammad an-Nasir.

47. Painting of al Khidr depicted standing atop a fish. Also known as 'the Green One', Khidr is a mystical figure believed to be the mysterious individual sent to guide the prophet Moses in Surah *al-Kahf* of the Qur'an.

Youssef was standing directly in front of the mihrab, 'is the greatest piece of classical European Muslim art in the world!'

Youssef peered in stunned silence over the black iron rails that stopped us going any further than the *maqsura* (Caliph's private praying quarter), in front of the mihrab, built by Caliph al-Hakam II around 965. His eyes slowly traced the dazzlingly spectacular horseshoe arch. Every inch was covered in a mosaic of gilded vegetal patterns over a fan of red, green and gold panels, framed by an alfiz of uber-delicate stucco and regal gold Kufic Arabic.

I waited as he took it all in. The Great Mosque of Córdoba, sitting in the heart of the capital of the Emirate and then Caliphate, became the archetype and artistic inspiration across al-Andalus not just for mosques, but also for its synagogues and even its churches.

'Beautifully ironic that the greatest piece of Muslim art in Europe was probably created by Christian artists,' I finally said.

'Christians?' asked Youssef, turning to me in disbelief.

In yet another example of the relations that existed between Christian and Muslim rulers during this period, Caliph al-Hakam, like his father when he constructed Madinah az-Zahra, sent a request to the Byzantine Emperor Nikephoros II Phokas in Constantinople to send him his finest mosaicists to help construct the mihrab. When al-Hakam built his masterpiece, merging Islamic features and techniques with Byzantine ones, he was in effect solidifying the distinctly Umayyad style started by his ancestors back in Syria with monuments such as the Great Mosque of Damascus, and in other early Islamic domains like the Great Mosque of Kairouan in Tunisia. In all of these, we see a cross-pollination of historical Graeco-Roman and Byzantine features with Islamic ones.

Youssef was trying to read the ancient inscriptions.

'Abd'al-Hakam . . .' he said tilting his head to try and follow the script as it turned ninety degrees around the arch. I could see other tourists were impressed by Youssef's effort. One or two waited to hear what else he could read.

'It's too difficult, the letters are missing the grammar marks and this style is very different to what we are used to,' he finally said.

Youssef told me he had been more successful in Granada, reading the words on the walls of the Nasrid Palace – a story that instantly reminded me of the one the author Washington Irving reveals in *The Alhambra*, where one day in the Court of the Lions he encounters a turban-wearing Moor from Tetuan, who was going around reading the inscriptions, lamenting the vanishing of the Muslims from the palace. Irving goes on to say that there were families still in the Maghreb who had ancient maps, deeds and even the keys to their ancestral estates and gardens in Granada, waiting for the day they could return.

'The tourists were so surprised I could read it.'

'Why were you able to read those words and not these?' I asked.

Youssef explained that both scripts were equally difficult to read, but because a lot of the writing on the Alhambra was from the Qur'an, it was easier to work out the sentences and verses.

'I couldn't read the poetry, it was just too hard!'

I read out what the larger text was supposed to say according to my notes. This included verses from the Qur'anic surahs *as-Sajdah, al-Mu'min* and *al-Hashr* – 'Prostration', 'Believer' and 'Exile', the titles of the selected Qur'anic chapters summing up the self-image of the Iberian Umayyads, believers in exile. The mihrab also included some text commemorating the expansion of the mosque by al-Hakam.

Just as I finished, an Arab man turned up. Youssef told me he thought the man was from the Middle East, before going up to him and giving him salaams. It turned out the slightly rotund man in a flat cap, who we both referred to as 'Ammu', the Arabic for 'uncle', was from Bethlehem in Palestine.

'So you must've been to the Umayyad's very first masterpiece, the Dome of the Rock, many times?' I asked, referring to the iconic golden dome that is part of the Masjid al-Aqsa complex, built by the fifth Umayyad Caliph, Abd al-Malik, around 692.

'He says he prays jumu'ah in al-Aqsa Mosque every week!' translated Youssef.

The uncle smiled at me. We were both extremely envious of this response. The Dome of the Rock was Islam's very first statement monument, built above the rock from which many Muslims believe the Prophet ascended to the heavens on his mystical journey known as the *Mi'raj* and where Jews believe Abraham prepared to sacrifice his son. The iconic monument, which may have also been constructed with the help of Christian artisans, used a dome and mosaic patterns for the first time in Islamic architecture — both borrowed from local Eastern Christian churches and palaces. Its completion is viewed by art historians as the Umayyads' announcement to the world that a new empire and religious art style had arrived.

'Ask him how he feels being here seeing this, and these bars,' I said, grabbing the iron bars with both hands, 'how does he feel that we are stopped from going near it?'

Youssef repeated the question and the Palestinian uncle was quiet at first. He then spoke slowly and deliberately, staring at the mihrab the whole time, putting his hands together, as if making dua. Youssef turned to me.

'He feels sadness and loss . . . As a Palestinian, these feelings are even more painful,' Youssef said.

We all fell silent. More and more people now came up to the mihrab and maqsura: some clearly had no idea what it was doing here inside a church, while others were stunned into silence by its beauty. They all then took the obligatory snap in front of one of the maqsura's entrance arches, framing the mihrab behind it, ideally under the most elaborate one in the centre, for which a queue began to form. We stood to the side, where the arches are just marginally less elaborate and dazzling. Here the entrance beneath them is covered by two gold-coloured doors with lines of notches going across horizontally. The space separating the maqsura from the main mihrab area is divided by Almohad-style arches with their distinctive smaller curves, creating that iconic cloud-like pattern. The colours are still a deep red, like the horseshoe arches that run through the entire building. Once upon a time a spectacular minbar, made from red and yellow sandalwood with gold and silver inlays, used to sit here. The minbar was described by the fourteenth-century Maghrebi polymath Shams al-Din Muhammad ibn Marzuq as one of 'the best works one can find'. The other, said Shams, was its twin, the minbar of the Kutubiyya Mosque in Marrakech, Morocco. The one in Córdoba is no more, having been destroyed sometime after the sixteenth century, but the one in Morocco is still in the Kutubiyya. I stared up at the sumptuous gilded cupolas above each arch. They were difficult to appreciate from behind the bars, which are set outside the maqsura chambers. When I finally craned my neck enough to get a glimpse, it took my breath away; as it did the last time I was here, and the time before. I noticed a patrolling guard watching the three of us carefully. Resembling the cupolas I had seen inside Sicilian Arab-Norman churches, every inch of the dome and its tambour were covered in gold mosaic, interlaced with vegetal, floral and geometric patterns, occasionally set against a rich navy blue. All of them were lit up by the only natural light entering the otherwise gloomy church, through the windows in the tambour of each dome, where once the eyes have adjusted to the dazzling patterns you notice, just above the rim, in goldleaf on a rich blue, Kufic Arabic inscriptions: verses from the Surah *al-Hajj* – 'The Pilgrimage'. I tried every possible way to get a full shot of one of the domes, even reaching my hand through the bars and pointing my phone upwards in selfie-mode, but each shot came back only with part of the dome in the frame or a blurry image as the phone struggled in the dim light. Quite why visitors were stopped from standing beneath the domes to appreciate their beauty was beyond me.

When Iqbal came to the mosque, and was lucky enough to pray in front of the actual mihrab chamber, it was an experience that made his soul sing.

'O magnificent mosque! In love and eagerness, we both are alike. / There is a mystical affinity between you and me.'

In the masterpiece, much of which he wrote in Córdoba, Iqbal talks about the finite nature of creation and how all material

The mihrab of Córdoba's Caliphate Mosque was built by Caliph al-Hakam II around 965 and is considered the finest example of classical European Muslim art anywhere in the world

Close-up of the mihrab shows the merging of classical Islamic art and calligraphy with Byzantine motifs and techniques

things, including spectacular and spellbinding art and architecture, will ultimately be reduced to rubble and ruin – consistent with the Sufi Iqbal's denouncement of the material – yet he singles out the Grand Mosque of Córdoba as an exception, because, he says, it has been crafted by the hands of a 'messianic man of God'. In the powerful poem, which has a total of eight stanzas, Iqbal believes it is love that inspired Abdu'r Rahman to build it:

'To Love, you owe your being, O haram of Córdoba.'

In traditional Muslim culture, such mosques were always more than just places of prayer, and it is estimated that at the height of the Caliphate Córdoba's Grand Mosque had a library of up to 600,000 books and manuscripts. That was more than most countries in

Northern Europe, where the average library had 200 or so. Even two centuries later, the whole of Paris could only boast 2,000 books. Al-Maqqari tells us this is because Córdoba's 'inhabitants were renowned for their passion for forming libraries', and the city was a place where 'any man in power, or holding a situation under government, considered himself obliged to have a library of his own', and would spare no expense to create one. This last quote by al-Maqqari is a bit misleading as it suggests only men possessed libraries, when in fact Córdoba was also home to many learned and scholarly women, like the tenth-century polymath A'isha bint Ahmad b. Muhammad b. Qadim, who was a serious collector of books and possessed an enviable library, many of them copied by herself, as she was a highly skilled calligrapher. A very wealthy woman who never married and was often asked to give speeches and read panegyrics at royal courts, she typifies the independent Muslim women of al-Andalus often overlooked in historical accounts. The famous historian Ibn Hayyan claimed there was no one in the peninsula who compared with her for knowledge, literary skills and poetic ability. The Grand Mosque's library was one of at least seventy in Córdoba filled with books copied and brought from all the equally luminous Muslim cities of the medieval world, like Baghdad, Kairouan, Cairo and Palermo. This was a city where if you found yourself speaking to a physician, be they Muslim, Jew or Christian, in all likelihood you would also be speaking to a philosopher, poet and linguist, such was the level of education of its residents.

The city was home to up to half a million people – by some estimates – many from parts of Asia and Africa. Córdobans, says al-Maqqari, were 'famous for their courteous and polished manners, their superior intelligence, their exquisite taste and magnificence in their meals, drinks, dress and horses'. They lived in over 120,000 houses, prayed in more than 800 mosques, bathed in 3,000 baths and, when they were sick, were treated for free in fifty major hospitals. This was a place with street lighting, paving and homes with indoor plumbing and running water. There were observatories, madrasas of higher education that attracted students from across the world, and pleasure gardens at every turn with innumerable fountains and pools of water. Córdoba had twenty-eight suburbs, each with its own thriving market, including those selling just books, and others overflowing with goods and luxuries from across the globe. Its river was lined with villas and pleasure palaces, its children could all read and write, and its fields were filled with fruit and vegetables of such abundance they 'have nowhere equal in the world' – the result of the advanced agricultural techniques introduced to Iberia by the Muslims. Ibn Hawqal claimed Córdoba was a city that surpassed those in Syria, Egypt and the entire Maghreb, while the nineteenth-century author Victor Robinson puts it most poetically when he compares Córdoba to the cities of Northern Europe in his *Story of Medicine*: 'Europe was darkened at sunset, Cordova shone with public lamps; Europe was dirty, Cordova built a thousand baths; Europe was covered with vermin, Cordova changed its undergarments daily; Europe lay in mud, Cordova's streets were paved; Europe's palaces had smoke-holes in the ceiling, Cordova's arabesques were exquisite; Europe's nobility could not sign its name, Cordova's children went to school; Europe's monks could not read the baptismal service, Cordova's teachers created a library of Alexandrian dimensions.'

I wanted to stay longer in front of the mihrab, but we knew the mass would start soon and so Youssef and I wandered off to see the rest of the monument.

'Can you see how the two arches look almost like a palm tree?' I said to Youssef, as we wandered beneath the gloom of the darkened forest of pillars.

'Firm are thy foundations, numberless are thy pillars.'

Soaring like ranks of palms over the Syrian desert,' wrote Iqbal in a nod to the theory that Abdu'r Rahman I built his mosque to create an allusion to the palm oases found in the Syrian deserts of his childhood and ancestral home. This is why he is said to have opted for a double horseshoe arch, to resemble large palm leaves, and built the mosque with open archways on all four sides that flooded the forest of pillars with light and air.

PART 3: EUROPE'S CALIPHATE CULTURE

Author on a previous visit photographing the iconic double horseshoe arches of Córdoba's Caliphate Mosque, reputedly designed to resemble a forest of palms

'Take a picture of me under these,' asked Youssef, handing me his camera phone.

I obliged, and showed him the results.

'No, no,' he said, 'I don't want the church things in the picture.'

Handing back the phone, he moved to avoid getting any of the framed images of saints hanging on the walls in the shot.

'That will be difficult,' I said.

I gave him the phone a second time and pointed out the little lamps containing upturned crucifixes that hung from the ceiling. Youssef zoomed in to see the crosses and grimaced, before putting the phone away. I could see he was visibly uncomfortable with the amount of Christian iconography now surrounding us. The lamps of the mosque were once crafted from bells stolen from the church of Santiago de Compostela in 997 by the Caliphate's *de facto* ruler, the wily chamberlain, al-Mansur, whose act, along with burning the city, would catapult the local cult of Matamoros to national symbolism in the coming centuries.

'Look,' I said, pointing to a pane of see-through glass in the floor, 'that's where they claim the foundations of the original church can be seen.'

Youssef peered down at the small collection of stones beneath our feet, as we entered the exhibition on the Visigothic era at the Basilica of Saint Vincent the Martyr. Here the finds included pieces discovered in excavations carried out as recently as 2017.

According to the historian ar-Razi, the mosque was originally part of the church of St Vincent, because when the Muslims first arrived in the peninsula, they had come to an agreement with the local Christians to share the space – apparently a common policy observed by the Umayyads in Syria too. Over time, as the size of the Muslim community grew, the mosque extended far beyond the church's footprint. By the time the Umayyad prince Abdu'r Rahman I came along, it was apparent something needed doing, and he bought the Christian side of the church for 100,000 dinars from the Christians, who were given another church to use instead, and in 784–5 the original structures were demolished and the foundations for the Great Mosque were laid.

'So only the mihrab, the maqsura and the pillars remain of the mosque?' Youssef asked.

'Yes, and the patio outside, the gates you were reading from before, also the minaret, but now it's a bell tower, and other details that you have to look carefully for,' I replied, before explaining to Youssef the tussle the building is at the centre of.

The reason Iqbal was allowed to pray here in the 1930s and would not be allowed to pray here today is because, in 2006, Spain's Catholic Church registered the Mezquita as its property through an obscure legal procedure called immatriculation, for the princely sum of thirty euros, during the conservative government of José María Aznar. For many locals, the questionable acquisition has led to 'abusive control' of the monument by a Church that wants to convert a symbol of 'tolerance into one of intolerance'. One example of this was the dropping of 'Mezquita' from the monument's branding, a policy also adopted by Google Maps in 2014. Both the Church and Google have since been forced to reinstate 'mosque' to the name following several campaigns by the local platform 'Mosque-Cathedral Heritage for All', which recently successfully lobbied the Andalusian Ombudsman to intervene after it felt the Catholic Church and Andalusian Department of Culture's Master Plan for the monuments failed to comply with the regulations and guidelines of UNESCO, which views it as a world heritage site primarily because it is 'an irreplaceable testimony of the Caliphate of Cordoba'. The campaigners who want to see the monument managed more transparently and with input from independent experts have questioned the legitimacy of the Church's acquisition of the Mezquita-Catedral and feel there has been a concerted effort to overstate the Christian aspect of the monument's history. This includes an increase in recent Christian discoveries being displayed inside and the reduction of text about the Muslim period in the official brochure, where there is no mention or acknowledgement in the timeline of the monument's period of shared usage by Christians and Muslims between 711 and 784.

Whether or not the Ombudsman's resolution that the Master Plan be adapted to integrate the unifying aspect of the monument's culture and history will be heeded by the Catholic Church remains to be seen. In recent years, it has been digging its heels in, insisting the monument be identified exclusively as a church and, more worryingly, repeating ancient Islamophobic tropes as lately as 2014, by claiming that during its Caliphate days 'any Christian who tried to enter the mosque would be killed'. This was in spite of the building's history of shared usage, and of the widely accepted fact that many Christians and Jews not only entered the mosque but helped to construct some of its most spectacular features, like the mihrab and maqsura, which al-Maqqari tells us 'Christians and Moslems repeatedly expressed their admiration for', something the former could not have done standing outside.

'Come, I want to show you something,' I said, leading Youssef towards the middle of the building, where the Renaissance and Gothic cathedral nave and transept, forming a new Capilla Mayor, was completed in the seventeenth century, smashing through the roof, and altering the aesthetics and atmosphere of the original building, for ever. Prior to this intrusive adaptation, the Christian additions had mostly been sympathetic and harmonious with the spectacular Umayyad monument, often integrating *mudéjar* elements. The Christian Renaissance addition was vigorously opposed by Córdoba's Christian city council, but an aggressive campaign eventually saw Charles V authorize the rebuild, a decision he would later regret. According to legend, when the King of Castile and Aragon saw what the builders had done, he is said to have lamented: 'You have built what you or anyone else might have built anywhere; to do so you have destroyed something that was unique in the world.'

I knew Youssef wasn't keen to see the Christian elements of the monument, but I wanted to show him the statue of Matamoros that remains near the altar, and began telling him the story of how a companion of the prophet Isa came to be the patron saint of Spain and dubbed 'Muslim killer'. But even before I finished, we were confronted by a guard near the chapel, who told us it was closed. I noticed the relief on Youssef's face, and so we both decided to leave.

The bright morning sunshine was blinding as we emerged from the gloomy interior of the cathedral, like two hermits from a cave. The pair of us walked around the patio, admiring the citrus trees and the baroque fountain – which probably replaced the original wudu fountain – and sat in the shade of the bell tower to share some fruit. I pulled out large ripe plums and Youssef handed me a satsuma.

'I was here a few days ago, listening to a guide talking to tourists,' began Youssef, as we watched streams of tourist arriving, 'and the guide said to them, "This used to be a mosque but we beat the Muslims and so now it is a church!"'

I smiled.

'When I walk around, I can tell they don't want us here, they feel it is theirs now, not ours,' Youssef continued, with more than a hint of sadness in his voice.

17

The City of Poets

Seville, Spain

When Abdu'r Rahman I arrived in Córdoba to found his Emirate in 755, one of the people who came to visit him was an intriguing woman from the Muslim town of Ishbiliyah (Seville) called Sara la Goda (Sara the Goth), the granddaughter of one of the last Visigothic rulers of Iberia, Witiza. The recent widow had come to greet the young Umayyad prince and Emir, who reminded her that they had actually met before in Damascus, when he was just a child, beside his beloved grandfather, the Umayyad Caliph, Hisham.

Sara had gone to the court of the Syrian Umayyad ruler, with her two younger brothers, Ardabasto and Romulo, to ask the Caliph to restore a thousand estates they had rightfully inherited but that had been confiscated by one of their Visigoth uncles. During the hearing, Sara told Hisham that the inheritance had been agreed under Caliph al-Walid I. After hearing her case, Caliph Hisham sent orders to his governor in Ishbiliyah to have the lands returned. While in Damascus, the Caliph helped arrange Sara's marriage to a local man, Isa ibn Muzahim, who returned to Ishbiliyah with Sara. Isa died the year the new Emir of Córdoba came to Iberia, and he thus recommended she marry Umayr ibn Sai'd al-Lakhmi, also from a pre-Islamic royal family and a supporter of the Umayyads, to strengthen their ties. The marriage was typical of the mixing of blue blood across al-Andalus that saw Christian aristocracy merge with the new Muslim rulers. One of

Sara's descendants, part of the influential Banu Hajjaj, would go on to briefly rule Ishbiliyah, as too a member of her husband's al-Lakhmi family, though their reign would be far more prosperous.

I rushed through the darkened streets, past a small band of performers outside a branch of the BBVA bank. Picking up my pace, I noticed a police patrol car, neatly parked beneath two of the famous Sevillian orange trees that line every street here, trees said to have been introduced by the city's medieval Muslim rulers. I followed the tram line as it wound its way past the stunning twentieth-century Edificio de La Adriática, a sumptuous display of neo-*mudéjar* art and architecture. I glanced at my phone, and the jog became a run, along the back of the huge Gothic Great Cathedral of Seville — where once I would have been running along the back of the Great Jamme Masjid of Ishbiliyah, before turning left to see the Alcázar's pink Lion's Gate, complete with its golden lion holding aloft the cross.

I had just made it — or so I gathered from the scowl on the face of the security guard as he checked the digital ticket on my phone and ushered me in while bemused tourists wondered if the Alcázar was still open. He grimly wagged his finger at them, before closing the gate in their faces.

Alcázar comes from the Arabic *al-qasr*, meaning fort, because that's what it was originally founded as in 913 by the Muslim Caliph of Córdoba, Abdu'r Rahman III, serving as a stronghold and a residence for his governors of Ishbiliyah. The fort evolved through the ages under various Islamic dynasties, most notably the Almohads in the twelfth century, who significantly expanded and beautified the complex and were the last Muslim rulers of Ishbiliyah before it fell to the Christians in 1248. Much of what remains today dates from between 1356 and 1366, when Pedro I of Castile, known as Pedro the Cruel or Pedro the Just, transformed the palace into a luxurious royal residence, incorporating *mudéjar* architectural elements that celebrated the legacy of its Islamic origins while integrating Gothic and Renaissance styles. Pedro I commissioned skilled Muslim craftsmen, sent to him by his allies, the Nasrids of Granada, to create elaborate tilework, carved stucco and intricate wooden ceilings, blending Islamic artistry with his own regal vision.

I had visited the Alcázar many times, but always in the day and always self-guided. This time I wanted to experience it differently, at night – which arguably, like the Alhambra it is modelled on, is how it was meant to be appreciated: when the heat of the day is done – and by candlelight. That way the exquisite craftsmanship visible everywhere in the monument can come alive with each flicker of a candle's flame in the twilight. But most excitingly, I was to experience the Alcázar in the company of its forgotten women, under the title 'Theatrical Night Tours of the Real Alcázar of Seville: Women'.

I'timad lifts her hand mournfully towards the inky-blue night sky, her white head-veil flowing behind her, and as she spins around like a dervish, her shadow dances in the nooks and crevices of the diamond-shaped *tsebka* pattern in the delicate Almohad muqarnas arch that frames her. In front, beyond the neatly trimmed row of myrtle bushes, her reflection – created by subtle uplighting – mirrored her every move in the central pool of the Patio del Yeso, or the Patio of Plaster. The actual name given to this delightful courtyard by the Muslim builders of the Real Alcázar has long been forgotten. Built by the famous Ishbiliyah royal architect Ahmad ibn Baso, who also constructed the Great Mosque of Ishbiliyah and its iconic minaret – now the symbol of Seville as the Giralda bell tower – it is the only part of the palace that can be traced back to the Muslim period. I'timad had been the wife of Muslim Ishbiliyah's poet king, al-Mu'tamid, a man who epitomized so much that was great about medieval Muslim Spain, and whose poetry was so spellbinding that the great thirteenth-century Moroccan polymath al-Marrakushi claimed that of all the beauty produced by al-Andalus, al-Mu'tamid might well be the greatest.

The legend of how he met the great love of his life, I'timad, is set on one of the banks of the city's famous river, the Guadalquivir, which to al-Mu'tamid and his great friend Ibn Ammar would have been the Wadi al-Kabir. It was as the two wandered along its banks one day that they came upon a slave girl known as Rumaykiyya – the slave of Rumayk. The two friends often challenged each other by improvising verses of poetry, and as al-Mu'tamid threw a line describing the river at his friend Ibn Ammar, before the poet could answer Rumaykiyya completed the verse in such a beautiful and poignant manner that it blew the two friends away. Struck by her intelligence and poetic talent, the young prince, al-Mu'tamid soon arranged for her freedom. The slave girl's name was I'timad, and King al-Mu'tamid took her hand in marriage, making her his beloved queen and muse.

The legend is probably just that, a legend. What it alludes to, and the reason I'timad had been chosen as the only Muslim female actor for the night, is the poetic essence of Muslim Ishbiliyah, a city that developed such a reputation for nurturing the arts during the rule of al-Mu'tamid that it attracted poets from far and wide, including the great Siqilliyan Ibn Hamdis, after he left the homeland he was devoted to in the wake of the Norman conquest.

Al-Mu'tamid was from a branch of the Banu Abbad, a tribe of Lakhmid origin. On the eve of the collapse of the Caliphate in Córdoba – officially abolished in 1031 – it was his grandfather who was the *de facto* ruler of Ishbiliyah, and upon his death in 1042 al-Mu'tamid's father, Abbad – known by his throne title, al-Mu'tadid – became king and began immediately expanding his territories, capturing much of Gharb al-Andalus and a number of cities in al-Andalus, including Granada. This made the kingdom of Ishbiliyah the most powerful taifa to emerge in the wake of the Caliphate. The young al-Mu'tamid, known as Abu al-Qasim Muhammad prior to adopting his throne title, was a brilliant statesman. His father made him governor of Huelva aged eleven, and asked him at fourteen to lead a campaign against Silves, before he became its governor, aged twenty-three. During his rule, after an initial period of expansion that saw him take the former Caliphate capital of Córdoba, things began to go wrong, and by the end of the eleventh century he and several other taifa rulers sent for help across the Mediterranean to the Almoravids, who would eventually oust al-Mu'tamid to become the new Muslim rulers of al-Andalus. Born out of a conservative mystical reform movement in the western and southern Sahara, the Almoravids – from the Arabic *al-Murabit* – already ruled over all Morocco and Mauritania, and parts of Senegal and Algeria. Their acquisition of the former Iberian Caliphate territories saw the Maghreb and al-Andalus politically and culturally unified once again. The Almoravids, who did not see themselves as caliphs and paid homage to the Abbasids in Baghdad, along with the Almohads who would replace them, really embedded the art and architecture of al-Andalus in Morocco and other parts of their territories. In fact, they often sent Muslim, Jewish and Christian artisans from Iberia to their Maghrebi territories to build monuments, such as the Almoravid Qubba in Marrakech, the Great Mosque in Algiers and parts of al-Qarawiyyin in Fez. This unity of culture across the Mediterranean between the cities and Emirates also allowed people to move seamlessly between them, which meant scholars like Ibn Khaldun and mystics such as Ibn Arabi studied, learned and taught on both sides of the sea. This culture continued long after the Almoravids and Almohads were gone, allowing even female scholars, including Sayyidah bint 'Abd al-Ghani bin 'Ali bin 'Uthman al-'Abdari, to move between Muslim Europe and the Muslim Maghreb safely and frequently. She was an orphan from Granada, raised in Murcia, who became such a proficient Qur'an teacher that she taught first in the palaces of Granada, then in Fez, and briefly again in Granada before heading to Tunis to teach in the royal palace there.

We had met I'timad in the adjacent Sala de Justicia, from where a slim channel beneath a small round fountain at floor level leads into the pool of the Patio del Yeso. She had marched in looking every bit the medieval European queen, her long flowing white robe as elegant as the draping veil that hung from one side of her face to the other. With the actresses all speaking Spanish, I had to consult my translated notes and script several times in the dim light of the Sala to realize exactly who we were in the presence of. Unlike the Patio, the Sala was commissioned by Alfonso XI of Castile in 1330 and is considered the finest example of *mudéjar* art in the entire palace, taking its name from the fact that it was later used as a courtroom. It is the first room anyone enters when visiting the palace and immediately makes clear where its inspiration comes from. I had looked around at the faces of the twenty or so entirely white European audience as they admired the mesmeric plasterwork of delicate vegetal patterns that surmounted the blind arches along the white-washed walls. The room was crowned by a coffered wooden ceiling featuring geometric patterns emanating from the Moorish star. To those of us who had visited the Alhambra in the past, it felt like we had suddenly been transported back there, and that is because the artisans Alfonso commissioned to create the Sala de Justicia, like so much of the Real Alcázar, had been sent over from Granada, and had also worked on the Alhambra – the only difference here, and you had to be really paying attention, was the Castilian emblems and their coat of arms, hidden among the classical Islamic design. Everything else was just like the Nasrid Palace in Granada.

After her recitation in the Patio del Yeso, I'timad led us out to the Patio de la Montería – a large flat featureless courtyard, surrounded by double- and triple-tiered arcades in the Islamic and later Castilian style – and performed again, this time standing on slabs beneath which were the ruined foundations of I'timad's original palace. It was here that the evening's Muslim performance ended. As she recited in a tone that evoked what Youssef called Andalusi music, I noticed slanted geometric Arabic inscriptions in blue, high above the courtyard's impressive three-tiered *mudéjar* facade, at the entrance to the Palacio de Pedro I. The same artisans that constructed the Sala built the Palacio, and it featured the same enthralling plasterwork, they had left an even bigger clue to their origins. The Arabic read: '*Wa la ghaliba illa-llah*' (There is no victor but God), the motto of the Nasrids of Granada. Momentarily, I was stunned. I had known about his close relationship with the Nasrids, but why had Pedro commissioned such a thing in so prominent a

PART 3: EUROPE'S CALIPHATE CULTURE

place? What did it say about his relationship with the Nasrid kings of Granada? What did it say about his admiration for them? What did it say about his own faith?

A gate inside the Alcázar commissioned by Pedro I in the middle of the fourteenth century and built by skilled Muslim craftsmen sent to Pedro by the Nasrids of Granada, whose motto, '*Wa la ghaliba illa-llah*' (There is no victor but God), is featured along the top in geometric Arabic script

Pedro I of Castile was born in 1334 and reigned from 1350 until his death in 1369. Popular history remembers him as a controversial monarch known for his complex and often brutal rule, which earned him the nicknames Pedro the Cruel and Pedro the Just. His reign was marked by internal strife, with numerous revolts and a civil war against his illegitimate half-brother, Henry of Trastámara. Pedro was also known for his empathy towards the Jewish community, offering them protection and high positions at court, earning him the epithet 'King of the Jews', fostering both support and resentment among his subjects, in particular because of his relationship with Samuel Ha-Levi Abulafia, a prominent Jewish financier and diplomat. Samuel served as Pedro's treasurer and was one of his most trusted advisers. During Pedro's reign, Samuel wielded significant influence, managing the kingdom's finances and assisting in diplomatic missions. Samuel's influence at court, however, also drew considerable envy and resentment from other nobles and courtiers, making him a target in the volatile political environment of Pedro's court. Eventually, in a dramatic turn of events around 1360, Samuel fell out of favour with Pedro and was arrested, tortured and executed. Pedro also maintained a strategic and sometimes turbulent relationship with the Nasrid kingdom of Granada, utilizing alliances and military engagements to navigate the complex landscape of Iberian politics. As well as sending Pedro architects and artisans to build his famous Alcázar, the Nasrid ruler Muhammad V gave him a large red 'ruby', the size of a hen's egg, as a token of their diplomatic relationship. The ruby, which was actually a spinel, was then gifted by Pedro I to Edward, the 'Black Prince' of England, who helped him regain his throne from his half-brother, Henry of Trastámara, by providing military assistance in the decisive victory at the Battle of Nájera in 1367. Edward brought the gemstone back with him to England, where it was at some point set in the Imperial State Crown of the United Kingdom and remains one of the most famous and storied gemstones in the British crown jewels, symbolizing the intricate web of medieval European and Iberian alliances and conflicts.

Among the most interesting visitors to Pedro's court was a certain Geoffrey Chaucer, dubbed the 'Father of English Literature'. Chaucer mentions in his work at least five of the great Muslim polymaths who revolutionized Northern Europe. In *The Canterbury Tales*, he talks about Ibn Sina, Ibn al-Haytham and Ibn Rushd, using their Latinized names; and he does the same when mentioning the two pioneering astronomers al-Farghani and al-Battani, in *A Treatise on the Astrolabe*, an instruction manual on how to use the innovative scientific instrument that became the key to navigation. Chaucer's ability to access Latin translations of works by the eleventh-century Córdoban polymath and astronomer Ibn as-Saffar to write what is regarded as the first work in English on a scientific instrument makes clear that work by such Muslim polymaths was a part of medieval England's and Northern Europe's intellectual landscape.

The rest of the acts for the evening brought back to life characters from the palace's Christian period; each spoke in a different mesmerizing room, atmospherically lit and bringing the Alcázar to life in a way that simply cannot be done in daylight. This included a performance inside the stunning Patio de las Muñecas – the Patio of the Dolls – where, unlike in the Alhambra, the breathtaking honeycombed plasterwork still has its original colours of bright reds, greens and yellows, and also features the famous Córdoban horseshoe arches. Another was in the dazzling Salón de los Embajadores – Hall of the Ambassadors – with its mesmeric dome of carved and gilded interlaced wood of geometric Moorish star patterns, built by craftsmen from Toledo in 1366. Then we were led out to the Patio de las Doncellas, or the Patio of the Maidens: yet another courtyard with a central water feature and a spectacular array of delicate arches built by Nasrid craftsmen and held aloft by elegant white pillars. These were in the poly-lobed style of the Almohads and featured the diamond-shaped tsebka, oyster shells, the hand of Fatima and Kufic Arabic calligraphy that refers to Pedro as 'Sultan Don Bidru'. Until 2005, the central courtyard was covered with marble slabs and featured a small Renaissance fountain in the middle. Then following excavations that uncovered the original central pool, flanked by a garden, dating from the fourteenth century, it was restored to its current state, one that mirrors in symmetry and design the Alhambra's famous Patio de los Arrayanes – the Court of the Myrtles. In spite of these obvious allusions to a deep affection and admiration for Muslim culture that existed among Christian rulers like Pedro, the court's modern name continues to perpetuate a myth that its name – Patio of the Maidens – commemorates the annual tribute of 100 Christian virgin girls delivered to Muslim rulers: a myth, like Matamoros, now widely accepted as yet another piece of Islamophobic propaganda constructed by the early Spanish Church.

It was in this stunning ode to Spain's Islamic past, created by Seville's Christian sultan, that we were treated to a hypnotic dance by a woman in a patterned dress. As the music played, merging classical Andalusi rhythms with contemporary ones, we watched enchanted as the woman moved like a whirling dervish at times and then like a flamenco dancer. The darkened garden and courtyard seemed to dance too, her shadow flitting around, playing tricks in the niches and bringing the plasterwork relief to life. We watched, realizing that this was how the palace was meant to be appreciated and this was how to bring that stunning artistry to life: using the interplay of dance, music, low light and rhythm.

Carved Arabic inscriptions alongside Islamic patterns and motifs on a wooden door inside the Alcázar, dating from the middle of the fourteenth century

We exited the Real Alcázar into the Patio de Banderas – the Patio of Flags – a cobblestoned courtyard neatly lined with Seville's famous orange trees. Beyond the arched entrance, completely dominating the night sky and beckoning me like a guiding star, bright and glorious, was Ibn Baso's stunning Giralda, which al-Maqqari considered a piece of architecture 'unparalleled in the world'. Like a moth drawn to a lamp, I wandered in its general direction and arrived beneath its haunting glow to find a clarinet player serenading the late-evening crowd of mostly romantic couples, as they drifted through holding hands. I sat beside him on a stone bench, where an orange tree hung low above my head, its young green oranges so small they resembled limes. The clarinettist had his music sheets on an open lectern, only they were not of paper but on a white tablet, fed by a large power bar. On the bench to my left was a young woman in a skirt lost in a book. As the bald busker sat down on a folding stool and played a slow melancholic piece that felt wonderfully familiar, I could hear the crickets overhead in the citrus tree, playing their own tune.

The Giralda was the minaret for the Great Mosque of Ishbiliyah, which was started by the Almohad 'Caliph' Abu Ya'qub Yusuf (Yusuf I) in 1172 to announce the arrival of the new regional Muslim power in al-Andalus. The Almohads seamlessly stepped into the vacuum left by the collapse of the Almoravids and, like their predecessors, made Ishbiliyah the capital of al-Andalus, also emerging out of a reform movement. Theirs was founded in Morocco's High Atlas Mountains town of Tinmal and called al-Muwahiddun, which means 'the asserters of unity' – Latinized to 'Almohads'.

The Giralda was designed by Ahmad ibn Baso and completed under Yusuf I's son and successor, Caliph Abu Yusuf Ya'qub al-Mansur in 1198. The minaret stood at 97.5 meters (320 feet) and was adorned with intricate brickwork and a series of ramps that allowed a rider on horseback to ascend to the top. Following the Christian conquest in 1248, the mosque was converted into a cathedral, with the Giralda used as a bell tower. This was with no major modifications until the sixteenth century, when a Renaissance-style upper bell section was added, which included a statue representing Faith, known as El Giraldillo, giving the tower its modern name.

Many of the passers-by stopped for a while to listen, couples embracing and friends hugging. There was a haunting melancholy to the clarinet player's choice of music, yet it wasn't wholly sad. I watched as a woman in a gold pleated skirt held the hand of her boyfriend and they selfied beneath the Giralda. Everyone who tried to do this had to do so from a considerable distance in order to get the full height of the former minaret in shot. A crowd now sat on the lip of the large stone Renaissance fountain with its Gothic faces, all of them watching the performer. The music was now filled with leaps and jumps as if telling a story, and a group of women playfully danced to it, much to the delight of the audience. An electric police patrol car slowly cut through the crowd.

As my eyes followed the length of the Giralda from the top down to where it becomes Ibn Baso's minaret, the juxtaposition was distinct and the contrast clear. There is a simple, understated confidence to Ibn Baso's design: the repetition of the tsebka and its ratio to the plain brickwork is perfectly balanced; the small horseshoe arches – nods to the Córdoban Caliphate – sit symmetrically in the middle, each slightly obscured by the stone rail of a balcony. The tsebka diamonds cover only the top half of the Giralda, and as my eyes fell towards the bottom half, there were only allusions to Ibn Baso's famous pattern in the arches of the final few windows, until right at the bottom, in a plain curved niche, completely out of context with what came before, was a small Madonna, a clear statement that the start and end of the Giralda were Christian. It was the Reconquest narrative in architectural form; Spain began Christian and remains Christian.

The clarinettist had now finished his repertoire for the evening and rose to bow, inducing enthusiastic applause from the gathered crowd as, one by one, they all came forward and dropped some change into his small woven basket. I also clapped, before thanking him and doing the same.

I returned to the Giralda in the morning and climbed up all thirty-four levels, just as the muezzin would have done five times a day. Only he probably did it on horseback, which is why the Giralda has no steps, but just a series of wide, gently sloping ramps. This means it is one of the tallest, yet one of the most pleasant, minarets to climb. At the top, which was extremely busy because half of the viewing platform was closed for restoration, I stared out over the white low-rise houses, many covered with the quintessential Mediterranean terracotta roofs. My gaze was westward, towards the neighbourhood of Triana beyond the Guadalquivir, a river so

PART 3: EUROPE'S CALIPHATE CULTURE

The Giralda of Seville was originally designed by Ahmad ibn Baso and completed in 1198 as the minaret of the Great Jamme Masjid of Ishbiliyah (Seville)

beloved of the historical Muslim Sevillians that the poet Ibnu Saffár wrote of it: 'the ring-dove laughs on its banks from the excess of his love, and the whole scene is covered with the veil of tranquillity and peace', while the historian Ash-Shakandí claimed it was more beautiful than the great Nile or Tigris, for the way its banks were lined with pleasure gardens and orchards, where the 'merriest people on earth could be found' singing, playing their instruments and drinking their wine – which the locals considered to be permissible in moderation – with Tarayanah (Triana) and Kabtál, islands in the great river, among the most popular spots for such 'recreation and indulgence'. In the foreground I could make out the beautiful round Plaza de Toros de la Real Maestranza de Caballeria de Sevilla – Bullring of the Royal Cavalry Armoury of Seville – where the controversial and cruel tradition continues to this day. Beyond it, outside the central areas, tall white apartment blocks rose up, far enough away to be exempt from Seville's laws that stop buildings exceeding the height of the Giralda.

I had picked this spot deliberately, for it was the only one available that offered a bird's-eye view of the cathedral's other remaining Muslim segment, the Patio de los Naranjos – Patio of the Oranges. The beautifully green courtyard where Sevillian orange trees were first planted in neat rows by Muslims is still enclosed by the original Muslim walls and gate, its series of pointed archways all bricked up now, where once they would have been open for worshippers to wander through. The sun was still low in the sky, and so the patio was darkened by the long shadow of the Giralda, but already there were huddles of large tourist groups, in shorts, T-shirts and sun hats, listening to their guide on small audio devices. The remaining Muslim wall, with its central archway, covered by a tiled roof, was reminiscent of the entrance to Fez's Qairouan University. The wall's simplicity jarred in contrast to the busy loud Gothic cathedral it now faced. The complicated patterns on each spire and large buttresses holding up Europe's largest cathedral looked out of place, against the rest of the muted cityscape. The Giralda, the Patio of Oranges and the original Muslim world really did appear to belong to an older, simpler time. I was awakened from my musings by a sudden gust of wind, even more fierce than the one that had been blowing, threatening to fling my sun hat towards the cathedral's huge gothic spires. I took it off my head and held on to it tightly. Two large groups of tourists, a Chinese and an American group, arrived noisily at the already busy viewing platform, making it feel even more claustrophobic. It was my cue to leave and so I began the descent down the brick ramps. Along the way I passed a beautiful set of large *mudéjar* doors, featuring stunning gold lion knockers and both Gothic and Arabic Qur'anic inscriptions. The doors, dating from the fourteenth century but clearly older, aptly represented the hybrid nature of the cathedral, where Islamic, Christian and *mudéjar* elements come together. The doors were on display in one of the chambers in the central column of the Giralda. The other featured a giant pair of Almohad bronze door knockers, two simple mosque lamps, and an interactive display that was meant to project Ibn Baso's original twelfth-century plans over the current cathedral, but sadly, along with a revolving display of the Giralda's different phases, it was not working.

A fountain sits in the centre of a geometric pattern in front of a horseshoe arch in the garden of the Great Cathedral of Seville, which was originally the garden of the Great Jamme Masjid of Ishbiliyah (Seville), begun by the Almohad 'Caliph' Abu Ya'qub Yusuf (Yusuf I) in 1172

It was a Friday, and had I been visiting Seville eight centuries ago. I could have descended the minaret and simply entered the city's Great Mosque to pray jumu'ah. But modern Seville is a very different place, and locating a mosque is no mean feat here. As in much of Spain, visible mosques are entirely absent in Seville. So instead I had to walk fifteen minutes north-west of the former Jami'a Mosque of Seville to the Fundación Mezquita de Sevilla, not just to perform the weekly congregational prayer but also to learn about the possibility that Seville may once again be getting an Ibn Baso-style minaret.

'Seville needs a Friday mosque,' said Nabeel Abdalhaqq, a volunteer at the Fundación.

Nabeel had kindly agreed to meet me after the Friday prayer, which was held in the Fundación's temporary premises, next to the Plaza Ponce de León bus terminal, secured with the help of ex-Premier League and FC Seville footballer Frédéric Kanouté. The devout Muslim from Mali paid 500,000 euros in 2007 to buy the section of the residential building for the community after struggling to find a mosque in the city.

'At the moment, we all pray in different little mosques scattered around the city, and only on Eid, we try to find a place to pray together, so all the mosques are working together to realize this dream,' Nabeel explained, as we made our way from the bus terminal towards a small coffee bar that spilled out onto the streets.

I pulled up a chair at a small metal bistro table and we both sat down.

'I found it very interesting those fronting the campaign for the new mosque appear to be largely white local converts,' I said, as Nabeel ordered us two coffees in perfect Spanish.

I was intrigued by this because earlier during the jumu'ah, I had found myself praying alongside mostly North Africans, black Africans and South Asians.

'Yes, it's an approach,' began Nabeel, a little tentatively, 'that kind of makes sense for the time we are in.'

Nabeel spoke with the hint of a South African accent, which is where he grew up, though his ancestry went back to India. He was also a convert, born a Christian and now married to the daughter of a local convert. Nabeel's background was in media, so he understood the importance of good marketing. Spain was a deeply Islamophobic nation and the Fundación was sensitive to this. This was why their campaign and the new mosque's design wanted to make clear Islam was not foreign to Seville or Spain. Their promotional video featured several Spanish converts to Islam talking to the camera about why a new mosque was important. It also featured a diagram of a mosque design that showed a series of simple low white buildings, with an unmistakable replica of the Giralda – minus the baroque features – looming over them. It was meant to resemble the minaret the Almohads built in Ishbiliyah in the twelfth century and is modelled on the surviving one in Marrakech, which they built thirty years previously, upon capturing the Almoravid regional capital. There they also constructed a statement grand mosque, the Kutubiyya – home of the twin minbar of Córdoba's Mezquita – complete with a minaret the Giralda would then be based on. The mission to create a new purpose-built mosque after nearly 800 years was something Nabeel's community had also taken to the Islamic Festival of Mértola, where they were regulars, along with members of the Muslim community in Granada. As well as hosting a series of stalls selling everything from Spanish Muslim literature to handmade artefacts, they led the acts of worship at the festival.

'We prayed near the historical mosque and held a dhikr there,' explained Nabeel.

'So you guys help to bring some more authenticity to the event?' I asked.

'Yes, we're not taking it over . . . But very respectfully saying, "We see what you're doing, and we're not saying it's *wrong*, with your belly dancers and whatever, but give us a chance to show you the *real* faith."'

Like myself, Nabeel and his community had some reservations about the exoticizing of Islamic culture by the festival's admittedly well-intentioned organizers, something I had realized when watching videos of the event, which featured clichéd belly dancers and sword-juggling 'Aladdins'. We both agreed these caricatures were wholly unnecessary and offensive, and ultimately reinforced the 'othering' of Muslim culture – something Manuel had said the festival was trying to avoid. For me, it was yet another clear example of why local Muslims like Nabeel needed to be involved in the process.

'We've kind of learned to deal with it with a benign neglect,' Nabeel said, smiling.

'Pragmatism?'

Nabeel explained that while there were certainly problematic aspects to the festival, like seeing visitors walking around, beer in hand, wearing a djellaba and a fez, they tried to do things to counter it, by making *their* section of the festival very distinct, so that it became immediately clear that this was a very different space.

'So it is obvious to visitors where "Aladdin" is and where you guys are?'

'Yes!' Nabeel said emphatically.

'Do all the Muslims that attend have this approach or are some deeply offended?'

Nabeel thought for a while.

'It's very early days,' he finally began, 'this is not England, this is not South Africa.'

'So, pragmatism has to be the order of the day?' I asked.

Nabeel nodded.

'There would have been a time,' he said, pointing to the bar, 'you couldn't enter without passing beneath legs of pork. If you came here even ten years ago, the entire ceiling would have been covered with hanging legs of pork, so you are forced to walk underneath them.'

Nabeel was talking about the overt display of *jamón*, the popular local hams seen hanging in bars and restaurants across Spain. The display of a food impermissible to both Muslims and Jews goes back to the Spanish Inquisition, during which diet was viewed as an indicator of religious allegiance and a way to flush out crypto-Muslims and crypto-Jews hiding in Catholic Spanish society. To refuse pork in those days was considered evidence enough that you were actually a Jew or a Muslim and thus you were likely to be burnt at the stake.

'Have you seen the film *Goya's Ghosts* about the painter Goya?' asked Nabeel.

I shook my head.

The film is a biopic about eighteenth-century Spanish painter Francisco de Goya, whose work is said to have often disturbed the Church's Inquisition.

'There is a scene in which Goya's model Inés – an ethnically darker woman – is drinking at a bar and is offered some pork tapas, which she declines.'

Nabeel explained how a spy from the Holy Office saw this and had her arrested and brought before the Inquisition on a charge of 'Judaizing' for refusing pork. Inés was then stripped and tortured using the notorious *strappado* method that resulted in the dislocation of her shoulders and led her to confess. She was then imprisoned. Nabeel was telling the story to make clear just how deeply anti-Semitic and Islamophobic historical Spanish culture was and alluded to the fact that this is something that doesn't go away overnight. It is part of the Spanish DNA, just as it is part of much of the Western European DNA. Nabeel, who had grown up with a priest for a father, before embracing Islam, understood better than most the need to be pragmatic and diplomatic.

18

On the Nasrid Trail

Granada, Spain

Nasrid Granada emerged during the second taifa period of al-Andalus. This followed the reunification of Muslim Iberia under the two Berber dynasties, the Almoravids and the Almohads. The Nasrids were an Arab dynasty founded by Abu Abdullah Muhammad ibn Yusuf ibn Nasr, the son of a humble farmer who claimed descent from a Companion of Madinah called Sa'd ibn Ubadah. Born at the end of the twelfth century in the town of Arjona in Jaén province, Ibn Nasr was known for his piety and asceticism, though he was no pacifist and was also highly respected for his fighting skills. Ibn Nasr witnessed the collapse of the region's last major Muslim dynasty, the Almohads, and the rise of the Christian kingdoms in the north. By the start of the thirteenth century, with the unification of Castile and León, the region's largest kingdom was no longer a Muslim one, and attempts by a local independent ruler, Muhammad ibn Yusuf ibn Hud, to step into the vacuum left by the Almohads were short-lived. Suffering several defeats at the hands of the Christians, Muslims across the region quickly lost confidence in Ibn Hud, leading to an outbreak of rebellions. One of these took place in Arjona, after the last jumu'ah prayer of Ramadan 1232, when the locals nominated their pious ascetic warrior, Ibn Nasr, as their leader and declared Arjona an independent taifa. Backed by his own tribe, the Banu Nasr, and the influential Banu Ashqilula, Ibn Nasr took the city of Jaén, before briefly grabbing Córdoba and Seville, but unable to hold on to these he temporarily gave his allegiance to Ibn Hud on the agreement that he would continue to rule over a small polity north of Granada. However, by 1236, seeing the rise of Castile in the north, Ibn Nasr switched his allegiance and helped Castile take Córdoba, turning his back on Ibn Hud. The following year, he took several other important cities in the south, including Granada, which he entered in Ramadan 1238, dressed like a humble Sufi murid wearing sandals, a woollen cap and the clothes of a commoner, before taking up his residency in the Alcazaba, which had been built by the Zirids, the Berber dynasty that ruled Granada for much of the eleventh century. In time Ibn Nasr identified a reddish hill known locally as *al-Hamra* ('the red hill'), upon which sat a small fort, as the site for his new palace, where he would build his fabled palace-city, the Alhambra.

When Ibn Nasr died in 1273, the Emirate of Granada was the last independent Muslim state left in al-Andalus. Over the course of the next two centuries, adopting the tactics of their founder, the Nasrid sultans would survive in what was now the Christian domain of Iberia

The motto of the Nasrid dynasty, '*Wa la ghaliba illa-llah*' (There is no victor but God), is repeatedly inscribed into the walls of the Alhambra, from where they ruled between the thirteenth and fifteenth centuries

by adapting to the changing circumstances at home and across the waters in the Muslim Maghreb, taking advantage of their enemies' weaknesses, and when needed making themselves useful to them, regardless of whether these were Christians or Muslims.

Nestled at the foot of the majestic Sierra Nevada mountains, Granada's urban sprawl straddles several hilltops around the valleys of the rivers Darro and Genil, and as it was the last major Muslim stronghold in Iberia is home to the largest collection of the remaining physical allusions to that pioneering culture – an offshoot of the Caliphate culture – left anywhere in Iberia. The sheer dominance of Ibn Nasr's Alhambra in the popular imagination of Muslim Granada means many of these other spaces get overlooked by most visitors who are either oblivious to their existence or simply not interested.

I jumped off the bus near the narrow street that runs alongside the Darro River in the immediate shade of the Alhambra. Clambering to stay on the narrow pavement every time a large vehicle came through, I wandered past the tall post-Renaissance houses that loomed overhead, stopping to admire the waters of the very low Darro, which resembled a stream surrounded by foliage. After briefly popping in to see the tiny Bañuelo, the eleventh-century remains of a hammam, largely modelled on the Roman set-up of cold and hot rooms, I walked up the tiny, narrow alley beside it, named after the baths. This had a steady incline of long wide steps that led upwards and away from the river where the buildings either side appeared to close in on each other, before reaching a freshly plastered wall on the right-hand side with a sign that read: *El Maristán*. I stepped in to be greeted by a number of low brick pillars and sections of incomplete walls. These looked equally fresh in construction. In front of me was a dusty barren courtyard that appeared to have a piece of astroturf covering a rectangular cavity in the centre. Directly opposite was an old wall with large chunks of plaster and broken bricks peppered with holes. A low-rise collection of ugly grey blocks had been constructed to my left, beyond which were a wire fence and a huge open space that resembled a construction site. The reason there was hardly anything here is that the fourteenth-century Maristán of Granada, the Muslim precursor to the modern hospital, was almost completely demolished in the nineteenth century. The building to my right was the reconstructed Maristán, which in style and look resembled a classical Islamic *funduq*, or caravanserai.

As with philosophy, medieval Muslims built upon the existing medical wisdom of the Greeks. In this case the likes of Hippocrates and Galen, and as with philosophy they massively improved those great foundations through a process of transference and countless innovations. These include Abu Bakr Muhammad ibn Zakariya al-Razi, the ninth-century Persian philosopher and physician par excellence, identifying for the first time that measles and smallpox were actually two different diseases. He was also the first to carry out controlled medical trials with groups – something we take for granted now but in the ninth and tenth centuries was a sophisticated approach way ahead of its time. Then there is the twelfth-century Syrian Ibn an Nafis, who was the first to describe the pulmonary circulation of blood, revolutionizing our understanding of the circulatory system, and the groundbreaking work in surgery of the tenth-century Córdoban physician Abu al-Qasim al-Zahrawi, known as Albucasis in Latin and considered the 'father' of surgery, for his many innovations and breakthroughs still relevant and in use a thousand years on – such as his discovery that haemophilia is hereditary and his use of catgut for internal stitching, still prevalent in intrusive modern surgical procedures. Born in Abdu'r Rahman's fabled Caliphate city of Madinah az-Zahra, hence his *nisba* (name indicating place of origin), al-Zahrawi had a career that spanned five decades, during which he is said to have pioneered neurosurgery and performed surgical treatment of spinal injuries and head fractures. Al-Zahrawi was the first physician to provide a description of a surgical procedure to relieve fluid from the brain of a child as well as of migraine surgery in his *Kitab al-Tasrif* (The Method of Medicine), which covered topics including surgery, medicine, orthopaedics, ophthalmology, dentistry, pathology and childbirth. Arguably though, al-Zahrawi's greatest legacy was the development of 200-plus surgical instruments for such procedures as cataract removal, caesareans and stillbirth. These appear in an illustrated guide in the final chapter of his book and many, including different types of scalpels, specula, retractors and pincers, would not look out of place in a modern surgeon's toolkit. Al-Zahrawi published his book in 1000 — at the same time on the other side of the continent, in Britain, 'leechbooks' were still the medicinal manual of the day — so named because leeches remained central to medicinal practices in North-Western Europe. Other remedies in these leechbooks included healing lower-back pain with the smoke of smouldering goat's hair. The *Kitab al-Tasrif* was first translated into Latin in the twelfth century in that famous school of translation in Toledo by Gerard of Cremona, becoming a standard text in Salerno, as well as other Western European centres of medical studies. It would remain the authority on surgery across the continent for at least the next five centuries.

The works of each and every one of these Muslim physicians — and countless more — were widely translated and studied across Europe's universities from the medical school of Salerno all the way north to the University of Oxford. The Latin translations of their work often remained core texts right up and into the Christian Renaissance, which is why most are known only by their latinized names, like Rhazes (al Razi) and Albucasis (al-Zahrawi). But arguably the Muslim to exercise the biggest influence in Europe and the West in the field of medicine was the great Persian philosopher and physician Ibn Sina, or Avicenna. His *Canon of Medicine* condensed and arranged the ancient Greek and modern Arabic theories so phenomenally that it became the standard medical text across all major European universities during the Renaissance — when it was one of the most printed books on the continent — right up until the eighteenth century. The *Canon* remains the most famous medical textbook ever written, and Ibn Sina the most influential medical author in history. He was a polymath who was a famous philosopher and a scholar of Islamic sciences, and had he been a Christian in later centuries would have been branded a Renaissance man by the West. While all the polymaths named above offered numerous pioneering contributions to Western medical practice: without any shadow of a doubt, the Islamic hospital, or *bimaristan*, was the real game-changer. These hospitals far outshone anything remotely comparable in Europe at the time, which were mostly hospices where patients were looked after by monks more concerned with the salvation of the patient's soul than actual medical practice, or as one popular book on medieval England puts it, 'the sign of the cross was the antiseptic of the year 1000'. Muslim hospitals on the other hand were sophisticated clinical modern places with large libraries and lecture theatres where not only was cutting-edge, research-based treatment offered, but doctors and nurses were taught, tested and qualified in them. Many bimaristans had departments that saw only women and were staffed solely by female physicians; they were open twenty-four hours a day; measures like being issued special in-patient clothes that are still in place today were the norm; and they were airy, light-filled spaces. Bimaristans were non-confessional and therefore Christians, Jews and Muslims were both patients and practitioners. So when a Frank found himself in a tenth-century Córdoban hospital – of which there were at least fifty in the city – needing treatment, he was left awestruck. Writing to his father, he explained that the hospital had clear and distinct departments, including those for disease diagnosis and even one for gynaecology run by women; a library beside his room where doctors listened to lectures and discussed treatment; and a space where music was used to speed up recovery. The Frank said everywhere was as clean as could be, beds and pillows were covered with clean white cloths, and there was plumbed fresh water in each room as well as a stove for heating. It is almost as if he was describing a hospital in the twenty-first century, except he told his father the food in the bimaristans was excellent, treatment was absolutely free, and discharged patients were offered a new set of clothes and an allowance to ensure they rested and did not feel the need to return to work too early. Nothing so progressive and advanced had ever been seen in Europe before – and arguably still hasn't, when we consider modern medical costs across the continent and the reputation of hospital food!

The very first Muslim hospital was actually opened in the early eighth century by descendants of Mu'awiyah in Damascus, but this was a leprosarium. The first general hospital opened in Baghdad a century later, during the reign of the Abbasid Caliph Harun al-Rashid. Over the next century or so hospitals appeared in all the major Muslim cities from Makkah in the Arabian Peninsula all the way to Córdoba in al-Andalus.

Granada as seen from one of the windows of the Alhambra's Nasrid Palace, the Islamic heart of the palatial city complex

I wandered into the reconstructed Maristán, past two bemused-looking tourists, and climbed the staircase into the small rooms once used for training doctors and treating patients. I began reading the various information panels; there were no artefacts and the ground floor was still not ready. Built between 1365 and 1367 by the Nasrid king Muhammad V, during what many consider to be the Golden Age of Nasrid rule, the name *Maristán* comes from the Persian word *bimaristan*, which means 'house of the sick'; in fact, the word for sick, *bimar*, is the same in my native Sylheti. The hospital was constructed in what was then a neighbourhood of aristocrats, in a rectangular layout with a total of four two-storey sections like the one I was standing in. These surrounded an open courtyard where there was a large pool fed by water spouting from the mouths of two stone lions. The lions are now in the Alhambra Museum and resemble sitting versions of those seen in the Nasrid Palace's famous Patio de los Leones, or Court of the Lions (the modern name for the court and its surrounding habitations), another section of the renowned palace built by Muhammad V. The Alhambra's museum is also home to the Maristán's most well-known physical remnant, a huge decorative marble foundation stone in the shape of the city's iconic doorways, with inscriptions confirming the purpose of the building and who commissioned it. This spectacular large relic was once positioned above the double wooden door at the entrance to the hospital, surrounded by a gorgeous decorated geometric frame. I stared at the reproduction of the sketch made by a Miguel Pineda Montón in 1873, when the entrance was still set with the stone and featured much of the original Nasrid decorative elements. Typically sumptuous in design and elaboration, it was easily the most spectacular entrance to any hospital I had ever seen. The next panel revealed how the hospital was a place for both teaching and treatment, with patients being those afflicted by conventional illnesses as well as those who were mentally unwell. The Maristán had spaces for recreation, including a garden where medicinal plants were grown. The complex was served by an advanced sewage and irrigation system and was connected to the Bañuelo I had visited earlier.

The final panel had an artist's impression of what the Maristán would look like upon completion of its reconstruction. The picture showed all four sides of the simple two-storey building, set around the large rectangular pool, where the two seated lions had been restored to their original fourteenth-century locations, facing each other as water fell from their open mouths. The artist had chosen to depict the Maristán from the opposite end of the courtyard: a conscious decision, as it allowed the inclusion of the Alhambra, high up on its perch, to loom over the hospital, like a parent standing over their child.

The Golden Age of Nasrid Granada began with the advent of Muhammad V's father, Yusuf I, who also left behind a spectacular legacy that few people visiting Granada ever appreciate. It sits inside a building called the Palacio de la Madraza, which is part of the University of Granada, right next to the Catedral de Granada – none of which is coincidental. As with most of the major cities and towns of medieval Iberia, Granada's main cathedral is built on what was once the town's Friday or Jama'at Mosque. The city's lavish Renaissance-era cathedral in the centre of the town, famed for its stained-glass domed chapel, was built on top of the destroyed foundations of Granada's Masjid al-Kabir, where, in a strange twist of fate, Yusuf I was murdered by a 'madman' while praying. But before he died, in 1349 Yusuf built a splendid place of higher education – or a madrasa, hence the building's modern name, Madraza – right beside the mosque. The subjects taught at the madrasa of Yusuf I included mathematics, medicine, mechanics, logic, literature, theology, astrology and law, and teachers included Ibn Marzuq (the former tutor of the Marinid Sultan Abu al-Hasan Ali ibn Othman) and the great Alhambra poet Ibn al-Jayyab. This was a place that produced great scholars like the two most illustrious viziers of the Nasrid court, the polymaths and poets Ibn al-Khatib – a name that means 'son of the sermon-giver' – and Ibn Zamrak, the former said by the great medieval geographer Ibn Khaldun to 'possess unequalled linguistic habit'. It also attracted great luminaries from across the Muslim and non-Muslim world. Education, as we have seen across the region's Muslim cultures, was a central pillar of those enlightened societies – inspired by scriptures that placed a significant weight on the seeking of knowledge, including famous hadiths like the one that claimed the Prophet said, 'seek knowledge even unto China', and by the fact that the very first word believed to have been revealed to Muhammad by God was 'Read!' This meant the earliest Muslims placed a huge emphasis on education and built some of the world's earliest institutes of learning, such as the University of al-Qarawiyyin in Fez, which like Yusuf I's madrasa was attached to a mosque. This is why children in the Caliphate of Córdoba and

Emirate of Sicily in the tenth century could read and write, while most adults across Northern Europe couldn't.

Although the university had an impressive library, halls of residence for students and laboratories for research, sadly, like the mosque, none of the original madrasa remains. Its invaluable collection of books and manuscripts – by some estimates numbering one million – were brought to the Plaza de Bib-Rambla near the university, piled high and burned in a huge bonfire, in December 1499, at the height of the country's Christian Renaissance on the orders of the Grand Inquisitor, Cardinal Francisco Jiménez de Cisneros. Modern historians have compared the disaster to the Roman destruction of the Library of Alexandria, and the burning of the Mayan codices, also by the Spanish in the following century. The building was then looted, closed and finally destroyed completely in the early eighteenth century. Or so it was thought. Around a century or so later a ludicrously stunning little prayer room or mosque, complete with its very own dazzling mihrab, was discovered. The square room with an octagonal upper section and a decorated wooden domed ceiling seemingly belongs in the Alhambra, such is the sumptuous nature of its delicate carvings, muqarnas and Arabic inscriptions, as well as the geometric patterns and the Nasrids' iconic curved and delicate archways. Unlike the Alhambra, much of the pigmentation of the paintwork on the carved stucco remains, offering a tantalizing glimpse of what the great education institutes of al-Andalus may well have looked like, and hinting at just how spectacular the rest of the madrasa would have been.

The historical mihrab is one of only two in Granada belonging to purpose-built places of worship. The other is a near-identical wood replica of Caliph al-Hakam II's spectacular mihrab in the Mezquita-Catedral in Córdoba that sits inside the 2003-built Mezquita Mayor de Granada, the first mosque to be opened in the city since the Inquisition and the fall of the Nasrids in 1492. Located atop the hill where the ancient district of Albaicín is found, the $4.5 million mosque was built by a largely convert local community close to where the oldest Islamic settlement in the city once stood, an eighth-century castle built during the country's earliest Umayyad period. The site also offers spectacular views across to the Alhambra.

The minaret of the Mezquita Mayor de Granada, the first mosque to be opened in the city since the Inquisition and the fall of the Nasrids in 1492; built in 2003, it features the iconic horseshoe arch and geometric Arabic inscriptions

Making up the last of the trio of exclusive Nasrid-era buildings few visitors to Granada even know exist is the fourteenth-century caravanserai, al-Funduq al-Jadida, also said to have been built by Yusuf I. Known today as the Corral del Carbón – a nod to its usage as a coal weighing station in the seventeenth century – the two-storey building has a magnificent entrance that can be found close to the university, off the busy Reyes Católicos. Its monumental portal of richly carved stucco, decorating the arched entrance, is framed in an alfiz, topped with verses from Surah *al-Ikhlas* in elegant ancient-Kufic script. Above the verses are a pair of delicately unmistakable Nasrid windows, peering out from in between a collection of modern shops, like the secret entrance to a fairy tale. However, when you step beneath the dizzying muqarnas of the portal's ceiling – some of it inlaid with Arabic calligraphy – and enter through the large double wooden doors, the fairy tale ends abruptly. The caravanserai was a highly functional and practical three-tier construction, the like of which can only be seen in Europe's furthest eastern parts and, of course, Cyprus. Stepping into the cobblestone courtyard, which had a small watering trough in the middle, I was immediately reminded of the Büyük Han in Lefkoşa, though this was considerably smaller. A stage with several speakers, behind a cordon in the central courtyard, hinted at the funduq's current usage as a frequent concert venue.

'Tomorrow there will be a jazz festival here,' explained the friendly female member of staff standing near the entrance, 'and it is free!'

'That is a shame,' I said, 'tomorrow I will probably be heading north to Toledo.'

'Ah, the city of three faiths,' she smiled.

I smiled back, though I did wonder why every city in southern Spain didn't have this tag as almost all of them, during Muslim rule, had been cities of three faiths.

The funduq was one of many built in the area during the Nasrid period and offered security and shelter to merchants and traders from across the country. Collectively they were part of a chain of such travellers' lodges scattered across the Iberian Peninsula and modelled on the pre-Islamic funduq of the Middle East. The Corral del Carbón had large well-guarded warehouses for merchants to store their goods; there were also stables for the beasts that carried the goods, as well as areas for the traders to meet, dine and sleep in. All of this would have been provided at the expense of the sultans – usually for a minimum of three days and three nights – as was the practice throughout the Muslim world. This display of benevolence and guarantee of safety encouraged traders and merchants to visit Muslim lands, making places like Granada thriving centres of trade and portals for luxury goods from the East to start making their way into Western and Northern Europe. The funduq was strategically located close to the main mosque and the numerous souks that once existed nearby. Today only a nineteenth-century reimagined 'souk' exists, the Alcaicería, a name derived from the original

Arabic name for the souk, al-Qaysariyya, which means 'Caesarean' and derives from the Byzantine markets of Syria – long arcaded structures containing rows of shops – copied by the Umayyads. The name is actually a common one for souks across the Arab-Muslim world, with the most famous al-Qaysariyya souk probably the one founded in the Muslim Quarter of Gaza city, which was built by the Mamluks in the fourteenth century, roughly the same time the Nasrids built theirs. Unlike the other markets in the area, the Nasrid sultans personally owned the al-Qaysariyya as it was the one where the most luxurious products were sold and therefore was the best protected. It once covered an area of 4,600 square metres, even after the Muslim period, when the Catholic Monarchs owned the souk, but then in 1843 the entire market was destroyed by fire and rebuilt on a much smaller scale in a mock-Nasrid style that feels more Aladdin than a real souk.

    I stared at the green canopy of vines two storeys up, created by the foliage trained to climb the sides of the funduq's main pillars. Once at the foot of the second floor, the greenery was supported by a series of strategically criss-crossing wires that allowed some of the vines to hang down and create a beautiful natural feature that also offered shade. It was easy to see why the city officials had chosen to host musical events here. Beyond admiring the vines, and the reconstruction work, like the Maristán, there is very little to see or do here, as most of the rooms are now occupied by small businesses and retailers and so, conscious of my evening booking to see the Alhambra at night, after admiring the funduq's spectacular entrance one last time, I made my way out into the busy streets of Granada again.

19

The Muslim Alhambra

Granada, Spain

The revolutionary poet of Granada, Federico García Lorca, grew up enamoured of the Alhambra, a place he would frequently visit in his youth, and is said to have loved dressing up as a Moor. Although his romanticism would shift to the other neglected minority in Spanish history, the *gitanos*, towards the end of Lorca's short life he began studying the translations of the poetry of al-Andalus. This offered him his first glimpse into a Spanish history that until then he had only seen through post-medieval, post-Catholic and post-Matamoros lenses. In 1936, at the outbreak of the Spanish Civil War, Lorca spoke on radio using the architecture of the Alhambra as a metaphor for the divide in his own city, suggesting it was like the contrast between the palaces built by the Nasrids and the later, Renaissance and baroque one built by Charles V. In the speech, Lorca also claimed the fall of Muslim Granada had been a disaster. Later that year, followers of the uber 'Catholic' and fascist General Franco murdered Lorca. His remains have never been found.

'Is that a crab on your phone?' I asked.

Mina got up from her crouched position in front of the slender pillars holding up the delicate muqarnas arches of the small arcade that protruded into the sumptuous Patio de los Leones. She looked a little embarrassed as she held aloft the bizarre silicone phone cover in her hand and started giggling, before explaining that she was not alone. She then pointed out three other girlfriends in the courtyard, who were busily snapping away with phones encased in equally ridiculous silicone covers. Mina and her friends were of Nepalese origin but now lived in Hampshire, England. She took a seat beside me on one of the wooden double-u-shaped chairs, strategically positioned throughout the Nasrid Palace for weary legs and modelled on the foldable Nasrid 'throne' in the Alhambra's museum.

'We always do this when we go away together. Each of us has to carry around a really silly accessory and pretend it is perfectly normal. We are not allowed to choose who gets what. Look, one of my friends got lucky, she has a smiley emoji . . . But look at hers!'

Mina pointed to a friend who appeared to be carrying around a large, brown silicone doughnut.

'That is not a doughnut – it is a turd!' Mina said, before falling about laughing.

I examined Mina's phone cover, which was indeed a crab, being cooked in a frying pan. The cover was about three times the size of her smartphone, and looked quite ridiculous as she wandered around the Alhambra using it to take pictures, though we both agreed she looked better than her turd-carrying friend. I had first noticed Mina in the Sala de los Abencerrajes – Hall of the Abencerrajes, named after a legend claiming it was the room that the prominent Ibn Serragh Muslim noble family was massacred in, for plotting against one of the Nasrid sultans. I was staring at the words of the poet-vizier of Muhammad V, Ibn Zamrak, on the walls, comparing the room's spectacular cupola muqarnas ceiling to the heavens, and it was as I began looking for the rust marks on the room's central fountain, which guides tell visitors are 'blood' stains from the massacre, that I could see Mina becoming frustrated trying to capture the delicate muqarnas that hung from each corner of the ceiling. The carvings were accentuated by the dim light, creating wonderful shadows in the niches, but awful conditions for photography.

'No matter how many pictures you take, or how you take them, it never feels like you capture just how beautiful it is,' I said, explaining that on my first few visits to the palace I was doing the

Looking through the slender pillars of the Alhambra's Court of the Lions to its famous fountain

same, frantically trying to capture the Alhambra on camera, but ultimately failing.

'It's so beautiful . . .' she said, now looking out to the courtyard again.

The fact that it was night-time seemed to have a muting effect on the visitors, who were all moving around in silence trying to photograph the lion fountain in the middle, from which the four canals of water linked it to smaller fountains inside rooms in the surrounding arcades, just like the Zisa. Commissioned by the eighth Nasrid sultan, Muhammad V, in the second half of the fourteenth century – the period considered the zenith of Nasrid architectural achievement – the marble fountain with its twelve sculpted lions is among the most iconic symbols of the Alhambra, which began life as a palace as early as the ninth century, though the remnants of the Muslim parts we see today were almost all built once the Nasrids, an Arab dynasty, took control of Granada and the Alhambra around 1238. Believed to have originally been called Dar Aisha – the House of Aisha – after the sultan's favourite wife, to whom it may have been dedicated, the current name of the Palace or Court of the Lions, like so many in the Alhambra, is a modern designation. The original Nasrid ones are no longer known and in truth even Dar Aisha is a later Eurocentric projection, suggesting such expressions were always rooted in the sensual and the sexual – i.e. the popular nineteenth-century European – 'Arabian Nights' view of Muslim cultures. This stands in stark contrast to another theory that suggests the complex around the lion fountain served a very different purpose, as either a madrasa, a zawiya or a *Bayt al-Hikmah* – house of knowledge. In this theory, the Sala de los Reyes, or Hall of Kings, and the Sala de los Mocárabes, or Hall of Muqarnas, would have served as the palace libraries, and the Sala de las Dos Hermanas, or Hall of Two Sisters (all modern names) – also added by Muhammad V – might well have been used for dhikr or halaqas while the southerly-facing Hall of the Abencerrajes, believed to have been known as al-Qubba al-Gharbiyya – the Western Dome – would have been a space for congregational salah for the students at the madrasa or zawiya. This theory is often dismissed out of hand because of the huge popularity and perpetual repetition of the historical Eurocentric versions. Yet there are almost no known surviving written accounts of exactly how the Alhambra was used prior to the Christian conquest – because all its archives were burnt by the Catholics – except for one. This was written by the poet-vizier Ibn al-Khatib, whose real name was Muhammad ibn Abdallah al-Salmani. Written upon the return of Muhammad V from exile in Morocco, it describes a celebration of *mawlid* – the Prophet's birthday – in December 1362, on the future site of the Court of the Lions. This places a highly religious event in the space, and yet the idea that a place so ornate, so spectacularly beautiful, might be used for worship or education remains implausible to most. However, we only need to cross the city to the University of Granada and its surviving mihrab of the historical madrasa to know this was very much the norm. In fact, if we were to cross the tiny strip of water to the region where the descendants of the builders of such magnificent places fled, and where a parallel al-Andalus culture flourished, we would find complete versions of madrasa and zawiya that could be the mirror image of the Court of the Lions. The famous historical madrasa attached to the Ben Youssef Mosque in Marrakech, which was founded by the Marinid sultan Abu al-Hasan, is a case in point. Interestingly, it was built in the same century when Muhammad V went into exile under Marinid protection in Fez. Meanwhile Fez is of course home to the most famous and equally sumptuous madrasa, now known as the University of al-Qarawiyyin. Both spaces resemble the Alhambra in terms of the tiles, the muqarnas, the central fountains and pools, and their canals leading into spectacular rooms beneath delicate muqarnas arches, where students learned fiqh, tafsir (commentary) on the Qur'an and *qira'at* – a method of pronunciation in reciting the Qur'an – or engaged in congregational dhikr. Even the floor plans of both institutes mirror that of the Court of the Lions. While al-Qarawiyyin is attached to its equally famous mosque, the Ben Youssef Madrasa has a large room with particularly rich stucco and a stunning mihrab that is reminiscent of the surviving one at the University of Granada. Had either madrasa been built on this side of the Bahr ar-Rum (and survived the systematic destruction), it would have no doubt been lauded as also reflecting the pinnacle of the 'Nasrid' architectural style. Although they are not, what they do confirm is that Muslims did build places of learning and spirituality that looked as spectacular as the Alhambra.

'What made you guys visit this place?' I asked Mina.

'We heard it was beautiful and thought we must visit it when we are in the city.'

'Did you know that it was an Islamic building?' I asked.

Mina looked at me, her eyes wide open.

'Really?'

'Yes, what did you think it was, when you were looking at these patterns and the Arabic on the walls?'

'There's Arabic on the walls?'

'Yep, some are actually verses from the Qur'an, and others are classical Arabic poetry,' I said.

Mina began looking around. Almost every inch of the stunning palace is covered with Arabic inscriptions. Researchers have found almost 10,000 across the entire site in three different styles, including the ancient Kufic and naskh, with the most common phrase, repeated over and over again, being the Nasrid motto. The same one I had seen copied in Sintra and Seville's Alcázar. Here it was often depicted diagonally on a shield like a European coat of arms. There is also the repeated use of everyday phrases that Granada's Arabic-speaking Muslims, Christians and Jews would have used to reflect their gratitude, servitude and humility before God. These included phrases like '*alhamdulillah*', which means 'Praise be to God', and '*subhanallah*', which means 'Glory be to God', phrases that act as a constant reminder for believers that everything is ultimately from God. Their use in the Alhambra's architecture reflects the humility of the Nasrid monarchs before God. The other inscriptions were the ones Youssef tried to read and Irving's Moor from Tetuan reportedly did read. These are the Qur'anic verses and poetry by the Alhambra's poet-viziers. I had seen examples of this earlier in the Hall of the Ambassadors, where beneath the spectacularly carved wooden ceiling, framing some of the gorgeous mashrabiya arched windows, are verses from Surah *al-Mulk*, the sixty-seventh chapter in the Qur'an. The title means 'The Kingdom' and is one of the chapters said to protect the reciter. Even the patterns used to frame the inscriptions have been found in the decorative margins of ancient handwritten Qur'ans of the time. The room also contained poetry, as did the bowl of the fountain in the courtyard we were staring at, which is adorned with verses by Ibn Zamrak. I pointed this out to Mina.

'I was looking at the patterns and thinking they looked like something from Bollywood,' said Mina.

She admitted, without any explanatory signs on display, that she did not realize what she was looking at was Arabic.

PART 3: EUROPE'S CALIPHATE CULTURE

Around 10,000 Arabic inscriptions have been found across the Alhambra's various sites, with many of them verses from the Qur'an and lines of poetry

'I wish I had bought the audio guide now!' she laughed.

I told Mina how some experts believed the courtyard we were staring at may well have served as the grounds of a madrasa or zawiya, and how, behind us, was where the Great Mosque of the Alhambra once stood, on the site of the Church of Santa María. In between was a place called the Rawdah – the royal cemetery, where all the Nasrid kings were once buried. The name is the same as that given to the space between the Prophet's pulpit in his mosque and his house (in Madinah), which he famously claimed was a 'garden from the gardens of paradise'. The fact that the Rawdah was in between the mosque and the Court of the Lions further supported the idea that it may well have been a spiritual place of learning. To be buried within 'earshot' of worship and the sound of Qur'anic recitation is for many Muslims the ideal resting spot, and why in some Muslim communities a *hafiz* – someone who has memorized the entire Qur'an – is hired to take up residence in a cemetery following a burial and paid to recite the entire Qur'an almost continuously for a set period of time.

'Nowadays, when Muslims visit the Prophet's Mosque in

304

Madinah, they try to pray in the Rawdah there as they believe it multiplies the reward,' I said to Mina, who was genuinely flummoxed by the Islamic links to the monument.

'Even these chairs we are sitting on are the same design as thrones that Islamic kings sat on.'

Mina got up to take a look at the double-u-shaped wooden chairs, which were certainly handsome but did not resemble anything regal. I explained how the Alhambra's museum, over in the Charles V Palace, which I had visited earlier, contained a mobile Nasrid throne that was essentially the same design, just more decorated and with a higher leather back rest. I had also seen an ornate lamp in the museum that belonged to the Alhambra's mosque.

So much of what might have brought the Alhambra and the Nasrid Palace to life authentically, and contextualized it as an actual Muslim space, felt absent in the way it had historically been – and continued to be – presented. The lack of historical accounts about the true usage of the palace during Muslim rule sadly meant that curators and guides all too often fell back on later projected and loaded clichés, as well as problematic tropes, which over time became accepted facts.

'Excuse me,' said a voice, when Mina and I stopped talking.

I looked across to the skinny white man clutching his bag, sitting on the 'throne' to her right. We had all been asked to wear our backpacks on our fronts rather than our backs at entry.

'Are you a tour guide?' he asked.

'Who, me?' I replied, looking around to make sure.

'Yes, you sound like you know so much about the Alhambra that I have not heard before.' Michael, it turns out, was a tour guide himself, working in Seville, his adopted home.

'No, not at all, just an enthusiast,' I said, feeling a tad embarrassed.

Just then, Mina's friends came over, and after briefly saying hello, the four of them continued onwards with their tour of the palace, while Michael and I stayed seated. When he moved into the seat Mina had vacated, the strong smell of alcohol emanating from his breath made it apparent that Michael had enjoyed a few beers before entering the Alhambra tonight. I was tempted to crack a joke about whether it was actual Alhambra branded beer he had enjoyed but didn't want to make him feel awkward. We left the Court of the Lions and entered the Hall of the Kings, used as a chapel and offices for the nearby Santa María de la Alhambra while the court's mosque was being dismantled to make way for its building. The Hall of the Kings is divided into seven sub-units using delicate muqarnas arches, above which are vaulted oval-shaped ceilings covered in leather with painted scenes in a style that suggests they were done by Christian artisans. The central one features ten Nasrids, who some believe to be dignitaries and others say are the first ten Nasrid sultans. The figures include several with red beards, hinting at the mixing of Northern European blood with the Muslims and their rulers. I stared up at the congregation and wondered what they might have made of how tourists appreciated their ancestral home today.

The author on a previous visit to the Alhambra admiring the intricate carvings on the walls of the Court of the Myrtles

Michael explained that he wanted to work as a guide in Seville, but one of his great frustrations was not being able to access the story of the city's Muslim past in ways other than the 'invader' perspective. I shared a little bit of my knowledge of Seville.

We were now outside the walls of the Alhambra, close to the main entrance for daytime tourists. It was 11 p.m. and there was hardly a soul up on the hill, where the businesses rely entirely on the footfall the palace-city brings. Despite being slightly inebriated, Michael could sense the visit had been a disappointment for me.

'You didn't enjoy it at all?' he asked.

'Look, it's the Alhambra, and the aesthetics are of course crazy, but that was maybe how I felt the first time I came . . . Now I feel kind of cheated,' I said, explaining that I had consciously not picked up an audio guide on this occasion to avoid the Eurocentric interpretation being impressed upon me in each space.

The first time I visited the Alhambra, I used the audio guide to wander through the halls, imagining the legends about the murder of the Abencerrajes, even rushing out to find the dead cypress tree in the Sultana's Courtyard, under which the 'legend' claimed one of them used to clandestinely meet the wife of the last Sultan of Granada, Abu Abdallah Muhammad XII, or 'Boabdil', before picturing giggling 'veiled' women in the 'harem' areas. Those narratives brought the palace to life in a way that reinforced the idea that Muslim rulers were all about brutality, decadence and sensual indulgence, clichés taken straight out of the exoticized nineteenth-century rulebook on how to 'other' Muslims, so that these – by then – Iberian Muslims, some – as the painted ceiling in the Hall of the Kings suggests – as blue-eyed and red-bearded as any 'European', would for ever remain 'foreign'. It was only when I had travelled to the Maghreb, and saw the 'Alhambra' everywhere, that I realized how badly I had been misled. I remember on one trip to al-Qarawiyyin making wudu while sitting on one of the stone seats around the courtyard's central fountain, using water from a bowl not too dissimilar to the one with the twelve lions, and remarking on just how much the pavilions positioned at each end of the courtyard mirrored those in the Court of the Lions. Where I had knelt beneath the slim pillars of the ones in the Alhambra to capture the beauty of the courtyard, next to the one in the Fez mosque a young Moroccan sat in its shade with an open Qur'an, gently reciting in hushed tones. I realized these courtyards – the elaborate muqarnas in niches and vaults, the stunning, slender pillars holding aloft arches so delicate that they were seemingly carved out of air – were not *just* found in palaces and stately homes, but in the everyday too. In fact, the most historically elaborate examples were often in places of worship and education. The places that resembled the Alhambra the most were the historical – often contemporaneous – zawiya, madrasas and mosques, and yet I had never heard any such connection mentioned in the many visits I had made to the Alhambra: there were no allusions to Islamic spirituality or worship; even the knowledge that the Alhambra had a large congregational mosque is something visitors would need to spend time researching beforehand. It was as if the Nasrids and by extension, the Muslims of Iberia had been something to only be feared, as brutal, barbaric and tyrannical rulers, or perversely and sexually desired as 'forbidden' veiled Moorish maidens.

The Nasrid Palace was of course an imperial space, but the almost complete de-Islamizing of a space home to thousands of salutations to Allah, and countless verses from the Qur'an, including many from the most revered surahs, like *al-Ikhlas* and *Ya-Sin*, was deeply problematic and, for me, unforgivable.

Michael nodded. He now understood why I felt the Alhambra was being so poorly presented and curated, but, more importantly, why that pained me as a Muslim.

Michael was originally from Poland, so as well as Seville we also spoke about the 'hidden' Muslim heritage in his own homeland, a place with a mind-blowing Islamic history that goes back over six centuries, and unlike the one in Spain still has a living legacy. Islam came to Poland and the Baltic region when Muslim Tatars from the Crimea arrived in what was then the Grand Duchy of Lithuania – of which Poland was at the time a part – in 1398, at the behest of the Grand Duke Vytautas. The Muslims, along with some Jewish Tatars, had been sent by one of the Crimean khans when Vytautas had sought help to defend his duchy against the invading Germanic Teutonic Knights. The Tatars fought alongside the duke in several key battles to defeat the Teutonic Knights and effectively save medieval Lithuania (and parts of modern-day Poland and Belarus). In return, the duke granted the Tatars permanent residency in his duchy, giving them land and telling them they were now part of his kingdom. The Tatars spent the next six centuries assimilating into Polish, Lithuanian and Belarusian society and were later joined by more Tatars from the East. Many continued to live in the original villages founded by the first settlers in the fourteenth century: villages like Keturiasdešimt Totorių and Nemėžis in the Lithuanian and Polish countryside, where to this day quaint wooden mosques that have integrated elements of local Eastern Orthodox design stand as physical testimony to their survival. In spite of the horrors of the fascist communism that ripped through the region and saw most of the Tatar mosques torn down and their customs and traditions wiped from memory, there are Muslim Tatars now in all three countries actively reviving their suppressed religion and cultures. Many of those involved in the revival claim direct descent from that very first generation of Muslims who came to help Vytautas.

'I remember travelling around the Baltic and almost nobody knew this story. When I spoke to Polish people, they looked at me like I was crazy,' I said to Michael.

'I know, very few Polish people know that we have Polish Muslims that are not converts in our country,' explained Michael, before revealing – to my astonishment – that he *did* know the history, though conceding this was only because he was curious why the street he lived on in Poland was called Tatar Street.

Meeting Michael after he'd had a few drinks might not have been ideal, but I was glad we had met. He joined a growing number of non-Muslims on this journey who had shown me all was not completely lost. Wandering through places where the memory of Muslim Europe has been either eradicated, horribly distorted or misrepresented often left me with feelings of loneliness, frustration, hopelessness and even anger. Coming upon a Thorsten, Manuel, Sebastián or Michael helped some of those feelings to subside. The fact that Michael was from a country where as recently as 2017 the far right was allowed to march through the capital city holding up a banner that read: 'Pray for Islamic Holocaust' made the encounter all the more important.

The Crimean Tatar Muslims arrived in the Baltic at exactly the same time as another group of Muslims got a foothold in Europe. Also of Turkic descent, the Ottomans were a rapidly rising power founded by a thirteenth-century Turkoman leader called Osman in Anatolia, who like Mu'awiyah in the seventh century began by taking advantage of weaknesses in the Byzantine Empire. Then, following the pivotal Battle of Kosovo in 1389, the Ottomans entered Europe. Almost exactly a century later, in 1492, the Catholic Monarchs Ferdinand and Isabella would step into the Alhambra to be ceremonially handed the keys to the palace by the last Nasrid sultan, Muhammad XII. Had it not been for the Ottoman success earlier, Muhammad might well have been handing over the keys to Muslim and Jewish Europe, given the expulsions that followed and the fact that almost nowhere else in Western Europe was safe for Jews. But he wasn't. Muslim and Jewish Europe would continue in the continent's Ottoman domains. When Bayezid II was transporting Sephardic Jews and thereby Sephardic Judaism to Ottoman lands, the Turkic empire had succeeded where Mu'awiyah had failed and conquered the new Rome, Constantinople. Within a few decades, its rulers would also become the undisputed Caliphs of Islam as part of an ascent that would make them the world's greatest superpower by the time Sultan Suleiman the Magnificent came to the throne in 1520, just twenty-eight years after Muslim rule in Southern Europe came to an end. While Muslims continued to live – under much duress – in the former Caliphate lands of Iberia, it was the global superpower of the Ottomans that would ensure Muslim Europe and Jewish Europe continued long after the Catholic Monarchs tried to extinguish them both.

PART 4
Echoes of al-Andalus

20

The Village of Murids

Órgiva, Spain

'O Lord bless Muhammad, the Messenger of God . . .
Sidi, Amadou Bamba, *madad* [protect us], *madad* . . .
Sidi Sheikh Muhammad Ahmed Adil Sultan *Awliyah, madad, madad* . . .
Sidi Abdul Qadir Jilani, *madad, madad* . . .
Blessings on all the followers of God . . .
Bless Master Hasan and Master Husayn, *madad, madad* . . .
Bless the Virgin mother, *madad, madad* . . . and Mistress Zahraaaa.'

The murid sang the names like he was riffing. He had a traditional drum under his left arm and his pointed felt hat moved slowly from side to side. Amadou Bamba Diawara waited for the elongation of the last line. That was his cue.

'*Laa ilaha illallah* . . . *Laa ilaha illallah* . . .' sang Bamba, leaning in towards the murid.

Bamba's arms were crossed and his short dreadlocks swayed from under his knitted white prayer hat. The murid leapt on Bamba's last word.

'. . . *haaa . . . Muuuhammaduur rasoool allah . . .*'

Before he finished, Bamba was back in with his slightly higher-pitched voice.

'Peace and blessings upon hiiiiiim . . .'

And so it went on. Occasionally the murid would play a beat on his drum, or Muhammad Boulaich, who sat opposite, would beat his, his slick black hair, tied in a bun at the back, glistening in the reflection of the bright lights. Many of us sitting around were still eating the delicious lamb shank with pilau, laid out in large mounds on communal silver dishes on the long wooden tables; others had moved on to the after-dinner sweets and tea. The starry sky above was an inky blue, and when I looked around the Chico River valley in which the Órgiva Haqqani Zawiya rested, I could see nothing but the odd tiny light of a rural Andalusian home – a stark contrast to the hive of activity here at the zawiya, where children of all different races ran around playing with each other, sometimes chased by a bearded murid in baggy clothes. Their mothers and older sisters wore colourful headscarves and sat at two long benches either side of a table, beneath the colourful canopy of textiles that covered the verandah of the lodge. Various tapestries and framed images adorned the zawiya's walls: some were inscriptions of duas of the Haqqani community, and others were more mystical and incomprehensible to the uninitiated. At the back was a large kitchen where several people wandered in and out, carrying food and tea. On my right were the men, our backs to the zawiya's herb and fruit garden, sitting along tables in an L-shape, listening to the dhikr or catching up like old friends. The standard dress code for men seemed to be loose baggy trousers and shirt, topped with a colourful hat. These were sometimes pointed or wrapped in a turban and married with colourful waistcoats. The segregation was not as strict here as at the dargah in Lefke, in Northern Cyprus: men and women often spoke to one another across the invisible divide, and the odd couple even sat together. The dargah was warm and welcoming, just as it had been in Lefke. Bamba had told me there would be a gathering here tonight to celebrate an anniversary from the life of his sheikh. A native of Senegal, Bamba was one of a number of African Sufis who had decided to join the otherwise largely white convert Sufi community residing in the mountain village of Órgiva, deep in the Alpujarras, south of Granada. He had kindly agreed to host me for the evening after a convert murid in Lisbon had made the introduction. Sitting just thirty miles north-east of Almuñécar, where al-Maqqari tells us Abdu'r Rahman I – the legendary Falcon of the Quraysh – landed in August 755, Órgiva and its residents are an echo of that great legacy.

Órgiva is one of Spain's most culturally diverse villages, home to around 6,000 people from more than 68 nationalities; this is in no small part down to the Sufis that now call it home. The majority of them follow the Naqshbandi order of which there are some 1,200 Spanish convert devotees across the country, with the largest collective based here. The Órgiva community began after Sheikh Nazim appointed local resident, and Sufi convert, Sheikh Umar (Felipe) Margarit as his Spanish Emir around the mid-1970s. Once news got out of the appointment, more and more Spanish murids left their existing homes and moved to Órgiva. In many ways the community is no different from any other rural Spanish one. Everyone works, their children go to mainstream schools, they use the internet and drive cars – the only *real* difference is that they have chosen to live close to each other so they can have gatherings, like the one I was privileged to attend, and take part in other regular acts of communal devotion and worship, including a weekly, congregational dhikr. The Órgiva zawiya is one of five located in four different European countries that were formally endorsed by Sheikh Nazim, whose teacher, ad-Daghestani, had made it clear his mission was to spread the word in the West. As well as the one in Lefke, there was one in Cologne, Germany, and two in London. Other followers of the sheikh had also set up smaller gathering spaces across the continent in countries like Portugal and Italy.

I had descended into the Alpujarras just as the sun was beginning to set, and by the time the road wound its way down into the bosom of the valley, where the phone signal was limited, I found myself lost on more than one occasion and was hugely relieved when I eventually saw the bright lights of the zawiya's outdoor area and the sound of communal worship in the otherwise silent hills. Bamba had greeted me with a big smile, and like any good Muslim instantly sat me down in front of a huge platter of meat and rice.

'So, you are not a follower of Sheikh Nazim?' I asked Bamba.

'No . . . of course he is a great teacher, but I follow the al-Muridiyyah tariqa,' Bamba said in wonderful English, despite speaking in his fourth language.

'And how long have you been a murid?'

'Since I was born,' Bamba said with a smile.

Depending on who I spoke to and how they perceived the labels murid and dervish, I had found the answers were always different. Some, like Bamba, believed we are born 'seeking' or 'learning' and that's what it means to be a murid, but I was interested in how long he had formally followed his sheikh.

'Ah, from the age of eighteen.'

'And when did this sheikh die?' I asked.

'Around nineteen . . . nineteen . . . twenty-seven, around nineteen twenty-seven,' Bamba said, noticing my surprise. 'Of course I did not learn from the sheikh directly, but indirectly he is my teacher.'

The order Bamba followed was founded by the late nineteenth- and early twentieth-century wali, or Sufi saint, from Senegal called Sheikh Amadou Bamba, who Bamba was named after and who famously led a pacifist struggle against the country's French colonizers. The mystic, also known as Khadimu r-Rasul, or 'Servant of the Prophet', and author of several works on meditation, tafsir and numerous rituals, was exiled twice and put under house arrest by the French colonizers when they became worried about his order's growing influence. However, later on, Sheikh Bamba was viewed as an asset by the French and allowed to take part in the independence process. The current caliph, which in this context simply means the leader of the al-Muridiyyah order, is Sheikh Bamba's eldest grandson, Serigne Mountakha Mbacké.

Bamba explained this was why he used the surname Bamba: it was to make clear whose teachings he followed. Bamba told me that there were many such teachers in his native Senegal and neighbouring Mauritania – both of which historically had parts in the Almoravid empire that ruled al-Andalus, and, later, the great medieval Islamic Mali Empire, which had rulers like Mansa Musa, still believed to have been the richest man that ever lived. I had assumed all those living in Órgiva and at the dargah were followers of the Haqqani order.

'No, there are people here from all over: London, France, Senegal, Ghana, Mali, Morocco . . . some live here, and some are visiting like you,' he explained, as a small boy came up and began tugging at his arm, a cup in his other hand.

'I think he wants your hibiscus juice . . .' I said, laughing at the little black boy in traditional West African Muslim attire.

Bamba spoke to him in what sounded like French, before pouring out some hibiscus juice for the boy.

'Yours?' I asked.

'No, no . . .' smiled Bamba, before explaining that he and his wife did not have children yet, 'the only family I have here is my sister.'

I had noticed the familiarity with which everyone greeted Bamba, just like the child. As well as his sister, it seemed Bamba had a lot of 'family' here. In that respect, Órgiva's dargah felt very different. Maybe it was because the families were more visible without a physical segregation. It also seemed that most people were locals. This wasn't a site of pilgrimage the way Sheikh Nazim's final resting place was; it felt more like a settled community, a place where people came to live rather than merely pass through.

'There are some people staying here at the dargah but it is not like the one in Cyprus, which is always full!' explained Bamba, when I mentioned this.

'And how long have you been living here in the village?'

'Six . . . no, seven years.'

'And what do you do?'

'Everything!' Bamba said, throwing his hands up, 'Building, selling stuff, clothes . . .'

Muhammad Boulaich came over and the two of them spoke in French. Bamba then turned to me and asked if I wanted tea.

PART 4: ECHOES OF AL-ANDALUS

I explained that drinking caffeine in the evening was not a good idea for me and politely refused. Somewhere in the group someone began banging a metal drum. Once they had established a rhythm, others joined in by clapping, before someone else loudly declared that there was 'no god but God' and another impromptu round of dhikr began.

I sat back and watched. The children continued to play in the open grass area close to the dargah's gardens; most adults joined in with the dhikr – some clapped, one or two pulled out a drum and riffed with the lead drummer. The main vocalist led everyone with words praising God and the Prophet. After a while, the rhythm picked up; the drumming intensified, the clapping did too, and only the words *'la ilaha illallah'* – there is no god but God – were repeated over and over again. The pace was ramped up another notch: now the only words said were *'illallah'*, and as it reached a climax, one or two women made the shrill, warbling cry, synonymous with Berber and Arab women, often heard at North African festivities. It was an exhilarating session, made all the more exciting by the setting: outside beneath the Spanish night sky in a valley that was one of the last to be called home by the historical Muslims of Iberia. In that respect, the gathering of Sufis here felt very apt; the Iberian Peninsula, like Sicily, Malta and Cyprus, had always been home to Muslims of a more mystical persuasion, as this journey had shown me, from the dargah in Lefke to the many zawiyas that Ibn Jubayr encountered.

After several minutes, the adhan cut through, to announce that it was time for the late-night *isha* prayer. The middle-aged muezzin wore a beige hemp top and baggy patterned trousers. His voice was thick and heavy and he made the adhan by simply standing at the edge of the covered verandah. Everyone slowly began making their way into the dargah's small mosque, which was entered through a wooden doorway to the left of the kitchen. I followed the men towards the door, and noticed a series of white shelves beside them, where either side of a climbing plant were pictures of Sheikh Nazim and his son Sheikh Mehmet Adil, the most striking of which was one of Sheikh Nazim sitting on a chair in front of the iconic tiled walls of the Nasrid Palace inside the Alhambra. The sheikh was seated on a Nasrid 'throne' and wore a green and white outfit with a large round white turban. He had the hint of a smile on his serene face, and as I stared at the picture, I realized it was the very first time I had seen a Muslim sheikh photographed inside the spectacular Islamic monument. I wondered what connection the sheikh would have felt to the space? How would he have perceived it, being able to read all the Qur'anic verses? Like all Sufis, he wouldn't have believed in coincidences, and I now wondered what was the *real* reason Órgiva had been chosen.

21

The Blood Runs Deep

Órgiva, Spain

I awoke the next day to a spectacular view from my balcony in Bamba's house, which sat at the northern edge of Órgiva, close to where the valley floor began to rise. There were clear blue skies above the terracotta-tiled roofs of the low-rise houses, hemmed in on all four sides by the green mountains of the Alpujarras, which seemed to go on for ever in every direction. Flanked by the Chico River on one side and the Seco River on the other, it was a beautiful location. I spied the awning of a coffee shop on the street below and decided to head down. By the time Bamba joined me, I had already enjoyed my first coffee at the pleasant little Bar Agustín, which had chairs and tables spilling out onto the street.

'Why do you think they chose Órgiva?' I asked.

'Forty years ago, they came because this area is full of alternative people, hippies, Gypsies, international people . . .' Bamba replied, as he ordered us some breakfast of fresh bread with honey.

Órgiva lay in the region through which Abdu'r Rahman I is said to have arrived in the eighth century to found the Emirate of Córdoba and it was also the region through which a defeated Boabdil would leave al-Andalus in the fifteenth century. This was an area steeped in Muslim history.

'Is there a mosque here in the village?'

'Yes, we have a small place near the Baraka restaurant. You go there and ask for the keys and they give them to you.'

'And do they have daily prayers there?'

'Not really . . . people are working and it is difficult for them to come all the way there,' Bamba said, 'but on Fridays the dargah is packed!'

The waiter brought over our fresh crusty bread, with local honey, and another murid from the dargah walked past. Nooruddin was a tall Spanish convert, with broad shoulders, and looked like he was in his fifties but was extremely fit and muscular. He had a small grey beard and wore a blue and white knitted hat. Nooruddin was the caretaker of the dargah and didn't speak any English, so Bamba explained what had brought me to Órgiva. I sat back as the two of them caught up. The morning birdsong was loud and the street extremely quiet, with no cars passing through. The bar was beneath a two-storey block of houses. Unlike Bamba's house, the buildings here were mostly new-builds and lacked any aesthetic appeal. In that respect, Órgiva could have been any modern Spanish village. Soon we were joined by another Spanish convert, who looked to be in his fifties as well. Known to everyone as 'Sevillia' because he was from Seville, the man had long flowing white hair and a pair of specs hanging on a cord around his neck. We salaamed him and he sat down to join us. Sevillia also didn't speak much English. So I again sat back as the locals caught up. Dressed in a yellow waistcoat, he looked every bit the hippy, but was wearing a green prayer hat, the only clue that he was actually Muslim. No sooner had Sevillia settled when Muhammad Boulaich arrived, wearing a dazzling pair of sunglasses and a stylish Maghrebi waistcoat. We embraced warmly. There were now five of us seated around the table drinking coffee. We had been at the café for almost an hour on what was a Tuesday morning, yet nobody seemed in any great hurry to go anywhere. After a while, Sevillia leaned in towards me and, using broken English, said that I needed to visit the museum in the village. Bamba had told him what I was looking for.

'The man is descendant of Nasrid,' he said, nonchalantly, while lighting a cigarette.

'What?' I asked in disbelief.

PART 4: ECHOES OF AL-ANDALUS

'The man of *museo* is a descendant of Nasrid kings.' Sevillia repeated the words as nonchalantly as the first time, before blowing out a large plume of smoke.

'The Muslim kings of Granada?' I asked, still not sure I had heard right.

Sevillia nodded and took another drag of his roll-up.

'Bamba! Bamba!' I said, pulling at Bamba's hand. 'Ask Sevillia to repeat what he said in Spanish to you.'

I watched as Sevillia, fag in hand, repeated what he had just said, but with far more detail, to Bamba. Bamba's eyes began to grow wide in astonishment and he asked in Spanish if this was *really* the case before turning to me. Sevillia was indeed suggesting that the family who ran the village's local museum, the Museo Ruiz de Almodóvar, claimed to be descended from the last ruling Muslim family of Spain, the Nasrids. This was through a cousin of Boabdil called Sidi Yahia al-Najjar, who was a grandson of the Nasrid sultan Yusuf IV. Al-Najjar converted to Christianity – some say before the fall of Granada – becoming Don Pedro de Granada and with his wife, Cetti Merien Venegas, founded the Granada Venegas family of converted Nasrid *moriscos*. Amazingly, the journey of ancestral rediscovery has led to Paloma Ruiz de Almodóvar, the daughter of the current owner, Miguel, embracing Islam.

That was not all, said Bamba, asking me to bring up the maps on my phone. Sevillia was pointing to my phone too, the ash from his cigarette falling to the floor as he did this.

'Type in Mulhacén,' Bamba said, tapping my phone screen with his thick fingers.

I did as I was told and a spot about fifty kilometres north-east of Órgiva, deep in the Sierra Nevada, popped up on the screen, surrounded by hiking signs.

'Boabdil *padre*!' said Sevillia pointing to the screen.

'This,' began Bamba, 'is where they believe the father of Boabdil – you know Boabdil?' he asked.

I nodded enthusiastically.

'This is where they say he is buried.'

'Wow, really? . . . Do they know exactly where?'

Bamba looked to Sevillia, asking him in Spanish if the exact location of the grave of Boabdil's father was known. I could see Muhammad was also now taking a keen interest in our conversation. Sevillia shook his head. The location of the grave of Boabdil's father was not known. Mount Mulhacén is actually the tallest peak on the Spanish mainland, standing at an impressive 3,482 metres above sea level, and is named after Abu l-Hasan Ali, the ruler of the Emirate of Granada between 1464 and 1482 and from 1483 until his death in 1485. Known as Muley Hacén, he is remembered for being cruel, almost warlike in nature, mostly because unlike previous Nasrid rulers he refused to pay tribute to the Catholic Monarchs, preferring to go to war with them if needed. This reputation may well have emerged also because he violently usurped his own father's throne in 1464, and is said to have had him imprisoned for the rest of his life in the castle at Salobreña on the south coast. Abu l-Hasan is also remembered for his weakness for the sensual, because he enjoyed the company of singing and dancing girls, though in all likelihood this reputation emerged because of the way he lusted after and married a Christian concubine called Isabel de Solís, who had been captured during one of the Nasrid raids into Castile. The raids were a response to those begun by the Castilians when the then newly crowned Abu l-Hasan had refused to pay tribute to the crown of Castile. After marrying Isabel, Abu l-Hasan abandoned his first wife, Boabdil's mother, Aisha al-Hurra, who was reportedly a direct descendant of the Prophet Muhammad. Isabel converted to Islam, took on the name Zoraya and bore Abu l-Hasan two sons, Nasr and Said. The marriage caused a scandal, and the arrival of the two sons posed a potential threat to Aisha's sons succeeding Abu l-Hasan to the Nasrid crown. The civil war that ensued saw Abu l-Hasan briefly deposed and Boabdil placed on the throne in 1482.

'Zoraya's castle is near here also,' said Bamba, as Sevillia offered up more nuggets.

Sure enough, when I pulled up my map, there was indeed a Castillo de Zoraya in Mondújar, just thirty minutes north-west by car. This was reportedly given to Zoraya by Abu l-Hasan as a wedding gift, and then, during the Nasrid civil war, they both took refuge there. I was beginning to get a familiar feeling, one I had experienced on almost every single journey I had made over the past two decades looking for Muslim Europe. It was a sickly feeling mixed up with intense excitement born out of the fact that in spite of my best efforts to research the places I wanted to visit, there was always so much more out there on the ground: hidden layers wrapped up in myth, legend and local lore. The fact that so much of the history had been systematically eradicated or just ignored by popular culture meant, all too often, that it was impossible to appreciate this Muslim heritage in any one book, website or source. Sometimes it was only by being on the ground, like this, talking to the locals, that I often learned about the other places I needed to visit; and frustratingly, all too often the discoveries came just as I was starting to run out of time.

'Wow, there is so much history in this area!' I said.

Sevillia nodded sagely.

The Nasrids famously left Granada by going south through the Alpujarras before making their way across the Mediterranean to North Africa. It was why the mountains I was now staring up at were littered with sites haunted by the memory of the rulers of the region for almost three centuries. In the case of the Castillo de Zoraya, almost literally. According to one tradition, upon realizing the end was nigh in 1491, a year before Boabdil would famously hand over the keys of the Alhambra Palace to the Catholic Monarchs and symbolically bring to an end eight centuries of Islamic rule in Spain, he had the bodies of his ancestors exhumed from the palace's royal cemetery – the Rawdah – that I had pointed out to Mina and Michael. The tradition claims he did this to move them to a cemetery in Mondújar near the foot of the castle. This legend was corroborated by the Alhambra's conservation architect, Leopoldo Torres Balbás, in the 1920s, when he discovered that seventy of the tombs in the Rawdah were empty. Mondújar, a mere half-hour drive north-west of Órgiva, could be the final resting place of Spain's last Muslim royal family. As I contemplated this possibility, and whether I had time to go and look for them, I became distracted by Muhammad and Sevillia, who were falling about laughing and high-fiving one another.

'What's so funny?' I asked Bamba.

'They are laughing because the whole time they have been friends they always fight over whose city is the most important, Seville or Tangier, where Muhammad is from . . . and now Muhammad find out he is originally from Seville!' Bamba was laughing too.

I stared at the three of them in disbelief.

'Do you mean Muhammad has traced his ancestral roots from Morocco back to Spain?'

Bamba nodded, before the penny dropped for him.

'Wait, you will be interested in this, Muhammad must tell you his story and how he find out his ancestors are from Seville!'

I laughed out loud.

'I can't believe I am actually in the presence of a Muslim who is part of the direct legacy here, Muhammad, please tell me your story!'

Muhammad looked at Bamba as he had no idea what I had just asked him, and Bamba translated.

The journey to look into his roots was actually prompted by Sheikh Umar, explained Muhammad, and came about after he experienced a kind of awakening and rebirth.

'I was twenty-one years old, living the life of a *jahil* in Madrid – smoking, drinking, womanizing,' said Muhammad, using the word used by Muslim historians to describe the Arabs before they were 'given' Islam: *jahil* means to be ignorant or act stupidly.

'Then one day an Egyptian came into my life. He saw what I was doing and said to me: "Your ancestors would be ashamed of you! This is not your way, man . . . You need to leave Madrid!'

'Where did you go?' I asked.

'Ibiza,' said Muhammad nonchalantly.

Sevillia, Bamba and I collapsed in laughter.

PART 4: ECHOES OF AL-ANDALUS

'More dangerous!' squealed Bamba.

Muhammad's face was a picture of seriousness. It turns out there is a small Naqshbandi community on Spain's most famous party island, and a friend of the sheikh there had offered him a bed, but before he even got to the house, a fire broke out, burning it to the ground. Muhammad saw this as a sign.

'The man told me to spend the night in the maq'am,' explained Muhammad.

The maq'am in Ibiza came about after Sheikh Nazim visited the community there in November 1997. During his stay, the sheikh identified a location where he had 'received' instruction to build a symbolic maq'am — a shrine that does not contain a real body — dedicated to his teacher, ad-Daghestani. That night, as Muhammad sat outside the quaint stone-built maq'am, he saw lots of young Moroccans just like himself, walking around, smoking weed.

'That's when I remembered my mother's words again.'

I could hear Sevillia laughing. Muhammad looked at him over the top of his dark sunglasses and grinned; he had told him the story already.

'What did she tell you?' I asked, expecting deep pearls of wisdom to tumble from his lips.

'She said, "Ibiza is not a good place for you!"'

We all burst out laughing again. Bamba was feigning clapping his hands. Sevillia was having a laughing-coughing fit, and Muhammad was grinning. After his brief stint in Ibiza, Muhammad made his way to Catalonia in the north-east of the country, close to the border with France, where in a place famed for its association with the region's patron saint, St George, called Sant Llorenç de la Muga, Muhammad worked for a time on a site where a mosque was being built also dedicated to Sheikh Nazim's teacher, Sheikh al-Faiz Abdullah ad-Daghestani. There Muhammad read the Qur'an for the first time as an adult.

'I read it from Surah *al-Fatihah* to Surah *an-Nas* in one go!'

Muhammad wiped his finger across the table to indicate that he read the entire holy book, all 114 chapters, containing over 77,000 words, in one sitting. I looked at him in disbelief.

'You read the whole Qur'an in one sitting!?' I asked, still not sure I had heard right. Muhammad nodded.

'In eighteen hours! I couldn't close the book . . . not because I didn't want to. I just couldn't!' he said.

Muhammad lived at the site for about two years, until one day Sheikh Hassan Dyck (sheikh at the Cologne zawiya in Germany) came to the site, and although he wanted to give his *bay'ah* – his allegiance – to the sheikh, he felt uncomfortable to do this as he didn't feel like he was a 'Muslim' any more.

'But you were born into a Muslim family and raised a Muslim, right?' I asked.

Muhammad nodded, before explaining that all the things he had done as a child that Muslim children do, he did without feeling anything and only because he was asked to do them. I wanted to say but that is the case for most Muslim children – myself included – but didn't want to detract from his story.

'I never did anything from the heart, and so I wanted to take the shahadah first and only then did I give bay'ah to the sheikh.'

The sheikh then handed Muhammad a microphone and told him to give the adhan. Muhammad tried for a whole twenty minutes, struggling to finish his sentences.

'Every time I started to say the words, I couldn't finish . . .'

'He cried,' Sevillia said, finishing his friend's sentence.

After twenty minutes of breaking down and restarting each sentence of the call to prayer, Muhammad finally finished the adhan. The incident left him exhausted and he soon fell into a deep sleep.

'I had a dream where I saw a light coming from the Ka'aba, like a thunderbolt, straight at me, and it stabbed me right here' – he pointed to his chest – 'I woke up and I could still see the light, and that was the beginning for me.'

Over the course of the next few years, Muhammad married twice, got his Spanish citizenship and found his way to Órgiva.

'It was Sheikh Hassan that said to me, "You don't know where you are from, you should go and make some investigations in Morocco", and that made me go back to Tangier and look for my grandfather's tomb.'

As he said this, Muhammad pulled out a battered old ID card, with its plastic laminate peeling back at the corners. There was a photo in the top-right corner of a sage-like old man staring directly at us. His eyes were kindly, and he was wearing a prayer hat. The old man's beard was white and large. I looked up at Muhammad to see the resemblance, but it was difficult with his large shades and greased-back black hair. The words were mostly in Arabic except for some numbers and a year, '1916'. The card had a signature in black ink in the bottom right and a round red seal that had been stamped across much of the text and photo, in the way documents were historically notarized. The seal had a domed structure on it, with a finial on the top. It resembled the dome of a mosque, but there was no crescent. I turned the card over to find the same logo on the back: it belonged to the Association of the Sharif Bani Aich, the issuing authority.

'When I went to Tangier and asked about him, people said, "Who are you the son of?"' explained Muhammad. 'When I gave them my father's name, they said, "Oh, you are from the Lishby family."'

Muhammad had never heard the name 'Lishby' and was confused by their response, but they were insistent that this was his tribe, and when he ran it by his father, the response left him flabbergasted.

'I told my father that the locals said we are from the "Lishby" family, and he said this was true, so I asked him why Lishby, what does that mean?'

'What did he say?'

'He said Lishby means the people that fled Ishbiliyah [Muslim Seville] and came here!'

Sevillia heard the punchline and howled with laughter, patting his friend's shoulder. Muhammad's family were part of the mass migration of Iberian Muslims that began following the fall of Granada in 1492, but gathered pace after 1567, when the practice of Islam and use of Arabic was made illegal across Iberia. During the Muslim period, Seville had been known as al-Ishbiliyah, from which his ancestral name, a geographic locator, had been reduced to 'Lishby'.

'The *morisco* families fled Seville and went to Africa and stopped when they felt safe, that's how my family ended up in Anjra,' said Muhammad.

He estimated there were probably around four or five hundred 'Lishbies' scattered across Morocco and maybe 700 more Christianized Boulaich in Spain.

Sevillia was still laughing.

'Do you remember when I used to say Seville is the most beautiful city in the world, and you used to say "No! Tangier! Tangier!"?' Sevillia teased Muhammad in his broken English for my benefit.

Muhammad laughed and nodded. He didn't need to understand all the words to know what Sevillia was saying. I laughed too, as much in disbelief as anything else. Sevillia was a blue-eyed, long-haired, white Spaniard, his waistcoat and green embroidered prayer hat the only hint of the East about him. In all likelihood he was descended from those 'barbarian' Franks — as Manuel had described them — that came from the North to 'reconquer' a place they had no real ancestral claim to. Meanwhile, Muhammad, with his black box-beard, slicked-back hair and North African waistcoat, looked every bit the Maghrebi, descended from those that were evicted from their ancestral home. Maybe centuries ago, as Irving described, his family still held maps, deeds and even keys of the houses they had been forced to give up. It was amazing that here they both now were: descended from Iberian Muslims and Christians sitting together in a café in a tiny village in the south of Spain, five centuries after fate had separated their families.

'We are now celebrating that we are family!' said Muhammad, putting his arm around his friend and handing him a Marlboro Light cigarette.

Sevillia took the cigarette and continued to poke fun at Muhammad. I sat and watched, still in disbelief at the moment and the surreal privilege of being part of it.

Almost every inch of Iberia harboured some Islamic heritage, but the area to the south of Granada, around Órgiva, was probably the richest of all. It was through this corridor that Abdu'r Rahman I arrived in Iberia, and it was through this corridor, eight centuries later, that Boabdil left. It was here that the last embers of Iberian Islam glowed the longest and why almost everywhere you look on a map there is an echo. To the south-west of Órgiva, near the Guadalfeo reservoir, was Vélez de Benaudalla, the second half of which is a Latinization of *Banu Wadi Allah*, meaning 'Children of the Valley of God', which is also home to the Jardín Nazarí. This is a quaint little classical Islamic garden, where the delightful interplay of water, landscaping and flora is so reminiscent of the Nasrid one near the Alhambra that locals have dubbed it 'Generalife Chico', or Little Generalife. Even the river that flows through the valley, Guadalfeo, has Muslim roots: the clue is in the prefix *guadi*, always a Latinization of *wadi*. One theory for the name's second half claims it comes from Wadi al-Fath, meaning 'River-Valley of Victory', because Abdu'r Rahman I reportedly landed at the mouth of the river when he crossed over from North Africa. That spot now sits in the town of Salobreña, where, in the heart of the original medina, there is still a castle built by the Muslims dating from the tenth century that was used to imprison several Nasrid kings, including Muley Hacén. Albuñuelas to the north-west of Órgiva is said to come from the Arabic for 'pretty things' or 'abundance'; further west is the great fourteenth-century Moroccan traveller Ibn Battuta's 'al-Hammah', now Alhama, where he passed a 'marvellously built mosque' and bathed in hot springs at a hammam decorated with Caliphate horseshoe arches still visible in the bowels of the Hotel Balneario; to the north-east, Guadix is surrounded by blue lines on satellite maps and comes from *wadi* – valley; while Purchena, to the east, is from *burj* – tower;

Almanzora, even further east, was 'The Victorious' – *Mansour*; and Almuñécar, along the coast and once a thriving Muslim port, is from *hisn al-Munakkar* – which means the fortress surrounded by mountains. The town's official flag still features the heads of three turbaned figures in the waters.

In truth it had been the same in every country I had visited on this trip. Once that radar is turned on and the Eurocentric perspective switched off, suddenly the heritage is everywhere and you're left wondering how you hadn't noticed it all before.

22

The Mosque-Churches of Toledo

Toledo, Spain

'Was this a mosque then?' asked Robert to no one in particular, as he stared up at the beautiful Arabic inscriptions on the large Umayyad-inspired horseshoe arches of the San Román Church.

'It started as a church and was briefly a mosque but that's not why it's got the Arabic, the Arabic was done by Christians,' I replied.

'Really?'

Robert blinked a couple of times, as if in disbelief, now staring at the slim ornate windows, framed by Arabic inscriptions and surrounded by frescoes of Christ and his Apostles. They sat above a sumptuous partially destroyed Nasrid-style muqarnas arched entrance. It was an easy mistake to make: Toledo's San Román Church was built on Visigothic remains in the thirteenth century, in the most spectacular *mudéjar* style. This alluded to the admiration medieval Christians of Spain had for Iberian Islamic culture by blending its architecture with Romanesque, using its distinctive horseshoe arches in such a magnificent manner that it felt like a homage to Abdu'r Rahman I's mosque and that pervasive Córdoban Caliphate culture I had encountered across the Mediterranean basin. In so many ways, the architecture of the church, built during the reign of Alfonso X, is an artistic metaphor of his Toledo. Known as 'the Wise' or 'the Learned', Alfonso loved acquiring knowledge, and early on in his reign, which started in 1252, he tried to set up a school of Arabic and Latin in Seville. Related to Frederick II of Sicily, to whom he is often compared and whom he hoped to emulate (but failed) in becoming Holy Roman Emperor, Alfonso was also a visionary. This was why just as the church was being constructed, absorbing and embracing all that was beautiful, good and useful about Muslim art and architecture, Alfonso was doing the same by establishing his pivotal school of translation, modelled on those previously established in Damascus, Córdoba, Baghdad and Palermo. In the same way that they revolutionized global Muslim culture, Alfonso's, following closely in the footsteps of Sicily's Frederick II, was about to revolutionize Northern and Christian Europe.

'Was it Seville, love, we visited where they have the church in the beautiful mosque?' Vanessa, Robert's wife, asked him, 'Or was it Córdoba?'

I had bumped into the warm and friendly English couple from London as I stared up at a fresco painted into the inner rim of one of the giant horseshoe arches. The cross-pollination was transporting me back to the Arab-Norman churches of Palermo, and I knew from the cultural corridor Toledo became, even more so than Palermo, that this was no coincidence.

'I think Córdoba,' said Robert.

He spoke much slower than his wife, either because he was tired or, as I suspected, due to illness. I was tempted to jump in and tell them it probably was Córdoba, but realized this journey had taught me that actually it could be any church across the Mediterranean.

'Where they put this Christian chapel right in the middle of this gorgeous mosque filled with arches.'

Vanessa's description, echoing the lament of the Catholic monarch Charles V, confirmed it was indeed Córdoba she was thinking of. A history lecturer by profession, she knew the legend well.

'Yes, that's right. He said, "What have you done here?"'

Vanessa laughed, in that very polite way middle-class English people do. I could see why she was reminded of the Mezquita-Catedral of Córdoba. The San Román's understated red and white horseshoe arches, to the untrained eye, look exactly like the Umayyad ones in the Mezquita, only bigger, and the church's later addition of a busy, gaudy baroque altar, all ivory and gold, appeared as invasive a presence as the chapel that Charles V regretted giving permission for. We spoke about the beauty of the layers in the Córdoba mosque and other monuments across Spain.

'To be honest, it's continuing to this day across Britain, where many of the deconsecrated churches have been taken over by Muslims who respectfully convert them into mosques,' I said, thinking of the dargah of Sheikh Nazim in North London.

'I recently developed a history walk in London near Aldgate –' began Vanessa.

'Oh, I grew up there!' I said, a little too excitedly.

'Then you'll know the place down Brick Lane, I always end there – it used to be a church, synagogue –'

'– and now a mosque!' I finished Vanessa's sentence.

We laughed about the chances of meeting someone in Toledo who knew one of the only mosques I had actually grown up with. We then spoke a little about the famous lane, its wonderful market and curry houses, and how it had changed over the years.

'Yes, I grew up with that mosque and the East London Mosque around the corner . . . Did you know there is a synagogue building at the back of the East London Mosque, in Fieldgate Street?' I asked.

'Er . . . no, I haven't been to that one,' said Vanessa.

Both mosques, just like what we were staring at inside the San Román, actually told a story of a forgotten *convivencia* in the East End of London. The Brick Lane Mosque began life as a Protestant chapel in 1743, before becoming a synagogue in 1891, and has been a mosque since 1976. Meanwhile, the East London Mosque started off as a small place of worship on the other side of the borough on Commercial Road in the 1940s, and was moved to its current site next to a synagogue in 1982. Over the years, the mosque grew and grew, consuming every building around the synagogue, until in 2015 the mosque trust also bought the listed synagogue building. I told the couple the stories my father's generation had told me of how the old Jewish community had also experienced prejudice from the locals, and were among the only ones willing to offer the new Bangladeshis work.

'It was the Jew down Brick Lane who would offer them work, even training them to use the machinery in his textile factory,' I explained.

This was how many of the historical Jewish factories were eventually inherited by the Bangladeshis, just like the synagogue, and in time the Sunday markets, first established by the Jews because they couldn't work on the Sabbath (Saturday). I told them about other great anecdotes I had heard over the years, like how the Bangladeshi men would buy kosher meat when they couldn't source halal (permissible to Muslims) and, my personal favourite, though in all likelihood an urban myth, how when the Jewish community began to dwindle and a funeral service didn't have the required number of men to go ahead, how they would go out to the Lane and ask the Bangladeshis to step in and make up the numbers.

After saying goodbye to the kindly couple, I wandered around the San Román for a little longer admiring the fascinating interplay of the classical Islamic with the Renaissance and baroque, before glancing at the Visigothic Museum and heading out.

I opened the small wooden door set within the horseshoe arch entrance of the San Román, stepped out and turned right, past the original baroque entrance to the church, where the tall bell tower that once served as a minaret loomed overhead. I began walking south-east along the pavement of Calle San Román, the high walls of the eighteenth-century Iglesia de los Jesuitas and those of the University of Toledo offering me welcome shade.

Perched high up on a hill above the Tagus River, Toledo is known as the 'City of Three Cultures'. Once the capital of the Visigothic Kingdom between the sixth and the eighth centuries, Toledo was where the influential Christian Councils of Toledo would meet. Al-Maqqari describes the region of Toledo as being home to 'pleasant orchards, a beautiful river, gardens, groves, fine fruits of every kind

PART 4: ECHOES OF AL-ANDALUS

A highly decorated Caliphate horseshoe arch inside Toledo's San Román Church, featuring Arabic on the upper tier

and description' and a place of 'good arable lands, rich meadows and pastures fine'.

With most of the buildings dating from the thirteenth century onwards, there is a distinctly medieval feel to the historical centre. The city became Toleytullah as soon as the Muslims arrived in Iberia, with Tariq ibn Ziyad's capture of the city around 711 marking the start of more than 250 years of Muslim rule.

Wandering beneath mashrabiya-style bay windows that looked over the narrow cobblestone alleyways, I was reminded of the medinas across the Mediterranean. As I turned left onto Bajada Corral Don Diego a familiar smell wafted into my nostrils – of fresh leather, emanating from a small store selling the kind of bags found all over North Africa. I took a left onto Calle Tornerías, where the cobbled street, devoid of any paving – like so many in historical Toledo – continued to slope downhill. I could now see the horseshoe arches halfway down the street even before I came upon them. The three arches were set in a facade of thin red bricks on the first floor, above large empty spaces that were once shop fronts. Two North African men carrying machinery entered the site. Another stood at the doorway of his little confectionery store opposite.

'*Assalamu alaikum,*' I said to all three.

The men replied in Maghrebi accents.

'Is this a mosque?' I asked, using my poor Arabic.

The workmen, both wearing T-shirts slightly too short, nodded.

'*Si, si, masjid!*' said the owner of the shop.

I stared up at the archways again. The two at each end had metal black bars criss-crossing through them to offer support, and the roof at the top looked flat and conventional. The Mezquita de las Tornerías was originally built in the eleventh century in what was the old Muslim neighbourhood of Arrabal de Francos. Online images of the interior showed a small square prayer space dominated by red-brick horseshoe arches which had to be built on the second floor because of the street's uneven nature. The mosque was only rediscovered in the late nineteenth century, and at first thought to be a synagogue, but was confirmed as a historical mosque in 1905.

The workmen had disappeared inside the building now, and I could hear loud banging. I turned to the shopkeeper who was casually picking his teeth.

'Do you know when it will open?' I asked him.

The man shook his head.

'Maybe they will open for jumu'ah?' I said, smiling at him.

This made him laugh.

'No, no jumu'ah here!' he said.

He was right. Toledo is now home only to historical mosques. There are no functioning ones in the city any more. To perform the Friday prayer, I would have to leave the old centre and make my way into the suburbs, but before I did, I was going to visit the ancient mosque the Mezquita de las Tornerías is believed to have been modelled on: Toledo's best-preserved mosque building, the tenth-century Mezquita del Cristo de la Luz. This was located near the ancient town's northern gate, the Puerta de Valmardón, a name that comes from the original Arabic Bab al-Mardum, meaning the 'walled-up' or 'condemned door'. This was close to the city's most 'Muslim'-looking gate, Puerta del Sol – Gate of

PART 4: ECHOES OF AL-ANDALUS

the Sun – which has a gigantic arabesque archway and was known during the Islamic period as Bab Mu'awiyah, possibly a direct reference to the Umayyad dynasty's founding father.

The tiny Mezquita del Cristo de la Luz is a beautiful little redbrick building that has three framed horseshoe arches open at the entrance and, above this, six decorative ones, featuring the Umayyad red and white pattern, that have now been bricked up. The southwestern wall features a grille made using thin red bricks. Above this, also made using thin red bricks, are Kufic Arabic words that tell us the mosque was financed by an Ahmed ibn Hadidi, in 999, and built by a Musa ibn Ali. The influence of the mosque in Córdoba can be seen in the use of the brickwork on the facade and the horseshoe arches inside. The mosque, originally known as Masjid Bab al-Mardum, because of its proximity to the gate, is one of ten that once stood in Muslim Toleytullah and easily the best preserved. Even the apse, added after Alfonso VI took the city and converted it into a church, was done sympathetically, using the same brick technique and similar arch designs, something that was probably executed by the city's Muslim architects and therefore considered *mudéjar*.

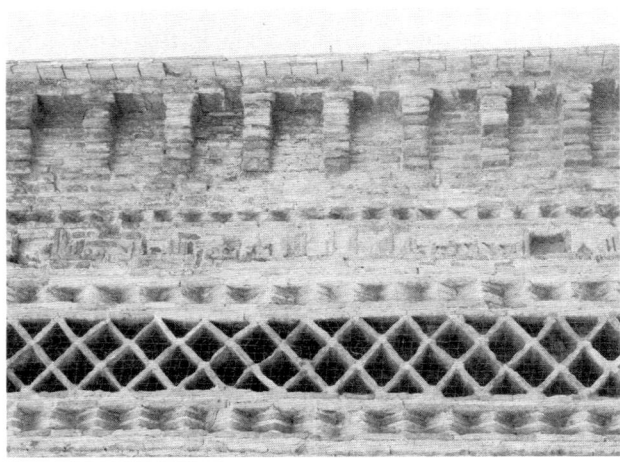

A close-up of the Kufic Arabic on the outer wall of the Mezquita del Cristo de la Luz which reveals that it was originally built in 999 by Musa ibn Ali as the Masjid Bab al-Mardum, in Toleytullah (Toledo)

I entered the square 8×8 metre Cristo de la Luz to be greeted by a mini-forest of pillars and a dim light coming through the thick lattice now covering the archways of the former mosque's outer walls. It felt like a miniature of Córdoba's Mezquita-Catedral, only the horseshoe arches here were white, in the Almohad style rather than the iconic Umayyad one. I wandered in between the grey marble pillars, which made the tiny space feel busy, and had clearly been installed with aesthetics in mind and a huge nod to Abdu'r Rahman I's archetype in Córdoba. Sensibly though, the pillars had all been aligned in such a way that they created straight rows facing Makkah, thus serving as a guide for worshippers lining up to pray, while minimizing their impact on the space. I looked above the pillars to the small vaults — a total of nine — some of which contained an eight-pointed star pattern. The wall opposite the entrance faced south-east and had a plain mihrab in the middle of three arches, now resembling a doorway, with small red tiles fanning along the curvature of the upper arch. The lattice covering was blocked from the back, so there was no longer a niche. I stepped through one of the three horseshoe arches and entered the Christian extension, a space that felt markedly different.

The addition was semi-circular in shape with no pillars running through it, though mini-horseshoe arches were used decoratively along the walls, where frescoes of angels and saints were painted into their niches. In the centre was a crucified Christ, suspended in mid-air using string. Painted above, in the semi-circular dome, was a faded image of Christ in a red oval frame, with the partial remains of two painted angels either side and the remnant of a four-legged winged animal underneath. The large arch that led from the congregation to the altar area contained Arabic inscriptions written in the same style as I had seen in the San Román Church. Smaller fragments further down suggested the Arabic had once run all the way to the ground. To move between the two 'sections' of the church felt like moving between two entirely separate buildings. The older part, devoid of any Christian iconography, could still be a mosque, whereas the extension with its imagery and the hanging crucifix felt like a chapel: the juxtaposition was fascinating.

I wandered back into the 'mosque' section, where a red-framed sign headed 'Antigua Mezquita' offered an explanation of the mosque for the uninformed using three close-up shots of its features. After a brief line about the founding of the mosque during the 'Caliphal Period' in the Muslim residential area of the city, the first image of the pillars spoke about how they resembled palm trees – just as they did in Córdoba; the second picture was of the vaults, and told us that there were indeed nine and these 'closed the mosque'; each piece of information was nicely displayed in both languages beside the pictures, but when I got to the last section about the mosque's mihrab, I had to read it twice. Next to a close-up image of the former mihrab, it said, 'Qibla: Wall of the mosque, looking to the city of Córdoba'. I looked up at the Spanish words, to check if it also had 'Córdoba' in the sentence. It did. I looked around to see if anyone else had noticed this schoolboy error by the Toledo Monumental – the touristic arm of the Archbishopric of Toledo – which had created the sign. A woman in a flowing summer dress was standing nearby, but she had clearly not read the sign or noticed the error.

'It's so, so beautiful,' she said.

'Yes, you can see they talk about the connections to Córdoba a lot,' I said.

'I am from Córdoba . . . did you see the Mezquita?' she asked, taking a picture of the vaults above our heads.

'You are from Córdoba?'

The lady nodded and explained that she was an architect by profession and had been drawn to the little church because of its architectural parallels with the famous church-mosque in her town. I told her I had also recently visited the Mezquita and loved the echoes of it inside the Cristo de la Luz, except for the last section of the sign we were both staring at.

'This is not the way to Córdoba,' I said, pointing first to the horrific error in the text, before pointing south-east and at the former mihrab.

The lady, who wore a large floppy hat and dark sunglasses, did a quick turn as if trying to assess what I had just said. As a non-Muslim, she hadn't quite grasped the point I was making. From Toledo, Córdoba actually lies to the south-west, so not only was the sentence on the sign theologically wrong – it was also geographically wrong.

'I . . . erm . . .' she began, before pausing as she tried again to figure out her bearings.

'This is the way to Makkah,' I finally said, before adding, 'We don't pray towards Córdoba, we pray towards Makkah . . . This is a big mistake.'

I smiled at her, but could see the woman still wasn't sure what it was I was saying, so she re-read the sentence I had pointed to.

'And . . . erm, Córdoba is this way.' I now pointed south-west, away from the mihrab and in the actual direction that the former Caliphate city was in.

'I don't know . . . I don't know,' said the lady.

I realized she was still assuming I was annoyed about the incorrect geography. Our conversation had now aroused the interest of a few other visitors inside the tiny space, including the lady's husband.

I remembered Miguel, the young Córdoban I had met at Madinah az-Zahra, and how little he had known about Islam. It dawned on me that maybe she had no idea what direction Muslims prayed in, or what, if any, relationship we still had with Córdoba.

'It's a big mistake. People that read this will think Muslims pray towards Córdoba,' I explained.

'Normally the orientation is for Jerusalem?' she asked.

Before I could answer, her husband jumped in.

'Mecca,' he said, pronouncing it in the anglophone way and making me wonder if my own pronunciation of Islam's holiest city had added to the confusion.

'For the Jews, Jerusalem, and for ancient Christians, but for

Muslims always Makkah,' I said, before realizing that too was not entirely accurate.

'*Si, si,*' said the woman as her husband repeated Mecca to her.

'Actually . . .' I began, hoping the mini-history lesson on early Islam I was about to give was not going to muddy the waters. I could see both husband and wife were genuinely interested, so I continued.

'When Islam first began, it was Jerusalem.'

The woman and the man's eyebrows rose with this new piece of information. For fourteen years, at the start of Muhammad's prophethood, the early community of Muslims directed their prayers towards Jerusalem, or al-Quds, as it was known to them. Then in the year 624 the revelation came that Muslims should face towards the Ka'bah in Makkah – the first clear message that Islam was a distinct faith and separate to the ones followed by the Jews and the Christians. Up until that point, much emphasis had been placed on the revelations to highlight the commonalities and reinforce the idea that the faith being preached by Muhammad was merely a continuation of the one preached by Abraham, Moses and Jesus. One great anecdote about the switch tells the story of how Muslims in Madinah were reportedly in mid-prayer when the news reached them of the qibla change.

'The story goes that when they heard this, they turned a full 180 degrees in mid-prayer to go from facing Jerusalem to facing Makkah,' I said, explaining that the mosque this happened in is now known as Masjid al-Qiblatayn – the mosque with two qiblas. None though, I reminded them, faced Córdoba.

I wandered over to the small roof garden connected to the mosque, passing beneath a canopy of jasmine. The garden, like the one attached to the Mezquita Mayor de Granada, was centred on a fountain which had four pathways symmetrically leading away from it; one of these also had a thin channel that connected it to another fountain built against the far wall. I stopped at the furthest wall, in between the two gates of Puerta de Valmardón and Puerta del Sol, and wondered if I should say something about the mistake in the text. It felt ironic that I would have to educate Toledo about the most basic of Islamic principles, when once upon a time it was hungrily devouring everything it could get hold of from the Muslim world.

The reason Toledo was able to become so pivotal to the re-awakening of Western Europe was that it was the first major city of the former Caliphate which the Christian kingdoms of northern Iberia – with their *very* different mono-culture – captured. In doing so, the northern Christians acquired a city with the perfect conditions to become a translation hub. Firstly, Toledo was a multilingual city, where most people were fluent in more than one language; it was a city in the mould of those found across the Córdoban Caliphate and Muslim Mediterranean. This meant differing communities did not just tolerate one another, but shared and engaged with each other's respective intellectual traditions and resources. Secondly, and maybe most importantly, Toledo's Arabized Christians – known as *mozárabes* – were already immersed in the Caliphate culture and therefore best placed to convince naysayers of the revolutionary potential al-Andalus's intellectual, cultural and scientific traditions possessed; in particular, those Christians from the North and parts of Western Europe who may have heard the suggestion that they should resist the progressive and 'heretical' ideas coming from infidel Muslim lands. Finally, and crucially, Toledo, like all the major cities of the Caliphate, was home to vast libraries filled with the books, manuscripts and treatises of the Muslim and Jewish Renaissances. The culture of Toledo in eleventh-century Iberia was very similar to the culture inherited and nurtured by the Arab-Normans of Sicily, which is why it is no surprise that the first major organized and systematic medieval Christian translation efforts took place in Toledo and Palermo, at almost the same time.

The Toledo School of Translators had two distinct phases. The first is in the middle of the twelfth century at the Cathedral of Toledo under the guidance of Bishop Raymond de Sauvetât, who commissioned *mozárabes*, Muslims and Jews to translate mostly Arabic and Hebrew philosophical and scientific texts into Latin. One of the most prolific translators of this period was Gerard of Cremona, who personally translated almost a hundred Muslim works essential to the later Christian Renaissance. Many of Gerard's translations of Ibn Sina, al-Khwarizmi, al-Kindi, al-Zahrawi and al-Razi were made widely available across Europe and used, virtually unchanged, for centuries to come. Another was John of Seville – possibly a converted Jew – who translated several treatises on how to use the Muslim-invented astrolabe, a century before the Portuguese invented the mariner's astrolabe – modelled on the former – which became essential to their seafaring exploits. John is also credited with translating works of Ibn Sina, al-Ghazali and the eleventh-century Jewish philosopher and poet Solomon ibn Gabirol (Avencebrol), as well as the highly influential *Secretum Secretorum*, a tenth-century Arabic encyclopedia on topics as varied as medicine, magic and statecraft. The translation became one of the most widely read texts of the Christian high Middle Ages, and was particularly important to the thirteenth-century English friar, philosopher and Oxford graduate Roger Bacon, who frequently cited it in his work. With the reputation of Iberia growing as a place of scholarship and translation, droves of knowledge seekers from across the Christian North made their way to the Iberian Peninsula, like Peter the Venerable, the Abbot of Cluny – the first Christian leader to approach polemic denouncement of the great Islamic threat academically, by studying the scriptures of the enemy. Peter commissioned the translation of five Arabic texts, including the Qur'an – the very first translation into a Western language and called *Lex Mahumet Pseudoprophete* (Law of Muhammad the Pseudo-Prophet). This was actually done by an Englishman, called Robert of Ketton, who also translated a history of the Muslim Caliphate and was part of a growing number of British translators, such as Michael Scot, working in Iberia during this period. Others included John of Toledo, who specialized in the translation of medical treatises and later became a personal physician to the pope; Alfred of Sareshel, who translated parts of

Ibn Sina's *Kitab al-Shifa*; and Robert Chester, whose translations included books on alchemy and al-Khwarizmi's book on algebra. These individuals, along with travelling knowledge seekers like Chaucer and the familial ties between Norman England and Sicily and Castile, created a crucial corridor that allowed the English to access this amazing body of work too. An example of this is when a man called Daniel of Morley, said to have been born in Norfolk, left England in the second half of the twelfth century in search of knowledge on the continent. Finding the education at the University of Paris thoroughly underwhelming – Daniel was scathing in his reflections – he set off for Toledo, the only place he knew where he could access 'the teaching of the Arabs, the wisest philosophers in the world'. Daniel stayed in Toledo for a while, and when he left for England again took with him a 'valuable collection of books'. He then presented these to Bishop John of Norwich – also 'John of Oxford' – who himself had seen the splendours of the Arab-Norman courts when accompanying Joan, Henry II's youngest daughter, to Sicily to marry Sultan Musta'izz, also known as William II. The bishop, who may have already acquired some manuscripts of Arab origin from his time in Sicily, told Daniel he was keen to establish a place of learning in the then relatively insignificant town of Oxford. The books Daniel brought back from Toledo are believed to have become the nucleus of the new Oxford University's library and central to the teaching of the new institution. Then there was Adelard of Bath, who referred to those he learned from as 'his Arab masters' and travelled through Spain and Sicily, where it is believed he learned Arabic, and brought back to England translations of works on astronomy, philosophy and alchemy, and, of course, Indo-Arab numerals.

The school of Toledo's most prolific phase came during the reign of Alfonso X in the thirteenth century. With the monarch rewarding translation work handsomely, the court – there was no formal 'school' at this point – quickly started to attract scholars from across the continent, with translation efforts in Toledo reaching new heights. One of the distinguishing aspects of this phase was Alfonso's desire to make translations more accessible by translating into a version of Castilian rather than Latin, thus also laying the foundations for the modern Spanish language. Many of Alfonso's translators were Jewish, including two of his personal physicians, Yehuda ben Moshe ha-Kohen, who translated numerous works on astrology, and Abraham of Toledo, who translated works by the tenth-century Iraqi polymath Ibn al-Haytham. Throughout this period, many translators – like Michael Scot – often went on to work in some of the other translation hubs across Christian Europe, in places such as Bologna, Salerno and Palermo. Many also returned to their home nations armed with entire libraries of translations – like Daniel – that revolutionized the intellectual landscapes of their home countries.

23

Madinat al-Yahud

Toledo, Spain

One of the fascinating stories al-Maqqari told when describing the Muslim conquest of Toledo was of its alleged connections to actual Abrahamic prophets. He claimed that it was once the abode of both the prophets Solomon and Jesus, as well as Alexander of Macedon, whom he referred to as 'Dhul-Qarnayn' ('the two-horned one') – a mysterious figure in the Qur'an some Muslim scholars have identified as Alexander. He then claimed that when Tariq ibn Ziyad took the city, he grabbed himself some interesting loot, including the Table of Solomon made out of 'one solid emerald' which was brought there during the sacking of Jerusalem by 'Ishban, King of the Romans and founder of Ishbiliyah'. Al-Maqqari claimed the table was then presented to the Caliph al-Walid and valued at 'one hundred thousand dinars', but said its whereabouts were no longer known, though it was probably in Rome. He also said that Tariq and his troops came upon a huge 'temple' filled with gold and silver vases, as well as numerous precious jewels and stones. It then became another city that the Berber general left in the care of the local Jewish population, before setting off to continue taking further towns and cities to the north.

The Madinat al-Yahud, or City of the Jews, was the Jewish quarter of Muslim Toleytullah, and almost a town in itself, taking up 10 per cent of the walled city, where everything Jews needed was available to them. It is in this historical area that the 'monuments' to memory which Sebastián felt the Sephardim did not have can be seen today, with the most spectacular and enigmatic being the Santa María la Blanca Synagogue – one of the oldest synagogue buildings in Europe. Everything about this twelfth-century place of Jewish worship screams mosque: row upon row of beautiful white horseshoe arches – the Almohad arch – held aloft by thick matching white pillars, resembling a beautifully preserved forest, just like Abdu'r Rahman's in Córdoba, except these resembled trees after the first snowfall of winter. The hypostyle construction combined with a lack of a women's balcony, and even the original name, Ibn Shoshan, all felt way too familiar to a Muslim. I could have been staring down the arcades of the twentieth-century Sheikh Zayed Grand Mosque in Abu Dhabi, or the twelfth-century archetypal Almohad Tinmal Mosque in the High Atlas Mountains of Morocco. The horseshoe arches of the Santa María la Blanca are found in thousands of mosques across the world built through the ages. Where they can't be found is in synagogues and churches. The deconsecrated Santa María la Blanca has been both of these, but never a mosque.

With a perplexed look on my face, I wandered around the near-empty synagogue-cum-church that in many ways epitomized the three faiths even more than did the church of San Román. I stared at the perfectly semi-circular arches topped by a neat row of smaller cursive Almohad ones, noting how they resembled miniatures of those I'timad had stood beneath in the Alcázar. It really was impossible not to assume that this had been a mosque at some point during the two and a half centuries of Muslim rule. With no garish altar sabotaging the aesthetic flow of the rows of arches, this former synagogue, converted into a church in the fifteenth century, felt more like a mosque than the Umayyad Mezquita in Córdoba or the Cristo de la Luz church just half a mile to the north-east. Such is the beauty of its construction that it is considered a masterpiece of both *mudéjar* and Almohad architecture and was almost certainly built by Muslim artisans, and most likely paid for by Joseph ibn Meir ibn Shoshan, the son of a finance minister to Alfonso VIII of Castile. I watched as tourist after tourist pulled back the thick curtain at the entrance of the synagogue and stopped, stupefied by the unexpected and stunning architecture. I then listened as more than a few queried its possible origins as a mosque in hushed tones. One particularly insistent young man called Ben kept asking his father David if he was sure that it hadn't been a mosque.

'After all, the Muslims and Jews got on really well,' he kept repeating, much to the bemusement of his mother. Nothing in the records shows that the Ibn Shoshan synagogue began life as a mosque when it was built in 1180, just a few decades before another horrific and murderous assault on the city's Jews by the Catholics in 1212, one of innumerable anti-Semitic revolts through the ages in Toledo — not one of them during the city's four centuries of

The 'forest' of stunning white horseshoe arches beneath smaller, Almohad ones in the Ibn Shoshan synagogue of Toledo, later the Santa María la Blanca church, built in the twelfth century almost certainly by Muslim architects and considered a masterpiece of *mudéjar* and Almohad architecture

Muslim rule. The reason for the synagogue's distinctive style is probably that at the time of its construction most of al-Andalus – not including Toledo – was under the sway of the Almohads, and it was artisans versed in their architecture who were most likely employed for its construction.

The unique synagogue-cum-church, like the equally unique mosque-cum-church in Córdoba, is now also at the centre of a tussle with the current custodians, the Catholic Church. Both properties – by today's standards – were seized illegally when Muslims and Jews were ousted from the respective cities. The Ibn Shoshan was seized by the Church following the Spanish Massacre of 1391, one of the worst displays of anti-Semitic mass murder in medieval Castile and Aragon. Numbers are difficult to establish, but with calls for the Jews to convert or be killed, the murder of 4,000 Jews on 6 June in Seville – by then Christian ruled – began the genocide, which continued through at least seventy Catholic-controlled cities for three bloody months. Jews were given the choice of being baptized or killed, as their houses and properties were sacked and looted indiscriminately. It is said that the man whose preaching instigated this anti-Semitic zeal, Vicente Ferrer, personally converted 4,000 Jews in Toledo in a single day and may also have been personally involved in the conversion of the Ibn Shoshan synagogue to a church. In Aragon, around 100,000 Jews are believed to have converted to avoid death – the number is said to be much greater for Castile – while many fled to Muslim lands, where they knew they would be guaranteed protection. Ferrer was made a saint by Pope Callixtus III on 3 June 1455, two decades before the start of the Spanish Inquisition by the Catholic Monarchs of Castile and Aragon. The Sephardic genocide of 1391 took place at the end of the same century as the fifteenth meeting of the ecumenical council of the Catholic Church, called the Council of Vienne, in 1311–12, which strongly criticized the religious freedom of Iberia in previous centuries, signalling the end of its, by then admittedly nominal, observance by Spain's Catholic rulers.

The modern community of Spanish Jews – all twentieth-century arrivals, mostly descended from those historically exiled to Morocco – believe the synagogue of La Blanca should be returned to them as a place of memory, so its original name and purpose can be fully acknowledged. However, as with the Mezquita, the Catholic Church is unrelenting on its position that in 1929 the ownership of the building passed from the government to the Church.

Jonathan Badichi and I headed towards the austere stone front of El Tránsito, with its fifteenth-century twin bells. The modern name comes from a painting called *El Tránsito de la Virgen* – The Dormitian of the Virgin – which hung on the altar in the seventeenth century after the synagogue had been converted into a church. We walked past the bronze statue of Samuel ben Meir Ha-Levi Abulafia, the builder of El Tránsito, who once upon a time was reportedly the richest man in Spain. The body-less, seemingly floating bald head wore a kippa with the Star of David on it, and was looking straight towards his former synagogue with an intent stare, his long beard draped over two tall Torah scrolls. At the foot of the statue, a sign explained it had been paid for by local property development firm Eprycon SL and sculpted by Rosa Hidalgo. Next to the sign was a collection of tea lights visitors had lit to honour the great Jew. Clearly this was done by non-Jews as Jews only light candles to honour family members, and even then only on their death anniversary. The statue was located in a new pedestrianized area, flanked by raised concrete plant beds. In front of Samuel, carved into a sandstone paving slab, was a menorah, to the left was carved a crescent, and behind the statue was a crucifix. There was one more stone, beside the crescent, with a Spanish inscription that loosely translated as 'Between the silence of its walls, the shadows of its memories are the Three Cultures', by an anonymous author. It was dated 2010.

'Oh wow!'

I gasped as I stepped into the main worship space of El Tránsito, where light came streaming into the rectangular hall through two small windows above the restored Torah Ark, which was a dizzying collection of geometric reliefs that belonged in a Nasrid palace. The windows were held up by three elegant Almohad arches, like those that ran along the top of the synagogue of La Blanca. El Tránsito was like the synagogue in Córdoba, on steroids.

'Pedro needed money for a war, but he didn't want to pay interest, and this is why he let Samuel build this synagogue,' Jonathan, a musician and tour guide to Jewish Toledo, explained as we sat down on a bench at the opposite end to the Ark.

Historical accounts suggest Ha-Levi, who was born around 1320 and descended from the influential old Andalusian Abulafia family which had provided leadership to the Jews of Toledo and Castile, lent significant sums of money to King Pedro I to support various royal expenditures, including military campaigns and administrative costs. Estimates of the amount he lent vary, but it is believed to be roughly 300,000 gold ducats, a fortune at the time. This, along with the fact that he was a highly influential adviser and treasurer to Pedro, gave Samuel the leverage to seek permission to build his grand synagogue in Toledo at a time when the construction of new synagogues had been banned across Christian Spain. The Catholic Church was outraged by the request and lobbied the king to refuse permission, but Pedro ignored this and Samuel's synagogue was constructed around 1356 – quite possibly the last Sephardic synagogue ever built in Sepharad – with Ha-Levi sparing no expense, employing the most skilled craftsmen, possibly Muslims sent from Granada by the Nasrids, where both Ha-Levi and Pedro had close ties: Ha-Levi often visited the 'Granada of the Jews' for diplomatic purposes and possibly to see extended family. The design incorporated exquisite *mudéjar* artistry, which blended Islamic and Jewish decorative elements, including actual Arabic writing. The synagogue's intricate stucco work, Hebrew inscriptions and stunning wooden ceiling, deeply reminiscent of the artistic and architectural style of the Nasrids, were more than just a nod to Muslim culture. Like the synagogue in Córdoba and the Ibn Shoshan around the corner, it was paying homage to what was then *the* high culture, the one the Sephardic Jews had welcomed to Toledo and Iberia, the one under which Sepharad flourished. In fact, integrated into the patterns of Ha-Levi's synagogue are Qur'anic verses, including the last verse of Surah *Luqman*, which discusses the omnipotent nature of God's knowledge and offers the cryptic lines, 'And no soul perceives what it will earn tomorrow, and no soul perceives in what land it will die.'

As I sat studying the Alhambra-inspired synagogue, trying to identify the Arabic in the patterns, Jonathan's phone went off, and he apologized. We had been together a mere twenty minutes and already he had answered a call and replied to several text messages about his guided tours. This was Jonathan's busiest time of the year, with coachloads of Jewish tourists arriving daily seeking his services. I had wanted to visit both Toledo's synagogues with him, but he just didn't have the time, so I had asked him to visit his favourite one with me, the synagogue of El Tránsito.

'I am always busy in Toledo, these big groups of Israelis are always coming from Madrid,' he said after ending the call.

Jonathan tells me he 'fell' into travel guiding. An accomplished music producer who had worked with some of Spain's all-time greats, including the legendary singer Raphael, he had come to Toledo wanting to do something different.

'I'm sorry, there is a bus, but the microphone is not working,' explained Jonathan, ending another quick call.

A trumpeter since the age of eight, Jonathan was in his midfifties, but looked young in his green-felt artist's hat, stonewashed jeans and white shirt. The son of a Dutch Christian mother and a 'tough' Yemeni Jewish father, he grew up in the Israeli city of Tzfat, surrounded by a large conservative community, which made things a little uncomfortable at times.

'Everybody knew our mother is not Jewish,' Jonathan said, checking I understood why that was important. In Judaism, the religion is passed down from your mother, which meant, as far as most Jews were concerned, Jonathan, his two brothers and his sister were not Jewish.

'They would say: "Your mother is *goya*!", a non-Jew.'

Goya is a derogatory term used to describe non-Jews. It comes from the word *goy*, meaning a gentile or non-Jew. In spite of this, his father's connections ensured the whole family received Israeli passports that did not identify them as non-Jews. Jonathan explained that as a family they never practised Judaism: he attended a secular school alongside Arabs, Christians, Muslims, Druze and Bedouins, but spoke fluent Hebrew and knows the faith well.

'Was there ever much trouble between the groups?' I asked.

Jonathan thought for a while.

'I remember when the black Jews arrived there was trouble,' he finally said.

Jonathan was only young, but recalls seeing white Jews throwing rocks and stones at the Ethiopian Jews when some of them first began moving to Israel.

'It was plain racism.'

I nodded in agreement, before asking him how he ended up in Spain. I wondered whether it was Spain's Jewish history that had brought him here. Jonathan quickly responded to a text message and then looked at me.

'I didn't know anything,' he admitted.

What he now knew, Jonathan learned during the pandemic, when he had nothing else to do. His relationship with Spain had nothing to do with his Jewish heritage.

'I fell in love with a Colombian woman in the Netherlands,' Jonathan explained.

This happened when he had gone to his mother's homeland to do a music course. After meeting his girlfriend, they moved to Barcelona together, but then went their separate ways. By then Jonathan had also fallen for Spain, though he still knew nothing about its fascinating Jewish history.

'Of course, I knew about Sepharad and that many Jews came from Europe, but when I came to Toledo I started to investigate everything really deeply, and I started to feel something very special in Toledo – because Toledo, it's . . . It's not Jewish, it's not Christian, it's not Muslim, it's everything together,' he said, before correcting himself, 'It *was* everything together.'

'So when you started learning this history, what stood out for you?'

'The history I learned that really stands out is the one of *la convivencia*, which the Christians messed up,' Jonathan said with more than a little disgust, 'because the Jewish and the Muslims they got along very well here . . . When the Jews were expelled in 1492, they searched for the Islamic countries . . . they went to the Ottomans.'

I was impressed by Jonathan's awareness of the continued protection of Europe's Jews by Europe's Muslims, who sheltered them for twelve centuries before the Nazis came along with their Final Solution. In fact, barring the odd despot, there was not one example of an anti-Semitic atrocity committed by European Muslims that was even remotely comparable to those committed by Europe's historical Christians. From the eighth century up until the twenty-first, Muslim Europeans were in effect the guardians of Europe's Jews.

Jonathan explained that the lack of awareness of this history was why he went out of his way to make clear to Israeli tourists the debt their ancestors owed to Iberian Muslims.

'They know but they don't *know*,' Jonathan said.

I found it refreshing that Jonathan made a point of getting this across to his Jewish tourists, the majority of whom hailed from Israel, where more than half the population have Sephardic roots and therefore largely owe their survival to the protection their ancestors were afforded by the likes of the Umayyads of Córdoba, the Nasrids of Granada, and later, when they were expelled, the Muslims of North Africa and the Ottomans of the Balkans. Even those Israeli Jews from the eastern half of Europe arguably owed much to the protection afforded them by Muslims in medieval and late-medieval Europe, when much of (Western European) Christendom was committing genocides like the Inquisition, issuing expulsion edicts and carrying out pogroms. By the fifteenth century, nowhere in Western Europe, barring isolated regions of Italy and Germany, was safe for Jews. Only Muslim

Europe was safe for Jews. It's true that by the time Western Europe became enlightened enough not to dismiss an entire people based on their religious beliefs or race, more and more post-Christian countries in the West of Europe were accommodating Jews, but arguably, had many of these communities not been protected by Europe's Muslims during previous centuries, there might not have been a European Jewish community to speak of.

'They [the Muslims and the Jews] were brothers, not cousins. They were *really* brothers, but they also had the common enemy that was the Christians, and the Christians won,' Jonathan said, summing up why this history was not a part of the popular European narrative. He then explained that in his opinion this was the reason why the synagogue we were sitting inside, the synagogue around the corner, the Ibn Shoshan, the synagogue in Córdoba and all the hundreds across the peninsula that were destroyed looked like 'Muslim spaces'; they were indeed paying homage to a culture, a creed and a people they respected, admired and looked up to.

In medieval Europe, the Muslims *were* the elite. They had been a cut above the rest, humanely, intellectually, culturally and artistically, and it was therefore only natural that all those around them, especially those enjoying their protection, would wish to emulate them (hence the San Román). Theirs was the high culture of the age, which is why when the richest man in Europe built himself a statement synagogue, he asked Muslim artisans to decorate it in the same way they decorated their palaces and mosques – in all likelihood, this was done by the same artisans that built Pedro's Alcázar.

'It was Muslims that built this,' Jonathan confirmed, pointing out the decorative Arabic on the synagogue's spectacular wooden *artesonado* ceiling of criss-crossing geometric patterns.

I stared up at the mesmeric intertwining woodwork in awe. We then wandered over to some of the artefacts of the Museo Sefardí inside the former convent of the Knights of Calatrava – an order named after a former Muslim castle, one of many that men joined vowing to engage in perpetual war against the Muslims. There were a bronze *hanukiyah* – a lamp used during *Hanukah* – an ornate silver case to hold sacred scrolls, and a tenth-century capital with Hebrew and Arabic inscriptions on it. The most interesting items though were segments of old tombstones.

'It says, when we die, we are all the same . . .' Jonathan began, reading and translating the Hebrew to me.

'Death is certainly a great unifier,' I mused, before asking, 'Whose tombstone is this?'

'It was a rabbi, and he died when there was an earthquake here . . . It shows that the Jews were here almost . . .' Jonathan worked out the date. '. . . a thousand years ago. They were talking in Hebrew, reading and writing in Hebrew, and singing in Hebrew, and then they took it with them'

'And now you're bringing it back,' I said as we began making our way to the exit.

I knew Jonathan had several tours lined up for the day, and I didn't wish to take up too much more of his time. Outside, in the bright sunshine, we took a seat at the Taberna Tristana, beneath its cooling parasols in front of windows with archways that echoed the synagogue of La Blanca. As we waited for our coffees, I asked Jonathan how his visitors responded to his tours.

'Some people cry . . . when they hear the music. Here, look . . .'

Jonathan pulled out his phone and showed me a video on a Facebook page, where he was playing a slow, melancholic number on his trumpet. He was very good. Within seconds, those around him – his Jewish tourists – began to sing to the tune he was playing. It was spontaneous, he assured me, they just knew the words to the songs, because singing them is a part of the Sephardic tradition they have retained in all the corners of the earth they fled to.

'The music is from here in Toledo, but they know it . . . immediately, they start singing to it.'

It was a powerful video, and I told him what he was sharing is a powerful history, with much potential given what we are witnessing in the world today. He nodded.

'I always point out to them that the longest period when Jews lived without conflict was here under the Muslims' control – in the Bible it says and now it was forty years of nothing happened, it was relaxed. Here it was nearly a thousand years, it was nine hundred years under the Muslims' control. It was not that long ago . . . they spoke Arabic.'

I believed it was longer, but I didn't correct Jonathan, the point didn't need labouring. I was just glad someone else recognized the amnesia prevalent among Europe's Jews and their descendants. Instead, I pointed to Samuel, who was now looking straight at us, and asked about the statue and the markings on the floor. Jonathan admitted he knew little about the statue but says the pushing of the historical *convivencia* in Toledo felt a tad empty.

'They sell here the past, but what about now? They are very anti-Semitic against the Jews and the Muslims now,' he said, correctly grouping both Semitic peoples together before adding, 'This is their example for them to learn, not me.'

I nodded in agreement, taking a slow sip of coffee. Jonathan was absolutely right: the memories of *convivencia* exemplified in its medieval form under the Muslims was something Spain, and by extension Europe, needed to learn from, not me and Jonathan, though our respective communities could clearly benefit from a refresher.

'It seems *convivencia* is just a nice thing to talk about when discussing what happened in the past. There doesn't seem much appetite for it now . . .' I finally said.

24

The Muslim Capital of Spain

Madrid, Spain

I stared at the ancient stones of the wall as it emerged from beneath a tall modern red-brick tower block and smiled to myself. The irony wasn't lost on me at all: the large roughly hewn rocks, stuck together using ancient techniques to create Madrid's oldest monument, rediscovered in the middle of the last century, was the most tangible evidence that a nation intent on denouncing its Muslim self had unwittingly picked for its capital one of the only cities in the entire country actually founded by Muslims, and again an Umayyad. Few of the other great 'Muslim' cities of medieval Spain could lay claim to that. Only Madrid, or al-Majrit as it would have been known to the founders, was created by Muslims. The ninth-century remains are those of the wall, which once measured two kilometres in length, built by the Emir of Córdoba, Muhammad I, the son of Abdu'r Rahman II, between 854 and 871, when he founded a military enclave on the very spot where I now stood. The wall, which only measured around 120 metres or so now, after much of it was destroyed in the fifteenth century, once protected the main citadel, or *almudayna*, complete with its very own grand mosque. I looked towards the area where that would have once been, now dominated by the striking baroque Catedral de Santa María la Real de la Almudena, which loomed high above the quiet Calle Mayor. The clue is in the name, Almudena. The cathedral, although completed less than half a century ago in 1993 after construction began a century earlier, was first mooted in the sixteenth century, when newly minted Spain, having 'discovered' the 'New World', switched its capital from Toledo to the then backwater of al-Majrit. Spain was too busy building its overseas empire, so despite al-Majrit not having a cathedral, the plans to build one dedicated to the Virgin of Almudena – the patroness of Madrid – were postponed. As with any major church or cathedral in Spain and its relics, the legends around the Virgin of Almudena statue – a copy of which now sits inside the cathedral – is built on anti-Muslim propaganda. The original statue is said to have been brought from the Holy Land by the patron saint of Spain himself, St James of Muslim-slaying fame, and according to the most popular Christian-centric legend the saint built the original military encampment nearby predating the Muslim one. In this version of history, the statue – complete with two lit candles – was hidden by the inhabitants in the defensive walls when they saw the Muslims advancing around the year 712, thus placing the legend right at the start of the Muslim conquest. The statue's location was closely guarded by the Christians until the eleventh century, when King Alfonso VI of Castile took the town from the Muslims. However, by this time the location of the Virgin had been forgotten by the little girl called María who had been entrusted with the secret by her mother just before she died. This apparently enraged Alfonso, who swore to tear down the walls, and was only placated by the townsfolk and María when they started praying for divine intervention. Then, as they marched around the walls, that intervention came in the shape of a sharp and 'unholy cry' from María, which brought the exact section of the 300-year-old wall hiding the statue tumbling down. This revealed the Virgin of Almudena sitting as it had been three centuries ago, complete with two lit candles. To honour the miracle he had just witnessed, Alfonso reportedly reconsecrated the citadel's mosque as the church of the Virgin of Almudena, and it was on this site, albeit ten centuries later, that the modern cathedral was finally built. The legend about the Virgin statue it harbours and the founding of the church is an article of faith, the only verifiable fact being that the cathedral stands on the site of the citadel's former grand mosque. The power of the legend remains to this day, with the Virgin's annual feast day celebrated in the city on 9 November, and Madrid's glamorous football club, Real Madrid, frequently paying homage to her by arriving with their – admittedly regular – haul of silverware and presenting it to the Virgin ahead of a city-wide parade.

I stared up at the colossal sandstone-coloured monument, topped by a modest grey dome and fronted by a fort-like design, complete with battlements above the entrance portico. Beyond the cathedral, to the east of the 3,000-plus-roomed Royal Palace of Madrid, was where the Muslims of al-Majrit built their medina. The area, now bisected by the Calle Mayor, was home to small neighbourhood mosques, a bazaar and even a court of law. Over time, the military encampment built to serve the dual purpose of controlling uprisings in nearby Toledo and defending against incursions from the north morphed into a fully fledged town.

'So this is the wall . . . I have never been,' Dr Javier Castaño said, wandering into the Parque Emir Mohamed I with his young son, as I studied a sign about lavender.

The original ninth-century wall of al-Majrit, built by the city's founder, the Emir of Córdoba, Muhammad I, and beneath it, the gardens now dedicated to him

PART 4: ECHOES OF AL-ANDALUS

Opened in 2010, the park backed onto the wall built by the Umayyad Emir and was located outside the original citadel perimeter. The small garden was laid out like a six-pointed geometric star, a pattern that emanated from the dry star-shaped fountain, tiled in blue and white, in the centre. Around this were a series of carefully planted botanical specimens, each containing a small display with the plant's Arabic name and how it was used historically by Muslims – a kind of living homage to the great Islamic culture of botany. Lavender, it turns out, was known as *al-juzama*, and the Muslims were using it as a potpourri by filling little fabric bags with dried lavender, long before the concept became popular in Europe. Meanwhile, in the twelfth-century the Sevillian Ibn al-Awwam was seasoning roasted meat with it.

'It's impressive,' Javier said, still looking at the wall, 'it gives you the idea that it was a very important small city, but still it was, from a military point of view, significant.'

Dr Javier Castaño belonged to the Department of Jewish and Islamic Studies at the Spanish National Research Council and had kindly agreed to spend the morning exploring what little remains of al-Majrit.

I told him I had learned rosemary was known as *al-ikli* or *kalil*, and that the oils of its flowers were recommended by Ibn Sina as a balm for a number of ailments, including stomach problems, and that cypress, or *sirw*, was used by local Toledan physician Ibn al-Wafid to treat bladder dysfunction, before I asked about his city's Muslim past.

'When Muhammad I founded Madrid, it was part of a chain of frontier encampments, along what was the Middle March of al-Andalus,' Javier said.

This was an area filled with towers, explained Javier. Another example was the town of Alcalá de Henares, thirty kilometres to the north-east.

'Alcalá is from the Arabic *al-qal'at* for citadel, it is on the road to Zaragoza and was the most important city in the area in the Muslim period,' explained Javier.

Known as Saraqusta by the Muslims, Zaragoza was also an important Muslim town in al-Andalus, with the Umayyads making it the capital of the Upper March. During the later taifa periods, it was home to one of the Muslim kingdoms that as-Sayyid, or El Cid – Rodrigo Díaz de Vivar – the Castilian mercenary knight, fought for. Today it is home to the most spectacular Muslim palace in the north of Spain, the Aljafería Palace, which like the Alhambra resembles an imposing fort from the outside and harbours stunning medieval Islamic architecture and artistry on the inside, though not quite on the scale of the Alhambra. The name comes from the eleventh-century ruler of the taifa of Zaragoza, Abu Ja'far al-Muqtadir. Like the Alhambra's Court of the Lions, the Aljafería has a stunning courtyard, with muqarnas arches topped with stucco decoration, but in a style now recognized as Almohad or Almoravid, as the palace inspired the architecture of both later North African conquerors. The Aljafería's rebuilt courtyard is much greener and has one small pool, and therefore may not reflect the original Muslim style. It leads off and into various smaller rooms, like the Alhambra, decorated with sumptuous stucco, muqarnas and Kufic Qur'anic inscriptions, but unlike the Alhambra the Aljafería's mosque has survived. There is a tiny false octagonal-shaped space of prayer featuring a mihrab in the style of the Mezquita in Córdoba, and large blind muqarnas arches that are topped first by a band of tall Kufic inscriptions and then smaller open muqarnas arches in the style seen in the Ibn Shoshan synagogue. Above these is a reconstructed dome. The Aljafería's mosque is the only surviving medieval mosque building identified north of Toledo. The palace's complex mix of delicate lacing, muqarnas and arabesque in relief was a precursor to later baroque styles and the more delicate versions we see in the Nasrid Palace.

I felt my phone go off and noticed that my relative, Somir, had messaged me. I had come to Madrid for two reasons: to end my trip learning about how Spain became the only Western European country with a capital city founded by Muslims, and secondly to catch up with family I had not seen for many years, someone who

PART 4: ECHOES OF AL-ANDALUS

wanted to show me *his* Madrid. I had asked Somir to come and first see the wall with me and Javier. His message said he was now on his way over. Somir had come to Spain almost two decades ago and slowly established himself among the growing Bangladeshi community in the capital. He had married the daughter of my maternal uncle and now lived here with his wife and two children. I had wanted to see the children and my uncle's daughter, but sadly my visit coincided with their own, 'back home' to Bangladesh.

I turned to Javier and asked him if there was much doubt about Muslims founding Madrid.

'Probably there were smaller settlements in the Visigothic time . . . Recent excavations have shown that this area was full of settlements, but Madrid as a village, as a small town, was founded by the Muslims, because from this hill you can control the Christian armies coming from the north,' Javier said, speaking slowly and deliberately, the way academics do.

Even in his third or fourth language, he was very articulate.

'And what about the name?'

'Some people say this is Islamic, some say it was Visigothic – it is difficult to tell . . . the Islamic meaning is "plentiful water".'

Javier explained this was because the fort was built close to the River Manzanares, which once flowed past where we were standing.

'Do you know the motto of the city?' asked Javier, with one eye on his son, who was climbing the dried-up fountain.

I shook my head.

'The motto of the city: "Madrid is built upon water and is surrounded by fire" – why? Because the stones of the wall are silex [flint] – it's a stone that you make fire with. One of the things in Madrid is that the city is very much related to water . . .'

That water was underneath the city, explained Javier.

'During the Arab period the Arabs built networks of tunnels to channel the water – the same kind you have in North Africa – and until the nineteenth century the people here took advantage of these underground water reservoirs. In the mid-nineteenth century, systems were built to channel the water from the mountains, which is why Madrid has one of the most high-quality water supplies. You can drink here with no problems, the water from the tap; in Barcelona it is not so good.'

Having climbed the disused fountain, Javier's son now came over to ask me what car I drove. I pointed to one of the cars he was playing with and said it was similar to that one. He wanted to know why I drove a yellow car. I laughed and told him that it was actually white. Javier allowed the interaction to arrive at its natural conclusion, before saying something gently to his son in Spanish. The little boy ran off again, but I could see how boring the garden was for him. After reading all the plant labels, it had become boring for me too.

'Maybe we can head to the high street in a bit and get him something to eat,' I proposed.

'Yes, we can do that,' Javier said, looking up at the looming cathedral of Santa María la Real de la Almudena. 'That building is awful!' he quipped, making me laugh.

It was true that the cathedral was not the most aesthetically appealing. Javier tells me it was almost certainly where the mosque of the citadel once stood, and I think we both secretly wished it was still there. He then told me that much of his research had been on Madrid's Jewish heritage, and that behind the cathedral there was once an area where the Jews were kept in an enclosed ghetto by the Christians. By then, he explained, the Muslim fortress had become a royal Christian fortress.

'It was the same building, rebuilt in the fifteenth, sixteenth and seventeenth centuries, and in the eighteenth century it was burnt down. In the early eighteenth century, the king decided to build a new palace and that's what you see today, but it was placed in the same location.'

Javier's son was back.

'He needs to use the toilet,' Javier said.

We both scanned the gardens, but there was nothing here.

'OK, let's go up to the high street, we can find a bar there,' I proposed.

Javier agreed this was the best idea, and we began walking towards the centre. Our route took us beneath the Viaducto de Segovia, and after telling me that many people consider the road that runs along it as being the start of historical Madrid, Javier offered a macabre contemporary fact about the bridge.

'Sadly many people have committed suicide here, that's why they put those fences up.'

I shielded the bright Madrid sun using my hand and stared up at the huge metal bridge. There was indeed fencing along the edge of the bridge's wall. Beneath it, on a platform around one of the foundation pillars, was a sleeping homeless person. We made our way up onto the busy Calle de Bailén, past the Almudena Cathedral's eastern facade, which was equally unappealing. I noticed Javier grimacing as it came into view.

'This area is called Barrio de Almudena . . . so the Muslim quarter was located in that area.'

Javier pointed to the other side of the busy street opposite the cathedral and royal palace. It was there, near a pleasant strip of green with a bust of the famous Romantic writer Larra, that we found a bar with a toilet. I filled my water bottle at one of the public drinking fountains outside and sat down on the stone bench beside it. My phone rang, and suddenly I remembered Somir was on his way to the Emir Mohamed I gardens. I answered the call by apologizing for not updating him and asked him to take note of the ancient wall and gardens before making his way to where we now were, promising him I would not move.

I looked behind me. Through the branches of two large splendid fir trees were pretty, low-rise apartment blocks that lined the edge of the green. Many clearly were of some age as their balconies and features were far more ornate and aesthetically pleasing. These were coloured a mellow peach or yellow, while the more functionally designed ones were plain white. An older woman walking a small dog and wearing outlandish sunglasses came waltzing through, closely followed by a guy in denim jeans and trainers. I wondered if either of them lived in the neighbourhood, and if they had any idea about its Muslim origins. Javier emerged from the bar with his son, who was now holding a large yellow ice cream.

'Aah, so that's what you wanted *papi* to buy you,' I said, smiling at the young boy, who was grinning away.

'Come this way,' said Javier, heading towards a narrow pedestrianized corridor to the left of the bar, 'I want to show you something.'

'Can we wait just a minute? My cousin is coming and I promised him we wouldn't move . . .'

No sooner had I said this than my phone rang again. It was Somir, and before I even answered the phone, I could see his white baseball hat peering inside the bar I had mentioned to him. I waved to get his attention, and he began walking over. We embraced and then I introduced him to Javier, who asked what language we were speaking. After I explained to him that we spoke Sylheti and the intricacies that distinguish it from Bengali, he and Somir became acquainted in Spanish. Javier then led us to the side street that ran between the bar and a smart, two-storey post-Renaissance apartment block. I read the sign on the wall, Calle de la Almudena. In the middle of this street was a large raised glass display area, surrounded by a low fence. This stopped people encroaching but I could see someone leaning on it at the far end. The structure was about two metres wide and four metres in length. As we got closer, I realized the person at the other end was in fact a bronze statue.

'These are the excavated foundations of the old church of Almudena, which was demolished in the nineteenth century,' explained Javier, before adding, 'It was built on the foundations of a mosque inside the walls of the medina.'

I translated this to Somir, pointing to what looked like nothing more than some old rocks behind a series of large, grubby glass panels.

'Why would they build a mosque down there?' he asked.

I explained how over time ground levels rise for various reasons, and that once upon a time that was street level. This didn't seem to satisfy Somir, who now turned to Javier and asked him about the excavations. As the two of them spoke and Javier's son happily licked his ice cream, showing no interest in the old rocks, I walked around to the bronze figure whose buttocks had lost their colour the same way Maimonides' shoe in Córdoba had, making me wonder if people also rubbed it for luck. I noticed a small bronze model of the original church on a pedestal against the wall. The Church of Our Lady of Almudena, also known as the Church of Santa María la Mayor, is believed to have been built on the site of the medina's Jami'a mosque, or 'Friday mosque'. This was where the main sermons of the week were delivered by the local imam; it was where local scholars and religious clerics would have met to discuss theological and societal matters, and where announcements from central government, i.e. the Emir or Caliph's offices, would have been made. During its first 200 years as a Muslim town, al-Majrit had been no backwater: the area we now stood in would have been home to several markets, including a large indoor one, a corn exchange and numerous hammams, like the ones I had seen in Granada and Sicily – in other words, a fully functioning urban space with that Córdoban Caliphate culture. In fact, al-Majrit also produced notable scholars, the most famous of whom was Abu al-Qasim Maslama ibn Ahmad al-Majriti – known by the Latin translators of his work as Methilem. The tenth-century Muslim polymath helped translate works of Ptolemy into Arabic, and introduced al-Khwarizmi – the Persian polymath and head of the Abbasid Bayt al-Hikmah, whose pioneering algebra revolutionized mathematics – to the West. Al-Khwarizmi was known as the best mathematician and astronomer of his age. Al-Majriti – known by his nisba – may have also had a daughter called Fátima, who some historians believe was an equally amazing polymath who worked on several mathematical and astronomical treatises with her father.

When Alfonso VI came and took the city as part of his conquest of Toledo, it was not done by military force, explained Javier, but with the agreement that existing non-Christian religious communities could remain. This meant that although some of the big mosques may have been immediately turned into churches as statement conversions, others continued to function as normal – something al-Idrisi noted in the twelfth century, stating that khutbahs were still being delivered regularly in the mosques of Madrid. Javier does concede, however, that shortly after the conquest of Toledo Manuel's 'barbarians' arrived and things changed.

'Right after the conquest, there was the arrival of the French ecclesiastical – French clergy – that were not used to seeing Muslims in France. So, they started a very anti-Islamic approach; the early agreements respected the mosque, but after the first bishop was installed in the see, he just converted the mosque into what is today the cathedral – here it was more or less the same.'

The bronze model of the church suggested it had a similar architectural style to the one in Mértola in Portugal, with a gently sloping apex roof. There was nothing to show us what the interior might have looked like and whether that too resembled the Mértola church. It was finally torn down in 1868 due to wholesale changes to the neighbourhood and to make way for the main road that now ran from north to south, Calle de Bailén, past the palace and cathedral. The model did, however, feature the church's tall bell tower, which felt extremely familiar.

'That looks like it could have been a minaret,' I said, as Javier read the Spanish inscriptions beneath the model.

'I have seen similar ones across Andalusia and Portugal that began life as minarets of mosques,' I said in Sylheti, turning to Somir, 'The Giralda in Seville is the most famous example, but they are literally everywhere.'

'I had no idea,' he said, raising his eyebrows in astonishment.

The excavations were only of the church's apse, and there was no way to ascertain if the bell tower had indeed started off life as the Friday mosque's minaret. I suspected it had. We left the ruins of the Church of Our Lady of Almudena and began heading north-east along the busy four-lane Calle Mayor. Somir wanted to show me where he worked, and Javier and his son decided to come along for the walk. It was a typically smouldering day in Madrid, and the road, which linked the city's popular Plaza Mayor to the palace and cathedral, was filled with tourists in their sun hats and shades, many sticking to the right-hand side of the road, where the tall neo-Renaissance blocks offered the most shade. We passed tourist shops selling fridge magnets and cheap polka-dotted flamenco dresses. A golf cart, branded 'Tuk Tuk Madrid', mounted the paved area and an amorous couple held hands as they stepped out, thanking the driver. After a little while the right-hand side of the road opened up to a large cobblestone square. Javier explained that this was the Plaza de la Villa, home to some of Madrid's oldest surviving buildings.

'That's the old town hall there, and that tower, in front of us,' Javier said, pointing to the five-storey Torre de los Lujanes and the attached palace, 'is the oldest building in Madrid. It is a fifteenth-century tower.'

'It's got a very Islamic . . .' I began, noticing five blind horseshoe arches at the very top of the tower.

'It's a Moorish style but it is Christian, from the fifteenth century,' explained Javier.

Known as the Tower and House of Lujanes, the complex is named after its fifteenth-century owner, Pedro de Luján, and is Madrid's oldest example of *mudéjar* architecture, with the horseshoe arches at the top – twenty in total, five on each side of the rectangular tower – the most prominent Muslim-inspired feature on the tower's facade. It was around here somewhere that Sheikh Nazim reportedly spoke to some jinn, according to one of the stories a murid told me. The Spanish murid said the sheikh was taken to the oldest part of Madrid, and stood high up in front of an open window in silence for such a length of time that those with him asked what he was staring at. The sheikh revealed he was not staring at anything, but addressing some jinn who had come to give him bay'ah. The jinn are part of the Islamic cosmology and are said to be 'beings' that exist in a parallel universe, and, like humans, some are Muslims and some are not. In fact, the Prophet Muhammad would state that he was sent as a 'mercy to mankind and the jinn'. The jinn are normally passive and do not interfere with the human realm. However, possessions by and interactions with jinn have been recorded throughout Islamic history. It is from the concept of the jinn that we have the modern Disneyfied 'genie'.

'And this statue . . .'

Javier was pointing to the only statue in the Plaza, a black figure on a large marble plinth.

'This is also relevant to Islamic history. This is Don Álvaro de Bazán. He was a Spanish admiral who led the Spanish navy at Lepanto – won the battle against the Ottomans in the second half of the sixteenth century. Lepanto means the victory of the West against the Ottoman Empire for supremacy in the Mediterranean in the sixteenth century.'

Named after the Ottoman naval base in modern-day Nafpaktos in Greece – Lepanto was the Venetian name given to the port – the Battle of Lepanto in 1571 saw a fleet of the Holy League, a coalition of Catholic states put together by Pope Pius V with the specific aim of breaking Ottoman control of the eastern Mediterranean, leave from the coast of Sicily to defeat the Ottomans in what was to become a pivotal moment in the history of both Europe and the Ottoman Empire. The Christian victory, taking place shortly after the end of the reign of Sultan Suleiman the Magnificent – seen as the zenith of the empire and a period in which the Ottomans were supreme across Europe – was the first chink in a previously impenetrable armour. This halted further European expansion by the Muslim empire and offered hope that the mighty Turk could be defeated. Bazán, who was lauded as *Padre de los Soldados* – the Father of the Soldiers – by Cervantes, was a member of the Order of Santiago (named after Matamoros), a religious group of soldiers founded in the twelfth century with the sole purpose of removing Muslims from the Iberian Peninsula, and incorporated into the Spanish Crown in the fifteenth century – thus institutionalizing it as part of the national Spanish identity. As a member of the aristocracy, Bazán was given *encomiendas* during the *Reconquista*, which in essence were the right to 'own' and 'enslave' conquered non-Christian people. Bazán was afforded this 'right' over Villamayor, La Solana and the Alhambra, which his grandfather, of the same name, helped to take from the Muslims. Bazán also held the title of Marquis of Santa Cruz, which was given to him in 1569, for his role in the sixteenth-century clash between the Crown and *moriscos* living in the mountainous area to the south of Granada who had had enough of forced assimilation. *Moriscos* were nominal Christians, first forced to 'convert' to Christianity at the start of the sixteenth century and gradually forced to assimilate with the introduction of laws that stopped them appearing 'Moorish', such as wearing 'Moorish' clothes, speaking Arabic and building and using public baths.

Madrid felt very different to the other major cities I had visited in Spain: the buildings here had none of the allusions to Islamic architecture that had been apparent in the streets of Seville, Córdoba, Granada and Toledo. Here everything felt distinctly Western European, in look and style. We turned right onto the Calle de Ciudad Rodrigo, a pedestrianized corridor that led to the Plaza Mayor, flanked on both sides by huge square pillars and decorated with large round black basalt stones. The Plaza Mayor is Madrid's main square, and was originally called Plaza del Arrabal when it was constructed in the early seventeenth century, during the reign of Philip III. The Plaza Mayor has a huge rectangular central square and is surrounded by three-storey residential buildings with 237 balconies facing onto the plaza. It has a harmonious and uniform architecture, featuring arcaded walkways and decorative frescoes, and has undergone several renovations, particularly after devastating fires in the seventeenth and eighteenth centuries. It has previously served as a gathering space for markets, bullfights and public ceremonies.

'This is where I work,' Somir said, pointing to a busy bar beneath the Renaissance-style arcade to our immediate right, as we entered through the Arco de Ciudad Rodrigo at the plaza's north-western corner. As we approached the wine-red-coloured bar, Somir greeted his colleagues, all of them dressed in white shirts and black trousers. I looked up at the bar's name, and nearly choked on the water I was drinking. The name of the bar was Cafetería Magerit.

'Isn't that the historical name of the city?' I asked Javier, laughing at the irony.

'That's where he works?' Javier asked back.

I nodded.

'He works in a restaurant with the original Muslim name for Madrid!' I said, laughing again.

Somir came back to us and we pointed this out to him. He looked at me blankly – it had never occurred to him at all. He had never even thought about the name.

'Fancy that!' I said to Somir in Sylheti, 'All this time you were working in a café using the Muslim name given to the city by its founding Muslim Emir!'

25

The Muslims in the Capital of Spain

Madrid, Spain

'Wow,' I said as Somir and I passed the umpteenth al fresco seating for restaurants serving 'Indian' food, 'this is just like Brick Lane, but in the sun!'

Somir smiled. He had promised to bring me to a 'home from home', and this resembled almost exactly the East End of London I had grown up in. The Bangladeshis of Madrid, like their British cousins, had quickly worked out that Europeans really love South Asian food. We were walking down the Calle de Lavapiés, a tiny one-way cobblestone street with a wide pavement along its north-western edge. Every single sign overlooking the al fresco eating area had a familiar name: the Shapla restaurant was named after the national (lotus) flower of Bangladesh; Baisakhi after the Bangladeshi New Year; and Calcuta (sic), after the 'Oxford of Bengal'. Each one had large brightly decorated menus with pictures of dishes like chicken tikka masala and aloo gobi. Even the spellings were the same. It was as if someone had asked a relative in Brick Lane to send across their restaurant's menu, and copies were distributed to all the Madrid Indian restaurateurs. And just like Brick Lane, the punters were all non-Bangladeshis. The only difference – and what a wonderful difference – was that here customers got to sit out in the warm Madrid sun, beneath wide parasols that lined the street. There was no need for the iconic flock wallpaper and pseudo-Mughal furniture made famous by their British equivalents in 1960s and 1970s London and Birmingham. Here it was practical patio chairs and tables, covered in red and white check cloth. As tempted as I was to see if the dishes tasted the same as the ones we had 'invented' in Britain, we didn't stop: we were making for a spot where the food was far more authentic – places Spain's hipsters were yet to discover.

Madrid has a population of almost seven million people, of which over one million are from immigrant backgrounds. Given Spain's history and colonial presence in the Americas, it is no surprise that the largest migrant group in the capital come from Latin American countries once ruled by Spain. It is also not surprising, given their shared history, that Madrid's largest Muslim immigrant group hail from Morocco. The Bangladeshis are in the minority here, with a mere 50,000 in the entire country, and yet, just as they had done in London in the 1960s and 1970s – even before there was a 'Bangladesh' – the tiny group in the capital had already begun to carve out a distinct little quarter of Madrid for themselves.

'Come, let's go and say hello to a friend,' Somir said, as we approached the junction with Calle de Caravaca, where a row of Bangladeshi greengrocers, just like those I had seen in Portugal, Sicily and Cyprus, lined one side of the street.

We walked into Spice Bazar, which was two doors from the Shah Jalal Supermarket – a nod to Bangladesh's most famous Muslim saint, Hazrat Shah Jalal, the thirteenth-century Sufi, from Konya in Turkey, credited with bringing Islam to the Bengal peninsula. The Spice Bazar sold everything a Bangladeshi kitchen needed, from halal meat to garam masala dried spice. We walked past every type of exotic fruit and veg you could imagine, including heaps of fiery Scotch bonnet peppers and green bullet chillis, both hugely popular with Bangladeshis. The middle of the store was an island of large packets of the Bangladeshi staple, rice; no pack was less than 20 kg in weight. At the back, a man in a navy-blue woollen hat and a bloodstained apron, was hacking away at a huge leg of mutton behind the meat counter, and hanging from the ceiling near the till were packets of spicy fried peanuts, fried mung dal and chanachur

(Bombay mix), the classic Bangladeshi street food snacks in packet form. A slightly rotund man with dark skin, in a blue polo shirt and a pair of leather desi sandals wandered over to us smiling at Somir. After greeting his friend with a handshake and a hug, Yusuf turned to me and did the same, before telling me Somir had mentioned I had come all the way from London to see them. Yusuf then informed his employees that he would be back shortly.

The three of us left the grocery store and walked down Calle de Caravaca, a cobblestone one-way street, with low black bollards marking out the pavement. The roads here were much grubbier than in central Madrid. The walls were stained and littered with graffiti. I noticed some of the blocks had windows at floor level with wrought-iron grilles across them. These were often covered to stop prying eyes looking in. We passed a small barber's shop with white doors and large Bengali letters down the side of the wall that read 'Salon'. A young man with a yellow beanie hat stood outside, waiting his turn. I peered in to see three Bengali men, two cutting hair and the other with a cup of tea in hand, all of them chatting away. The next few stores had their shutters down; these were covered with illegible scribblings by bored vandals. I was again reminded of the East End of my youth. As we neared the end of the road, where it met Calle del Amparo, on the corner was a small eatery with the sign 'Bangla Town' above the door. We walked in and both Yusuf and Somir immediately greeted the bucktoothed chef with the familiarity of family.

'What's good today?' asked Yusuf.

'I have *beri* [mutton] biryani and *shobzi* [vegetable curry],' replied the chef.

'Give our brother who has come from London a biryani and . . . do you want *shobzi*?' Yusuf turned to me.

'I'll eat whatever you brothers eat,' I replied, smiling.

Soon we were joined by another friend, Mashuk, who came in and salaamed everyone, before enquiring after me. We all spoke Sylheti as I explained to Yusuf and Mashuk what I had been up to. They listened carefully, with Somir occasionally jumping in to provide the location of a place I had visited in Madrid in relation to where we were seated. I told them that Madrid was a Muslim city by birth and they were impressed with this information, asking Somir where the medieval wall was. Mashuk also ordered the biryani and asked the chef to bring us some rotis too. I went to the bathroom and washed my hands in preparation to eat. When I returned, a delicious, steaming plate of colourful red, yellow and white spiced rice, with mounds of melt-in-your-mouth lamb, masala and a curried boiled egg, sat in the middle of our table. Beside it were two small bowls: one contained a dark-brown meat curry sauce to pour over the dry biryani, and the other contained thinly sliced curried potato with onion, tomatoes and coriander – the *shobzi*. In front of Yusuf were the two rotis, and a small plate of chopped lettuce, cucumber, lemons, onions and enough bullet chillis to spoil an entire weekend: the classic Sylheti salad. It was a comforting and reassuring sight, and grabbing an empty plate, I put some biryani on it, poured some of the spicy meat curry sauce over it and began mixing with my right hand. Yusuf, who had a deep gruff voice, barked at his chef friend for more food, wondering out loud how this amount of *shobzi* and biryani was meant to feed four of us. His friend snapped back that he should come in the kitchen and cook it himself if he wanted it done so fast. The pair of them then laughed at each other's insults. Mashuk asked me about the things they were all really interested in.

'Where's your *bari* [village] in Desh?'

'I'm from near Chandrapur, Kali Dhor . . . on the river bank,' I replied.

They were Sylhetis, I didn't need to give them any further particulars. Mashuk and Yusuf nodded away. They knew it well.

'So not far from your in-laws, then?' Mashuk said to Somir.

Somir's in-laws lived in my maternal grandparents' *bari* in Dhakadakshin, a place I had fond childhood memories of, as it was where I would go for all my holidays to Bangladesh. Both Mashuk and Yusuf also loved the area because of how lush and hilly it was. We began to reminisce about Dhakadakshin bazaar's great atmosphere, the taste of freshly cooked street bites like *chana* (curried chick peas) and *daalir bora* (lentil fritters), and the joy of watching a football tournament at the local high school, jostling for space in the heaving crowd of villagers from every local homestead.

Nobody mentioned Spain's Islamic history once; they had all feigned interest out of politeness, just as Somir had when he met me earlier. I didn't mind at all. In a way, I was kind of relieved. I had spent almost two months on the road exploring Europe's Islamic heritage and in spite of finding it almost everywhere I looked, I had often felt alone, uneasy and like I didn't belong. Now, in Western Europe's only Muslim capital, sitting in an early incarnation of the Banglatown of my East London childhood, among Sylhetis, eating the food we loved and speaking in our mother tongue, I finally felt at home.

As Yusuf and Mashuk bemoaned the size of the remittance they were having to send back this month to support their extended family in Sylhet, I realized that this 'new' Muslim quarter of Madrid, established by the Bangladeshis, lay less than a mile southeast of where the New Moorish Quarter was founded in the middle of the fifteenth century, just as Muslim Iberia was coming to an end; and a mere half a mile west of where the ancient Majrit Maqbara (Madrid Cemetery) used to be. I didn't mention any of this to Somir, Mashuk or Yusuf; I knew these guys were not interested in European Muslim heritage or trying to belong in Spain. The way they spoke about Bangladesh, like my parents' generation, told me they had no dilemma about where they felt they belonged: they knew they belonged 'back home'. They were not stuck between the two worlds; they were not feeling like the eternal migrant that I was. The dilemma of belonging would be a burden carried by Somir, Yusuf and Mashuk's children. I knew this because I *was* their children: the children of a generation that came to Britain and built a life for themselves – many by opening Indian restaurants just like this one. They had also started off showing no interest in local Muslim heritage, or pondering whether they belonged in Britain or not. They accepted they didn't. But it became my home, and when Somir, Yusuf and Mashuk's children grow up, Spain will be theirs, and they, like me, will look for ways to belong. They will look for heritage to help anchor and secure their identity right here, so they can create those narratives of belonging and forge a 'place identity' that includes *their* European Muslim history. As I spooned another portion of deliciously spicy *shobzi* onto my colourful biryani, I felt confident they would. In fact, I was certain they would.

Glossary

Adhan – Muslim call to prayer
Alfiz – A decorative architectural feature that encloses or frames the outer edges of an arch
Allah – Arabic word meaning 'God'
Asr – Third of the five daily Muslim prayers; performed mid-afternoon
Awliyah – Literally, 'friends of God', these are holy men and women usually equated with the concept of a saint
Barakah – Blessing
Bay'ah – Pledging one's allegiance to a leader or the taking of an oath to follow a spiritual teacher
Bayram – Turkic term for widely observed festivals like the two Eids
Bhai – 'Brother' in many languages of the Indian subcontinent
Bimaristan – A classical Persian term meaning 'house of the sick' used across the Muslim world for 'hospital'
Bismillah – Meaning 'In the name of God'
Dargah – A Sufi lodge or complex usually built around the tomb of a revered *wali*
Dervish – Student or follower of a Sufi order
Dhikr – Remembrance of God through various acts
Dhimmi – Protected, tax-paying non-Muslim citizens within a Muslim state
Dhuhr – Second of the five daily Muslim prayers; performed in the middle of the day
Djellaba – Moroccan name for a long, flowing gown-like garment worn by men and women across North Africa
Dua – Invocation; a prayer of supplication or request
Eid al-Adha – Festival to mark the end of the *Hajj* in Makkah
Eid al-Fitr – Festival to mark the end of the month of fasting, Ramadan
Fajr – First of the five daily Muslim prayers; performed at dawn
Fatihah – The first chapter in the Qur'an, read at the start of each *rakat* of prayer
Fiqh – Islamic jurisprudence or process of establishing law (sharia) by examining the Qur'an and other sources like the *hadith* collections.
Funduq – A caravanserai

Hadith – Saying or doing of the Prophet recorded in scripture

Hafiz – Someone who has memorized the entire Qur'an

Hajib – Court chamberlain

Halaqa – A communal gathering or meeting to learn about Islam

Hammam – Public bathing facilities; also used to refer to toilets or washrooms

Hijrah – Migration, usually for the sake of Islam

Hoca – A religiously learned or scholarly person in Turkic countries

Imam – Person who leads the prayer (in Shi'a Islam this is also the title for the spiritual leader of the entire community)

Iqama – The call to start the congregational prayer

Isha – Fifth of the five daily Muslim prayers; performed late in the evening

Jama'at – Congregation (usually in reference to a congregational prayer)

Jami'a – A gathering and in reference to a mosque; one that is for larger congregations

Janazah – The funeral prayer

Jinn – Supernatural beings Muslims believe live in parallel with humans

Jubba – Tunisian name for a long, flowing gown-like garment worn by men and women across North Africa

Jumu'ah – Weekly midday Friday prayer performed in congregation

Ka'aba – The revered, cube-shaped structure at the centre of Islam's holiest mosque, the Masjid al-Haram in Makkah, Saudi Arabia, considered the 'House of God'. Muslims face the Ka'aba to pray and when they are laid to rest in their graves

Khutbah – The sermon delivered by an *imam* usually at the *jumu'ah* prayer on a Friday and other important ones like the Eid prayer

Kiswa – The decorated cloth used to cover the *Ka'aba*

Kufic – Ancient Arabic script with angular and rectilinear letters that now comes in different forms, including square and knotted, and originated in Kufa, Iraq

Kunya – Teknonym or name derived from one's child, usually the eldest

Madad – Asking for protection through the blessings of those being called upon

Madrasa – Educational institute; elementary, secondary or higher education

Maghreb – Classical Arab term to refer to North Africa

Maghrib – Fourth of the five daily Muslim prayers; performed at sunset

Mahvil – Balcony in a mosque, usually at the back of the central hall and reserved for female worshippers

GLOSSARY

Maq'am – A spiritual station or stage on the Sufi path or a type of shrine for a Sufi teacher

Maqsura – Enclosed area close to the *mihrab* of a mosque set aside for a ruler and their family to pray in

Marranos – Sephardic Jews forced or coerced into converting to Christianity but who continued to secretly practise Judaism during the fifteenth and sixteenth centuries

Mashrabiya – Traditional balcony-like bay window featuring carved wooden screens, originating in the Muslim world

Masjid – A mosque

Mawlid – The annual celebration of the birth of the Prophet Muhammad

Mechouar – Large open courtyard at the front of a palace, common across North Africa

Medina – Arabic for a city, town or urban centre

Mescit – Term common in Turkic countries to mean 'mosque'

Mihrab – The niche in the direction of the *Ka'aba* in Makkah where the *imam* stands to lead prayer

Minbar – Pulpit inside a mosque used by the *imam* to give sermons

Moriscos – Muslims who were forcibly converted to Catholicism in Iberia

Mudéjar – Art and architecture by Christians inspired by those of historical al-Andalus

Muezzin – The person who makes the *adhan*

Muqarnas – Style of pattern common in classical Islamic architecture: ornamental stalactite-shaped features that form small pointed niches

Murid – A student or disciple of a Sufi teacher or sheikh

Musafir – Traveller

Musafirhane – Traveller's lodgings, usually found in a Sufi lodge

Namaz – *Salah* or daily formal prayers (used mostly in Persian-influenced cultures)

Naskh – A round and cursive ancient style of Arabic lettering

Nikah – Islamic marriage contract between a man and a woman

Nisba – Arabic word for the part of a person's name that indicates their geographic place of origin or birth

Niyyah – The intention in one's heart

Qadi – A legal judge of sharia law

Qasr – A palace, castle or fortified residence

Qibla – The direction of prayer (towards the *Ka'aba* in Makkah, Saudi Arabia)

Qur'an – The holiest scripture in Islam, believed to be the literal word of God

Rakat – Segments of *salah*, the formal prayer; usually in twos, threes or fours

Riadh – Arabic for 'garden'

Sahabah – The Companions of the Prophet Muhammad; his followers from the first generation of Muslims who saw or met him

Salaam – The shortening of the Muslim greeting '*Assalamu alaikum*' ('Peace be with you')

Salaf – Also *as-Salaf as-Salih* to mean 'the pious predecessors', a term used to refer to the revered first three generations of Muslims

Salah – Formal prayer performed by Muslims, like the ones performed five times a day

Salawat – Offering blessings upon the Prophet and his family

Shahadah – The declaration of faith in Islam

Shahid/shuhada – Martyr/martyrs

Shi'a – One of the two main branches of Islam

Shirk – Equating others with Allah; considered the gravest of sins in Islam

Sitara – Highly decorated curtain-like section covering the door of the *Ka'aba*

Sufi – Term used to describe a follower of Sufism, a mystical branch of Islam

Sunnah – When something is believed to have been done by the Prophet and considered part of the model for Muslims to follow (especially Sunni Muslims)

Sunni – Larger of the two main branches of Islam; comes from the term *sunnah*

Surah – Chapter of the Qur'an

Tabi al-Tabi'in – The 'successors of the Successors'; the generation of Muslims who followed the *Tabi'un*

Tabi'un – The followers or 'Successors': the generation of Muslims who followed the Sahabah

Taifa – An independent Muslim principality

Takbir – The name for the phrase *Allahu Akbar*, meaning 'God is the greatest'. Used in *salah*, the *adhan* and various sacred rituals, as well as informally by Muslims

Tambour – Architectural feature on mosques holding up the dome

Taqiyya – The practice of denying one's faith when one's life or property might be threatened because of it

Tariqa – A formalized Sufi order or its teachings with distinct rites, rituals and a teacher or sheikh

Tasbih – Collection of thirty-three or ninety-nine beads on a thread that aids with *dhikr*

Tawheed – The oneness of God or absolute monotheism

Tsebka – Architectural feature of interlacing rhombus-like motifs

Tughra – Signature of an Ottoman sultan, usually in artistic calligraphy

Türbe – The Turkic term for mausoleum, tomb or grave

Ummah – The global or collective Muslim community

Umrah – The shorter pilgrimage performed all year round that involves carrying out rites and rituals in Makkah; often referred to as the lesser *Hajj*

Wadi – The Arabic for a river valley

Wali – A 'friend of God', who has a special relationship with the Divine and is often equated with the Western concept of a saint

Waqf – Donation of an asset as endowment for religious or charitable purposes

Wudu – Ritual ablutions performed by Muslims before praying

Zawiya – A Sufi lodge or complex sometimes built around the tomb of a revered *wali*

Ziyara – A pious visitation or pilgrimage, usually to a holy place, grave or shrine

Further Reading

AL ANDALUS (PORTUGAL, SPAIN AND THE MAGHREB)

AbdoolKarim A. Vakil. 'The Crusader Heritage: Portugal and Islam from Colonial to Post-Colonial Identities.' In Robert Shannan Peckham (ed.), *Rethinking Heritage: Cultures and Politics in Europe*. London: Routledge, 2003.

W. J. Austin. *Sufis of Andalusia: The Ruh al-quds and al-Durrat al-fakhirah of Ibn Arabi*. Woking: Unwin Brothers Ltd, The Gresham Press, 1971.

J. Black. *A Brief History of Portugal*. London: Robinson, 2020.

Pascual De Gayanas. *The History of the Mohammedan Dynasties in Spain*, Vols. I & II. London: W. H. Allen and Co., 1843.

E. Drayson. *The Moor's Last Stand: How Seven Centuries of Muslim Rule in Spain Came to an End*. London: Profile Books, 2017.

W. Elliott. *The Career of Ibn Qasi as Religious Teacher and Political Revolutionary in Twelfth-Century Islamic Spain*(PhD thesis). Edinburgh: University of Edinburgh, 1979.

J. S. Gerber. *The Jews of Spain: A History of the Sephardic Experience*. New York: Free Press, 1992.

John Gill. *Andalucia: A Cultural History*. New York: Oxford University Press, 2009.

Adam Hopkins. *Spanish Journeys: A Portrait of Spain*. London: Viking, 1992.

W. Irving. *Tales of the Alhambra*. León: Editorial Everest S.A., 1981.

R. Irwin. *The Alhambra*. London: Profile Books, 2005.

María Rosa Menocal. *The Ornament of the World*. New York: Back Bay Books, 2002.

María Rosa Menocal. *Culture in the Time of Tolerance: Al-Andalus as a Model for Our Own Time*. New Haven: Yale Law School Occasional Papers, 2000.

Museum with No Frontiers. *In the Lands of the Enchanted Moorish Maiden*. Lisbon: Cultural Tourism Growth Programme, 2001.

M. A. Nadwi. *Journey to Andalus*. Translated and edited by A. Zayd. London: Angelwing Media, 2019.

M. Rosser-Owen. *Islamic Arts from Spain*. London: V&A Publishing, 2010.

A. Vakil. 'Muslims in Portugal: History, Historiography, Citizenship.' *Euroclio Bulletin*, no. 18 (2003): 9–13.

W. Montgomery Watt. *A History of Islamic Spain (Islamic Surveys 4)*. Edinburgh: Edinburgh University Press, 1965.

J. Webster. *Andalus: Unlocking the Secrets of Moorish Spain*. London: Black Swan, 2005.

SIQILLIYAH (SICILY AND MALTA)

A. Ahmad. *A History of Islamic Sicily*. Edinburgh: Edinburgh University Press, 1975.

G. Bonello. 'New Light on Majmuna's Tombstone.' In *Histories of Malta: Deceptions and Perceptions*, Vol. 1. Malta: Fondazzjoni Patrimonju Malti, 2000, 9–12.

J. M. Brincat. 'Maltese: Blending Semitic, Romance and Germanic Lexemes.' *Lexicographica* 33 (2017): 207–224. https://doi.org/10.1515/lexi-2017-0011 (Accessed: 7 July 2025).

J. M. Brincat. *Maltese and Other Languages: A Linguistic History of Malta*. Malta: Midsea Books, 2011.

Roland J. C. Broadhurst. *The Travels of Ibn Jubayr*. London: The Camelot Press Ltd, 1952.

Patrick Brydone. *A Tour Through Sicily and Malta in a Series of Letters to William Beckford Esq.*, Vol. I. London: W. Strahan and T. Cadell, 1773.

Leonard C. Chiarelli. *A History of Muslim Sicily*, 2nd ed. Malta: Midsea Books, 2018.

C. Dalli. 'A Muslim Society under Christian Rule.' In *Melitensium Amor: Festschrift in Honour of Dun Gwann Azzopardi*. Malta: Midsea Books, 2002, 37–56.

Charles Dalli. *Malta: The Medieval Millennium*. Florence: Midsea Books, 2006.

J. Johns. 'The Arabic Inscriptions of the Norman Kings of Sicily: A Reinterpretation.' In *Nobiles Officinae: The Royal Workshops in Palermo During the*

Reigns of the Norman and Hohenstaufen Kings of Sicily in the 12th and 13th Century. Catania: Giuseppe Maimone, 2006, 324–337.

L. Kapitaikin. ' "The Daughter of al-Andalus": Interrelations Between Norman Sicily and the Muslim West.' *Al-Masaq: Islam and the Medieval Mediterranean* 25, no. 1 (2013): 113–134.

L. Kapitaikin. *The Twelfth-Century Paintings of the Ceilings of the Cappella Palatina, Palermo* (DPhil thesis). Oxford: University of Oxford, 2011.

H. Kennedy. 'Sicily and al-Andalus under Muslim Rule.' In *The New Cambridge Medieval History*, Vol. 3. Cambridge: Cambridge University Press, 2000, 646–669.

Karla Mallette. *The Kingdom of Sicily, 1100–1250: A Literary History*. Philadelphia: University of Pennsylvania Press, 2005.

J. J. Norwich. *Sicily: An Island at the Crossroads of History*. London: John Murray, 2015.

A. Nef (ed.). *A Companion to Medieval Palermo*. Leiden and Boston: Brill, 2024.

D. Polidano. *Al-Dafin in Medieval Muslim Malta: A Characterisation of Funerary Material Culture in Arab and Norman Period Malta* (BA dissertation). Malta: University of Malta, 2022.

Habeeb Salloum. 'Palermo's Arab Heritage.' *Arab America*, July 25, 2015. https://www.arabamerica.com/palermos-arab-heritage/

J. Shakespear. 'Copy of an Arabic Inscription on a Tombstone at Malta.' *Journal of the Royal Asiatic Society of Great Britain and Ireland* 6, no. 1 (1841): 173–181. https://www.jstor.org/stable/25207545 (Accessed 26 Feb. 2024).

C. Thake. 'Envisioning the Orient: The New Muslim Cemetery in Malta.' *Muqarnas: An Annual on the Visual Cultures of the Islamic World* 33 (2016): 221–251.

QUBRUS (CYPRUS AND THE TURKISH REPUBLIC OF NORTHERN CYPRUS)

Merve S. Arkan. 'Mapping the Ottoman Cyprus Through Travellers' Eyes.' In *Proceedings of the International Cartographic Association*, 8th International Symposium for the ICA Commission on the History of Cartography. Florence: ICA, 2021, 1–10.

Association of Cypriot Archaeologists. *Muslim Places of Worship in Cyprus*. Nicosia: Association of Cypriot Archaeologists, 1990.

Tuncer Bağişkan. *Ottoman, Islamic and Islamised Monuments in Cyprus.* Nicosia: Cyprus Turkish Education Foundation, 2009.

Eleni Bouleti. 'The Muslim Community on Cyprus and British Colonial Policy, 1878–1915.' *The Cyprus Review* 23, no. 2 (2011): 39–56.

Claude Delaval Cobham. 'The Story of Umm Ḥarám.' *Journal of the Royal Asiatic Society of Great Britain and Ireland* (1897): 81–101. http://www.jstor.org/stable/25207826.

Lawrence Durrell. *Bitter Lemons.* London: Faber & Faber, 1957.

Peter M. Fischer. 'Hala Sultan Tekke, Cyprus: A Late Bronze Age Trade Metropolis.' *Near Eastern Archaeology* 82, no. 4 (2019): 236–247. https://www.jstor.org/stable/48569977.

Rupert Gunnis. *Historic Cyprus: A Guide to Its Towns and Villages, Monasteries and Castles.* London: Methuen, 1936.

Philip K. Hitti (trans.). 'The Origins of the Islamic State.' *Studies in History, Economics and Public Law* 68, no. 163 (1916): 235–243.

Thorsten Kruse. *The Religious Heritage of Cyprus: A Survey in the Districts of Kyrenia and Larnaca.* The Hague: Ministry of Foreign Affairs of the Kingdom of the Netherlands, 2019.

Thorsten Kruse. *The Religious Heritage of Cyprus: A Survey in the City of Nicosia and Its Suburbs.* Nicosia: Friedrich-Ebert-Stiftung, 2021.

M. Corneille Le Bruyn. *A Voyage to the Levant: or Travels in the Principal Parts of Asia Minor, the Islands of Scio, Rhodes, Cyprus, etc.* London: Gray's Inn-Gate, 1702.

Henry Light. *Travels in Egypt, Nubia, the Holy Land, Mount Libanon and Cyprus in the Year 1814.* London: Rodwell and Martin, 1818.

Ryan J. Lynch. 'Cyprus and Its Legal and Historiographical Significance in Early Islamic History.' *Journal of the American Oriental Society* 136, no. 3 (2016): 535–550. https://www.jstor.org/stable/10.7817/jameroriesoci.136.3.0535.

Sir Harry Luke. *Cyprus: A Portrait and an Appreciation.* London: George G. Harrap & Co., 1957.

Robert MacLean and Nicholas Danziger. *Beneath the Carob Trees: The Lost Lives of Cyprus.* Nicosia: Armida Publications, 2016.

Abbe Mariti. *Travels Through Cyprus, Syria, and Palestine with a General History of the Levant.* London: G.G. J. and J. Robinson, 1791.

G. and M. Micula. *Eyewitness Travel: Cyprus.* London: Dorling Kindersley, 2016.

Rita C. Severis. *Travelling Artists in Cyprus 1700–1916*. London: Philip Wilson Publishers, 2000.

Prof. Dr. Salahi Sonyel. *The Struggle of the Turkish Muslims of Cyprus for Survival*. Lefkoşa: TRNC Ministry of Foreign Affairs and Defence, 1999.

Colin Thubron. *Cyprus*. London: Penguin Books, 1987.

GENERAL

S. T. S. Al-Hassani (ed.). *1001 Inventions: The Enduring Legacy of Muslim Civilization.*, 3rd ed. Washington, D.C.: National Geographic, 2012.

Al-Ṭabarī, Abū Ja'far Muhammad ibn Jarīr, *The History of al-Ṭabarī* (40 vols.), 1985–2007: State University of New York Press (Albany)

Samar Attar. 'Conflicting Accounts on the Fear of Strangers: Muslims and Arab Perceptions of Europeans in Medieval Geographical Literature.' *Arab Studies Quarterly* 27, no. 4 (2005): 17–29. http://www.jstor.org/stable/41858512.

O. Bush. 'The Architecture of Jewish Identity: The Neo-Islamic Central Synagogue of New York.' *Journal of the Society of Architectural Historians* 63, no. 2 (2004): 180–201.

Basil Anthony Collins (transl.). *Al-Muqaddasi: The Best Divisions for Knowledge of the Regions*. Reading: Garnet Publishing Ltd, 1994.

E. E. Curtis (ed.). *The Bloomsbury Reader on Islam in the West*. London: Bloomsbury Academic, 2025.

N. Davies. *Europe: A History*. London: Pimlico, 1997.

J. S. Field. *The History of Europe in Bite-Sized Chunks*. London: Michael O'Mara Books, 2019.

Rev. B. Gerrans. *Travels of Rabbi Benjamin, Son of Jonah, of Tudelah: Through Europe, Asia and Africa*. London: Stationers Hall, 1783.

Claudia Gold. *King of the North Wind: The Life of Henry II in Five Acts*. London: William Collins, 2018.

David J. Goldberg and John D. Rayner. *The Jewish People: Their History and Their Religion*. Middlesex: Penguin Books, 1987.

Camille A. Helminski. *Women of Sufism: A Hidden Treasure*. Boston: Shambhala Publications, 2003.

Paul Johnson. *A History of the Jews*. London: George Weidenfeld & Nicolson, 1987.

R. Lacey and D. Danziger. *The Year 1000: What Life Was Like at the Turn of the First Millennium*. London: Little, Brown, 1999.

Bernard Lewis. *Islam and the West*. Oxford: Oxford University Press, 1994.

Josef W. Meri (transl.). *A Lonely Wayfarer's Guide to Pilgrimage: Ali ibn Abi Bakr al-Harawi's Kitab al-Isharat ila Ma'rifat al-Ziyarat*. Princeton, NJ: The Darwin Press, 2004.

Douglas Murray. *The Strange Death of Europe: Immigration, Identity, Islam*. London: Bloomsbury, 2018.

A. al-H.A. Nadwi. *The Glory of Iqbal, 1877–1938*. Translated by M. Waseef. London: Youth of the Ummah, 2003.

Stephen O'Shea. *Sea of Faith: Islam and Christianity in the Medieval Mediterranean World*. London: Profile Books, 2006.

J. Quinn. *How the World Made the West: A 4,000 Year History*. London: Bloomsbury Publishing, 2024.

J. M. Roberts and O. A. Westad. *The Penguin History of Europe*. London: Penguin Books, 2013.

I. Shoval. *King John's Delegation to the Almohad Court (1212): Medieval Interreligious Interactions and Modern Historiography*. Turnhout, Belgium: Brepols, 2016.

Sally B. Smith. *Charles: The Misunderstood Prince*. London: Penguin Books, 2017.

T. Wallace-Murphy. *What Islam Did for Us: A Discovery of Europe's Hidden and Borrowed History*. London: Watkins, 2006.

Index

Page number in *italics* indicate an illustration.

Abbadid dynasty, 200, 227
Abbasid dynasty, 91, 194, 216, 217, 222, 270
'Abd al-Mu'min, 103
Abd al-Rahman ibn Muhammad ibn 'Abd Allah al-Bakri al-Siqilli, 95
Abd Allah, 216–17
Abd al-Wahhab, Muhammad ibn, 4
Abdul Qadir al-Gilani, 42
Abdulaziz Khan, Ottoman sultan, 140
Abdu'r Rahman I, Emir of Córdoba, 216, 259, 263, 266–84, 315, 330
Abdu'r Rahman II, Emir of Córdoba, 91
Abdu'r Rahman III, Caliph of Córdoba, 216–17, 218, 223, 225, 236, 266–84
Abdu'r-Rahman, Uthman ibn (Ibn as-Susi), 170
Abraham of Toledo, 346
Abu al-Qasim al-Zahrawi (Albucasis), 288–9, 344
Abu Bakr, 37, 52
Abu Bakr Yahya ibn Abd Allah Ibn al-Huwari, Sheikh, 202, 205

Abu l-Hasan Ali of Granada (Muley Hacén), 322–3, 330
Adelard of Bath, 111–12, 345
adhan (call to prayer), 9, 39–40, 133, 327
Adil, Sheikh Mehmet, 318–19
Afonso Henriques I of Portugal, 175, 189, 210
Africa, 108, 316–17; Fez, 248, 248–9, 249, 302; Libya, 148–9, 152, 153; Morocco, 244, 258, 302, 328–9; Tunisia, 88, 89, 93–4, 132, 142–3; *see also* Morocco
Aghlabid dynasty, 91, 146, 217
agriculture, 135
Ahmad ibn Baso, 268
Aisha al-Hurra, 323
Albania, 10, 196
Albucasis: *see* Abu al-Qasim al-Zahrawi,
Alcock, Antony, 8
Alemdar, Imam Şakir, 68–75, 78–82, *82*
Alexander III, Pope, 77
Alfonso VI of León and Castile, 338, 360, 368
Alfonso VII of León and Castile, 189

INDEX

Alfonso X of Castile and León, 249, 251, 332–3, 345–6
Alfred of Sareshel, 344–5
Alhambra, 232, 286, 287, 298–310; Alcazaba, 286; architecture of, 307–8; Court of the Lions (Patio de los Leones), 292, 298, *300*, 300–301; Court of the Myrtles (Patio de los Arrayanes), 274, *306*; de-Islamizing of, 307–9; fountains, *300*, 300–301; Great Mosque (Church of Santa María), 304; Hall of the Abencerrajes (Sala de los Abencerrajes, al-Qubba al-Gharbiyya), 299, 301; Hall of the Ambassadors (Salón de los Embajadores), 303; Hall of the Kings (Sala de los Reyes), 301, 306; Hall of the Mocárabes (Sala de los Mocárabes), 301; Hall of the Two Sisters (Sala de las Dos Hermanas), 301; inscriptions, *286*, 303, *304*; Nasrid Palace, 245, 246, 256, 271, *291*, 292, 319; Rawdah, 304, 324
Ali ibn Abi Talib, Caliph, 37, 83
alienation, Muslim, 11–12
Aljafería Palace, Zaragoza, 363
Allah, names of, 104
Alloui, Jaafar, 138
Almohads, 200, 270, 276, 349–50; arches, 257–8, 339, 348, *349*, 352; architecture of, 117, 200, 205, 274, 348–50, *349*, 352
Almoravids, 117, 189, 200, 270, 281–2
Amr ibn al-As, 23–4
al-Andalus, 263; al-Gharb (Portugal), 174–6, 186; *taifa* periods, 226–7, 237, 269–70, 285, 363

—, Almohad Caliphate (1147–1238), 200, 276, 285, 349–50
—, Almoravid Empire (1085–1145), 270, 281–2
—, Córdoba, Caliphate of (929–1031), 13–14, 186, 248–9; Alcázar, Seville, 267; collapse of, 269; development of, 216–17; *fitna* (civil war), 225–6; Jewish community, 231, 233–41, 245–7
—, Córdoba, Emirate of (750–929), 91, 194, 216; al-Gharb (Portugal) as part of, 174–6, 186; cultural development of, 222–3, 233–4; founding of, 266
—, Nasrid Emirate (1238–1492), 249, 285–7, 293–4, 296–7, 322–5; Alcázar, Seville, 268, 271–2, *272*; architecture of, 295, 300–301, 352; Jewish community, 237; motto, 182, *286*, 303; Pedro I of Castile, relations with, 273; surrender, 310; *see also* Alhambra
—, Umayyad Caliphate (711–750), 193–5, 235–6, 336, 359–60, 361–3, 368
—, Zirid Emirate (1013–1090), 237, 286
Andrew, Saint, 56
Ansar (Helpers), 201
al-Ansari, Ishaq Ibn Faras, 201
Andalusians, 226–7
anti-Semitism, 9, 237, 241, 243–5, 283–4, 349–50, 355
Arabic language, 142–4, 148, 152–3, 303–4
Arabic numerals, 111–12
archaeology, 163–4, 190–92, 208–9; Muslim artifacts, destruction of, 195–6

394

INDEX

arches: Almohad, 257–8, 339, 348, *349*, 352; Córdoban, 126, 182–3, 184; Umayyad, 200–201, 206–7, 218–20, 261–2, *262*, 336, *336*

architecture: Almohad, 117, 200, 205, 274, 348–50, *349*, 352; Almoravid, 117; cupolas, 119, 258; English, Muslim influence on, 112–13; Islamic, 185; *mashrabiyya* (window), 115; *mechouar* (courtyard), 218–19; of mosques, 60, 104; Mughal, 141, 174; *muqarnas*, 104, 107, 113–14, 116–17, 119, 299, 363; Nasrid, 295, 300–301, 352; neo-Islamic, 180–81, 184; neo-Moorish, 228; neo-Mughal, 184; Norman, 104–7, *106*; Ottoman, 140–41; *tsebka* pattern, 268, 274, 277; of *türbesi* (mausoleums), 31–2; Umayyad, 184, 206–7, 219, 255, 256–7; ventilation and cooling systems, 114–15; *see also mudéjar* architecture; star motifs

Aristidou, Ekaterini Chr., 7, 82

Aristotle, 109, 111

asceticism, 52, 285

Ash-Shakandí, 287

astronomy, 109–10, 273, 368

Averroes: *see* Ibn Rushd

Avicenna: *see* Ibn Sina

awliyah ('friends of God'), 25, 34, 40, 316

Al-Aziz palace: *see* Zisa (Al-Aziz) palace

Aznar, José María, 263

Bacon, Roger, 344

Badichi, Jonathan, 351–2, 353–8

Baghdad, 104, 111, 216, 222, 251, 270, 291

Bamba, Sheikh Amadou (Khadimu r-Rasul), 316

Bangladesh, 60–62, 377–8

Banu Hudhayl tribe, 169

Barnabas, Saint, tomb of (Cyprus), 51–2, 56

baths/bathhouses, 330; Bañuelo, Granada, 287; Hisn al-Hammah (Calathamet, Sicily), 123–7; Malta, 158–60; Terme Arabo-Normanne di Cefalà Diana, Sicily, 126–7

al-Battani, 273

Bayezid II, Ottoman Sultan, 244

Bazán, Don Álvaro de, 371–2

belonging, 11–12, 378–9

Ben Ali, Zine El Abidine, 88

Berbers, 89, 226–7, 235; Zirids, 285–7; *see also* Almohads; Almoravids

Black Prince's Ruby, 273

Boabdil (Muhammad XII of Granada), 310, 322–3

Bonnici, Owen, 151

books: burning of, 294; guidebooks, 71; medical treatises, 108, 289; *see also* libraries; literary culture

Bosnia and Herzegovina, 10, 196

botany, 362

Boulaich, Muhammad, 314, 321, 325–9

Brincat, Joseph, 144

Brown, Thomas, 111, 113

Bruijn, Cornelis de, 72

Burton, Sir Richard, 107, 180

Byzantine Empire, 23, 83, 89–90

Camões, Luís Vas de: *The Lusiads*, 189–90

caravanserais, 295–7

cartography, 122, 191

INDEX

Casa de Sefarad, Córdoba, 228–33, *229*, 239–45
Castaño, Javier, 361–2, 364–5
Catholic Church, 263–4, 350–51
Caxaro, Pietru: *Il Kantilena*, 142, 144
cemeteries: excavation of, 163–4, 165–6; Gozo, 172; Ottoman Cemetery, Malta, 137, 139–42, *140*; Rawdah, Alhambra, 304, 324; Valletta, Malta, 154; *see also* tombs; *türbesi*
ceramics, *188*, 199–201, 202–4, *204*
Charlemagne, Holy Roman Emperor, 194, 195
Charles III of the United Kingdom, 10, 76–7
Charles V, Holy Roman Emperor, 265, 333–4
Chaucer, Geoffrey, 108, 273
Chelebi Khalifa, 36
Chester, Robert, 345
Christianity, 51–2; Catholic Church, 263–4, 350–51; Europe, arrival in, 68; Frankish adoption of, 194–5; iconography, 167, 205, 262, 277, 339–40; *see also* conversions to Christianity
Christians: Arabized, 343; artists' work in mosques, 255; *moriscos* (nominal/forced Muslim converts), 239, 322, 372; Muslims, marriage to, 266–7; pilgrims, 51–2, 72; Portugal, conquest of, 175, 176, 189, 197; prayer towards Makka, 204–7; Spain, conquest of, 343, 368–9
churches: Holy Trinity, Palermo, 104; mosque-churches, 35, 60, 95–6, 129, 201, 204–7, 332–4, 369; mosques, shared with, 263; Muslim prayers prohibited in, 254; Our Lady of Almudena, Madrid, 367–9; Saint John of the Hermits, Palermo, 100–102; San Román, Toledo, 332–4, 335, *336*; Santa María la Blanca (Ibn Shoshan synagogue), Toledo, 348–51, *349*; São Pedro de Canaferrim, Sintra, 178; St Mary of the Admiral, Palermo, 97, *98*; *see also* Alhambra; Mezquita-Catedral (Great Mosque), Córdoba
citizenship, 238–9
clothing: fashion, 223; head coverings, 151–2, 205; *thobe*, 152
Cobbold, Lady Evelyn, 78
commerce: in Portugal, 192, 194, 195; in Sicily, 92, 135; in Spain, 238, 296–7, 352
Companions of the Prophet: *see* Sahabah
Constans II, Byzantine emperor, 83
Constantine the African, 108
conversions to Christianity, 51, 145–6, 322; forced, 129, 194, 230, 239, 350
conversions to Islam, 42, 75–8, 281–2
convivencia (coexistence), 110, 120, 235–7, 244–5, 349, 355–8
Copernicus, Nicolaus, 109–10
Córdoba, 215–50, *247*, 286; Casa de Sefarad, 228–33, *229*, 239–45; Jewish community, 233–4, 236; Jewish Quarter, 231; Madinah az-Zahra, 215–16, 217–22, 225–6; al-Morabito mosque, 224–5; Muslim community, 260–61; synagogue, 231, 233, *240*, 245–7; Torre de la Calahorra, Museo Vivo de

INDEX

al-Andaluz, 248, 249–51; *see also* Mezquita-Catedral
—, Caliphate of (929–1031), 13–14, 186, 248–9; Alcázar, Seville, 267; collapse of, 269; development of, 216–17; *fitna* (civil war), 225–6; Jewish community, 231, 233–41, 245–7
—, Emirate of (750–929), 91, 194, 216; al-Gharb (Portugal) as part of, 174–6, 186; cultural development of, 222–3, 233–4; founding of, 266
cosmetics, 223
Critchlow, Keith, 76
Crusades, 105, 121, 189
Cyprus, 10, 13; Caliphate conquest of, 23–4; civil war, 19, 29, 35; female cults, tradition of, 81–2; historical record of Muslims in, 71–2; *Sahabah* (Companions of the Prophet) buried in, 19–20, 22, 26, 26, 27–8; UN Buffer Zone (Green Line), 29
—, Republic of, 58–64; Bangladeshi community, 62; Nicosia, 58–64; Ömeriye Mosque, Cyprus, 58–64, 63; *see also* Larnaca
—, Turkish Republic of Northern Cyprus (TRNC), 19–33; Girne (Kyrenia), 26–8; Hala Sultan Camii mosque, 28; Hazret Omer Türbe and mosque, 19–26, 33; Kırklar Türbesi ('Forty Tombs'), 28–33; mosque-churches, 35; *see also* Lefke (Lefka, Cyprus)

ad-Daghestani, Sheikh Faiz Abdullah, 36, 40, 315, 326
Dagobert I of the Franks, 194–5
dance, 274–5

Daniel of Morley, 345, 346
Darro (river), 287
Davies, Norman, 9, 10
death, 44–5
dervishes, 21, 32–3, 54, 56, 316
Diana, Princess of Wales, 75
al-Din, Abu Bakr Siraj (Martin Lings), 76
diplomacy, 236–7, 272–3
Durr-i-Shahvar, HIH, 78
Dyck, Sheikh Hassan, 51, 327

Ebubekir, Mehmet Bey, 36
education, 147–8; *halaqa*, 147; literacy, 293–4; *madrasa*, 21, 89, 293–4, 301–2; universities, 109, 248, 249, 302; *see also* scholarship
Edward, the Black Prince, 273
Elizabeth I of England, 77
Enlightenment, 14–15
Erdoğan, Recep Tayyip, 28
Eschwege, Baron Wilhelm Ludwig von, 179
Eugenius of Palermo, 108
Euphemius, 90–91
exoticization, 180, 282, 307
extremism, 11, 88
Ezabe, Sara, 151

al-Farghani, 273
Fátima de Madrid, 368
Fatimids, 91, 92, 119, 134, 217
Ferdinand II of Portugal, 176, 177, 179–80
Ferrer, Vicente, 350
festivals: Eid al-Adha, 3; Iberian reconquest, Islamophobia in, 189–90; *mawlid*, 301; Mértola, Festival Islamico (Islamic Festival), 189, 190–91, 197–8, 207, 210, 282

Fez, 302; Jama'a al-Andalusiyyin (Andalusian Mosque), 248–9
Fibonacci, Leonardo, 111–12
Field, Jacob, 8
al-Fihriya al-Qurashiyya, Fatima bint Muhammad, 248
Firman, Armen (Abbas ibn Firnas), 253
Florian, Stephen, 151
Fonseca, António Tomás da, 183
Fonseca, Manuel Pinto da, 183
food culture, 160–62, 222, 223, 283–4, 376–7
fountains: Alcazár, Seville, 274; Alhambra, 292, *300*, 300–301; 'drinking doves' image, 164; Fonte, Sintra, 179–82, *181*; Great Jamme Masjid mosque (now Our Lady of the Annunciation), 280; Madinah az-Zahra, 219; Mezquita del Cristo de la Luz, Toledo, 341–2; Zisa (al-Aziz) palace, Palermo, 106–7
Franco, Francisco, 223–4
Franks, 193, 194–5, 237, 290, 329
Frederick II, Holy Roman Emperor, 108–12, 121, 130, 136, 333
al-Funduq al-Jadida, Granada (caravanserai), 295–7

Gaddafi, Muammar, 148, 149
Galizia, E. L., 140–41
gardens: Cathedral, Seville, *280*; Jardín Nazarí, 330; Mezquita del Cristo de la Luz, Toledo, 341–2; Parque Emir Mohamed I, Madrid, *361*, 361–2; Pena Palace Lakes, Sintra, 178–9; Zisa (al-Aziz) palace, Palermo, 104, 106–7, 115
Geaves, Ron, 19–20, 26–7
geography, 122, 191–2, 273, 344
Gerard of Cremona, 289, 344
al-Ghafiqi, Abd al-Rahman, 194
al-Ghazali, 344
Gómez Martínez, Susana, 199, 202–4, *204*
Goya, Francisco de, 283–4
Gozo: l-Ghajn il-Kbira bathhouse, 160; Museum of Archaeology, 166–8
Granada, 223, 285–97; Alcaicería, 296–7; Bañuelo, 287; Carlos V Palace, 304–5; Catedral, 293; al-Funduq al-Jadida (Corral del Carbón), 295–6; Jewish community, 236; Jewish Quarter, 232; Maristán, 287–92; Masjid al-Kabir, 293; Mezquita Mayor, 294–5; Palacio de la Madraza, 293, 294; *see also* Alhambra; Nasrids of Granada
Guadalquivir (river), 268–9, 277–8
Guarna, Romuald, Archbishop of Salerno, 108
Guénon, René Jean-Marie-Joseph (Abdalwahid Yahia), 76

hadiths, 4, 20, 66, 67, 99, 171, 293
al-Hakam II, Caliph of Córdoba, 225, 226, 254, 256
Hala Sultan (Umm Harâm), 33, 57, 67–8, 78–82; tomb, 70–73, *72*
Hala Sultan Mosque and *türbe*, Larnaca, 2–3, 5–7, 56–7, 65–73, *68*, *72*, 80–82
haLevi, Judah (Yehuda), 230, 235, 237

Ha-Levi Abulafia, Samuel ben Meir, 272–3, 351
Hamilton, Sir Abdullah, 78
Hammadid dynasty, 113
al-Hanafi, Alam al-Din, 121
Hanagid, Shmuel (Samuel ibn Naghrillah), 238
Hand of Fatima, 131–2, 274
al-Harawi, Ali ibn Abu Bakr, 90; *Kitab al-ishara ila ma 'rifat al-ziyara*, 71
harems, 116, 117
Hasan ibn Ali, Caliph, 83
HIH Hayriya Aisha Durr-i-Shahvar, 78
al-Haytham, Hasan Ibn, 111
Hazrat Shah Jalal, 44
Headley, Rowland Allanson-Winn, 5th Baron, 78
Hebrew language, 233–4, 357
Hejaz, 169
Henriques, João, 179
Henry II of England, 77, 105, 111, 112–13
Henry of Trastámara, 272, 273
Hidalgo, Rosa, 351
hijab (headdress), 151, 205
hijrah (migration), 5–6, 52–3
Hill, Derek, 75
al-Himyari, 144, 146
Hirst, John, 8, 10
Hisham II, Caliph of Córdoba, 225
Hisham III, Caliph of Córdoba, 225
Hisham X, Umayyad Caliph, 266–7
historiography: European, 8–10; Islamophobic, 196–7; of Portugal, 189–90, 192–4, 195–7
Holy League, 371
hospitals, 287–8, 290–92

al-Hudali, Hassan ibn Ali (Ibn as-Susi), 169
Hugo de Fer, 130
Hussein (Prophet's grandson), 31

Ibn Abbad, Muhammad, 130
ibn Abu Amir, Muhammad ibn Abdullah: *see* al-Mansur
ibn Ahmad ibn Jubayr, Abu'l-Husayn Muhammad, 93, 94, 96–7, 103–4, 122–4, 128–9
ibn al-Furat, Asad, 91, 131
ibn Ali, Musa, 338
Ibn an Nafis, 288
Ibn Arabi, 42–3, 249–51, 270
Ibn as-Susi (Uthman Ibn Abdu'r-Rahman), 170
Ibn as-Saffar, 273
Ibn al-Awwam, 362
ibn Baso, Ahmad, 268, 275, 276, 277
Ibn Battuta, 330
Ibn Daud, Abraham, 237
Ibn Firnas, Abbas (Armen Firman), 253
ibn Gabirol, Solomon, 235, 237, 344
ibn Hammud, Qa'id Abu 'l-Qasim, 129
Ibn Hawqal, 91, 261
Ibn al-Haytham, 273, 346
ibn Hud, Muhammad ibn Yusuf, 285, 286
Ibn al-Jayyab, 293
Ibn Khaldun, 249, 293
Ibn al-Khatib, 293, 301
Ibn Marzuq, 293
Ibn Mas'ud, Abd Allah, 169–70
Ibn Naghrillah, Joseph, 238
Ibn Naghrillah, Samuel (Shmuel Hanagid), 238

ibn Nasr, Abu Abdullah
  Muhammad ibn Yusuf, 285–6
Ibn Qasi, Abu 'l-Qasim Ahmad Ibn
  al-Husayn, 209–10, *211*
Ibn Ramadan, Abd'ur-Rahman
  (al-Qadi), 170
Ibn Rushd (Averroes), 109, 230,
  231–2, 249–51, *250*, 273
Ibn Sab'in, Abd al-Haqq, 121
Ibn Serragh family, 299
Ibn Shaprut, Hasdai, 236–7, 238
Ibn al-Shatir, 109–10
ibn Shoshan, Joseph ibn
  Meir, 348–9
Ibn Sina (Avicenna), 108, 111, 273,
  289–90, 344, 345
Ibn Zamrak, 293, 299
ibn Zayd, Rabi (Recemundo,
  Bishop of Elvira), 219
Ibn Ziyad, Tariq, 235–6, 347
Ibn Zur'ah, 129
identity: cultural, 138, 144–5, 197,
  379; European, Islamophobia
  in, 9–11, 14, 187, 197, 241, 371–2;
  Jewish Sephardic, 239; national,
  138; place, 11, 379; Spanish,
  241, 371–2
iftars, 154–5
imams, 21, 24–5, 134, 152–5
Innocent III, Pope, 77
Inquisition, 240–41, 284, 294
inscriptions, 255–6; Alcázar,
  Seville, 271, *272*, *275*; Alhambra,
  286, 303, *304*; Fonte, Sintra, 179;
  Hala Sultan Mosque, Larnaca,
  2, 69; Hazret Omer Türbe and
  mosque, Cyprus, 22; Maimuna
  Stone, 167–8; Mezquita del
  Cristo de la Luz, Toledo, *338*,
  338, 339–40; Mezquita Mayor de
  Granada, 294–5, *295*; Mezquita-
  Catedral (Great Mosque),
  Córdoba, 248, *252*, 251ff.;
  Palermo Cathedral, 97, *98*;
  Quinta do Relógio, Sintra, 182–3;
  Qur'anic, in synagogues, 353;
  on tombstones, 165, 171, 172,
  201, 202
intolerance, religious, 194–5
Iqbal, Muhammad, 251–3, 256–7,
  261, 263
Irving, Washington, *Tales of the
  Alhambra*, 180, 256
Isa (Jesus), 51–2, 121–2, 171, 347
Isabel de Solis (Zoraya), 323–4
A'isha (niece of Muhammad), 90
A'isha bint Ahmad b. Muhammad
  b. Qadim, 260
Islam: British Royal interests in,
  75–8; conversions to, 42, 75–8,
  281–2; European historiography, omissions from, 8–10; as
  European religion, 51, 68; familiarity with, 220–21; forty, sig-
  nificance of, 31; founding of, 12;
  fundamentalism, 88; green, sig-
  nificance of, 37, 181; holiest sites
  of, 66–7; Jesus (Isa) in, 52, 171; in
  Ottoman Empire, 310; religious
  tolerance of, 233–4; Salafism, 3–5;
  Shi'a, 3, 77, 134; Sunni, 3–4, 20; in
  Turkish Republic of Northern
  Cyprus, 27; in UK, 5, 75–8, 78,
  112–13, 184; Wahhabism, 4, 42,
  43; *see also* conversions to Islam;
  Muslim culture; Muslims;
  mysticism; Sufism
Islamic calendar, 52–3
Islamic State (Daesh/ISIS/
  ISIL), 197–8

Islamophobia, 5, 6, 138; in Balkan Wars, 244; in European identity, 9–11, 14, 187, 197, 241, 371–2; in Iberian reconquest festivals, 189–90; in Malta, 151–2; myths of, 241–2, 274, 360; pork, display of, 283–4; Spanish, 241–2, 263–4, 281–2, 371–2
I'timad, 268–9, 270, 271

Ja'far, 220
James, Saint (Matamoros/the Moor Slayer), 241–2, 262, 265, 360
al-Jawzi, Sibt ibn, 110
Jerusalem, 121, 341; al-Aqsa Mosque, 66, 121, 252, 256–7; Dome of the Rock, 121, 256–7
Jesus (Isa), 51–2, 121–2, 171, 347
Jewish–Muslim relationships: anti-Semitism, 237; *convivencia* (coexistence), 110, 120, 235–7, 244–5, 349, 355–8; Jewish refugees, support for, 244–5
Jews: al-Andalus conquest, role in, 235–6; conversion to Christianity, forced, 230, 350; Córdoba community, 231, 233–4, 233–41, 236, 245–7; expulsion of, 244, 350; Granada community, 236, 237; Iberia, expulsion from, 230; in London, 334–5; Madrid community, 365; persecution of, 194, 244–5, 365; Sephardic, 228, 229–30, 233–9, 357; in Spain, 230–31, 232–3; Toledo, 236, 347–58
jinn, 21, 370–71
Joan of England, 105, 345
John of Oxford, Bishop of Norwich, 345
John of Palermo, 111
John of Seville, 344
John of Toledo, 344–5
Judaism: cultural influence of, 233–4; Europe, arrival in, 68; Golden Age, 233–8; heritage of, 230–31, 232–3; in Ottoman Empire, 310; *see also* anti-Semitism; Jews
jurisprudence, 20, 113

Ka'aba, Makkah, 25, 66, 95, 341
Kagi, Gabriella, 246
al-Kamil, Sultan, 111, 121
Kanouté, Frédéric, 281
Karim, Abdul, 77
Karpeles, Gustav, 14
al-Khidr, 42–3
al-Khwarizmi, 344, 345, 368
El-Kibrusi, Seyh Muhammed Nazim Adil: *see* Nazim, Sheikh
al-Kindi, 344
al-Kirkinti, Abu Uthman Sa'id ibn Sallam, 95
Korkut, Derviš, 244
Kosovo, 10, 244; Battle of (1389), 310
Kruse, Thorsten, 65–6

lafif (jury), 113
languages: Arabic, 142–4, 148, 152–3, 303–4; Castilian Spanish, 346; Hebrew, 233–4, 357; Maltese, 138–9, 142–4, 146; multilingualism, 110, 114, 122; Portuguese, 156, 192; Siculo-Arabic, 142; *see also* translation
Larnaca, Hala Sultan Mosque, 2–3, 5–7, 10, 12–13, 15, 28, 56–7, 65–73, 68, 72, 80–82
law, 20, 113
Lazarus, Emma, 241

Lefke (Lefka, Cyprus), 34–57; Piri Mehmet Pasha Mosque (Pir Pasa Camii), 36–8, 46–50, 52–3, 54–5; Sheikh Nazim's *dargah* (lodge), 36, 37–9, *38*, 42–3, 50–51, 53–7; Sheikh Nazim's *türbe* (tomb), 44–5, 49–50
Leighton, Fredric, 107
Lepanto, Battle of (1571), 371
libraries: Alhambra, 301; burning of, 294; Córdoba, 259–60, 261; Sicily, 108; Toledo, 343, 345
Libya, 148–9, 152, 153
Lings, Martin (Abu Bakr Siraj al-Din), 76
Lisbon (al-Ishbun), 175, 177–8, 195
literacy, 293–4
literary culture, 135, 168–70, 180, 233–4, 268–9, 303–4
Lithuania, 10, 308–9
London: Brick Lane Mosque, 334–5; East London Mosque, 334; Leighton House, Arab Hall, 107, 184; Ramadan Mosque, London, 78; Tower of London, 104–6
Lorca, Federico García, 298

Macias, Santiago, 199
al-Madani, Sheikh Dr Badri, 87–92, 93–6, 98–100
al-Madani, Sheikh Muhammad ibn Khalifa, 94
Madinah, 37, 52–3, 201, 304–5; Masjid al-Qiblatayn, 341; Prophet's Mosque, 66
Madinah az-Zahra, Córdoba, 215–16, 217–22, 225–6
madrasa, 21, 89, 293–4, 301–2
Madrid, 359–79; Bangladeshi community in, 374–5, 377–8; Catedral de Santa María la Real de la Almudena, 359–61, 365; Christian conquest, 368–9; Church of Our Lady of Almudena, 367–9; Jewish community, 365; al-Majrit, Muslim name of, 359, 373; al-Majrit walls, 359, *361*, 362; mosques, 367–9; Muslim quarter, 366–8; under Muslim rule, 359–60, 362, 368; Parque Emir Mohamed I, 361–2; Plaza de la Villa, 370–71; Torre de los Lujanes, 370; water systems, 364–5
Mahmut II, Ottoman Sultan, 69
Maimonides (Musa ibn Maimon), 109, 237, 249, 251; Córdoba statue of, 246–7, *247*; and Ibn Rushd, 230, 231–2
Maimuna, 166, 169–70
Maimuna Stone, 166–8
al-Majriti, Abu al-Qasim Maslama ibn Ahmad (Methilem), 368
al-Majusi, Ali ibn al-Abbas, *Kitab al-Maliki*, 108
Makkah, 25, 52–3, 341; Ka'aba, 25, 66, 95, 341; *qibla* (direction of prayer), 127–8, 204–5, 246, 340–42
Malta, 13, 137–66; Arabic, teaching of, 148, 152–3; Centru Islamiku ta' Malta, 146–9, *150*, 152–5; Domus Romana museum, 163–6; food and drink, 160–62; Ghain Hammet, 158–60; Islamophobia in, 151–2; Knights of the Order of St John, 144–5, 157, 160; Libya, relationship with, 148–9, 152, 153; Mariam al-Batool school, 148; Mdina,

156–60; migration from, 142–3; mosques, 141–2; Msida, 151–2; Muslim community, 147–55, 169–70; Muslim cultural influence on, 144–5; Muslim expulsion from, 130, 146; Ottoman Cemetery, 137, 139–42, *140*; Rabat, 156–66; Siege (1565), 140; *see also* Gozo
Maltese language, 138–9, 142–4, 146
maluf (nuba) music, 222–3
al-Mansur (Muhammad ibn Abdullah ibn Abu Amir), 225, 226, 262
al-Mansur, Abu al-Abbas Ahmad, 77
al-Mansur, Abu Yusuf Ya'qub, 276
maq'am, 68, 326
al-Maqdisi, 14
al-Maqqari, 217, 249, 275; on Córdoba, 223, 236, 260; on Toledo, 335–6, 347
Margarit, Sheikh Umar (Felipe), 315
Marrakech: Ben Youssef Mosque, 302; Kutubiyya Mosque, 258
Martel, Charles, 194
martyrdom, 33, 67–8, 90
Matamoras: *see* James, Saint
mathematics, 121, 368
Mauritania, 316–17
Mazara del Vallo, Sicily, 88, 131–2, 133, 134
Mbacké, Serigne Mountakha, 316
Mecca: *see* Makkah
medicine, 108, 288–90, 362
Mehmet 'Adil ar-Rabbani, Sheikh, 40–42, *41*, 45, 49, 53–4, 55–7
Mértola, 185–211; Abu 'l-Qasim Ahmad Ibn al-Husayn Ibn Qasi statue, 209–10, *211*; Bairro Islâmico (Islamic Quarter), 208–9; Castelo de Mértola, 209; Festival Islamico (Islamic Festival), 189, 190–91, 197–8, 207, 210, 282; Great Jamme Masjid mosque (now Our Lady of the Annunciation), 201, 204–7; Islamic Art Museum, 199–201, *204*
Methilem (Abu al-Qasim Maslama ibn Ahmad al-Majriti), 368
Mezquita-Catedral (Great Mosque), Córdoba, 231, 251–65, *252*; arches, 261–2, *262*; architectural influence of, 112, 182, 220, 338–9, 340; Basilica of Saint Vincent the Martyr, 263; Capilla Mayor, 264–5; Catholic ownership vs Muslim heritage, 263–4; Christian artists' work on, 255; inscriptions, 248, 255–6; library, 259–60; *mihrab*, 254–8, *259*; minaret/bell tower, 248–9, 253, 263; *minbar*, 258
migration, 61–3; expulsions, 129–30, 146, 244, 350; *hijrah* (migration), 5–6, 52–3; from Iberia, 328–9; from Malta, 142–3
mihrab: Aljafería Palace, Zaragoza, 363; Ċentru Islamiku ta' Malta, 149; Great Jamme Masjid mosque (now Our Lady of the Annunciation), 205; Hala Sultan Mosque, Cyprus, 2, 24; Hala Sultan Mosque, Cyprus, 69; Mezquita del Cristo de la Luz, Toledo, influence on, 339; Mezquita Mayor, Granada, 294–5, *295*; Mezquita-Catedral (Great Mosque), Córdoba,

mihrab – cont'd.
254–8, *259*; Moschea di Tunisia, Sicily, 99; Mount Barbaros mosque, Sicily, 127, *128*; Ömeriye Mosque, Cyprus, 60; Ottoman Cemetery, Malta, 142; Palacio de la Madraza, Granada, 294; Piri Mehmet Pasha Mosque (Pir Pasa Camii), Cyprus, 37, 39

minarets: bell towers, converted to, 239, 268, 275–7, *278*, 369; Ċentru Islamiku ta' Malta, 147; Great Jamme Masjid mosque (now Our Lady of the Annunciation), Mértola, 205, 207; Hala Sultan Mosque, Larnaca, 2, 65; Hazret Omer Türbe and mosque, 20; Mezquita Mayor, Granada, *295*; Mezquita-Catedral (Great Mosque), Córdoba, 248–9, 253, 263; Ömeriye Mosque, Cyprus, 58–9; Ottoman Cemetery, Malta, 137; Piri Mehmet Pasha Mosque (Pir Pasa Camii), Cyprus, 36–7

miracles, 21, 43–4, 70

Moheb, Yishaq, 246

Morocco, 244; Ben Youssef Mosque, Marrakech, 302; Iberian Muslims' migration to, 328–9; Kutubiyya Mosque, Marrakech, 258; *see also* Fez

mosaics, 107, 114, 121, 164, 255

mosques: Alhambra Great Mosque (Church of Santa María), 304; architecture of, 60, 104; Ben Youssef Mosque, Marrakech, 302; Brick Lane Mosque, London, 334–5; Ċentru Islamiku ta' Malta, 146–9, *150*, 152–5; churches, shared with, 263; East London Mosque, London, 334; Fundación Mezquita de Sevilla, 280–83; Great Jamme Masjid mosque, Mértola, 201, 204–7; Great Jamme Masjid, Seville, 268, *280*, 280; Hala Sultan Camii mosque, Cyprus, 28; Hala Sultan Mosque and *türbe*, Larnaca, 2–3, 5–7, 10, 12–13, 15, 28, 56–7, 65–73, *68*, *72*, 80–82; Hazret Omer Türbe and mosque, 19–26, 33; Kutubiyya Mosque, Marrakech, 258; in Madrid, 367–9; in Malta, 141–2; Mezquita de las Tornerías, Toledo, 337; Mezquita del Cristo de la Luz, Toledo, 337–43, *338*; *minbar*, 2, 37, 60, 142, 149, 258; al-Morabito mosque, Córdoba, 224–5; Moschea di Tunisia, Palermo, 87–9, 95–6, *96*, 98–100; mosque architecture, influence on, 104; mosque-churches, 35, 60, 95–6, 129, 201, 204–7, 332–4, 369; Muslim prayers prohibited in, 254; Ömeriye Mosque, Cyprus, 58–64, *63*; Piri Mehmet Pasha Mosque (Pir Pasa Camii), Lefke, 36–8, 46–50, 52–3, 54–5; Prophet's Mosque, Madinah, 66; Ramadan Mosque, London, 78; in Seville, 268, *280*, 280–83; Shah Jahan Mosque, Woking, UK, 78, 184; in Sicily, 97, 101–2; *sitara*, 25; tombs in, 2–3, 4; *see also* Mezquita-Catedral (Great Mosque), Córdoba; *mihrab*; minarets

Mount Barbaros mosque, Sicily: mosques, 127–9, *128*

Mu'awiya ibn Hudayj al-Sakuni, Hassan ibn, 90
Mu'awiyah, 186
Mu'awiyah ibn Abi Sufyan, 23–4, 67, 71, 83–4, 89–90
mudéjar architecture: Alcázar, Seville, 267–8, 271–2; Cathedral, Seville, 279–80; Ibn Shoshan synagogue (Santa María la Blanca church), Toledo, 348, *349*, 352; in Mértola, 188; Mezquita del Cristo de la Luz, Toledo, 338, *338*; neo-*mudéjar*, 176, 177, 370–71; San Román Church, Toledo, 332
muezzins, 39–40, 277
Muhammad, Prophet, 31, 66–7, 370–71; *Ansar* (Helpers), 201; biographies, 112; death, 23; *hijrah* (migration), 52–3; prayers for, 49; *salat ad-duha* (Victory Prayer), 52–3; tomb, 37, 52, 54; *see also Sahabah*
Muhammad I, Emir of Córdoba, 359, 361–2
Muhammad V of Granada, 273, 291, 292, 300, 301, 302
Muhammad XII of Granada (Boabdil), 310, 322–3
Muley Hacén (Abu l-Hasan Ali of Granada), 322–3, 330
al-Mu'min, Abd, 199–200
al-Mu'min, Abu Sa'id Uthman ibn 'Abd, 103–4
muqarnas, 104, 107, 113–14, 116–17, 119, 299, 363
al-Muqtadir, Abu Ja'far, 363
Murad III, Ottoman sultan, 77
murid, 313–14, 316, 321
Muscat, Joseph, 154

music, 135, 222–3, 248, 274–5; *ghana*, 138–9; Sephardic Jewish, 228–9, 357
Muslim: Malta community, 147–55, 169–70; Portugal community, 173, 174–6, 178, 186; Sicily community, 89–93, 128–9
Muslim culture: artifacts, destroyed during archaeological digs, 195–6; European culture, influence on, 12–14; heritage, effacement of, 263–4, 305, 307–10, 324; in Malta, 144–5; in Portugal, 174, 176, 179, 190–95, 195, 196–7; in Sicily, 92–3, 104–7, 131–6; in Spain, 222–5; *see also* architecture; food culture; gardens; literary culture; music; scholarship; visual art
Muslim–Jewish relations: anti-Semitism, 237; *convivencia* (coexistence), 110, 120, 235–7, 244–5, 349, 355–8; Jewish refugees, support for, 244–5
Muslims: alienation of, 11–12; Christians, relationships with, 120–21, 266–7; in Cyprus, historiography of, 71–2; as Europeans, 10, 11, 12; *hafiz*, 304; Madrid community, 366–8; medieval status of, 356; migration/expulsion, 328–9, 350; *moriscos* (nominal/forced Christian converts), 239, 322, 372; persecution of, 129–30, 151–2; representations of, 189–90; Western stereotypes of, 239; *see also* Islamophobia
Musta'izz: *see* William II of Sicily
al-Mu'tamid (Abbad), 269

al-Mu'tamid (Abu al-Qasim Muhammad), 268–70
mysticism: Almoravid, 270; in Cyprus, 21, 34, 42–4, 74; in Sicily, 94–5, 125; in Spain, 249–51, 316, 318

al-Najjar, Sidi Yahia (Don Pedro de Granada), 322
Naples University, 109
Nasi, Gracia, 230
Nasrids of Granada, 249, 285–7, 293–4, 296–7, 322–5; Alcázar, Seville, 268, 271–2, *272*; architecture of, 295, 300–301, 352; Jewish community, 237; motto, 182, *286*, 303; Pedro I of Castile, relations with, 273; surrender, 310; *see also* Alhambra
navigation, 191–2, 273, 344
Nazim, Sheikh (Seyh Muhammed Nazim Adil El-Kibrusi), 25, 30, 34, 35, 315, 318–19; Charles III, relationship with, 75, 77; childhood, 65; *dargah* (lodge), Lefke, 36, 37–9, *38*, 42–3, 50–51, 53–7; death, 45; *Hakkani Kulliyati*, 25; in Ibiza, 326; in Madrid, 370–71; miracles, 43–4, 73–5; *türbe* (tomb), 39, 44–5, 49–50; Umm Harâm, mystical encounters with, 78–9
Neugebauer, Otto, 109–10
Nietzsche, Friedrich, 15
nuba (maluf) music, 222–3
numerical systems, 111–12

Obra, Sebastián de la, 228–33, *229*
Offa of Mercia, 77
Omer, Hazret, 21–3, *26*, 27–8
Omer, Hoca, 29–30

Órgiva, 313–22; Haqqani Zawiya *dargah*, 314–19; Museo Ruiz de Almodóvar, 322
Orientalism, 180, 301
others/othering, 180, 307
Ottoman Empire, 36, 310; Cyprus, conquest of, 22; Hala Sultan Mosque and *türbe*, reverence of, 67–8; Jewish refugees, welcomed by, 244–5; Lepanto, Battle of (1571), 371
oud (instrument), 222

Palermo (Bal'harm), 87–122; Anna, tombstone of, *114*, 114; Arab-Norman palaces, 103–8, 115–19; Cappella Palatina, 119–20, 121–2; Cathedral, 97, *98*, 131; Church of Saint John of the Hermits, 100–102; Church of St Mary of the Admiral, 97, *98*; Church of the Holy Trinity, 104; Giardino della Zisa, 104, 115; al-Madinah name for, 124–5; Moschea di Tunisia, 87–9, 95–6, *96*, 98–100; Palazzo dei Normanni (Royal Palace), 117, 119–20, 121–2; Palazzo della Cuba, 115–19; Zisa (al-Aziz) palace, 104–8, *106*, 112, 113–15, *114*
Palestine, 256–7
Palma, Manuel Passinhas da, 185, 186, 193, 195–8, 200, 202–11, *204*
Papo, Mira, 244
Patricolo, Giuseppe, 101–2
Paul, Saint, 145–6
Pedro Afonso, Count of Barcelos, *Livro de linhagens*, 190
Pedro de Granada (Sidi Yahia al-Najjar), 322
Pedro I of Castile, 267–8, 271–3, 274, 352

INDEX

people-smuggling, 61–3
Pepin the Short, 194
Peter of Ireland, 109
Peter the Venerable, Abbot of Cluny, 344
Petrus Alphonsi, 112
philanthropy, 236
philosophy, 109, 111, 345; Greek, translation of, 233–4; Islamic, 112, 121, 135; Jewish, 235
physiology, 288
pilgrimage, 28, 30–31; *Arbaeen*, 31; Christian, to Muslim sites, 72; to Christian sites, 51–2; guide-books, 71; *Hajj*, 80, 103; in Sicily, 90, 93; *umrah*, 5; *ziyara*, 20, 28, 51–2, 90
Pimenta, Rosinda, 188–93, 196–8
Piri Mehmet Pasha, 36
Pisani, Alex, 151–2
Pitrè, Giuseppe, 136
Plato of Tivoli, 108
pleasure palaces, 103–8, 112–13, 115–19
Poland, 10, 308–9
Porcus, William, 130
Portugal, 13, 173–211; Christian conquest, 175, 176, 189, 197; as al-Gharb al-Andalus, 174–6, 186; Lisbon (al-Ishbun), 175, 177–8, 195; Muslim community, 173, 174–6, 178, 186; Muslim cultural influence on, 174, 176, 179, 190–95, 195, 196–7; *see also* Mértola; Sintra
Portuguese language, 156, 192
prayer, 304–5; *adhan* (call to prayer), 9, 39–40, 133, 327; Christian, towards Makkah, 204–7; churches, prohibited in, 254; *dhikr*, 40, 46–50, 74, 282, 313–14, 318; *dua*, 49; *isha*, 318–19; *janazah*, 142; *jumu'ah*, 54–5; *maghrib* (sunset prayer), 39–40; *qibla* (direction of prayer), 127–8, 204–5, 246, 340–2; *salah*, 24–6, 63–4; *salat ad-duha* (Victory Prayer), 52–3; *salawat*, 25; *takbir*, 25, 102, 139, 145
Prophet: *see* Muhammad, Prophet
prophets, 51–2, 59
Prophet's Mosque, Madinah, Saudi Arabia, 66
Publius, Saint, 145–6

Qasid dynasty, 209
qibla (direction of prayer), 127–8, 204–5, 246, 340–42
Qur'an, 326–7; *al-Fatihah*, 47, 49; framed verses, 31–2; Jesus (Isa) in, 52, 171; names of Allah, 104; Surah *al-Ikhlas*, 295; Surah *al-Ankabut*, 'The Spider', 152; Surah *al-A'raf*, 'The Heights', 97, *98*, 172; Surah *as-Sajdah*, 'Prostration', 256; Surah *al-Hajj*, 'The Pilgrimage', 201, 258; Surah *al-Hashr*, 'Exile', 256; Surah *al-Ikhlas*, 'The Purity', 171; Surah *al-Mulk*, 'The Kingdom', 303; Surah *al-Mu'min*, 'The Believer', 256; translation of, 154, 344
Qur'an inscriptions: Mezquita Mayor de Granada, *295*, 295; Mezquita-Catedral (Great Mosque), Córdoba, 256; Palermo Cathedral, 97, *98*; in synagogues, 353; on tombstones, 165, 171, 172, 201, 202

Recemundo, Bishop of Elvira (Rabi ibn Zayd), 219
Ramadan, 154–5
Raymond de Sauvetât, 344
ar-Razi, 263
al-Razi, Abu Bakr Muhammad ibn Zakariya, 288, 344
Renaissance, 14; Christian, 109–10, 344; Jewish, 233–5; Muslim, 195
Respighi, Ottorino, 167–8
Richard I of England (the Lionheart), 105
Robert of Ketton, 344–5
Roberts, John M., 8–9
Robinson, Victor, 261
Roger II of Sicily, 113, 119, 121, 122
Roman Empire, 145–6
Romanus I Lekapenos, Byzantine emperor, 237
Ruiz de Almodóvar, Paloma, 322
Rumi, Jalal al-Din Muhammad, 32, 44–5
ar-Rumi, Mugheyth, 236

Sadegh, Ibtisam, 137–8, 147–8, 149–51
Sadruddin, Imam, 19–20
Sahabah (Companions of the Prophet), 26, 27–8, 36, 50–51; Cyprus, active in, 36, 60, 69, 71–2; Cyprus, buried in, 19–20, 22, *26*, 56, 71; *Sahabiyyah* (female Companions), 81, 90
Sahih al-Bukhari, 20
Said, Edward, 180
Salaf (first three generations), 3, 7, 13, 36, 90; see also Sahabah
Salazar, António de Oliveira, 187, 195
al-Samantari, Atiq ibn, 95
al-Samti al-Maliti, Abd Allah Ibn, 170

Sara la Goda (Sara the Goth), 266–7
Sarajevo Haggadah, 241
Sassanid dynasty, 23
al-Saud, Muhammad ibn, 4
Saudi Arabia, 4–7, 54, 169; see also Madinah; Makkah
Sayyidah bint 'Abd al-Ghani bin 'Ali bin 'Uthman al-'Abdari, 270
Schneider, Felix, 246
scholarship, 293–4, 301; astronomy, 109–10, 273, 368; botany, 362; cartography, 122, 191; flight, 253; geography, 122; Jewish, 237–8; jurisprudence, 20, 113; mathematics, 121, 368; medicine, 108, 288–90, 362; Muslim, influence of, 108–10, 121, 135, 273, 343–6; navigation, 191–2, 273, 344; numerical systems, 111–12; physiology, 288; status of, 122; by women, 260, 270; see also libraries; philosophy
Scot, Michael, 110–11, 112, 344–5, 346
Secretum Secretorum (encyclopedia), 344
Selim I, Ottoman sultan, 36
Senegal, 316–17
Serbia, 10, 244
Seville (Ishbiliyah), 195, 235, 266–84; Alcázar, 267–8, 270–72, *272*, 274–5, *275*; Cathedral, *280*; Fundación Mezquita de Sevilla, 280–83; Giralda bell tower (former minaret), 268, 275–7, *278*; Great Jamme Masjid (Great Mosque), 268, 280, *280*; mosques, 281; Patio de los Naranjos, 279
Şeyh Hacı Osman Yeşilbaş, 20–21
Shah Jalal, Hazrat, 375

shahadah (declaration of faith), 8
Shams al-Din Muhammad ibn Marzuq, 258
Sicily, 13, 87–136; Catania, 90; Emirate of Siqilliya, 89–91, 93–5, 97, 124–5, 134–6, 146; Hisn al-Hammah (Calathamet), 123–7; Marsala, 90; Mazara del Vallo, 131–4, *132*; Messina, 105; Moschea Ettakwa, 134; mosques, remains of, 97, 101–2; Mount Barbaros mosque, 127–9, *128*; Muslim community, 89–93, 128–9; Muslim cultural influence on, 92–3, 104–7, 131–6; Muslim expulsion from, 129–30; Muslim uprisings, 129–30; Norman conquest, 92, 93; Prizzi, 90; Qasr Sa'd *zawiya* (lodge), 94, 96–7; scholarship in, 108, 111–12; Sufism in, 124–5; Terme Arabo-Normanne di Cefalà Diana, 126–7; Trapani, 90; *see also* Palermo
Sintra, 173–84; Castelo dos Mouros, 173, 174–8, *175*; Church of São Pedro de Canaferrim, 178; Fonte, 179–82, *181*; Pena Palace, 173–4; Pena Palace Lakes, 178–9; Quinta do Relógio, 182–4
al-Siqilli, Abd al-Rahman ibn Muhammad ibn 'Abd Allah al-Bakri, 95
Slavs, 226–7
Solomon, 347
souks, 296–7
Sousa, Marcelo Rebelo de, 191
Spain, 13; Alcalá de Henares, 362; Castile, 286, 323; *Guardia Mora* (Moorish Guard), 224; Ibiza, 325–6; Inquisition, 240–41, 284, 294; Islamophobia in, 241–2, 263–4, 281–2, 371–2; languages, 346; Mondújar, 323–5; Mount Mulhacén, 322–3; Muslim cultural influence on, 222–5; place names, Muslim influence on, 330–31; Purchena, 330–31; Sant Llorenç de la Muga, 326–7; synagogues, 233; Vélez de Benaudalla, 330; Zaragoza, 103–8, 363; *see also* al-Andalus; Córdoba; Granada; Madrid; Órgiva; Toledo
star motifs: Alcázar, Seville, 271, 274; Fonte, Sintra, 179, 180–81; Mezquita del Cristo de la Luz, Toledo, 339; al-Morabito mosque, Córdoba, 224; Parque Emir Mohamed I, Madrid, 362; La Sinagoga, Córdoba, 245
Star of David, 69
Stefano of Pisa, 108
Sufism, 25, 42–3, 76, 121; Madaniyya order, 94; Mevlevi order, 32; al-Muridiyyah order, 316; Muridun movement, 210; Naqshbandi Haqqani order, 25, 34, 37, 40, 43, 314–15, 326; in Sicily, 94–5, 124–5; in Spain, 314–15
Suleiman the Magnificent, 36, 230, 310, 371
synagogues, 228, 334–5; Ibn Shoshan synagogue (Santa María la Blanca church), Toledo, 348–51, *349*; La Sinagoga, Córdoba, 231, 233, *240*, 245–7; Synagogue of El Tránsito, Toledo, 351–3, 356; Toledo, 233, 348–53
Syria, 23

Tahmasp, Shah of Persia, 77
Tancred of Sicily, 105
tasbiyyah (beads), 25, 189
Tatars, 308–9, 310
technology, 135; astrolabes, 191, 273, 344; water systems, 158–60, 209, 364–5
Theodore of Antioch, 111
Thomas Aquinas, 109
Toledo, 332–58; Christian conquest, 343; Ibn Shoshan synagogue (Santa María la Blanca church), 348–51, *349*; Jewish community, 236, 347–58; Madinat al-Yahud (Jewish quarter), 347–8; Mezquita de las Tornerías, 337; Mezquita del Cristo de la Luz, 337–43, *338*; Museo Sefardi, 356–7; Puerta del Sol, 337–8; San Román Church, 332–4, 335, *336*; Synagogue of El Tránsito, 351–3, 356; synagogues, 233, 348–53
Toledo School of Translators, 251, 289, 333, 343–6
tombs: of Saint Barnabas, 51–2, 56; Hazret Omer Türbe and mosque, 19–26, 33; Kırklar Türbesi ('Forty Tombs'), 28–33; looting of, 107; of Sheikh Nazim, 39, 44–5, 49–50; see also Hala Sultan Mosque and *türbe*
tombstones, 166–72, 201–2; Jewish, 357; Maimuna Stone, 166–8
Torres, Cláudio, 174, 187, 199
trade: *see* commerce
translation: into Castilian, 346; of Greek philosophy, 233–4; of Maimuna Stone inscription, 167–8; of Qur'an, 154, 344; of scientific works, 108, 109, 110–11; Toledo School of Translators, 251, 289, 333, 343–6
travel, 296–7; *see also* pilgrimage
tribute, 227; Islamophobic myths of, 242, 274; refusal of, 323
TRNC: *see under* Cyprus
Tunisia, 88, 89, 93–4, 132, 142–3
türbesi (mausoleums): architecture of, 31–2; Hazret Omer Türbe and mosque, 19–26, 33; Kırklar Türbesi ('Forty Tombs'), 28–33; *see also* Hala Sultan Mosque and *türbe*
Turkish Republic of Northern Cyprus: *see under* Cyprus
al-Tusi, Nasir al-Din, 109–10

Ubada Ibn as-Samit, 67
Umar ibn al-Khattab, 2nd Caliph of Islam, 23–4, 59
Umayyad dynasty, 23, 174, 186, 217; Emirs of Córdoba, 91, 175–6; Ummayad Caliphate, 193–4, 195; *see also* Córdoba
Umm Harâm (Hala Sultan), 33, 57, 67–8, 78–82; tomb, 70–3, *72*
United Kingdom: Arabic scholarship, access to, 344–5; Brookwood Cemetery, 78; Canterbury Cathedral, 112; crown jewels, 273; Durham Cathedral, 112; English Common Law, 113; Everswell palace, 112–13; Muslim cultural influence on, 112–13, 184; Shah Jahan Mosque, Woking, 78, 184; *see also* London
universities, 109, 248, 249, 302
Uthman, 3rd Caliph of Islam, 24, 67, 83

Venegas, Cetti Merien, 322
Victoria of Great Britain, 77
Visigoths, 235, 236, 262, 266, 364
visual art, 76; Alhambra, Sala de los Reyes, 306; Cappella Palatina, Palermo, 119–20, 121; ceramics, *188*, 199–201, 202–4, *204*; Mazara del Vallo, Sicily, 131–2, 133; mosaics, 107, 114, 121, 164, 255; neo-*mudejar*, 176

walis (*awliyah*, 'friends of God'), 25, 34, 40, 316
water systems, 158–60, 209, 364–5
Wettinger, Godfrey, 144
William I of England, 105
William I of Sicily, 104, 106
William II of Sicily (Musta'izz), 104, 105, 108, 115–16, 117, 129, 345
William of Conches, 112
women: harems, 116, 117; physicians, 108; *Sahabiyyah* (female Companions), 81, 90; scholars, 260, 270

World Islamic Call Society (WICS), 153
wudu (ablutions), 24, 60, 307

Yahia, Abdalwahid (René Jean-Marie-Joseph Guénon), 76
Yazid I, Caliph of Islam, 71
Yehuda ben Moshe Cohen, 346
Yusuf, Abu Ya'qub, 276
Yusuf I of Granada, 293
Yusuf al-Kalbi, Ja'far Ibn, 134–5

Zammit, David, 138, 142–3, 156–8, 168–9
Zammit, Martin, 154
Zammit, Sir Themistocles, 164, 165
Zaragoza, 363; Aljafería Palace, 103–8, 363
Zarfati, Isaac, 244
zawiya (lodge), 94
Zirids, 285–7
Ziryab (Abu al-Hasan 'Ali ibn Nafi), 222–3
Zisa (al-Aziz) palace, Palermo, 104–8, *106*, 112, 113–15, *114*
Ziyadatallah, Aghlabid emir, 91
Zoraya (Isabel de Solís), 323–4